גב'נ ו,

תודה רבה לכ על העזה
והתרכבה שלין אצלך רב.
בהצרכה ונה,

שמעון

Jewish Rights, National Rites

STANFORD STUDIES IN JEWISH HISTORY AND CULTURE

EDITED BY *Aron Rodrigue and Steven J. Zipperstein*

Jewish Rights, National Rites

Nationalism and Autonomy in Late Imperial and Revolutionary Russia

Simon Rabinovitch

STANFORD UNIVERSITY PRESS

STANFORD, CALIFORNIA

Stanford University Press
Stanford, California

Parts of Chapters 6 and 7 have been adapted from "Russian Jewry Goes to the Polls: An Analysis of Jewish Voting in the All-Russian Constituent Assembly Elections of 1917," *East European Jewish Affairs* 39.2 (2009): 205–25. Republished with permission.

This book has been published with the assistance of Boston University's Elie Wiesel Center for Judaic Studies.

Printed in the United States of America on acid-free, archival-quality paper

Library of Congress Cataloging-in-Publication Data

Rabinovitch, Simon, author.
  Jewish rights, national rites : nationalism and autonomy in late imperial and revolutionary Russia / Simon Rabinovitch.
      p. cm. — (Stanford studies in Jewish history and culture)
  Includes bibliographical references and index.
  ISBN 978-0-8047-9249-3 (cloth : alk. paper)
  1. Jewish nationalism — Russia — History — 20th century. 2. Jews — Russia — Politics and government — 20th century. 3. Jews — Civil rights — Russia — History — 20th century. 4. Jews — Legal status, laws, etc. — Russia — History — 20th century. 5. Russia — History — Nicholas II, 1894–1917.
  I. Title. II. Series: Stanford studies in Jewish history and culture.
DS134.84.R33 2014
320.540956940947'09021 — dc23

                                    2014011851

ISBN 978-0-8047-9303-2 (electronic)

For Jodi, for everything

Contents

A Note on Transliterations and Dates

Transliterations follow the style of the Library of Congress for French, German, and Russian, the style of the YIVO Institute for Yiddish, and the Academy of the Hebrew Language 2006 guidelines for Hebrew (omitting diacritical marks). Most surnames have been transliterated from Russian, and I have primarily used Russian rather than Yiddish given names (although, where appropriate, both are indicated). For proper names that have conventional English spellings (e.g., Chaim Zhitlowsky, Vladimir Jabotinsky, Semyon An-sky, and Maxim Gorky) I have used those instead. In the case of Dubnov, as per scholarly convention, I have used his Anglicized/Germanized first name, Simon.

For events that occurred in Russia and works published there, pre-revolutionary dates are given "old style" (according to the Julian calendar) unless indicated otherwise.

Acknowledgments

It is my pleasure and privilege to thank those who helped this book to see the light of day. I feel fortunate to publish a book in the Stanford Studies in Jewish History and Culture series, and I am very grateful to Steven Zipperstein and Aron Rodrigue for supporting this project. I am indebted to Steven Zipperstein for his patience and feedback, as both were ultimately crucial in bringing this book about.

This project benefited from the generous financial support of a number of institutions: Brandeis University's History Department and the Tauber Institute for the Study of European Jewry; the Memorial Foundation for Jewish Culture; the Center for Studies of the Culture and History of East European Jews in Vilnius, Lithuania; the University of Florida's Center for Jewish Studies and History Department; Boston University's History Department, Elie Wiesel Center for Judaic Studies, College of Arts and Sciences, and Center for the Humanities; and the Helsinki Collegium for Advanced Studies at the University of Helsinki. The European University at St. Petersburg also provided crucial logistical and visa support in 2005–6 and on intermittent visits in 2011–12. The Goldstein-Goren Center for Diaspora Research at Tel Aviv University kindly provided me with an office and support for a visit in 2012. All the archives listed in the notes provided me with assistance and access to their collections. I would like to single out for special thanks the three archives where I conducted most of my research: the Central State Historical Archive (TsGIA) in St. Petersburg, the YIVO Institute for Jewish Research in New York, and the Central Archive for the History of the Jewish People (CAHJP) in Jerusalem. In particular, both Benyamin Lukin at the CAHJP and Fruma Mohrer at YIVO went above and beyond in helping and accommodating me.

The seeds for this book were planted at Brandeis University. Antony Polonsky was a source of support, level-headed advice, and wisdom during my whole time at Brandeis and beyond. Antony, Gregory Freeze, and Eugene Sheppard all provided valuable feedback on the first iteration of this project that helped to transform it into this book. Jonathan Sarna went out of his way, and still does, to ensure my success, as did the late Eugene Black. My comrades—Karen Auerbach, Michael Cohen, Adam Mendelsohn, Eric Schlereth, and the whole comparative history crew—made the supposed daily grind in actual fact a pleasure.

The University of Florida proved a stimulating intellectual and social environment in which to reconsider some of the key assumptions in this book. During my two years there I had countless helpful conversations with many colleagues, but I would like to thank in particular Nina Caputo, Stuart Finkel, and Mitchell Hart for reading parts of the manuscript, and Jack Kugelmass and Ken Wald for their mentoring.

I'm very thankful to have found a wonderful and supportive home at Boston University. I've turned to many people for support here, with this project and others, but the sage advice of Charles Capper, Charles Dellheim, Louis Ferleger, Tom Glick, Deeana Klepper, Pnina Lahav, Bruce Schulman, and Michael Zank helped directly to bring this book to the finish line. I owe a tremendous debt to Mr. Peter T. Paul for his generosity, as my Peter T. Paul Career Development Professorship allowed the travel, teaching leave, and other research support necessary to complete this book.

What was a manuscript and work in progress finally took shape as a book during my year as a research fellow at the Helsinki Collegium for Advanced Studies. I'm very thankful to the HCAS director, Sami Pihlström, as well as the staff there, especially Maria Soukkio and Minna Franck, for assisting with several crucial ingredients: freedom, finances, and logistical support. Svetlana Kirichenko worked diligently as a research assistant. Among my fellow fellows in Helsinki, conversations with Dmitry Dubrovsky, Alejandro Lorite Escorihuela, and Monique Truong kept my spirits buoyed.

I benefited over the years from many eyes on many drafts, and the following people (in addition to those specified earlier) read bits, pieces, or the whole at one stage or another: Eugene Avrutin, Tom Glick, Semion Goldin, Vladimir Levin, James Loeffler, Adam Mendelsohn, David Rechter, Jeffrey Veidlinger, and Polly Zavadivker. In the final stage of revisions, Phillip Haberkern read the book from cover to cover and helped me to get it publication ready. I'm pleased also to acknowledge much collegial advice, conversations, and guidance over the years from Israel Bartal, Valerii Dymshits (who kindly provided the photo on the cover), David Engel, the late Jonathan Frankel, Zvi Gitelman, Eric Goldstein, François Guesnet, Gershon Hundert, Kenneth Moss, Derek Penslar, Andrew Sloin, and Ruth Wisse. Galina Georgievna Lisitsyna provided invaluable guidance with navigating St. Petersburg's archives.

Working with the editors at Stanford University Press was a pleasure, and my thanks go to Eric Brandt, Friederike Sundaram, Stacy Wagner, and Kate Wahl for getting things up and running, and to Tim Roberts and Mimi Braverman for their help during the production stage. Kelly Sandefer and Jonathan Wyss at Beehive Mapping were responsible for the beautiful maps. I would also like to thank Elise Alexander for her research assistance and Shaina Hammerman for her help compiling the online bibliography.

Finally, my greatest joy is to acknowledge my family. My parents Martin and Belinda, my in-laws Rhoda and Eddie, and my Aunt Tovah all helped in innumerable ways to make this project, and this career, a possibility. My only regret is that my father Martin did not have the opportunity to hold this book in his hands. He read and edited every page of every draft until becoming ill, and I hope his spirit pervades its pages.

My wife, Jodi, has been with me since before I ever considered writing this book or, for that matter, becoming a historian. Against all good sense she embraced this project, this life, and everything that came with it. There is nothing I feel more grateful for than her support, and the fact that we've lived these experiences together. She walked the streets in this book's cities, learned its languages, and lived in its terrain. In recent years my children, Zoe, Jonah, and Mia, have also been able to share in these adventures, and for that, and for them, I'm thankful too. Now, on to the next adventure . . .

Introduction

This is the most difficult test of national maturity: when a nation is deprived not only of its political independence, but also its territory; when the storm of history isolates it from its physical foundation, scattering it in foreign lands where it gradually loses its unifying language. If for all that, in this rupture of external national bonds a people continues over the course of many centuries to create a distinctive existence, manifested in the persistent striving for further autonomous development, then this people has attained the highest stage of cultural-historical individualization and may be considered indestructible if *under subsequent conditions it intensely maintains its national will.*

S. M. Dubnov

In a full-color poster for elections to the All-Russian Jewish Congress in 1917, the Yidishe Folkspartey, or Jewish People's Party, entreats the residents of a small Jewish town to vote for their list. The poster depicts a ramshackle shtetl with broken posts and crumbling wooden homes; the townspeople gathered around a Folkspartey banner include a mix of elderly men with beards and women with covered heads, along with clean-shaven men (one with a newspaper under his arm) (see Figure 7 in Chapter 6). This outwardly populist Jewish party sought to enlist the support of the broadest possible segment of Russia's Jewish population. It forsook neither traditional religious and economic life, like the Jewish socialist parties did, nor life in Europe, like the Zionists did. It embraced Hebrew, Yiddish, and Russian as fulfilling different roles in Jewish life. It sought the democratization of Jewish communal self-government and the creation of new Russian Jewish national-cultural and governmental institutions. Most important, the self-named folkists believed that Jewish national aspirations could be fulfilled through Jewish autonomy in Russia and Eastern Europe more broadly.

Despite its pretensions to populism and its claims to represent all of Russian Jewry, the Folkspartey only superficially penetrated the kind of small Jewish town depicted in this poster. In fact, Jewish life in Eastern Europe had for some time been shifting away from this kind of small Jewish town as a result of massive internal migration, emigration, urbanization, and dislocation due to war. Yet, ideologically and organizationally, the Folkspartey leadership profoundly influenced the course of Russian Jewish politics. The principal tenet of the Folkspartey—nonterritorial autonomy for the Jews of Russia, or autonomism—became the central thrust of Jewish political life in Russia before the party's founding during the revolutionary years of 1905–7. Thus well before the creation of a Russian republic in 1917, autonomism had taken hold of the Jewish political mainstream. The fact that Jewish autonomy had become the single positive political demand that spanned the Jewish ideological spectrum is reflected in how, following the tsar's abdication, all Jewish political groups and parties took part in organizing an all-Russian Jewish congress and in establishing local Jewish communal governments and, at the same time, called for guaranteed legal rights to an independent Jewish cultural and national life.

Jewish autonomism, the idea that Jews in the Russian Empire should demand not only civil equality but also national or collective rights, was first articulated by the historian, journalist, and political theorist Simon Dubnov (1860–1941) at the end of the nineteenth century. As Dubnov himself defined it (with scant modesty), "autonomism [was] the name given by Simon Dubnov in 1901 for the practical program for national-Jewish politics in the *galut* [exile, or Diaspora] which developed from his championing of a national ideology."[1] Dubnov's "letters," a series of essays published between 1897 and 1906, constructed a diaspora-nationalist political philosophy that was centered on the demand for Jewish local and national self-government and rooted in a historical claim to Jewish autonomy in Eastern Europe.[2] In essence, Dubnov sought to apply the territorial demands made by other national minorities in the Russian Empire to the nonterritorial situation of the Jews by calling for Jewish autonomy over education, culture, and communal welfare and the reconstitution of Jewish autonomy. In doing so, he called for the Jews of the empire to reject the "Western" model of Jewish emancipation, in which Jews gave up their collective rights in return for civil equality for Jews as individuals. In his influential essay "Autonomism," published in 1901, Dubnov proclaimed: "The new epoch must combine Jewish civil-political equality with considerable sociocultural autonomy like that enjoyed by other nations in similar historical conditions. Jews must demand *civil*, *political*, and *national* equality, without sacrificing one for the sake of the other, as was the case in the past."[3] In the years following this essay's publication, Jewish political discourse shifted decisively toward discussion of national rights and self-government and became dominated by much of the agenda set out by Dubnov in his political treatises. Although Dubnov suggested that the term *autonomism* applied specifically to his own "practical program," many Jewish political groups in the Russian Empire developed programs that could be characterized as autonomist (but within a socialist, Zionist, or even liberal-integrationist framework) and adhered to Dubnov's position that the "fundamental principle [of autonomism] is the acknowledgment that the Jews exist as a nation in its dispersal among other nations."[4]

Like other nationalists, Jewish and not, Dubnov used historical arguments to justify political demands and pointed to historical parallels with other nationalities. The urgency with which he argued his case, however, rested on his belief that for Jews, arriving at the moment of emancipation was akin to coming to a dangerous precipice overhanging a sea of assimilation, into which whole Jewish communities had previously thrown themselves, thereby erasing their Jewish national identity. In essence, autonomism's adherents sought to fortify the Russian Jewish community—linguistically, culturally, and politically—for the moment when it eventually reached this precipice. As we will see, Jewish autonomists came to cast themselves as soldiers in a battle against assimilation, a foe with multiple and changing forms. We now know that the Western and Central European "assimilated" Jews of Dubnov's imagination experienced a more complex assimilative process than he suggests.[5] Nonetheless, what actually occurred is less important than how autonomists viewed the Jewish experience with emancipation in the West, how they perceived the threat of assimilation at home, and how they believed this danger should be countered. The autonomist movement included different interpretations of what autonomy had meant for Jews historically and what it should mean in the future. But all the interpretations included the idea that Jewish citizenship in the Russian Empire, when it came, should take a very different form from what already existed in the states of Western and Central Europe.

A single characteristic shared by most of the Jews who built a national movement in Russia was a period (or lifetime) of immersion in the Russian linguistic and cultural milieu. Similar to the empire's other national minorities, the Jewish cultural and political elite's internal struggle with questions of integration and national self-consciousness occurred, if not in isolation, then separate from the larger population. Some members of the Jewish elite were drawn from the small number of Russified (or in the Kingdom of Poland, Polonized) Jewry, others had left small towns for educational opportunities in bigger cities, and still others had participated in Russian political movements. Yet the legalistic nature of Jewish religious life combined with the traditionalism of Russian society created a situation in which an individual's personal secularism often led to an especially sharp break with family and community. Secular Jewish intellectuals raised in traditional Jewish environments felt no desire to return to the rigors of religious life—its restrictions on diet, dress, and Sabbath rest—even while they mourned the attendant erosion of traditional Jewish life and culture. Furthermore, even the most emancipated and radically enlightened Jews feared the degenerative effect that emancipation might have on the Russian Jewish collective.[6] As a result, many Jewish intellectuals turned to Jewish nationalism and autonomy to fill both psychological and practical needs. If Jews could find a means of achieving national self-determination while remaining in an Eastern European world, then a reconstructed Jewish communal life might serve as a bridge between the traditional and the modern.

Reestablishing Jewish autonomy became a matter of Jewish survival or disappearance in the minds of autonomist activists, and the greatest challenge was overcoming their own sense of disconnection from the people and culture they hoped to protect. To take one example, in 1912, Yisroel Efroikin pleaded with Jewish intellectuals in the Russian Empire to reconnect with the Jewish people—"the folk"—from whom he believed they had become hopelessly alienated. According to Efroikin, "There are no deep, inner, or intimate threads binding him to the folk: instead there is a different lifestyle, a different worldview, and a different language. Only the sword hanging over all of our heads today, only the heavy whip whistling over our backs, and a pallid sentimentality without skin and bones still hold him [the intellectual] to the people."[7] Efroikin went on to suggest that the Jewish intellectual in Russia was moving down a path similar to the one taken by his Western brethren, "in yearning to break and tear this last thread that binds him" to his community.[8] Efroikin's own story suggests that he was writing for and about himself as much as his audience, the readers of a new and struggling Yiddish magazine published in St. Petersburg. The product of a small Lithuanian town, Efroikin received a heder and yeshiva education before moving to Switzerland, where he attended the University of Bern. Efroikin's study of law and economics in Bern was second in importance to his radicalization there, and when he returned to the Russian Empire in 1910 as a socialist, he must have been a very different person from when he left in 1904.[9]

We can see in Efroikin's words much of the tension and irony inherent in the political objectives of the Jewish intelligentsia in the late Russian Empire. No different from the non-Jewish intelligentsia there, Jewish intellectuals argued among themselves about who best understood the needs and desires of their "people." Of course there was no single kind of "Jewish intellectual" in the Russian Empire at the time: Jews subscribed to the widest possible variety of political ideologies, including, perhaps most commonly, no ideology at all. Nonetheless, it is possible to identify a set of issues and institutions that preoccupied politically active Jewish intellectuals in the empire's dying days, and foremost among those issues was the reform and reconstitution of Jewish communal autonomy. Efroikin understood the potency of the forces tempting Jews to break free from tradition, and he argued that if this desire to break free could not be fought, then it should be channeled into reshaping Jewish communal life.

Because the transformation of the Russian Empire was still an open question (not only whether it should happen, but if so, when and into what), Jewish intellectuals considered how Jews might affect and be affected by that transformation. Those Jews who debated the "national idea" had already become part of the modern world and naturally presumed that with emancipation much of the rest of Russian Jewry would modernize as well. Modernity would confront Russian Jews, whether Russian Jews liked it or not, and Jewish intellectuals offered differing solutions to the problem. The most radical socialists sought to do away with tradition completely; in inverse, the Orthodox movement Agudat Yisrael later sought to co-opt the political process to protect Jewish tradition. But for many Jews, nationalism was the bridge between the traditional world and the modern world. The autonomist movement (and different varieties of autonomism) thus resulted from an accommodation of traditional conceptions of Jewish community and peoplehood to the pressures of modernization. On a practical level, Jewish autonomism attempted to transform a premodern system of Jewish corporate autonomy into the secular and national institutions of Jewish self-government that would form the foundation of Jewish autonomy within the modern state. Finally, autonomy came to be viewed as the best defense against the threat of assimilation (real or imagined), the aspect of modernization that came to worry Russian Jewish intellectuals most.

Defining Nationalism in Late Imperial and Revolutionary Russia

How one explains nationalism historically depends primarily on how one defines it. Can nationalism be defined as a collective striving for sovereignty? Is it the attempt by groups to achieve a correlation between state boundaries and ethnicity? Or is it simply a sense of belonging to some cohesive political body? Each question will yield a different explanation for the emergence of nationalism and its relationship to modernization, and in my mind this is the fundamental problem with the most widely cited contemporary theorists of nationalism.[10] Interestingly, one of the key theorists of Jewish socialism, Vladimir Medem, came to a similar conclusion during the early-twentieth-century debates over how to define nationalism and the Jewish nation: "It is obvious that the argument is futile, for each proceeds on the basis of what it needs to prove. Build the definition of a nation on the basis of its characteristics, and derive the sum of these characteristics from the definition of a nation."[11] While readers may detect in my analysis the influence of certain recent theorists, I have avoided fitting the development of Jewish nationalism into a procrustean bed framed by one theory or another.

The approach taken in this book is to examine the moment when Jews began to call themselves nationalists and believed themselves to be participating in something called nationalism. Clearly, a sense of Jewish peoplehood existed before that point, as Jews had a legal framework regulating their lives and a national and religious narrative understood by all members of the group. Nonetheless, Jewish "nationalism" is a reflection of the ideological transformation of Am Yisrael—the People of Israel—into something that was new and that, although related to religious culture, was not defined solely by it.

Dubnov and other nationalists took active measures to promote and strengthen Jewish national self-consciousness and, in doing so, knowingly developed a distinctly modern form of Jewish nationalism that went beyond peoplehood while breaking with (or modifying) the biblical idea of Jewish chosenness. In fact, in tying together religion, language, peoplehood, and place (whether Eastern Europe or Palestine), all varieties of Jewish nationalism in Russia shared the same basic ingredients as Russian and Polish nationalism. In their application of history to the development of a "national idea," Dubnov and his followers similarly seemed to exemplify the role of intellectuals in creating national movements. On the one hand, Jewish nationalism in Russia engendered a new secular understanding of the Jewish nation, one that allowed for national identification based on culture and history rather than on religious observance. On the other hand, the religion at the heart of Jewish culture and history was difficult to divorce from the new modern Jewish nationalism. Autonomists thus saw their primary task as solving the problem of how to provide secular Jews with a national culture and polity while constructing a communalist ethos that would bind traditional Jews (the folk) to people like themselves (the intelligentsia).

Contemporary understandings of autonomism ranged from limited demands for cultural autonomy to maximalist visions of a Jewish national assembly and a minister for Jewish affairs in the government. Unsurprisingly, the extent of a given political group's autonomist demands integrally related to how it viewed the Jewish "nation." In the early years of the twentieth century a major transformation occurred among both Jewish socialists and liberals away from cosmopolitanism and toward more overt identification of the Jews as a nation in need of particular rights as a group. Where one desired autonomy—in religion, language, land, or spirit—depended on one's political views and how one viewed the essence of Jewishness. A number of scholars have recently reexamined the period between 1881 and 1917, an era generally associated with the Jewish move away from liberal integrationism and toward more radical identities, both socialist and nationalist, to suggest that in fact Jewish political identity remained multilayered.[12] The past few years alone have seen a burst of studies (e.g., those by Nathaniel Deutsch, James Loeffler, Kenneth Moss, Gabriella Safran, and Jeffrey Veidlinger) that take as their subject the relationship between Jewish cultural production and identity construction in late imperial and revolutionary Russia.[13] Not unlike Jews in other parts of Europe and in the Americas, many Jews in late imperial Russia attempted to create a personal identity that would allow them to feel part of a group (the Jewish people) and yet benefit from the cultures and societies in which they lived. In the Russian Empire such identity construction was rather obviously and self-consciously manifested in the abrupt turn to Yiddish by Russian-speaking Jewish intellectuals between 1905 and 1917 or in the gradual embrace of Jewish nationalism by highly acculturated Jewish lawyers. Nevertheless, not every shift in mentality should be viewed as a crisis of identity. The Jewish intellectuals described in this book, though no doubt often aware of the many contradictions related to their personal identity, were primarily concerned with solving the "Jewish question" in Russia in a manner suitable to Russian Jewry.[14] In other words, they did not invent the notion of a Jewish nation; they came to feel part of one, often after a prolonged absence from the fold.

Jewish Sovereignty and Autonomy

It is almost taken for granted today that a people's national sovereignty is linked to territory and defined by borders. The world's national liberation movements since the mid-nineteenth century overwhelmingly focused on wresting political sovereignty from imperial control in a given place. If we look back, however, at the national diversity of the Russian Empire's western provinces and the Austro-Hungarian

Empire's eastern regions, we find that solutions to the burning national issues of the day did not always revolve around territory. In this part of Europe before the two world wars, different linguistic and religious groups frequently lived in cities and towns where no single group formed a majority. The possibility of guaranteed national minority rights in both the Russian and Austro-Hungarian Empires was one of the most discussed issues of the day, as national minorities sought greater control over their affairs. Although Jews could not demand territorial autonomy in Russia like the Poles, Finns, Ukrainians, or Baltic peoples did, they could claim the right to use their own language, educate their own children, establish their own universities, and generally govern their own affairs.

Furthermore, Jewish autonomism presented a solution to the complex historical problem of Jewish sovereignty in the Diaspora. The issue of the Jews' power and sovereignty throughout their long history has been the topic of more than one comprehensive treatment.[15] To appreciate the resonance of such questions, one need look no further than recent popular fiction. In 2007 a novel set in a counterfactual parallel world, in which millions of Jews found refuge and a form of self-government in Alaska, became a bestseller in the United States.[16] In this novel, by Michael Chabon, Franklin Roosevelt's administration, reluctant to take in Jewish refugees but sympathetic to their plight, established a Jewish autonomous district in Sitka, Alaska (the premise for Chabon's story was a real proposal made by Secretary of the Interior Harold Ickes in 1938 to use Jewish refugees from Europe to help settle the Alaskan frontier). In the novel Sitka becomes home to several million Jews. Chabon's story, and its commercial success, reflects the hold that the potential courses of Jewish history and the possibilities of Jewish sovereignty continue to have on the popular imagination.[17] The Jews in recent history are often seen as a people both with and without agency. They were able to establish their own national movement and sovereignty over their historical birthplace, far from their major population centers, yet at the same time they were unable to save millions of Jews trapped by war and genocide. At the core of the question of Jewish fate and agency one finds the question of sovereignty and autonomy. In the mind of Chabon, no less than those of the early

Zionists, territorialists, and much of the public, sovereignty is something that can be achieved through population concentration and territorial separation. In the 1930s even Stalin and the Soviet government briefly warmed to such an idea and established a Jewish autonomous region in the Soviet Far East (Birobidzhan), because in Soviet thinking the Jews could not be a real nationality without territory.[18] Yet Jews did not always equate autonomy, self-government, and sovereignty with territory, even when they made up a plurality—in some cases, a majority—in many towns and cities in Eastern Europe.

With the benefit of hindsight, Jewish autonomism may seem ill-fated or unrealistic. Yet autonomism merely reflected the nearly universal belief at the time that Jews would continue to live as Jews in the territories of the Russian Empire for many years to come. It is important to remember that in the early years of the twentieth century, many political possibilities still remained open for Russian Jews. Most of them did not feel compelled to choose between Zionism and socialism, or some combination of the two. Jewish intellectuals, whether liberal or radical, expected the empire's imminent or eventual transformation and sought to prepare the way for Jews to participate politically as equal members of a new society in a reconstituted state. Such political preparation took place noisily and in an atmosphere of intense competition between parties and ideologies and emerging rivalries between nationalities. Autonomism's seeming attainability was the very quality that drew Jews to the idea. Jewish autonomy required neither the complete overthrow of the tsar's regime nor the mass emigration of Jews. Jewish autonomy required only one thing: that when the empire became unsustainable in its existing form, Jews would be treated equally with other nationalities.

A New History of Jewish National Politics

The turn to autonomism by Russian Jewish intellectuals played a central role in both the politicization of Russian Jewry and the development of Jewish national self-consciousness. Although scholars have concentrated on the influences of Austrian socialism, Russian populism, English utilitarianism, or German Romanticism on the

intellectual development of Dubnov and other Russian Jewish nationalist theorists, Jewish autonomism was predominantly a product of its
times. The movement for Jewish autonomy developed in the context of
changing notions of political sovereignty, decentralization, and federalism among the many national groups of Eastern Europe and should
be seen as a key element of both the political campaign for Jewish
individual and collective rights and the cultural mission to create an
alternative to religious traditionalism. Various parties and individuals
incorporated autonomism into their ideologies for different purposes:
to aid the class struggle, as a waystation on the road to Jewish statehood in Palestine, or as a means of finding an answer to the Jewish
national question in the places where most of world Jewry then lived.
The widespread dissemination of the autonomist idea, and with it the
conviction that through autonomy the Jews might attain their national
aspirations under a future constitutional or revolutionary regime, thus
helps to explain the general Jewish turn to nationalism in Russia. By
claiming that Russia's Jewish question could be solved as part of a
general solution to its nationalities question, Russian Jewish nationalists fostered the belief that Jewish national claims, whether in Palestine
or Russia, deserved to be redressed alongside their demands for civil
emancipation.

I originally intended this book to be about the influence of an idea—
autonomism—on Jewish political life in late imperial and revolutionary
Russia. Although Dubnov's fame ensured that "Dubnov literature" has
flowed like a steady stream since his death and in fact has only increased
in recent years, most contributors to that literature have focused on his
life, on a historiographic approach, or on relationships with other well-
known public figures.[19] What remained to be completed was what one
historian called a systematic assessment of the "sociopolitical impact on
Russian and Polish Jewry of Dubnow's ideology."[20] This is the task, still
relevant twenty-five years after this observation was made, that I set out
to complete. Indeed, Dubnov's ideas influenced not just the political
discourse of the period but also the national self-consciousness of an
expanding number of educated and self-taught Jews—and, on a practical level, the objectives and demands of every Russian Jewish political party and communal organization in the early twentieth century. In

attempting to define Dubnov's sociopolitical footprint, however, I also discovered several interesting stories that help to explain the relationship between Jewish autonomy and the genesis of Jewish nationalism more generally, and these became the primary themes of this book. The first theme is that a small number of intellectuals made a sizable impact on Jewish national self-consciousness in the Russian Empire and on ideas about what the Jewish community, people, or nation needed to do to reconfigure itself for survival in the modern world. The second theme is that practical efforts toward Jewish autonomism closely followed attempts within Russian imperial society more generally to create more local self-government, a more decentralized state, and what we today call civil society. And the third theme is that Jewish nationalism developed in a changing legal environment, where the idea that nations had legal rights was beginning to take hold. Much of the debate about Jewish nationalism in the Russian Empire was therefore about what legal rights Jews were entitled to, as individuals, as a group, and as a nation.

This is the first book to examine in totality the movement for Jewish autonomy in late imperial and revolutionary Russia. I aim to explore the role of autonomism in the process of Jewish politicization, to identify the various streams of Jewish autonomism as they developed, and to determine how and why different Jewish political parties and figures took up autonomism. I also take into account the wide range of ideological and circumstantial factors that contributed to the ascendance of Jewish national rights. The actions of the Russian state and Russian intellectuals, the struggles of other national movements in the western provinces of the Russian Empire, questions of national minority rights in the Austro-Hungarian Empire, the mixing of new Jewish socialist and nationalist ideologies, urbanization in the Russian Empire, and the development of a Jewish intelligentsia that was actively engaged in the political questions of the day—these are just some of the elements necessary for a full view of Jewish politics in late imperial and revolutionary Russia.

The book moves approximately chronologically from the turn of the twentieth century until the early 1920s. In the first chapter I provide an explanation of the intellectual and historical origins of autonomism.

In Chapter 2 I explain how ideas about federalism and state decentralization that were popular among Russian intellectuals influenced their Jewish counterparts, and I consider the development of parallel conceptions of nonterritorial autonomy among Jewish and non-Jewish socialists. Here I make a key argument, one that runs through the rest of the book: that Jewish autonomism followed the Russian movement to create a self-governing public sphere and national life independent from the state. In the third chapter I examine the role of the Russian Revolution of 1905–7 in politicizing Russian Jewry and bringing the issue of national rights to the fore. During these revolutionary years and thereafter, politically active Jews in Russia became convinced that if the Jews did not create a program for nonterritorial Jewish autonomy, they would be left without the autonomous rights of the other national minorities. The decade leading up to World War I saw the creation of new autonomist initiatives and growing nationalism across the Jewish political spectrum. Jewish intellectuals, lawyers, and communal activists debated the nature of the national idea and the ideal form of Jewish self-government. In Chapter 4 I analyze the Jewish conferences, organizations, and publications established during the interrevolutionary period where the "national idea" and the possible means of implementing Jewish autonomy in Russia were debated.

Both the war and the February Revolution of 1917 opened new opportunities to advance Jewish autonomy. As discussed in Chapter 5, Jewish political activists worked during World War I to centralize Jewish communal organizations and establish local and Russia-wide self-government. In the midst of war, widespread anti-Jewish violence, and a refugee crisis, Jewish activists (like those of other nationalities) seized the opportunity to build institutions that could actualize their national autonomy. Finally, in Chapters 6 and 7 I evaluate not only the lively Jewish experiment with legal autonomy in Russia, Ukraine, and Eastern Europe made possible by the February Revolution and the tsar's abdication but also how the historical processes that led to autonomism's eventual failure between the world wars reflected the broader conflicts that arose from the dissolution of the Russian and Austro-Hungarian Empires and their transformation into new states. In Chapter 6 I pay particular attention to Jewish voting in the wide array of Jewish and general elections that took place over the course of 1917 because it provides a rare opportunity to assess how political ideas about nationalism, national rights, autonomy, liberalism, and socialism made their way (or didn't) into Jewish public opinion. As discussed in the book's final chapter, Jewish claims to national minority rights made their way to the deliberations and eventual treaties of the Versailles Conference, and the issue of collective Jewish rights—and in particular whether the Jews should be recognized as a nationality—was a question with considerable ramifications in the early Soviet Union, a state that came into being by promising national self-determination for all. Even though full-fledged Jewish autonomism was suppressed in Eastern Europe and the Soviet Union, the concept of Jewish collective rights persisted and was in fact imported in different forms to the Western liberal democracies and the Jewish community in Palestine, known as the Yishuv. In sum, with many bumps and much disagreement, between the turn of the twentieth century and the early 1920s, Russia's Jewish political, intellectual, and financial elite managed to develop the institutional and ideological framework for an autonomous community (or nation, depending on whom one asked). That process was alternately enabled by circumstances and then curtailed by them, because ultimately the Jews in the new states that emerged following World War I lacked the power to enforce Jewish claims to national rights and autonomy.

The tragic fate of European Jewry has for many compounded the difficulty in understanding that in the early twentieth century many Jews believed that their national expectations could be fully realized in Eastern Europe, and others, such as Zionists and socialists, adopted demands for Jewish national rights in Russia (and the Austro-Hungarian Empire) alongside their platforms for a Jewish state or proletarian revolution. Yet at the turn of the twentieth century, the Russian government faced intense pressure from both its emerging civil society and national groups in the western provinces to reform itself and decentralize its powers. Jewish autonomism emerged in this context and became not merely an ideology but a principle around which Jewish political and social life in the Russian Empire could be organized.

One Jewish Autonomy Imagined and Remembered

The Jewish historian Simon Dubnov constructed his theory of autonomism as both a political philosophy and a historical model. In his writings Dubnov argued that Jews historically had used communal institutions to establish and maintain their collective autonomy, thereby preserving Jewish national consciousness through millennia of settlement and migration in the Diaspora. By the early twentieth century, many Russian and Eastern European Jews agreed with Dubnov's belief that to avoid the supposed "assimilation" accompanying secularization among Western Jewry, Russian Jews needed to reconstruct Jewish communal autonomy.[1] Although Dubnov undoubtedly romanticized medieval Jewish communal structures, he tapped into the concerns all Jews faced in the modern world about how to preserve Jewish community and identity in an age of increasing secularization.

The political, ideological, and philosophical components of Dubnov's historical work were the subject of considerable discussion in his own day, and recent years have seen a veritable renaissance of scholarly interest in his historiography.[2] Dubnov was both a historian and a political figure, but his scholarly work was hardly the crude tool of his political ambitions. In fact, while for much of his life Dubnov had faith in the rightness and eventual triumph of his political philosophy, in terms of time and effort spent, his political activities typically came second to his scholarly work. Yet Dubnov himself clearly believed in the unity of his scholarly and political—or, perhaps more accurately, national—work. A particular concept of Jewish history in the Diaspora, and in particular of the emancipation process in Western Europe, underpinned his political ideology. The story that Dubnov tells in his writings is, to use his term, "sociological": It prioritizes people and institutions over texts. And the historical institutions that Dubnov valued were those that preserved Jewish autonomy, in various forms of self-government, throughout the long history of the Jews in the Diaspora. To Dubnov the structure of Jewish life and society in the Diaspora always reflected a collective will to preserve Jewish national difference, and this is where his politics and historiography most clearly come together. He believed that the modern state's attack on Jewish communal autonomy was particularly dangerous because by holding out the promise of integration, the state made Jews into eager accomplices in their own denationalization; the possibility of real national integration all the while remained illusory.

This chapter explains how Dubnov's political and historical theories developed, with attention to his philosophical influences. It also considers what Jewish autonomy meant historically and what actually happened to Jewish autonomy in the Russian Empire in the nineteenth century that led Dubnov and others to conclude it should be revived. To Dubnov the only way to ensure Jewish national continuity in the future was to rebuild the structure of Jewish autonomy along secular national lines, with legal recognition from the state. Thus the final section of this chapter gives a view of how the significant legal and economic changes affecting the Russian state and its inhabitants generally over the course of the nineteenth century altered Jewish society in particular.

Simon Dubnov and the Origins of Jewish Autonomism

Born in 1860 in the shtetl of Mstislavl, in the Mogilev Province of the Pale of Settlement, to a family of established talmudic scholars, Dubnov rejected the traditional religious observance of his family in favor of, first, the *Haskala* (Jewish Enlightenment) and, later, European philosophy, languages, and literature.[3] Although Dubnov's grandfather was a rabbi and religious pillar of the Mstislavl community, at the age of 13 Dubnov refused to continue his yeshiva education. Unable to enter university—he failed to qualify for a secondary school certificate or to obtain a permit to reside legally in St. Petersburg—in 1890 Dubnov moved with his family to Odessa, where, surrounded by other Jewish intellectual and literary figures, he began his intellectual transformation into a Jewish nationalist.[4] Whereas between 1882 and 1884 Dubnov had argued that the Jews should be considered a religious group and transformed into a confession along the lines envisioned by the Jewish Reform movement, in Odessa his perspective changed.[5] There, as he began to delve into historical research, Dubnov came to view the Jewish people not only as a nation but also as one whose history in the Diaspora had caused it to evolve to a higher stage of spiritual development than other nations that could develop a culture within their own geographic territory.[6] Dubnov's membership in Odessa's small yet influential circle of Jewish nationalist intellectuals, especially his friendship and ongoing dialogue with the founder of spiritual Zionism, Ahad Ha'am (Asher Ginzberg, 1856–1927), helped to shape his view of the Jews as a distinctly "spiritual" nation.[7] In the last decades of the nineteenth century a number of *maskilim*, as the adherents of the *Haskala* were called, in Odessa and elsewhere who had been committed to effecting the reform and acculturation of Russian Jewry through such institutions as the Society for the Spread of Enlightenment Among the Jews of Russia (known most commonly by its Russian acronym OPE) began to shift their energies toward more overtly nationalist enterprises and writings. Dubnov was also a lead protagonist in the so-called Odessa *Kulturkampf* when a group of intellectuals formed a "national committee" in an attempt to lead the OPE to a program of national education.[8] Yet while the prominent Hebraists of this group believed that the road to national redemption led to Palestine, Dubnov's evolution into a professional historian affirmed to him the importance of the Diaspora in both the Jewish past and future. It is through his historical works that Dubnov developed a sociological explanation of Jewish history that would inform all his political writings.[9]

In his political essays, known as the letters, Dubnov outlined his interpretation of diaspora nationalism and called for autonomism to be adopted by all Jewish political groups. On a practical level he discussed emigration and "national education," and he advocated the reinstitution of the *kehila* (the historical body of local Jewish communal authority) as a secular organ of Jewish government within the Russian state. Dubnov insisted that neither territory nor the Talmud had preserved the Jewish people; rather, Jewish communal autonomy had maintained national self-consciousness throughout the Jews' long history in the Diaspora. Applying positivist evolutionary theories to Jewish history, Dubnov argued that the Jews historically had sought to establish spheres of Jewish autonomy to preserve their distinct national cultural and spiritual life, even in adverse conditions. In this way the Jews had survived in the Diaspora by turning the disadvantage inherent in a lack of territory into an evolutionary advantage for national development. Influenced by John Stuart Mill, Auguste Comte, Henry Thomas Buckle, and especially Herbert Spencer, Dubnov explained the history of Jewish society since its dispersion as a succession of changing hegemonic Jewish centers in the Diaspora. Thus Dubnov's evolutionary view of Jewish history broke dramatically with what was then the dominant understanding—espoused, for example, by the German Jewish historian Heinrich Graetz (1817–1891)—that Judaism was an unchanging religious concept. Although influenced by Hegel, Graetz believed that only Judaism's external features (i.e., its practices) changed over time, leaving in place the religion's core ethical values.

In Dubnov's evolutionary historical conception, Jews did not merely survive as a society; they evolved as a nation. In each diasporic center (e.g., Babylonia, Iberia, and Central and Eastern Europe), Jews used communal institutions to carve out a sphere of Jewish autonomy that preserved and even strengthened the Jewish sense of nationality. As one center declined or suffered pressures from the outside, an alternative center emerged, established its autonomy, and became hegemonic. Dubnov's historical theory thereby became the basis for his political ideology. If throughout their long history in Europe the Jews had been able to realize their "national life" through communal self-government, then the current challenge must be for the Jews to reassert their "social autonomy"—the ability to arrange their communal self-government according to historical traditions and the community's internal needs—which he considered to be crucial to keeping a nation spiritually and culturally strong.[10]

In addition to blurring the distinction between history and politics, Dubnov's personal influence on the historical consciousness of educated Russian Jews was significant. When more than 1,000 Jewish students in institutions of higher education in Kiev were surveyed in 1910 about who had most shaped their understanding of Jewish history, 43 percent listed Dubnov alone or among other writers, making his name by far the most popular answer.[11] All the respondents may not have agreed with Dubnov's diaspora-nationalist politics, but the popularity of Dubnov's historical texts and, accordingly, his autonomist interpretation of Jewish history, served to spread his political philosophy. Dubnov formed his historical and national theories from an eclectic mix of positivism, Herderian philosophy, Russian populism, and the classical liberalism of Mill.[12] The Russian opponents of historical materialism were particularly influential to Dubnov's conception of nationality, and three in particular left indelible marks on his historical and national theories: Petr Lavrov, who stressed the historically important role of individual intellectuals in the moral development of nations; Konstantin Aksakov, who separated territorial sovereignty from spiritual development; and Vladimir Solov'ev, who differentiated between positive and negative forms of nationalism.[13] Dubnov, like Solov'ev, argued for the compatibility of nationalism and a "universalist" ethos. Dubnov also further clarified Solov'ev's distinction between cosmopolitanism, which, according to Dubnov, required abandoning national distinctions and was therefore a negative phenomenon, and universalism, a positive phenomenon that saw each people as a member of the family of nations.[14] In his letters Dubnov engaged the theories of Solov'ev, Lavrov, Ernest Renan, and Johann Gottfried von Herder to demonstrate the philosophical and historical basis of Jewish national self-consciousness in the Diaspora.

In his political and philosophical writings Dubnov argued for the collective pursuit of an ethical and humanistic Jewish national idea. According to him, religious and national ideals were morally and psychologically similar, and therefore the transition from religion to Jewish nationalism occurred as part of a natural process. In his first four letters, the most purely philosophical ones in the series, Dubnov differentiated between national egotism and national individualism, arguing that Jews should opt for the latter. As national individualism did not aim to rob any other nationalities of political freedom or cultural autonomy, its expression did not violate the "ethics of society."[15] Thus the Jews must seek to use spiritual and ethical Jewish nationalism as a legal foundation for Jewish autonomy. Dubnov considered the fore-most challenge to establishing the principles of nonterritorial autonomy to be how to define both the privileges and the legal limits that would govern each nationality's autonomy so that larger or more powerful nationalities would be prevented from impinging on the autonomy of others.[16] Because Dubnov believed that the Jews historically existed and continued to exist in a state of national individualism, he considered them particularly well suited for such a legally delineated autonomous arrangement. Furthermore, in equating the ethical ideal in Judaism to spiritual nationalism and framing this nationalism as a force of histori-cal preservation in the Diaspora, Dubnov constructed a form of Jewish nationalism that included secular and religious Jews alike: "The ideal of a spiritual nation is in its essence an ethical one, and such is precisely the national ideal of *Judaism*."[17]

Dubnov was not the first to see the Jews' history in the Diaspora as having played a role in the spiritual development of Jewish people-hood. In the 1870s, Perets Smolenskin (1842–85) used his Vienna-based journal *Ha-Shahar* to steer maskilic thought toward an embrace of Jew-ish national self-consciousness and peoplehood. Although Smolenskin had made similar arguments before, his influential essay of 1872, "Am olam," may be his most famous presentation of the idea of the Jews as an "eternal people."[18] Smolenskin argued that the Jewish religion in the Diaspora preserved the Jews as a "spiritual nationality," a concept that both Dubnov and Ahad Ha'am would develop further. Smolen-skin was also among the first and most influential thinkers to propose that Jewish religious observance was something different from frater-nal spiritual bonds and that these bonds could remain strong even if the observances frayed.[19] And though he still believed in the necessity of preserving religion, by presenting nationalism as a response to the challenges of secularization and advocating the creation of a "national history" to further national self-consciousness and political activism, Smolenskin prefigured not only Dubnov but also arguably all Jewish nationalist movements.[20]

Some Jews sought to define themselves in solely religious terms, whereas others completely abandoned religious observance and a distinct Jewish identity. In contrast, Dubnov saw the question of

Figure 1 Simon Dubnov, Odessa, 1913. Courtesy of the YIVO Institute for Jewish Research, New York.

whether the Jews would continue to seek out spheres of autonomy in the Diaspora in the starkest terms of "national extinction or national revival."[21] He concluded that the willingness of both Jewish intellectuals and European governments to trade Jewish autonomy for civic rights—the basis of Jewish emancipation in the West—had been psychologically damaging, historically unnatural, and an incalculable mistake.[22] When addressing the National Assembly in Paris in 1789, Count Stanislas de Clermont-Tonnere may have famously claimed, "A nation within a nation is impossible,"[23] but in late imperial Russia, where the Russian language itself distinguished between *russkii* (Russian) and *rossiianin* (a subject of the Russian Empire), there appeared to be considerable room for many "nations" to live within a nation. As Theodore Weeks observes, unlike in France or Germany, "the nationalist's desire to see the state as the embodiment of the nation—or national spirit—was quite alien to the conservative Romanov state."[24] Given that many groups in the Russian Empire were then developing demands for national recognition, autonomy, and even independence, Dubnov was determined that the Western European "mistake" be avoided in the East.[25] As a polar opposite to what he called the "doctrine of national suicide" promoted by so-called assimilationist Jews, Dubnov created a nationalist ideology and a set of national demands that were not based on territorial sovereignty but rather on the legal recognition of Jewish rights to self-government and therefore appropriate to the situation of the Jews in the Russian Empire.[26] As growing numbers of Jews began to join radical and liberal Russian political groups and formulate demands, Dubnov concluded that anything less than full civil equality and national rights would deny Jews their freedom.

Dubnov saw historical consciousness as the basis for Jewish national self-consciousness, and he viewed building Jewish national self-consciousness as the very purpose of his historical activities. He also called on other Russian Jewish intellectuals to take up the task of historical study for the purpose of national activism.[27] The foundation of Dubnov's diaspora nationalism was his belief that Jews were a historical nationality with a legitimate claim to self-government in Europe. The argument that Jews had no historical claim to a permanent existence as a nation in Europe he labeled a falsity, spread by both antisemites and

Zionists. Dubnov argued instead that just as Jews had preserved their national self-consciousness in the Diaspora by carving out an autonomous Jewish life, they must continue to do so even when faced with the breakdown of communal authority as a result of state pressure.

Dubnov lived in a multiethnic empire that was undergoing a significant socioeconomic and political transition. Within this context his proposals for legal recognition of the Jews as a nationality, Jewish self-government, and the Jews' management of their own affairs were consistent with the demands of other nationalities, despite the Jews' lack of territorial claims. Although radical in its desire to replace traditional Judaism with diaspora nationalism and a national culture, both Dubnov's historiography and his political ideology were notable more for their idealization of Jewish autonomy in history than for a utopian vision of the future.[28] In reality, Jewish autonomy was neither as complete in the premodern world nor as willingly abandoned as Dubnov presented in his historical and political work, and it is worth briefly examining the historical context for Jewish autonomy—its decline and resurrection—from a more objective standpoint.

Self-Government and Autonomy in Jewish History: An Overview

Dubnov's autonomist theories were rooted in a long tradition of Jewish self-government in Europe and beyond.[29] The necessity for Jews, wherever they might live, to administer their own affairs according to the laws of their religion was considered by them to be sacrosanct at least since the composition of the Babylonian Talmud in late antiquity. In practice, the Jews' rights to autonomy were perfectly consistent with, and in fact replicated, those of other religious groups in the Persian and Roman Empires, the Islamic world, and Christian Europe. Jews managed their autonomy in the Diaspora as a self-governing community, known in Hebrew as the *kehila* (or *kehile* in Yiddish; *kehilot* is the plural form in both languages). In medieval Christian Europe, especially the areas of France, Germany, and Italy, the *kehila* developed the organizational characteristics that came to be imported to Eastern Europe. In most cases the *kehila* was run by an elected council of lay leaders known as the *kahal*.[30] Among its other responsibilities, the *kahal* appointed representatives to the local authorities and was held collectively responsible for the actions of individual Jews in the community (whom, in the case of misbehavior, it had to hand over or deal with accordingly). The *kahal*'s main activities were collecting taxes for the king or lord and managing the employment of the religious functionaries necessary for the Jews in a town to live in accordance with Jewish law and tradition.[31]

In medieval Germany Jews began to receive written charters that defined Jewish obligations and privileges. General charters were issued by a king and gave Jews the right to live in the king's realm; specific local charters stipulated the terms of Jewish residence in a municipality. Charters were usually negotiated when Jews gained the right to live in a given place, but they were often later altered, renegotiated, or even canceled by succeeding rulers. The medieval and early modern Polish municipal structure was based on German law, and it followed the German practice of defining Jewish residential privileges and autonomy according to written charter. In 1264 Bolesław the Pious, the duke of Wielkopolska, granted the first charter allowing Jews to live in Poland. Bolesław's charter became the model adopted by Kazimierz the Great (r. 1333–70) and subsequent kings to apply to all of Poland and Lithuania. As the source of power and authority in Poland-Lithuania (united by the Treaty of Krevo in 1385) shifted from kings to the great nobility between the sixteenth and eighteenth centuries, Jews received more and more charters from the nobility and came to live increasingly on their lands and in their private towns.[32] As Poland-Lithuania merged and expanded, Jews played an integral role in the colonization of new lands in the east (in the fifteenth century), the entrenchment of feudalism (in the sixteenth century), and the growth in wealth and power of the Polish noble magnates (in the seventeenth century). During that time the Jews in Poland-Lithuania as a whole became the largest Jewish community in the world.

As was the case with Christian burghers, the royal charters that determined the legal basis for Jewish settlement in Poland-Lithuania granted Jews wide-ranging corporate autonomy. Jews who settled progressively farther east brought with them the institutions of the *kehila* and *kahal*.

In Poland-Lithuania, as was the case elsewhere, the *kahal* levied taxes for the crown and the nobility. And like elsewhere, the *kehila* in Poland-Lithuania functioned much like a separate municipal administration, with legal jurisdiction over a town's Jewish population and powers to regulate all social, economic, and political contact between Poles and Jews.[33] But the system of self-administration that developed there went beyond the autonomy of earlier French and German communities and, for that matter, went beyond the significant autonomy that developed throughout much of early modern Europe and the Ottoman Empire.[34] The *kehilot* in Poland developed a complex governing system with different tiers of leadership within the *kahal* (*roshim*, *tovim*, and a rotating president known as the *parnas*) and had specialized officers for writing rules, supervising their observance, and acting as judges (sometimes with higher and lower courts). The various positions were determined by electors, chosen once a year from among the town's prominent married men (those who could afford high taxes and fees paid to the *kehila*).[35] The *kahal* was charged with protecting the collective interests of the Jewish community, and its decisions carried the weight and authority of Jewish law.[36] It appointed the town's chief rabbi (*av beit din*), who also served as the head of its law court. Because the *kahal* also held the ability to fire the chief rabbi and other paid religious officials, power in the community sat firmly in the hands of the lay leadership.

The medieval *kehila* and its institutional successor in the Polish-Lithuanian Commonwealth were tied together by the *va'adim*, leagues of local *kehilot* that were connected by intercommunal institutions and responsible for the general welfare of the Jewish community, as well as its representation to the governing authorities.[37] Much of the structure of Jewish autonomy that developed in Poland deliberately followed the structure of the Polish nobility, who had a representative governing body (*sejm*) that deliberated on laws for the entire Commonwealth as well as many local parliaments (*sejmiki*).[38] Unique to Poland-Lithuania, from the sixteenth to the eighteenth centuries, Jews possessed a level of self-government above the regional councils, known as the Council of Lithuania and the Council of Four Lands (Va'ad Arba Aratsot). The Council of Four Lands (so called even after the number of regions represented in it came to exceed four) met twice a year to write regulations

and decide on matters of disagreement between *kehilot*. Most important, they ratified and collected taxes from the communities, which is
why they had the support of the crown, who referred in official documents to this super-*kehila* as the Congressus Judaerom or the Jewish
Sejm.[39]

Within Polish society Jews existed as a corporate, self-governing
group, not unlike a Polish estate, though without officially composing one. To Dubnov the Jews' historical autonomy also provided an
example of how local Jewish autonomy in his own time might find
national coherence. The idea that the *kehilot* and the councils historically served as a substitute for Jewish statehood infused Dubnov's historical and political writing. In his descriptions of the medieval *kahal*
in particular, what was in effect a corporate entity in a corporate society resembled instead an instrument of modern national politics.[40] Yet
Dubnov overdetermined the completeness of Jewish autonomy; in reality, its specifics were constantly negotiated between the Jews and the
Gentile authorities. Even with their autonomy, Jews always depended
on the crown, the nobility, or the municipality for their security and the
maintenance of their privileges. The *kahal* ultimately derived its authority and powers of coercion from the Gentile authorities, who ensured
the *kahal* leadership's status as the sole intermediary between the Jews
and the Gentiles. The *kahal*'s power depended on individual Jews not
appealing directly to Gentile authority, a dynamic that Eli Lederhendler
termed the "contingent basis" of Jewish self-government.[41]

European states never ceased to involve themselves in internal Jewish affairs, but they began to trim back effectively the *kehila*'s autonomy
at least as early as the eighteenth century, resulting in what has been
considered the loosening of the bond between Jewish community and
individual.[42] In Poland-Lithuania the large landholding, or magnate,
nobility, on whose lands the majority of Jews lived, increasingly saw
the *kahal* as a rival authority over its Jewish subjects, and throughout
the eighteenth century the nobles sought to control, influence, and,
where possible, even select the Jews' leadership.[43] In his historical writing Dubnov painted the eighteenth century in Poland as a period of
internal schism, external threat, and the decline of communal authority,
and this view came to dominate Jewish historiography.[44] The extent,

however, to which a crisis in Jewish society and the weakening of Jewish autonomy in seventeenth- and eighteenth-century Poland-Lithuania took place is unclear.[45] It is certainly true that the regional councils and the Council of Four Lands lost their relevance in the eighteenth century. Financial problems associated with the councils' growing debts and the authorities' preference for more efficient and centralized means of taxation led to their abolition in 1764. But locally, until Poland's loss of statehood through the partitions (in 1772, 1793, and 1795) and absorption into Russia, Prussia, and Austria, the *kahal* in most places functioned as it always had, as an oligarchy with control over most aspects of Jewish religious, social, and economic life.[46]

Between 1750 and 1844 the Prussian, Austrian, and Russian governments all enacted reforms aimed at stripping the Jews of their legal autonomy.[47] Still, Jewish autonomy never fully disappeared in the lands of the former Polish-Lithuanian Commonwealth, or elsewhere in Europe, due to Jewish desire for community and the need of governments for expediency. For example, even though Jewish autonomy technically ended in the Grand Duchy of Poznan with the second Polish partition of 1793, the central government in Berlin found it useful to preserve existing Jewish communal structures.[48] And although the Prussians formally dissolved the legal authority of the *kehilot* in the Polish territories they acquired, the communities continued to organize institutions of self-government in all possible areas of Jewish life.[49] In a series of legal changes the rabbinate became subsumed under the new *Gemeinde*, or community, a situation that facilitated secular rather than religious Jewish communal control and with it the Prussian Jewish communities' integration into the dominant society to an extent not seen in other formerly Polish Jewish territories.

Napoleon briefly brought Poland back to life by creating the Duchy of Warsaw out of territory conquered from Prussia and then Austria (and he presumably would have enlarged it further had he defeated the Russians) and gave it a constitution and the Napoleonic Code. Most of the Grand Duchy (with the exception of Poznan) went to Alexander I at the Congress of Vienna in 1815, but in an attempt to diffuse Polish discontent, the new Kingdom of Poland was created (also known as the Congress Kingdom, or Russian Poland), with the tsar as king and with a liberal constitution. The Kingdom of Poland also set its own policy with regard to its Jewish population, and in 1822 it abolished the institution of the *kahal* and all Jewish fraternal organizations. Thus within the Russian Empire, the autonomous Kingdom of Poland actually abolished Jewish autonomy on its own, and more completely, more than twenty years before the 1844 law abolishing the *kahal* throughout the rest of the empire. Even so, Jews preserved their autonomy in the Kingdom of Poland by illegally organizing exclusively Jewish associations (*khevres* in Yiddish; *khevrot* in Hebrew). The 1822 reforms replaced the *kahal* with congregational councils that came to be controlled by integrationists (as was the intention), but the religiously traditional simply found a different means to exercise power over the community, namely through the *khevre kadisha* (burial society).[50] The Kingdom's autonomy was progressively curtailed after two disastrous failed revolts in 1830 and 1863, but the Jews' full emancipation in Poland, granted in 1862, was not rescinded after the Russians put down the revolt. The Kingdom of Poland after 1863 (formally renamed the Vistula-Lands) was thus a completely anomalous legal entity and geographic space for Jews: part of the Russian Empire but free of anti-Jewish legislation.[51]

The dismantling of Jewish communal autonomy and the corporatist structures remaining from the medieval world was the hallmark of every European government's attempt to integrate their Jewish communities, like other corporate bodies, into the modern state.[52] In contrast to Dubnov's presentation of Western and Central European Jewry's eagerness to trade autonomy for civil emancipation—whether in Austria, Prussia, France, or Poland—Jews had little power to fight the centralizing tendencies of the state when it sought to eliminate their inconvenient corporate privileges.[53] For example, the very phrasing of the decree in 1791 granting the rights of citizenship to all French Jews (extending to Ashkenazic Jews the privilege already granted to the Sephardic community) stipulated that taking the civic oath "shall be considered as a renunciation of privileges in their favor."[54] Jews tended to resist efforts to do away with their autonomous privileges, yet even concerted opposition and petition-writing campaigns could do little to sway governments. And as Jews tended to discover later, states rarely sought the complete integration of the Jews and used the remaining Jewish communal structure for a variety of practical purposes.

Jewish Self-Government in the Russian Empire

Before the first partition of Poland, the Russian Empire had only a small Jewish population (and only then since the 1720s) living within its borders. Almost immediately after 1772, however, when those borders moved west past the Dnieper and Dvina Rivers and incorporated a large slice of eastern Poland, the Russian state began to consider the question of what to do about the Jews in their newly acquired territory, and their autonomy. Because what concerned the state most were taxes and stability, the Russian government initially reinforced the legal authority of the *kehilot* and their courts and even briefly allowed the reinstitution of the regional councils and the creation of the Va'ad Medinat Rusiya (Council of Russia).[55] The government began to rethink these policies in the 1780s, and the drive to curtail Jewish autonomy that soon followed was a natural corollary to the desire of tsars from Catherine the Great to Alexander III to find an appropriate means of integrating the Jewish population into the Russian estate (*soslovie*, pl. *sosloviia*) system. Catherine the Great, whose reign included the three partitions of Poland and the Russian Empire's annexation of most of the territory that had been Polish, was the first to be faced with the question of the Jews' legal status. Seeing an opportunity to expand her new cities and towns, Catherine attempted to incorporate the Jews into the two urban estates. Such efforts were in keeping with her Enlightenment-inspired desire to form a well-ordered state, and, if pursued, this reform might have fully merged Jewish autonomy into that of the urban estates.[56] But notably, Catherine did not eradicate Jewish autonomy, as she did with the autonomy of other groups, such as the Polish nobility or the Baltic German barons.[57] Efforts to resolve the legal status of the Jews were stepped up under Alexander I, when the so-called Jewish Committees he appointed recommended that Jews be required to join the estates of farmers, artisans, merchants, or townspeople. Such suggestions reflected the government's desire to remove the Jews from their role as economic intermediaries between the Polish nobility and the mainly Russian Orthodox peasantry.[58]

The Russian government's approach to the legal status of the Jews and their autonomy was shaped most strongly by Russian society itself. Until 1905 (or, arguably, 1917), all Russian subjects were exactly that: subjects and not citizens, because the tsar had a monopoly on power. Within the largely hereditary Russian estate system, Jews, like everyone else, were subject to specified privileges and limitations. Furthermore, rather than transforming itself from a feudal society into one based on individual rights and the rule of law, as was happening in Western and Central Europe, Russia saw its legal and social boundaries fluctuate throughout the nineteenth century. Russian rulers even belatedly attempted to categorize into estates those of their subjects who had been outside the estate structure. Separation between estates grew in the nineteenth century, as did estate self-consciousness among groups. But the system also perpetuated the existence of many subgroups and included a significant component of individuals (known as *raznochintsy*) who did not belong to any hereditary estate. Although the *soslovie* system was highly flexible, by the late imperial period a person's estate had become the primary marker of self-identification, and endogamy within estates reinforced distinct cultural and social differences between groups.[59]

In considering the Jewish population acquired by the empire's westward expansion, the central question for Russian governments was always whether the Jews should be integrated into the new legal categories (and if so, which ones) or excluded completely.[60] As Benjamin Nathans points out, the result was a particularly chaotic classification with regard to Jews, who simultaneously fell under a Jewish and another (usually merchant) estate.[61] Jewish members of the urban and merchant estates had certain anomalous privileges and restrictions, especially regarding residence. Jews were prevented from living in many cities where other merchants could live, but unlike other merchants and members of the urban estates, Jews were permitted to live in the countryside and distill alcohol (privileges that were periodically rescinded and reinstituted by the government). Especially in the first quarter of the nineteenth century, such legal discrepancies more often than not worked in the economic favor of the empire's Jews.⁶² Still, efforts to reclassify Jews along new estate lines and to merge the Jews with their corresponding Russian estates accelerated under Count Pavel Dmit-rievich Kiselev's Jewish Committees, which lasted from 1840 to 1863. Kiselev's work represented the apex of attempts by Russian bureaucrats to apply Enlightenment-inspired ideas to the task of transforming Jews into Russians.⁶³

Consistent with its haphazard efforts to merge the Jews into the estates, the Russian government also periodically attempted to scale back or do away with Jewish autonomous institutions. To reduce Jewish political autonomy, in 1804 Alexander I in theory strictly limited the powers of Jewish communal leaders in the *kahal* to tax collection and the jurisdiction of the *kahal*-appointed rabbinic courts to religious matters.⁶⁴ In reality, the *kahal* maintained broad control over all aspects of Jewish governance because the government depended on its taxing power. Under Nicholas I the state attempted to increase its administrative reach into all religious communities, and its efforts to curtail the Jews' legal autonomy were consistent with Nicholas's attempt to reform the empire through centralizing it and minimizing cultural differences among the empire's diverse inhabitants. Some of these efforts took the form of attempting to make religious law compatible with civil law; other efforts attempted to end customs that marked the separateness of a particular religious community. The best example of the latter can be seen in the statutes passed by Alexander I and Nicholas I regulating Jewish dress, the intention always being to eliminate the Jews' visible distinctiveness.⁶⁵

The bureaucratic campaign against the *kahal*, which lasted until the institution's abolition throughout the Russian Empire by Nicholas I in 1844 (and was then succeeded by a campaign against the supposed "secret *kahal*"), occurred as part of the general centralizing efforts of the state, yet in practice the state merely supplanted the existing Jewish autonomist institutions with ones more directly under its control.⁶⁶ Thus the 1844 law abolishing the *kahal* throughout the Russian Empire did not abolish Jewish autonomy or even—as its designer, Count Kiselev, intended—suspend the community's funding through the tax on kosher meat (known as the *korobka*). The state thereby failed to solve the problem it had faced since its original absorption of large Jewish populations. The real dissolution of the official Jewish community, although possible from a legal standpoint, would have required, among other things, the integration of Jews into the general corporate professional structure, an outcome unwelcome to the non-Jewish population. Even though as a community the Jews lost their legal right to self-governance, in requiring that their taxes be paid collectively, the state left in place the instruments of Jewish autonomy.[67] In other words, the Jewish community remained largely autonomous, even as its institutional leadership lost state sanction. Indeed, by abolishing the *kahal*, the government lost its ability to influence the Jewish community directly and at the same time created or bolstered alternative social organizations that would prove ever more resistant to integration.[68]

In addition to abolishing the *kahal* and transferring its juridical authority to municipal courts, the Russian government simultaneously recreated the Jewish community in a new legal entity, the *evreiskie obshchestvo* (literally, Jewish society, and ironically the term in Russian that the government had always used for the *kahal*), which it required to collectively provide the state with taxes and military recruits and to make key decisions on behalf of the community, such as electing "official" or "crown" rabbis. Furthermore, the government preserved the community's power of adjudication in Jewish law, and so a framework for the Jewish community continued to exist. The Senate even declared that the new entity should be legally recognized as a "juridical personality" (*iuridicheskoe litso*).[69] The *kahal*'s responsibility for the provision of Jewish military recruits (after 1827) and the often corrupt methods it used to meet that obligation had already badly damaged the moral authority of the official Jewish communal leadership.[70] Thus, even after the *kahal*'s abolition, some Jews in the second half of the nineteenth century continued to see its successor, the *evreiskie obshchestvo*, as an arm of tyranny. One of Russia's first Jewish lawyers, Il'ia Grigor'evich Orshanskii (1846–75) argued that although Jews faced the same individual civic obligations as non-Jews, they were required to fulfill these obligations as a group, through a state-empowered community.[71] Therefore, Orshanskii argued, the Jewish *obshchestvo* bore some resemblance to the peasant *mir* (commune), only unlike the peasant *mir* the state viewed the Jewish *obshchestvo* with distrust.[72] Orshanskii thought that the legal impossibility of remaining Jewish outside the official Jewish community resulted in an impediment to Jewish integration, and he believed that Jewish communal life would need to end as the empire became a secular state. Nonetheless, as Olga Litvak points out, Orshanskii's "radical Jewish individualism" proved exceptional to Jewish thinking in Russia at the time.[73]

If the Russian government abolished the *kahal* but not its function within the state or community, what did Jewish communal self-government look like after 1844? It is not clear whether the government's primary motivation in abolishing the *kahal* was social (to integrate and secularize the Jews) or economic (to tax more effectively and eliminate corruption), but the real substance of the law was simply to put Jews under the jurisdiction of the municipalities they lived in. In essence, Jewish communities paid taxes collectively to municipal governments and continued to govern themselves in varying ways, depending on their locations, while hiding many of their activities from the authorities and gaining official state sanction for others.[74] As in the Kingdom of Poland, the Jewish associations in the Pale of Settlement (where they remained legal) took on new importance by maintaining the status and authority of the elite in a given town. So too did the leadership of the *obshchestvo*, synagogue board, or communal board, depending on the local system. So in Vilna, for instance, which became a major Jewish economic, cultural, and religious center in the nineteenth century, the so-called Tsedaka Gedola (greater charitable board) became the overseer of the many associations, charitable responsibilities, and property of the community, including the burial society, education for the poor and orphans, and upkeep of the Great Synagogue. Because the Tsedaka Gedola also fulfilled the functions of the *obshchestvo* for the government (i.e., collecting taxes and providing conscripts), it received official state sanction.[75] The directors of the Tsedaka Gedola were selected from among the city's financial elite in a manner similar to the selection of leaders of the *kahal*, with the major difference being that the nomination and election process was now run through the city's municipal office.[76] Similar sorts of communal boards or councils regulated the various aspects of Jewish communal life in a number of other cities, such as Mogilev, Vitebsk, Ekaterino-slav, and Berdichev.[77]

Odessa, in contrast, ran its thriving Jewish communal life through synagogue boards and Jewish welfare organizations, many of whose deputies held seats on the city council.[78] Odessa was a port city founded in 1794 (it was previously an Ottoman fortress town called Khadzhi-bei) that over the next thirty years became a major commercial center, attracting Jews (especially from Galicia), Greeks, Italians, Armenians, Turks, and many others who came for economic opportunities and especially the grain trade. Although a *kehila* was founded in the first year of the city's founding, as a frontier town on the empire's periphery and a new city, Jewish migrants created their own version of commu-nal self-governance. Modernizing *maskilim* played a large role in Jewish communal affairs there from nearly the beginning. In the 1820s a small group of prominent Jews received permission from the government to establish a modern Jewish school using funds from Jewish taxes col-lected by the *kehila*, and modern synagogues came to dominate the city's religious life in the 1840s.[79] The law abolishing the *kahal* there-fore had even less effect in Odessa than elsewhere, especially as religious observance declined over the years. Like the city's many other nationali-ties, Jews threw their energies into Jewish social and professional clubs, communal organizations, and philanthropies—running schools, creat-ing cultural organizations, and building hospitals—as they would have done regardless of the law of 1844.[80]

Finally, it is important to highlight that throughout the nineteenth century internal changes in Jewish religious life played a significant role in eroding the authority of Jewish communal authorities, independent of any actions by the state. The growth of the modern yeshiva as an educational model and its institutionalization as the seat of scholarly expertise and learning meant that the goal for the brightest students was to stay within the yeshiva system rather than to take a position on the payroll of a town.[81] Hasidism, a movement of religious revival based around charismatic spiritual leaders who founded independent dynas-tic courts, provided yet another model of religious authority. Hasidic courts throughout Eastern Europe and regional yeshivas in Lithu-ania (especially the famed Volozhin Yeshiva) emerged to fill the power vacuum created by the dissolution of legal autonomy and, with the acquiescence of the authorities, they came to fill many of the political functions previously played by the *kehila*.[82] The yeshiva and the Hasidic court, together with newly created Jewish voluntary organizations, also aggregated many of the religious and social functions of the *kehila* and recreated for their members the sense of belonging to the *kehila kedosha* (holy community).[83] At the same time, members of a new Jewish merchant aristocracy and self-described *maskilim* (who were often one and the same) sought recognition from the government as the sole representatives of Jewish interests in the empire. In the absence of Jewish institutional representation, prominent individual Jews came to play an important role in advocating on behalf of Russian Jewry as a collective. The internal competition over who represented Russian Jewry that followed the *kahal*'s abolition may even have put in place the framework for Russian Jewry's political modernization.[84]

Reclaiming the *Kahal* from Its Critics

Governmental suspicion of Jewish communal autonomy intensified in the late nineteenth century as a result of the work of Iakov Brafman (1824–79), a Jewish convert to Russian Orthodoxy whose publicizing efforts were responsible for the widely held view that a covert *kahal* continued to perform a host of nefarious deeds. Orphaned at a young age, Brafman came from a poor Jewish family in Ketsk (in Minsk Province). After converting to Russian Orthodoxy, he became a missionary among the Jews and came to blame communal control by elites for both the negative impact of the Jews on Russian society and the inability of the church to liberate oppressed Jews from their Judaism. From the late 1860s until the 1880s (at which point his son took over his work), Brafman published a series of articles and books of annotated documents supposedly from the *pinkas* (communal record book) of Minsk between 1794 and 1833. Brafman's various editions of what collectively became known as *The Book of the Kahal* went far beyond reproducing the minutiae of Jewish self-government. He sought to use these documents to prove that the continuing mission of the *kahal* was to oppress and segregate Jews, exploit Christians, and generally maintain a "talmudic municipal republic."[85]

Brafman changed the nature of Russian Judeophobia by altering the diagnosis of what was wrong with the Jews. Whereas previous Russian anti-Jewish sentiment tended to blame the Talmud for supposed Jewish fanaticism and separatism, Brafman blamed the *kahal*, which he claimed not only predated the Talmud but also had in fact created the Talmud for the purpose of communal control. Brafman further argued that the *kahal* defied the law abolishing it and continued to operate secretly in every town in the Russian Empire and that the existing Jewish organizations, such as the Society for the Spread of Enlightenment Among the Jews of Russia and the France-based Alliance Israélite Universelle, were actually arms of an international or "world-*kahal*."[86] According to Brafman, the *kahal* continued its reign over the Jews through the use of excommunication, separate law courts, and *hazaka* (the granting of monopolies). The purpose of his work was to argue that Jewish self-government was not merely an obstacle to Jewish reform and eventual emancipation; rather, the actions of the *kahal* proved the impossibility of ever emancipating the Jews *as Jews*. Brafman's writings were distributed widely throughout Russian government offices and were commented on extensively in the Russian press. Brafman himself advanced through the Russian bureaucracy, eventually becoming Censor of Jewish Books in the Chief Office for Press Affairs in St. Petersburg. Once in that position, Brafman proposed that the government seek to dismantle any and all forms of Jewish communal organizations, a proposal fiercely opposed by many of the empire's prominent Jews.[87] The chief effect of Brafman's influence was to focus the attention of antisemites in the Russian government and the public on the harmful nature of Jewish autonomy.

The impact of Brafman's publications was to reinforce the accusation that the Jews constituted "a state within a state."[88] Though the phrase "a state within a state" suggested the existence of a more direct governmental conflict than the term "a nation within a nation"—a description that was not by definition negative—both implied that the Jews' loyalties lay with an authority that was separate from the tsar and the Russian state (or, in other countries where the phrase was often heard, the French National Assembly or the Prussian crown). Yet even the claim that the Jews represented a nation within a nation, with its con- notations of ethnic solidarity and separatism, reflected at best a wary ambivalence about Jewish civil equality regardless of Brafman's work. As an example, in 1872 the Russian Geographical Society stated: "The Jews represent a nation within a nation; they are an isolated tribe, with its own language, its own religion, its own economic base and its own community—in administrative as well as civil terms."[89] The Jews were not the first to be accused of forming "a state within a state," a political slogan initially directed at the French Huguenots and later the Jesu- its.[90] When applied to the Jews, however, as it was throughout Europe by the nineteenth century, this slogan took on new meanings. In some cases it was used as an argument against the Jews' qualification for citi- zenship; in other cases it was a reason to deny the Jews the right to maintain a separate sociopolitical community.[91]

Because the accusation of dual loyalty threatened to disqualify the Jews from emancipation, the publication of *The Book of the Kahal* put members of the acculturated Jewish elite on the defensive, forcing them to deny the *kahal*'s continued existence and to downplay the sig- nificance of the remaining Jewish communal organizations. Dubnov's focus on reinstituting Jewish communal autonomy through the *kahal* was therefore revolutionary, in part because he reclaimed the concept of the *kahal* from the severely negative associations the term conjured up in the Russian imagination as a result of Brafman's work and in part because, unlike other acculturated Russian Jews at the time, he openly embraced the concept of Jewish self-government. Dubnov reaffirmed the importance of the *kahal* and *kehila* in Jewish history, fully accept- ing their protostate functions and promoting the idea that Jewish self- government should expand its responsibilities under state sanction.[92] Dubnov's position was, in effect, a mirror of Brafman's. Not only did Dubnov deny the existence of a pernicious secret Jewish *kahal*, but he also treated the erosion of Jewish autonomy as the source of Jewish troubles in the modern world. To Dubnov, greater Jewish autonomy was the solution for the present-day Jews, not the problem.[93]

Like several before him, such as Graetz, Smolenskin, and the Gali- cian Jewish theologian Nahman Krochmal (1785–1840), Dubnov revised the Hegelian pattern of thesis, antithesis, and synthesis in his own vision of Jewish history. For Dubnov the thesis represented the period in which communal self-government served in place of Jewish citizenship, the antithesis represented attempted assimilation, or the Western model, and the synthesis stood for the coming realization of secular autonomy through the reestablishment of Jewish self-government.[94] "The thesis was called 'isolation,' the antithesis 'assimilation,'" Dubnov wrote. "What is the name of the newborn synthesis? *Autonomism*. Autonomism represents the aspiration of any viable nation for the maximum internal independence or autonomy possible under the present political conditions."[95] Reflecting a number of theoretical trends at the time, Dubnov's synthesis envisioned the state's decentralization in favor of greater local governance. Yet Dubnov cast the reconstruction of Russian Jewish communal life as a deterministic historical process by which Russian Jewry, as it approached its emancipation, would seek to reconstitute legally its lost autonomy and to rebuild itself as an equal and autonomous member within the community of nations.

Dubnov argued that because the historical *kehila* had cared for both the secular and religious affairs of the Jews, the *kahal*'s management of the community's "national" and religious affairs should have split simultaneously and in a manner similar to the way religion and state had separated in Western Europe.[96] In other words, as the scope of the *kahal*'s religious authority narrowed, the communal government should have compensated by expanding its secular responsibilities and may thereby have facilitated the transition for the Jews from religion to nationalism. In Dubnov's view, however, instead of the French and German Jewish religious communities transforming themselves into national communities, they continued to exist merely as a fiction. Even though the concept of autonomism was still in its infancy when Dubnov wrote his treatise "Autonomism," he established that one institution—the *kehila*—should be at the center of Jewish autonomism, and he identified its historical secular responsibilities: for communal welfare and the supervision of economic life, criminal and civil justice, and tax collection for the government. These responsibilities had been part and parcel of the religious community's role, but the secular and religious functions of self-government could be separated administratively, as was the case in most European governments.

Like the attempts to merge Jews with the Russian estates, attempts to dismantle Jewish communal self-government in the Russian Empire occurred in the context of Western-facing reformers seeking the progressive transformation of Russian society. Awareness of the peasant commune entered public consciousness in the nineteenth century in a similar way, becoming a target of reformers who saw an institution representing peasant communal solidarity as an impediment to modernization. At the same time, some Russian philosophers came to idealize the peasant commune, seeing it as the epitome of the Russian "people" and as a particularly Russian response to the problems of modernity. Anke Hilbrenner places Dubnov squarely within the Russian intellectual tradition that saw collective institutions as the ultimate defenders of a particularly Eastern European way of life against modernization (equated with the West).[97] Hilbrenner is correct that, no less than the populist "father of socialism," Alexander Herzen (1812–87), Dubnov sought to adapt traditional life to the modern demands of postreform Russia and believed the situation of Russian Jewry to be dramatically different from that of Western and Central European Jewries. Nonetheless, while Dubnov may have been influenced by the antimodern discourse, popular among some Russian thinkers, that differentiated between Eastern and Western paths to social harmony—and in his historical work Dubnov may have idealized medieval and early modern Jewish autonomy—his political philosophy was radically modernizing. Dubnov emphasized the role of Judaism in preserving Jewish nationality throughout exile, but he advocated the radical secularization and democratization of communal self-government and its operation by secular professionals, the creation of a program for "national" education, and the institutionalization of formal bilateral relations between the Jews as a minority and the central government. In effect, Dubnov proposed the complete reconstruction of Jewish life in Russia along the lines of a "national" group. More than simply seeking to preserve Jewish collectivity in a battle against a centralizing state and dramatic Jewish urbanization, Dubnov sought to reconfigure and even, it might be said, modernize Russian Jewish life before the possibilities for doing so vanished. He saw Russian Jewry at the type of crossroads of emancipation that French, Prussian, and Austrian Jewry had reached earlier, and he believed that if Russian Jewry could preserve and even strengthen its national identity in the process of emancipation, it might serve as a model for all Jewish communities in the Diaspora.

In the context of nineteenth-century state and empire building, to "modernize" was to centralize, integrate, and homogenize—processes sure to meet resistance from national minorities when modernization meant the elimination of certain local privileges.[98] For the Jews this process of modernization through centralization, which arguably began with the abolition of the Council of Four Lands in Poland in 1764, took a major step with the elimination of the *kahal* in 1844, but remained incomplete.[99] Even in the Russian army, an institution considered by Jews to be a bastion of assimilation and forced conversion, the government not only granted Jewish religious autonomy but also allowed Jews to establish their own self-governing societies, mimicking the structure and responsibilities of Jewish voluntary societies in the Pale of Settlement.[100] The government may have erratically scaled back and delegitimized Jewish autonomy in the nineteenth century, but because of its reluctance to completely merge the Jews with the Russian estates, it removed many of the roots and branches without fully uprooting the tree. To understand how and why Jewish nationalists sought to reconstitute Jewish autonomy in late imperial and revolutionary Russia, it is first necessary to see how autonomism emerged from the particular circumstances of late imperial Russian society.

Russian Economy and Jewish Society in the Nineteenth Century

Dubnov was born in 1860 in the town of Mstislavl and wrote his first public meditation on the nature of Jewish nationalism in 1897 in Odessa, which was then his home. In those thirty-seven years the Russian Empire had changed enormously. The economic and social currents that carried Dubnov from Mstislavl to Odessa, from Yiddish to Russian, and from religious education to political theory had carried millions of other Jews to other destinations. Like much of Europe and the United States, the Russian Empire had been transformed in the second half of the nineteenth century, and it is worth considering what this process of modernization entailed for the empire's residents, particularly its Jews. In 1897 the empire's 4 million Jews still overwhelmingly spoke Yiddish, practiced Judaism, and worked as artisans and traders. Yet Dubnov's political philosophy stemmed from the changes in Russian Jewish society over the previous four decades.

Dubnov and his generation were products of what became known as the Great Reforms, undertaken by Alexander II to remake Russian society and restore Russian military power in the wake of the country's embarrassing performance in the Crimean War. Alexander implemented a range of reforms—to the agricultural economy, the military, and the legal and educational systems—that affected all aspects of life and society in the Russian Empire.[101] And, although he opposed removing Jewish legal disabilities too quickly, Alexander was considerably less heavy-handed than his predecessor, Nicholas I, in his approach to merging the Jews into Russian society. Even so, Alexander's 1861 edict emancipating the serfs adversely affected many Jews who were intimately tied to the peasant economy, and most Jews did not benefit from the transition to industrialization. As mechanized industry began to emerge, freed peasants moved to towns and cities in large numbers. Because non-Jews had fewer technical skills and therefore made lower wage demands, they were preferred to Jews as workers by Jewish and non-Jewish factory owners alike.[102] When shrinking opportunities for trade and commerce combined with greater competition and a higher than average birthrate, the result was the relative pauperization of the Jews in the Pale of Settlement over the course of the last forty years of the nineteenth century.[103] More and more Jews were forced from trade, commerce, and highly skilled artisanship into labor-intensive manufacturing and low-skilled handicraft work, such as leather tanning, bristle making, and cigarette manufacturing. More than anything else, the limited opportunities for sustainable employment explain the mass migration of Jews out of the Russian Empire—nearly one-third of the Eastern European Jewish population—especially from its northwest regions. One historian has called the impact of the late-nineteenth-century decline in Jewish fortunes a "de-classing" that removed the economic niche which had allowed Jews a better standard of living than their neighbors and that left most Jews without a means to make a living, relegating them to a "marginal caste."[104]

Yet the Great Reforms also opened up dramatic new opportunities for Jews to advance in Russian society and enjoy new privileges. In 1861 the government took the important step of removing restrictions on place of residence and choice of occupation for Jewish university graduates, and some Russian Jews saw this act as a Jewish emancipation equivalent to the abolition of serfdom.[105] Jews flooded Russian gymnasiums in order to enter universities, and then flooded the universities themselves. By 1886 nearly 15 percent of students at Russian universities were Jewish, with a much higher percentage in cities within the Pale of Settlement, such as Kharkov and Odessa.[106] The newly educated and other Jews with residential privileges extended the acculturated Jewish elite from a tiny group to one numbering in the tens of thousands (albeit still proportionally small).[107] The effective emancipation of the population's most educated segment created a tangible incentive for those Jews with the ability to do so to break their ties to traditional society, and that incentive by itself could be transformative. For example, Dubnov never managed to pass the university entrance examinations, but the hope of doing so provided the impetus for him to enter a gymnasium rather than a yeshiva and guided his self-education for a long time thereafter. Dubnov went from his traditional upbringing in Mstislavl to becoming a member of the growing Russian Jewish intelligentsia because the universities first created a Jewish intelligentsia—that is, Jewish students adapted the ideas of the Russian intelligentsia about the special role of intellectuals and their distinction from the *narod*, or people.[108] Adopting an invented term in the 1860s to describe themselves, the *intelligenty*—members of the Russian intelligentsia—gave themselves exceptional purpose, as the "intelligent or intellectual ones."[109] And it was in the universities where this new class was formed. As Martin Malia suggests, "For the unlettered mass of the population, an *intelligent* was anyone with a gymnasium or a university training," a fact that makes perfect sense when one considers what a tiny percentage of the population those with an education formed.[110] For educated

Russians (and Poles), it was the intellectuals outside the professions and civil service who especially became the frustrated agents of change most associated with the *intelligentsia*.[111]

Conveniently for our purposes, 1897 was also the year of the last complete Russian imperial census, which allows us to see a profile of the empire's Jewish population at that moment. It is immediately obvious that the Russian Empire generally and the Jews in particular had become considerably more urban since the Great Reforms. The shtetl (or Polish market town, the *miasteczko*) had no meaning except to Jews, and it was given a legal definition, as *mestechko* (small town), only in 1897. Despite its iconic status in Jewish collective memory, by 1897 only one-third of Russian Jews lived in shtetls, according to the census. Even that figure may be inaccurate (most likely too high) because there was no clear definition of *mestechko* and because people did not always live where they claimed they did.[112] People were moving from the countryside to small towns, from small towns to large towns, and from everywhere to cities.[113] Jewish migration inside the Russian Empire, although difficult to track, moved mainly from north to south, due to the pressure of peasant migration to the towns of the northwest and the ensuing occupational shift. Because of their high birthrate and competition for jobs, Jews were forced to be highly mobile, and the 1897 census shows that half of the empire's Jews no longer lived where they had been born.[114] In fact, a few more numbers from the 1897 census can help paint a picture of the extent of Jewish urbanization. Within the Pale of Settlement there were still many towns that were almost entirely Jewish: 35 locales in 1897 with over 1,000 people were more than 90 percent Jewish. But a rapidly growing number of Jews were also living in large towns and cities, where Jews made up a substantial proportion of the population. For example, 37 locales in the Pale of Settlement with more than 10,000 inhabitants were majority Jewish, and 4 metropolitan areas with more than 100,000 inhabitants were at least one-third Jewish (those cities were Kishinev, Vilna, Ekaterinoslav, and Odessa). In addition, 21 cities in the Pale had a Jewish population of at least 20,000 in 1897, and many cities elsewhere in the empire had large Jewish populations, especially in the Kingdom of Poland (which included Warsaw, Europe's single largest Jewish community) but also in Kurland and in the imperial capital, St. Petersburg.[115]

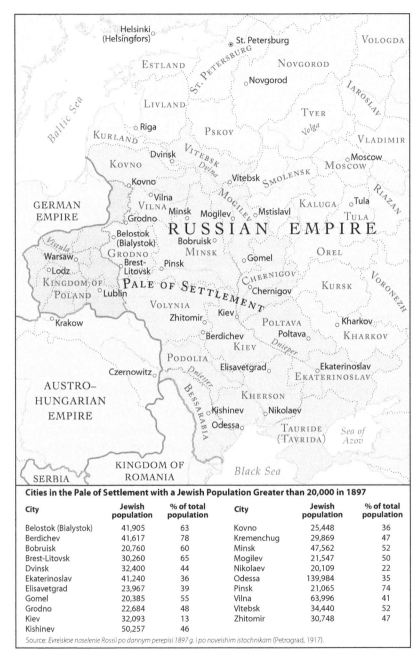

Cities in the Pale of Settlement with a Jewish Population Greater than 20,000 in 1897

City	Jewish population	% of total population	City	Jewish population	% of total population
Belostok (Bialystok)	41,905	63	Kovno	25,448	36
Berdichev	41,617	78	Kremenchug	29,869	47
Bobruisk	20,760	60	Minsk	47,562	52
Brest-Litovsk	30,260	65	Mogilev	21,547	50
Dvinsk	32,400	44	Nikolaev	20,109	22
Ekaterinoslav	41,240	36	Odessa	139,984	35
Elisavetgrad	23,967	39	Pinsk	21,065	74
Gomel	20,385	55	Vilna	63,996	41
Grodno	22,684	48	Vitebsk	34,440	52
Kiev	32,093	13	Zhitomir	30,748	47
Kishinev	50,257	46			

Source: *Evreiskoe naselenie Rossii po dannym perepisi 1897 g. i po noveishim istochnikam* (Petrograd, 1917).

Figure 2 Western provinces of the Russian Empire, 1897–1914.

Given that, despite urbanization and internal migration within the empire, estates continued to be used as the primary category of collective rights and restrictions in the Russian Empire, it is important to keep in mind the lack of clarity and continual disagreement about what was Russia and who was Russian. Critics of the estate system, especially on the left, considered the legal divisions within Russian society to be anachronistic (and of lessening importance to class), and some argued that regardless of Russian law, all the Russian and non-Russian peoples living within the Russian state composed a collective Russia. As Jane Burbank points out, the *soslovie* system continued to define the legal rights of all the empire's subjects until 1917, however much Russian and Jewish intellectuals might have preferred this not to be the case.[116] Yet at the same time, urbanization and greater mobility also created challenges in how the state categorized its subjects. For example, at the end of the nineteenth century the Russian Empire still depended on religion to classify its subjects and their privileges, but doing so had become more difficult. Russian Orthodoxy became destabilized in the wake of the Great Reforms and migration and urbanization made religious observance and affiliation harder to compel. If a Ukrainian peasant and a Jew moved to a city and both avoided religious observances and the jurisdiction of their respective religious communities, how was the government to classify those individuals by estate? By the time of the 1897 census, even if the government still officially used religion to differentiate its subjects (and would continue to do so until the end of the tsarist regime), the reality of life required new criteria to classify people and bureaucrats came increasingly to view the distinctions between subjects in national terms.[117]

It would be surprising if the tremendous economic, demographic, and legal transformations that affected individual Jews' lives in the last half of the nineteenth century did not also transform Jewish society and values, and indeed one can see significant changes. For instance, the disparity between the fortunes of the very rich and the growing number of impoverished Jews led the wealthy to create a wide range of Jewish philanthropic institutions. Increased urbanization, combined with the shift in communal authority from the religious elite to the economic elite (the two categories having previously been more closely intertwined), led to a fairly rapid institutionalization of Jewish social welfare. Philanthropists thereby filled the holes left by the legal dissolution of the official Jewish community in 1844.[118] Jewish old-age homes, homes for orphans, homes for the ill, and asylums all became part of Jewish urban space after the 1840s.[119]

Communal rabbis, on the other hand, began to disappear. By 1900 most of the large and important urban centers did not have a communal rabbi, and it was unusual even for smaller Jewish communities to maintain a communal rabbi.[120] By dissolving Jewish communal government and requiring communities to maintain a crown rabbi for administrative record keeping and official representation, the state undermined the institution of the communal rabbi, who, as the ultimate religious authority of a given place, was elected by the *kahal* and later the *obshchestvo*. Whether or not to circumvent the crown rabbi and elect a communal or spiritual rabbi as the town's real religious authority became the choice of communities and individuals. The crown rabbinate failed to fill the immediate modernizing function the state believed it would precisely because communities continued to elect a spiritual rabbi, but over time this practice declined.[121] As Shaul Stampfer suggests, the decline of the communal rabbi can best be explained by the increasing diversity of opinions and values among Jews in the Russian Empire, made even more complicated by the large migrant populations in each city. Rabbis reflect the ideals of a community, and consensus on those ideals became more difficult to reach as the number of Jews in a given place increased.[122]

Changes in attitudes toward philanthropy and communal services gave rise to a secular communal bureaucracy linked indissolubly to the modernization process. In some cases, as in the educational initiatives of the empire's wealthiest Jews, what Brian Horowitz refers to as a "Jewish enlightenment society" sought to use its resources to integrate the Jews into Russian imperial society.[123] Yet many local philanthropic initiatives represented an expansion of the preexisting communal framework, responding to a perceived increase in need for communal services. For instance, the *korobka*, the community's tax on kosher meat, was already being collected and spent on communal welfare. As ever greater numbers of the empire's Jewish elite settled in St. Petersburg in the second half of the nineteenth century, they attempted to develop that city's religious community as a model for the modern Jewish municipality in the Russian Empire. As they introduced new communal structures and reshaped others, the Jewish reformers looked for examples in the postemancipation municipalities of Western Europe with large Jewish populations, and they naturally stressed the importance of their own role in the community's leadership.[124]

Jewish legal rights within the Russian Empire declined in the 1880s and 1890s. Failure by the state to modernize the Russian economy sufficiently fed conspiracy theories, and the emergence of Russian nationalism spread popular antisemitism. Governmental policy continually aimed to restrict Jewish economic activity. A wave of popular anti-Jewish violence in 1881 and the government's reaction to it turned many Jews who had previously favored integration toward national self-consciousness. That the propagators of the violence made no distinction between religious and secular Jews, and that the government chose to blame the Jews instead of their attackers, shocked many Russian Jews who had believed that education and cultural assimilation would eventually erode the barriers between Russians and Jews. The pogroms also disillusioned many Jewish populists (*narodniks*), who shifted their concerns from the Russian peasantry to the oppressed Jewish masses. The precise impact of the events of 1881 on assimilated Jews, both socialist and nonsocialist, continues to be debated.[125] On an individual level, there is no doubt that the violence served as a call to arms for a number of budding Jewish nationalists. Yet it also served more as a trope for disillusionment (not unlike the Dreyfus affair) than as its direct cause. In the wake of 1881, early or proto-Zionists in Russia such as Moshe Leib Lilienblum (1843–1910) argued that the racially based antisemitism resulting from European nationalism would be a permanent phenomenon.[126] Dubnov read Lilienblum's autobiographical novel *Hat'ot ne'urim* (The Sins of Youth) when he was in his late teens, and he may have taken from it the conceptual apparatus of self-realization through crisis that he used to understand his own life and craft his own autobiography.[127] Perhaps the best example of the turn to Zionism by the disillusioned maskilic segment of Russian Jewry was Lev (Yehuda Leib) Pinsker (1821–91), the author of *Autoemancipation*.[128] As a decorated doctor who had served in the Crimean War, Pinsker exemplified the success of integrated Jews as well as their vulnerability. After 1881 he concluded that the hatred of Jews by Gentiles, or Judeophobia, was rooted in what he considered the pitiful condition of diasporic Jewry. The most influential element of *Autoemancipation*, Pinsker's manifesto, was that Jews cannot rely for their emancipation on the beneficence of Gentiles, who will always regard them as aliens in their midst; the Jews must therefore work to improve their own condition.[129]

Dubnov's claim that the "Jew who was a slave of little value outside the ghetto was a free man inside the ghetto, within his Pale of Settlement, in his community, in his spiritual realm" may seem both romantic and nostalgic.[130] But even though Dubnov found an element of spiritual freedom in Jewish isolation—a view shared by Zionist thinkers such as Max Nordau—he did not advocate the denial of Jewish civil equality.[131] He believed that in a constitutional, liberal, multiethnic state, civil equality and national self-determination were complementary. Indeed, such a formula similarly formed the basis for the demands of Polish liberal nationalists in the Russian Empire after the collapse of the revolt of 1863. The Polish response to failed national aspirations and lack of political sovereignty redefined the Polish nation as a shared cultural and linguistic heritage preserved among the Polish people and therefore not dependent on statehood or borders for survival. Through self-government, language rights, and national education, Dubnov believed that the Jews in the Russian Empire—and, for that matter, in the Austro-Hungarian Empire, Germany, and France as well—could similarly redefine the Jewish nation and achieve their civil and national emancipation.

Like other nationalist figures in Europe, Dubnov expected that the success of the nineteenth century in indelibly establishing concepts of personal rights and freedom would be followed by the twentieth-century challenge of firmly establishing "the ideal of freedom or autonomy for national individuals."[132] Yet Dubnov extended the concept of national rights beyond the territorial definition, insisting that all nations within a free state should be entitled to the same rights. Such a distinction was, of course, important because Dubnov formulated his national theories contemporaneously with the development of a competing and at times overlapping Jewish national movement: Zionism. At the core of Dubnov's historical and political autonomism lay the belief in the Jews as a diasporic people, and he considered autonomism—the constant striving for Jewish autonomy in the Diaspora—to be the "law of Jewish survival."[133] To deny a Jewish national existence in the Diaspora, then, was to deny history and, in Dubnov's view, to deny the Jews a decent future.[134] The contemporary challenge for Dubnov, and for those autonomists and diaspora nationalists who drew on his thinking, lay in building a modern means to address the Jews' budding national expectations on the edifice of historical Jewish self-government.

Conclusion

In nineteenth-century Western and Central Europe, many factors— from industrialization, urbanization, and the growth of capitalist economies to greater legal protections for all citizens—combined to erode the Jews' autonomy, regardless of any direct actions taken by states to end it.[135] The Russian Empire was pulled in different directions in the nineteenth century by Westernizers and those who favored a separate Russian path, but the same processes that affected the Jews in Western and Central Europe, where there was no single model for either capitalist development or Jewish emancipation, affected the Jews in Eastern Europe, albeit to different degrees. Both Dubnov and his philosophy were of course products of such changes, and like other Jewish intellectuals of his day, Dubnov grappled with the question of Jewish continuity in the modern world. In his historical writing Dubnov attributed Jewish national survival over two millennia in the Diaspora to Jewish adaptation to changing circumstances. In his political theories the idea of a return to self-government that formed the heart of Dubnov's autonomism was not an antimodern theory; rather, it was a reinterpretation of modernity. The notion that the civic and religious responsibilities of the *kehila* could be disentangled, given the historical lack of differentiation between the two, in effect was a form of radical secularism. Both autonomists and those favoring Russification held such a notion equally, with the crucial difference between them being whether communal institutions should serve the purpose of national regeneration (as the autonomists believed) or integration (according to the supporters of Russification). In fact, it was the *maskilim* who first sought to manage the Jews' transition from corporate identity to citizenship by creating institutions that were both Jewish and imperial and, in doing so, planted the seeds of early Jewish nationalism.[136] The development of Jewish autonomism continued this trend and (as elaborated in the next chapter) borrowed Russian liberal ideas about the benefits of decentralizing and localizing the empire's administration.

Dubnov saw the erosion of autonomy among Western European Jewry as something that Eastern European Jewry should do their utmost to avoid. And indeed the Jews of the Russian Empire seemed much better equipped to resist demands for total assimilation in exchange for civil equality, which in any case was not forthcoming. The Russian Empire was not a nation-state, and Jews lived among other nationalities that were demanding some form of autonomy. In addition, more than just a kernel of the superstructure of Jewish autonomy remained. No grand conspiratorial *kahal* existed in the Russian Empire, but neither the framework of a separate Jewish community nor the communal power of compulsion ever completely disappeared.

Like many Zionists, Dubnov came to his nationalist ideology through a spiritual search for a way to give a reconfigured secular Jewish nation a status equal to that of its European counterparts. This personal evolution began long before Dubnov considered himself a nationalist. What the followers of Dubnov shared with the forerunners of Zionism in Russia was a rejection of individual responses to the problems facing European Jewry in favor of collective answers. Where they differed was in their turn to Jewish diaspora culture instead of Zion (and statehood) for the material to build a new Jewish society. Sovereignty, in the minds of autonomists, was a goal that could be achieved without uprooting the Jews from the birthplace of their contemporary culture and what had become their historical lands. The turn, or return, to the *kehila* by highly acculturated Jewish intellectuals represented not only dissatisfaction with the incompleteness of emancipation but also a revision of old forms of traditional Jewish authority for the essentially modernizing task of making Russian Jewry a national community.

In the end, autonomism offered Jews a way out of a problematic national dynamic. In the late imperial period, liberals, radicals, and others expected the empire's transformation, either through evolution or revolution. Within this context, national minorities—especially in the western provinces, where most Jews lived—were making increasingly noisy national demands, including for the devolution of powers and greater autonomy. Some Jewish intellectuals came to realize or fear that Jews would be expected to assimilate fully into the national movements of other minorities—Polish, Ukrainian, or Lithuanian—or throw in their lot with the imperial Russian culture. In the Kingdom of Poland, Jews had faced such a dilemma since at least the early nineteenth century. And in the Pale of Settlement the Jewish elite, surrounded as it was by other nationalities, had begun to feel Russian as early as the 1850s.[137] In translating the national demands of other minorities to the nonterritorial case of the Jews, autonomism was thus attractive in part because it offered the Jews a way out of a dilemma that they could not otherwise resolve.

Two Jewish Autonomy and Europe's
Changing Legal Landscape

The emergence of the idea of Jewish autonomism in part reflected growing secular Jewish national self-consciousness among individuals who had left traditional Jewish life and religious practice. Autonomism, however, was also a movement for a clearly defined Jewish public space that reflected societal changes in late imperial Russia: urbanization, increasing separation of religious and private life, and a growing freedom of association. Similar processes had previously affected other European Jewish communities. Although possessing different aims than the twentieth-century Russian Jewish autonomists, the educated Jewish elite in eighteenth- and nineteenth-century Western and Central Europe also created a Jewish public sphere and sought to reshape Jewish society to match its own ideals.[1] The roots of twentieth-century Jewish communalism in the Russian Empire can similarly be found in the state reforms and social changes of the nineteenth century. The *maskilim*, who sought in the nineteenth century (with mixed success) to establish a leadership role for themselves as the representatives of Russian Jewry, were infused with a sense of communal responsibility, based in no small part on their belief in the erosion of traditional Jewish leadership and their own exceptional qualifications as replacement leaders.[2] By the time the internal struggle for Jewish leadership came to involve not only *maskilim* and traditionalists but also Jewish nationalists and socialists, Jewish politics was already revolving around questions of what kind of communal framework might best ensure the collective Jewish well-being.

52

Although Dubnov played the key role in introducing autonomism to a Jewish audience, he had borrowed the concept from Russian liberals and Polish nationalists, both of whom advocated decentralization of the Russian Empire. For Russian liberals autonomism meant devolution of power to local governments; for Polish nationalists it meant Polish sovereignty short of independence. For Jewish nationalists autonomism combined both ideas: local self-government and national autonomy through the creation of new Jewish communal institutions. The most pressing reason for the development of Jewish nationalist politics was the need for Jews to adapt to a changing political landscape in which other national and religious groups were increasingly demanding the recognition of their collective rights. The development of Jewish nationalism was thus consistent with the way different groups in Europe evolved according to changes in the law and their expectations as groups. Within the mix of evolving European nationalisms, Jews needed both to define what they were and to articulate what legal privileges they wanted as a collectivity.

This chapter looks at the intellectual ferment in which ideas about autonomism percolated among Jewish liberals and socialists. Jewish socialists in Russia (and Russian Jewish socialists living abroad) looked to Austria to see how the solutions proposed by Marxist jurists and legal theorists about resolving the simmering disputes among that empire's many nationalities might apply to Russia. On the other hand, Jewish liberals, and the emerging Jewish intelligentsia in general, watched a wide-scale experiment with local self-government in Russia and emulated the Russian activists who sought to decentralize the empire and regenerate it. Socialist and liberal conceptions of Jewish autonomy shared certain similarities but sought to solve different root problems. For socialists attracted to autonomism, the Jewish workers would not be truly liberated by a revolution if the Jews were not recognized as equal to the other nationalities in the struggle for socialism and in the implementation of a new socialist society. For all other autonomists, Jews as individuals would never truly achieve civil equality in Russia without Jewish national rights to guarantee their communal self-preservation. In sum, socialists, liberals, and others who took up ideas about Jewish autonomy adapted the prevailing intellectual trends to the Jewish situation in order to argue that Jews in the Russian Empire must attain equality not just as individuals but also as a group.

Chaim Zhitlowsky, the Austro-Marxists, and Jewish Autonomism

Dubnov crafted his autonomist political ideology from many different sources, but in language, argument, and structure autonomism idealized self-government at the local level and envisioned federalism at a national level. Of course, Dubnov was not the only source of inspiration for all Jewish discussions of the national idea in Russia, but such debates centered on the validity, or nonvalidity, of many of his central concepts, not least of which was the idea of Jewish communal self-government through the reinstitution of the *kehila*. Although Dubnov's writings influenced socialist conceptions of Jewish autonomism, his own philosophy remained fundamentally liberal. In economic terms he continually opposed any attempt to reconfigure Russian society in a manner that he believed would deprive most Russian Jews of their livelihood as artisans and traders. Nevertheless, socialist versions of Jewish autonomism—which tended to view autonomy as a means of achieving the victory of the proletariat—circulated and mixed with liberal versions, shaping political conceptions of the Jewish future in Russia. In 1897 a group of socialists of Jewish extraction founded the General Jewish Workers' Union in Lithuania, Poland, and Russia. The Bund, as it came to be known, was the most successful Jewish socialist party, but it limited its conception of autonomy to rights over language and education. Nonetheless, some socialists came to see Jewish autonomism as a valuable initiative in its own right, and others later joined the liberal autonomist movement.

Parallel to the development of Dubnov's conception of autonomism, Russian Jewish socialists, especially those in exile, developed an ideology that synthesized socialism and Jewish national demands. These groups of socialist Jewish nationalists, both in Russia and in exile, were in part influenced by the writings of Chaim Zhitlowsky (1861–1943).[3] Like Zhitlowsky's close friend and fellow townsman, the writer and socialist revolutionary best known as S. An-sky (Shloyme Zaynvl Rapoport, 1863–1920), Zhitlowsky left Judaism and Vitebsk to join the Russian populist movement. Zhitlowsky moved to Tula and joined the Narodnaia Volia. Both Zhitlowsky and An-sky were products of

Vitebsk heders who rejected traditional Judaism in favor of Russian radicalism.[4] Zhitlowsky, whose father was a successful timber merchant, came from a family of some wealth, which made possible not only his move to St. Petersburg in 1886 but also the publication in 1887 of his first book, *Thoughts on the Historical Fate of Jewry*.[5] Like Dubnov, Zhitlowsky had no tolerance for those radical Jews who eschewed the Jewish past, similarly believing that the Jewish religion historically served to preserve Jewish national identity. But unlike Dubnov, Zhitlowsky believed that Jewish cultural, educational, and linguistic autonomy, without self-government, would be enough to preserve Jewish national identity in the future.

Zhitlowsky was important because he was among the first to call for a unification of socialism and Jewish nationalism at a time (around 1883–84) when Jewish socialists generally opposed all variations of nationalism. While in political exile in Switzerland in the late 1880s and 1890s, Zhitlowsky was part of a small group of socialist Jews sympathetic to Jewish nationalism who were also attempting to combat the assimilationist tendencies of Jewish socialists and intellectuals.[6] In 1892 Zhitlowsky published "A Jew to Jews" under the pseudonym I. Chasin, and he called on Russian Jewish radicals and revolutionaries to embrace Jewish nationalism.[7] In this work Zhitlowsky began by attacking the premise that the majority of Russian Jewry was in any way "parasitic" (as was commonly believed by Jewish socialists); on the contrary, he claimed that most Jews were exploited as cheap labor. And like Dubnov, Zhitlowsky contended that Western-style civil emancipation had not preserved Jewish national life in the West and would not work for Eastern European Jewry. According to Zhitlowsky, mistakes had been made in granting civil equality in the West, "mistakes that have rendered the cultural, national, and spiritual (though not legal) conditions of European Jewry quite distant from the splendor that we are accustomed to imagining."[8] Along with An-sky and Viktor Chernov, Zhitlowsky was among the organizers of the Russian Socialist Revolutionary Party in Berne in 1893.[9] Zhitlowsky argued for the recognition of Jewish national rights and tirelessly advocated the use of the Yiddish language, but he defined Jewish national rights in a relatively narrow linguistic sense.

Dubnov gave Zhitlowsky no credit for his contribution to diaspora nationalism because Zhitlowsky was active outside Russia before 1905 and his publications were consequently rare and little known there.[10] Indeed, Zhitlowsky's first chance to propagate his ideas among Yiddish speakers came only in 1904, and it was in the United States rather than Eastern Europe.[11] Zhitlowsky's significance lies, however, in his largely successful efforts to convert Jewish socialists to the cause of nationalism, or at least to the acceptance of the position that socialism and national self-consciousness need not be considered mutually exclusive. Zhitlowsky may have found little audience for his ideas in the 1890s, but when the Bund eventually took up the cause of Jewish cultural autonomy, it espoused a conception that was close to Zhitlowsky's. And Zhitlowsky was in no small part responsible for initiating this debate within the Jewish social democratic movement.[12]

Zhitlowsky and other Russian Jewish socialists in Switzerland, such as John Mill (1870–1952), clearly came under the influence of the federalist ideas that were being developed in Austro-Marxist circles. Austria-Hungary was, like Russia, a multiethnic empire split by disputes among its nationalities. As a result, debates about how to solve Austria-Hungary's national divisions produced proposals for nonterritorial autonomy, some of which undoubtedly moved east. But unlike Russia, Austria-Hungary, albeit not a liberal democracy, had a parliament and a relatively free political life. A number of Austrian Social Democrats perceived Austria-Hungary's existing constitutional system to be inadequate for guaranteeing the rights of all nationalities, leading to a constant state of internecine struggle and interfering with efforts to unite the proletariat. As a way to solve this problem, some proposed endowing each national group with legally established autonomous rights. Conflict between Austria-Hungary's nationalities, especially in the Czech-speaking territories, led Karl Kautsky in 1897 to devise a socialist solution for the problems of multinational countries. Kautsky argued that territorial independence for national minorities in a state such as Austria-Hungary would lead only to the oppression of minorities in the new states. His solution was to separate self-determination from territory and to allow each linguistically defined nationality a degree of autonomy over its national affairs through a supraterritorial national organization.[13]

Kautsky's theory led first to the creation of a federally organized All-Austrian Social Democratic Party, and then to the so-called Brünn Resolution, accepted at the reorganized party's first All-Austrian Social Democratic Congress in 1899.[14] Between the party's transformation in 1897 into a federative organization with six national parties and the congress in Brünn in 1899, discussions of strategy and organization gave way to a developing theory of national autonomy.[15] The Austrian socialists had concluded that class struggle could not be conducted in an atmosphere of antagonism between nationalities, so the congress's top priority was resolving the conflicts among national groups. Although international socialism during this period remained decidedly dismissive of national issues, the origins of Austrian social democratic concern for national policy must be understood, as Arthur Kogan argues, against "a whole background of a paralyzed parliament, of the thinly veiled rule of the bureaucracy, and of nationalism running riot."[16] The Brünn Resolution included various demands, for example, that Austria be transformed into a federation of nationalities, that both self-governing regions and national unions be created to jointly manage each nationality's autonomous affairs, and that a special parliamentary law be enacted to guarantee the rights of national minorities.[17]

Not all the social democratic groups were satisfied by the initial resolution linking national autonomy to geographic boundaries, and the idea that national autonomy be decoupled from territory had its proponents. The South Slavs (speakers of south Slavic languages), for example, argued that the idea of a nation must be separated from territory, because nations such as their own were spread throughout the empire. In the words of the South Slavs' delegate from Trieste, "We have to make it clear that equality of rights is possible only if the nation is defined not as the population living in one territory but as the sum total of all individuals claiming a particular nationality."[18] The South Slavs were a diverse group, including Catholic Croatians and Orthodox Serbians, and the South Slav Party pushed the idea of "personal" autonomy because its members suspected they might not win autonomy over a single territory within the empire. Although the compromise resolution referred to "nationally delimited" self-governing regions, the Brünn Resolution nonetheless envisioned a version of national autonomy that was based entirely on territory. In other words, only groups with national autonomy in a given territory would gain autonomy for their members in other territories, a position that never changed in the official Austrian Social Democratic Party program.[19]

Zhitlowsky's treatise "Socialism and the National Question," prepared in advance of the Austrian Social Democratic Party's congress of 1899, was not aimed specifically at the Jews, but it was intended to apply to them. Eventually Zhitlowsky concluded that in the socialist movement, cosmopolitanism—or antinationalism—was too often used as an excuse for demanding the integration of smaller national groups into the Polish, Russian, or German social democratic movements. For that reason Zhitlowsky scathingly criticized the attitude of social democrats toward national movements, especially in Poland and Austria-Hungary: "Clearly, that superficial antinationalism which for a long time identified itself with international principles, in practice here degenerates into unadorned chauvinism and overt national oppression."[20]

Despite the limited scope of the Austrian Social Democratic Party program, two jurists, Karl Renner and Otto Bauer, seized on the issue of nonterritorial national autonomy. In "State and Nation," Renner argued that individuals as well as nations should be entitled to clearly defined public rights within a heterogeneous Austria, and he popularized the concept of "personal autonomy."[21] Renner pointed out that religious denominations have administrative structures that coexist at each bureaucratic and geographic level. Individuals are born into such denominations, but as adults it is their right to change their religious affiliation. Renner argued that nations also could coexist administratively and geographically in a legal relationship, so long as the individual retained the right to choose his or her national affiliation. Still, the state needed to legally recognize national entities in order to protect the individual's rights from encroachment by other nationalities and the state itself as well as to provide certain positive national rights, such as education.[22] According to Renner, "If it is a law of organic development that a particular organ is produced from the general organism for each separate function, then the people as a constitutional unit, as a totality of material and social interests, and the nations as cultural and spiritual communities, also require separate organs for their separate functions."[23]

These separate organs belonging to each national group would protect the group's members, provide access to cultural assets, and contribute to the health of the state as a whole. What Renner envisioned was a distinction between the legal rights corresponding to membership in the state—by definition, a territorial entity—and legal rights corresponding to membership in a nation.

One peculiarity of Austrian socialist conceptions of nonterritorial autonomy was the extent to which theorists considered the Jews a special case of a group that did not merit autonomy. This may have been related to the fact that several of the theorists were of Jewish origin. Both Kautsky (who was not Jewish) and Victor Adler (who was, but who converted to Protestantism shortly after his marriage) favored Jewish assimilation. Adler fiercely opposed any and all forms of Jewish nationalism and separatism as a result of both his personal experiences with antisemitism and his desire to avoid having the Austrian Social Democrats successfully labeled the party or protectors of the Jews. Otto Bauer, the theoretician who most comprehensively developed the principles of national autonomy for Austrian social democracy, argued vociferously that Jews should not be granted autonomy, educational or otherwise, but rather should be encouraged to assimilate into the ethnic groups among whom they lived.[24] Bauer suggested that Jews were an exception to his theory of national minority autonomy in Austria, arguing that Jewish national autonomy and even separate Jewish schools would harm the Jews' relations with their neighbors.[25] Bauer, unlike Adler, remained a member of the official Jewish community (the Israelitische Kultusgemeinde), but he was no less committed to Jewish assimilation.

Kautsky favored Jewish assimilation, but, in contrast to his Jewish Austrian Social Democrat colleagues, he supported the Bund and Jewish socialist movements as a necessity for the time being.[26] In general, Kautsky's position on the national question developed from a socialist reasoning common among Jewish socialists: "When the Jews shall have ceased to be persecuted and outlawed, the Jews themselves will cease to exist."[27] Proletarian democracy was the Austrian Social Democrats' ultimate goal, and as such, they viewed solving the conflict between nationalities in Austria as necessary to move on to the greater goal of class struggle. They did not, however, see nationalism in and of itself as a particularly positive phenomenon, and for that reason all the key Austrian social democratic theorists favored Jewish assimilation in the long or short term.

Jewish Renaissance and Socialist Autonomy

By 1904 Zhitlowsky ended his loose affiliation with the Bund and began to lean instead toward some form of socialist Zionism or territorialism. Around the same time, a group of socialists in Kiev were in the process of forming the Vozrozhdenie, or Renaissance, group, anticipating what would become a broader trend toward diaspora nationalism among leftist Zionists.[28] Within the Russian Empire the development of labor Zionism between 1902 and 1904 led a number of Jewish nationalists to search for more immediate solutions to the Jewish national question than a socialist Jewish state, and many would eventually become diaspora nationalists and folkists. Although the social democratic party Poalei Zion was mostly concerned with the application of Marxist thought to Zionism in Palestine, other groups to emerge from labor Zionism separated the socialist Zionist principle from Palestine. For instance, the Zionist Socialist Labor Party (known by its Russian initials, SS) became closely associated with the territorialist wing of Zionism and similarly advocated emigration and Jewish agricultural settlement but not necessarily in Palestine. The Vozrozhdenie group meanwhile believed that, although the Jewish national question would ultimately have to be solved by the creation of a Jewish state, Jewish national rights in the Diaspora would have to come first.

Vozrozhdenie originated in the fall of 1903 with a conference of socialist Zionists organized by a group of young Jewish students in Kiev that included Moyshe Zilberfarb (1876–1934), Avrom Rozin (Ben-Adir, 1878–1942), and Nokhem Shtif (Bal-Dimyen, 1879–1933).[29] The result of this conference demonstrated that Zhitlowsky was not alone in believing that the Bund and labor Zionism should not be the only frameworks for Jewish socialism in Russia. Although the conference attendees failed to reach a consensus on the goals of socialist Zionism, they established a publication, called *Vozrozhdenie*.[30] The group's united vision of Jewish socialism and nationalism was close to that of Zhitlowsky, but he had not yet come to accept territorialism. The group immediately began to attract others who were disenchanted with labor Zionism, in particular, the younger followers of the early ideologist of socialist Zionism, Nahman Syrkin (1868–1924), such as Zilberfarb and Zelig Kalmanovich (1881–1944). A Jewish movement began to take root in Russia that was simultaneously revolutionary, socialist, and nationalist. Nonetheless, as made clear in Vozrozhdenie's publications, the socialist autonomists were fighting for a revolutionary state that would recognize national difference rather than the establishment of Jewish national rights in the context of a new constitutional Russian Empire.

The essence of the group's philosophy lay in the belief that in order to attain socialism and true Jewish liberation, Jews must pursue both a national agenda and the class struggle, but not necessarily in the Palestinophile context offered by the labor Zionists in Poalei Zion.[31] For the members of Vozrozhdenie, like so many Jewish political groups at the time, the Kishinev pogroms of 1903 were an awakening moment, and Vozrozhdenie subsequently concluded that "vulgar Zionism" or "official Zionism" could no longer ignore the needs of the Jewish masses in the Pale of Settlement.[32] The logical outcome of such conclusions was to prioritize the attainment of national rights for the Jews in Russia as the first step in the long-term revolutionary struggle, but the members of Vozrozhdenie also argued that territorialism should be pursued together with the class and national struggle in Russia.[33]

Much of the first issue of *Vozrozhdenie* described how nationalism could play a role in social democratic thought, explained why national autonomy for the Jews under a socialist framework was desirable, and criticized the Bund. The *vozrozhdentsy*, as the group's leaders were called, not only took exception with the Bund's reduction of "national autonomy" to merely national-cultural autonomy but also attacked the Bund's general social democratic view of the national struggle's subordinated and utilitarian role in the class struggle.[34] In the second issue of *Vozrozhdenie* (published in Paris), Rozin traced the intellectual history of the group's ideology from socialism to socialist Zionism and then to a form of socialism and nationalism that envisioned national rights in the Diaspora and, some time in the future, a Jewish territory.[35] The *vozrozhdentsy* further argued that the demand for Jewish autonomy in Russia must not stop at the demand for national-cultural autonomy. Building on an idea circulating in Socialist Revolutionary circles, they argued that each nationality in the empire would be truly autonomous only if permitted a national assembly, or *sejm*, with the right of taxation and responsibility for administering national affairs. Without a *sejm* for the Jews and other *sejm*s for the other nationalities in the empire, the *vozrozhdentsy* argued that even a reformed and more enlightened Russia would be no better than the Austro-Hungarian Empire, which privileged the German and Hungarian cultures despite constitutional guarantees for other national minorities.[36] The *vozrozhdentsy* argued that the Russian proletariat must learn from the Austrian example in theory and practice. Naïve opinions about the benefits of declaring legal equality for all citizens, irrespective of nationality, must be dispelled when the predominant nationality has no interest in bringing about a real change in the hierarchy of nationalities or reducing "spaces of national friction."[37] The *vozrozhdentsy* made a clearly articulated legal argument for state decentralization, attacking the Enlightenment-inspired notion that a modernizing state should not tolerate dual loyalties or partial unions within its borders. This doubt in the protections of constitutionalism echoes the views of the revolutionary Aron Liberman (1845–80), who had argued much earlier that constitutionalism would do nothing to help the oppressed, least of all the Jews. Because political rights do not help those without power, radical economic reconfiguration is first necessary.

Most significant, the *vozrozhdentsy* rejected the dominant socialist understanding of nationalism's utility: that the national struggle should progress toward cosmopolitanism, until the dawn of an era in which national differences would disappear from the face of the earth. "No, we don't think so," stated the members of Vozrozhdenie. "We claim that this point breaks from the course of the legitimate analogy between class and national struggle."[38] In contrast to the cosmopolitan view, the group posited that national struggle complements class struggle and that national differences would continue to exist in the future, when different nationalities would coexist peacefully if given their legitimate autonomous rights. Vozrozhdenie's importance lies in its members' development of a socialist conception of Jewish autonomism based on a combination of Zhitlowsky's and Dubnov's ideas. Most important, their reasoning was fundamentally grounded in legal arguments, which provided a counter to the accepted wisdom among liberals that constitutionalism and civil equality, even on a federal basis, would provide guarantees for Jewish national equality. Many of both Dubnov's and Zhitlowsky's intellectual followers, who began in the socialist Zionist milieu and later developed their ideas as part of Vozrozhdenie, would become Russia's leading Jewish autonomists.

In 1906 the group became an official party, called the Jewish Socialist Labor Party (Sotsialisticheskaia Evreiskaia Rabochaia Partiia, or SERP). Like Vozrozhdenie, SERP was ideologically and organizationally close to the Russian Socialist Revolutionary Party, and it took a maximalist position in its demand for national autonomy.[39] The newly formed party, led by Yisroel Efroikin (1884–1954), Nokhem Shtif, and Zelig Kalmanovich (who would all later join the Folkspartey), as well as Moyshe Zilberfarb, Avrom Rozin, and Mark Ratner, wrote a platform for Jewish national self-government based on a *sejm* at its head, with the authority to legislate for and tax the Jews of the Russian Empire; as a result, the party's members came to be known as Sejmists.[40] After returning to Europe in 1906 from a lecture tour in the United States, Zhitlowsky moved to Lvov (Lemberg), in Austrian Galicia, and participated in the early formation of the party.

The Bund did not reach the same conclusions as Vozrozhdenie about the benefits of sociopolitical Jewish autonomy. Nonetheless, in its transformation from a doctrinaire Marxist group that viewed Yiddish only as a means of disseminating its ideas and agitating among Jewish workers to the standard-bearers of cultural Yiddishism, the Bund did increasingly incorporate autonomist ideas into its ideology.[41] At its party's founding in 1897, the Bund argued that Jewish nationalism would harm the cause of class struggle and might also awaken chauvinism in the Jewish proletariat. In Zvi Gitelman's words, the aim of the Bund, as envisioned by its early leaders, "was to prepare highly conscious socialist workers who would become thoroughly assimilated into the Russian culture and who could eventually go out to the centers of the Russian proletariat to preach the socialist doctrine."[42] Yet immersion in the Jewish working class would soon weaken many Jewish revolutionaries' commitment to assimilation and would convince them that the only possible way to advance the revolution among Jewish workers was to form a Jewish movement with "roots in its own environment."[43]

Despite its avowedly internationalist beginnings and to the dismay of certain wings of the Russian Social Democratic movement, the Bund quickly embraced Jewish national identification, resolving at its fourth convention, held May 24–28, 1901, that in Russia "various nationalities, should become a federation of nationalities with full national autonomy for each, regardless of the territory it occupies. . . . The concept of 'nationality' should also apply to the Jewish people."[44] The change in the Bund was partly a natural consequence of its absorption of unassimilated Yiddish-speaking workers, who came to outnumber its Russified intelligentsia leaders. More important, however, the deductive logic in this proclamation can be seen in the Bund's emphasis on federalism. If the Russian Empire is to become a federation of nationalities, then the Jews must be counted as one of the nationalities entitled to autonomy, regardless of where they live. The change also reflected the rise in prominence of spokesmen such as John Mill, who, while living in Geneva in the late 1890s, became the editor of *Der yidisher arbeyter* and introduced the ideas of Karl Kautsky to a Bundist readership.[45] Mill found that he could use Kautsky's arguments for a nonterritorial solution to national questions in countering attacks against the Bund by the Polish Socialist Party.[46] Although the Bund rejected Mill's proposal for Jewish national rights at the group's third convention, in 1899, by the fourth convention, in May 1901, the Bund was already more inclined to view the Jews as a distinct nationality.[47] Still, the 1901 resolution did not embrace Jewish nationalism; it was an argument for the equality of rights among nations. Given the national character of other socialist groups then forming, the Bund acknowledged that the Jews were a nationality and should not be deprived of rights demanded by socialists among other national minorities.

Two varieties of socialist autonomism developed in the early twentieth century. The Bund sought to incorporate claims to Jewish national rights to education and language rights into its platform without embracing either Jewish nationalism or sociopolitical autonomy. This nuanced Jewish national identification, balancing Mill's and Zhitlowsky's unabashed Jewish nationalism with more traditional socialist cosmopolitanism, found its clearest expression in Vladimir Medem's theory of neutralism. In "Social Democracy and the National Question," published in 1904, Medem argued that the Jewish workers' movement should stay neutral in the fight between assimilationists and nationalists because both served the ends of the bourgeoisie. The workers' movement should neither promote nationalism nor suppress it; rather, it should fight national oppression by actively attempting to secure from governments the right to control education.[48] Unlike the Bund, the members of Vozrozhdenie developed a theory of Jewish socialist autonomism, embracing a full sociopolitical model. It must be remembered that whereas the Bund was a party with thousands of members, Vozrozhdenie was composed of a small coterie of intellectuals who would eventually transform their group into a party. Thus the branch of Jewish socialism favoring sociopolitical Jewish autonomy remained small compared to the much larger wing, which, though leaning toward accepting Jewish national self-consciousness, limited its advocacy for autonomism to guaranteed rights over language and education.

Federalism and the Rights of Nationalities

Like other national minorities in the Russian Empire, Jews continued to watch how their multinational neighbor to the west, Austria-Hungary, dealt with the brewing discontent among its national minorities, and Austrian proposals to institute national and cultural autonomy according to language groups found a ready audience among Jewish socialists in Russia. Yet the discussions among Austrian socialists also indicated that national rights for minorities, whether in Austria-Hungary or Russia, would not necessarily translate into national rights for Jews. In fact, for many Russian Jewish socialists, Austria provided a negative example, demonstrating the pitfalls of constitutionalism and the need for a revolutionary socialist state that could guarantee national rights. For example, the members of Vozrozhdenie articulated the view that Austria-Hungary's dominant nationalities used constitutionalism to subordinate smaller groups "to the lowest step on the public ladder," thereby provoking the nationalities to agitate for equal rights through the parliament or on the street.[49] They believed that not only would a constitutional Russia be doomed to repeat Austria-Hungary's grueling national struggles but also that the coming national struggles in a revolutionary Russia would be much worse. In each place that Jews lived, their national bourgeoisie would have to fight a two-front struggle against the bourgeoisie of the newly liberated nationality—whether Polish, Ukrainian, Lithuanian, or Russian—and that of the previously dominant one. In the view of the socialist autonomists, in this struggle it would be the Jewish proletariat that would suffer most, made the pawn of local economic competition and political struggle. The answer could be found only in a new legal arrangement that clearly and plainly delineated the rights of national collectivities and created a national institution for each group to serve as the intermediary between the state and individuals.[50] In essence, genuine individual freedom could be guaranteed and protected only by national representation, and in order for a national organization to have internal authority and the ability to express the collective will externally, it must have the sanction of the state.

Like the Austrian Social Democrats, Vozrozhdenie saw state recognition of "nationalities as juridical persons" as the only way to guarantee the rights of all nationalities.[51] The evidence was supposedly to be found in the Austrian constitution itself, which read, "All nationalities of the state possess equal rights, and each of them has the inviolable right to keep and develop their culture and language."[52] But the obvious question remained whether Jews in both empires should be legally recognized as a nationality, and Austrian Social Democrats—Jewish and non-Jewish—disagreed with the Jewish political movements about the answer to this question. In fact, in 1906, the same year that SERP was founded, Avrom Rozin published a booklet attacking Kautsky's assimilationism and what was, in Rozin's mind, Kautsky's deeply flawed analysis of the Jewish question.[53] Nonetheless, there is no doubt that the members of first Vozrozhdenie and then SERP sought to understand from the debates among the Austrian Social Democrats what might be possible in Russia.[54]

Some Jewish autonomists found hope in recent Austrian socialist proposals, at least those arguing that autonomy need not be defined solely by territory, despite Austrian socialists' insistence on excluding Jews from this formula. Other Jews who favored autonomy, mainly socialists, welcomed the momentum for national rights that was developing within a socialist context. In 1907, the same year that Dubnov published his collected letters, Otto Bauer published his first edition of *The Question of Nationalities and Social Democracy*, and Jewish autonomists responded to Bauer's publication by making it accessible to a Russian Jewish readership. SERP published a Russian translation in 1909 that included a 54-page introduction by Zhitlowsky.[55] This introduction is one of Zhitlowsky's most interesting interpretations of autonomism. In it he examines the relationship between class and national struggles, discusses the historical basis for national autonomy in Russia for Ukrainians and Belorussians (similar to Bauer's evaluations of the Austrian context), and criticizes the Bund and other Jewish socialist groups for their supposedly muddled view of Jewish national rights. To Zhitlowsky, what Bauer said specifically about the Jews was less relevant than the fact that the process of Jewish national self-consciousness had been set in motion and that, from then on, the Jews had a socialist framework within which to assert their own national-cultural rights in the midst of other peoples' national struggles. "Regardless of [the national demands of] these little-Russian groups," Zhitlowsky proclaimed that "theorists raised their voices from representatives of a different oppressed nation—the Jewish people."[56]

Many scholars consider Russian Jewish theories of nonterritorial autonomy, both Dubnovian and socialist, to have come from the debates of the Austrian Social Democrats.[57] It would be fair to say that a consensus exists as to the practical origins of Dubnov's autonomism, and in fact the same intellectual genealogy is usually ascribed to the ideas of Zhitlowsky, Dubnov's socialist rival.[58] Even the Bund, which was often perceived to be intellectually indebted to the Austrian Social Democrats and was clearly influenced by Kautsky, was unaffected by later theorists such as Karl Renner and Otto Bauer.[59] Dubnov claimed that he developed his ideas independently of the Austrians and the Jewish intellectuals who brought Austrian ideas to the Russian Empire.[60]

For example, when Dubnov's letters were reprinted in a collected volume in 1907 (*Pis'ma o starom i novom evreistve*), he wrote in a footnote that after reading part 1 of Renner's *Der Kampf der österreichischen Nationen um den Staat* (The Austrian Nations' Struggle Surrounding the State), published in 1902, he was pleased to note the similarity between his own propositions for the Jews and those of Renner for national minorities in Austria (Dubnov also claimed that he read Renner's 1899 essay "State and Nation" only after completing his own letters).[61] Otto Bauer published much of his key work only in 1907, long after Dubnov's theories had been in circulation through his original letters and their revised versions. In truth, Dubnov was neither as influenced by the Austrians as one might think nor as original as he wanted his readers to believe. Austrian social democratic approaches to the national question likely reached Dubnov, if not through Renner and Bauer, then through Adler, Kautsky, and the influential journal of socialist theory, *Die Neue Zeit*, edited by Kautsky from 1890 to 1917. Kautsky gained a following in Russia as his journal was widely read by Russian Marxists and others.[62]

Because both Renner and Bauer were jurists, it is likely that their autonomist legal frameworks influenced Dubnov as he reformulated his theories in 1906. But unlike the Austrians, Dubnov did see an intrinsic value in nationalism. Thus liberal nationalist theories stand out as his most important influences. One need only read John Stuart Mill, Dubnov's hero, to understand the origins of his theory of nonterritorial autonomism. Unlike socialist theorists who stressed language as the key component to nationality, Mill pointed to a variety of factors that make up a nation: language, religion, community, geography, and, most of all, shared historical experience. Furthermore, Mill argued that any nation will naturally "desire to be under the same government, and desire that it should be government by themselves exclusively."[63] The context in which Mill framed this argument, as a response to colonial rule, was particularly adaptable to the case of the national minorities in the Russian Empire. Mill argued for the value of nation-states or, where they were impossible, federations. Although he did not consider the case of nonterritorial autonomy, Mill believed that in a perfect federation individuals owed their allegiance to two governments with separate and clearly defined bounds of authority—an idea much closer to what Dubnov envisioned for Russian Jewry than the nonterritorial linguistic and educational autonomy envisioned by the Austrians.[64]

Dubnov, Zhitlowsky, and the Bund all denied the Austrian influence on their own theories. Yet Renner's work inadvertently explains why different theorists may have reached similar conclusions at approximately the same time. Renner observed that the collective rights of groups were being recognized in more and more areas of society, ranging from commercial law to the rights of workers: "And yet, as far as the legal system is concerned the most important groups for our state system, the nationalities, still constitute transcendental natural entities that do not fit into the civil garments of state legislation."[65] Imperial Russia was not Austria-Hungary, and its subjects had fewer individual rights. Yet the Russian estate system, with its legally defined privileges and restrictions, fostered an even greater awareness of group rights. Thus, while Renner's claim that conceptually "the nation is not a territorial entity" seems identical to the position reached by Dubnov, in fact they came to the same conclusion by means of different routes. Renner saw the acceptance of the nonterritorial principle as the means of solving national disputes in heterogeneous Austria (and avoiding any one group's domination over another), whereas Dubnov generally accepted the territorial basis for nationality while seeing the Jewish historical experience in the Diaspora as exceptional (and even, in evolutionary terms, more advanced). Dubnov wrote his "Ethics of Nationalism" in 1899 because he feared the association between French nationalism and antisemitism in the Dreyfus affair was convincing Jews that all forms of nationalism were poisonous. It was therefore apprehension about the national excesses of others affecting Jews that led Dubnov to the necessity of establishing, in his own words, "criteria for defining what in nationalism is good and what is evil," in order to save Jewish nationalism from the antisemites.[66] In essence, Renner's dilemma was a juridical one about how to ensure that the members of each nationality would maintain their rights regardless of where in the empire they lived, whereas Dubnov's was a philosophical dilemma revolving around the preservation of national self-consciousness without territory and, in the future, probably without religion.[67]

Ideas of Self-Government in the Jewish and Russian Public Sphere

Underpinning Dubnov's philosophy was the idea that the Jewish autonomist movement in Russia would achieve its goals through cultural production and communal activism. Culture would replace Jewish religious practices with a secular Jewish national identification, and communal activism would carve out spheres of Jewish autonomy in the present and implement Jewish autonomy in the future.[68] Although Dubnov began with a theory of Jewish nationalism and national development, one can see an evolutionary process in his writing as he moved toward a more specific conception of Jewish autonomy. In 1897 his "Doctrine of Jewish Nationalism" established the basis for that nationalism historically through the development of national self-consciousness and the preservation of a unique culture in the Diaspora. In 1898 he established the historical basis for Jewish national life in Europe.[69] In 1899 he developed an ethical system to mediate relations between nations. And in 1901, when he wrote "Autonomism, the Basis of the National Program," he again looked to Jewish history to determine what mechanisms Jews had used to preserve their autonomy in the Diaspora and how such mechanisms could be adopted to ensure that secular national self-consciousness could firmly supplant the waning religious self-consciousness. Because of his theory of spiritual and cultural-historical nationalism, and ideas about reinstituting Jewish communal self-government that developed in these works, Dubnov was widely recognized at the time for having introduced the idea of Jewish autonomism.[70]

From his understanding of historical autonomy, Dubnov identified three pillars for a future Jewish national autonomy: community, language, and national education. Education was perhaps the most important aspect of Jewish autonomy, because a secular cultural education might solve the problem of Jews' being torn between their Jewish ethnic nationality and their adopted cultural nationality.[71] A host of different individuals progressively developed more specific details of Jewish autonomism. Yet Dubnov's three pillars of Jewish autonomism consistently remained the fundamental elements of sociopolitical

Jewish autonomy. Most important, Dubnov's elevation of these three elements of autonomism was perfectly consistent with the shifting legal and political environment in Eastern Europe. They mirrored (intentionally or not) the demands of other federalists, they were rooted in the legal demand that the state recognize the Jews as a nationality, and they were tied to the growth of communal and political activism by the Jewish intelligentsia, who were constructing new institutions of Jewish public life.

Autonomism echoed the efforts of Russian liberals and self-described progressives to create a sphere of public and national life separate from the state because, in a sense, autonomism was at base an attempt to create a separate sphere of public space for Jews within Russian society. Similar to the way the term *intelligentsia* served as a mode of self-description for people involved in the spread of ideas and culture in late imperial Russia, the word *obshchestvennost'* was used universally to describe people devoted to improving the empire through various forms of public activism.[72] Before the 1860s the term used by the educated elements in Russian society to describe themselves, *obshchestvo* (literally "society"), set them apart from the common people and connoted both Westernization and aristocracy.[73] Over time, however, "society" democratized beyond the nobility to educated professionals, and a new term, *obshchestvennost'*, arose to describe educated Russian society, their aspirations, and their programs. Nineteenth-century changes in Russian life—the Great Reforms, urbanization, and economic transformation, to name only the most significant—led to the emergence of professionals who did not fit into any of the Russian legal estates.[74] Such individuals, a "third element" defined by what they were not (nobility or peasants), came to be a driving force for change in twentieth-century Russia, and the term *obshchestvennost'* came to describe a social movement for change, reform, and work for the public good in which the third element played a crucial role.[75] *Obshchestvennost'* came to have two components in the context of late-nineteenth- and early-twentieth-century Russian politics: It described both the educated and politically conscious segment of society and the attributes of public-spiritedness and social responsibility.[76] Although *obshchestvennost'* has no English equivalent, recent scholarship suggests the word referred to a group "whose sense of identity rested on a keen perception that the Russian 'nation' differed from the Russian 'state'; that is, that Russia's future depended on achieving a proper and harmonious balance between autonomous social initiative and state power."[77]

Theories of *obshchestvennost'* emerged from debates between the 1860s and 1890s over the relative autonomy of the *zemstvo* (pl. *zemstva*), which was created in 1864 as the local seat of self-government in the thirty-two central provinces of European Russia (the Polish provinces being excluded). In the second half of the nineteenth century, Russian liberal thinkers such as Vladimir Solov'ev argued that "societal organization" (*obshchestvennaia organizatsiia*) should be cultivated to work for the public good, and B. N. Chicherin argued that state and society were independent yet fully autonomous spheres. Although Chicherin came to accept the necessity of constitutionalism only in 1900, much earlier he had introduced Russia to his theory of a civic community (*grazhdanskoe obshchestvo*), the idea that Russia's subjects must create a public life separate from that of the state.[78] Because of Solov'ev, Chicherin, and others, the demand for self-government as a means of development and a substitute for an inept state became popular among both liberals and conservatives.

The Russian experience with the *zemstvo* played a role in alerting Jewish leaders to the power of local self-governance. The original *zemstvo* statutes incorporated the Slavophile-inspired "societal theory of self-government," which enshrined the *zemstvo's* autonomy from the state and its responsibility to the people.[79] The institution of the *zemstvo* and the new proliferation of organizations not directed by the government eroded the considerable control over public life previously enjoyed by the tsar's bureaucracy.[80] Though the *zemstva* became increasingly conservative after the 1905 revolution, until that point they had been the primary base of liberal opposition to the central government and had provided a way for professionals to take responsibility for education and health at a local level.[81] Members of the nobility and other estates, and especially professionals, who fell outside the estate framework, filled the administrative ranks of the *zemstva* and organs of self-government, helping to institutionalize both it and *obshchestvennost'*. The development of an educated segment of the population committed to public service was to have long-term effects on the empire, because by the turn of the twentieth century this group shifted its efforts toward civil equality and the struggle against absolutism.[82]

As originally created, the *zemstvo* system established self-government at the district and provincial levels. District assemblies were elected locally, and these assemblies elected delegates to the provincial assemblies. Due to the lack of clearly delineated responsibilities, the *zemstva* constantly struggled with local administrators representing the central government over questions of jurisdiction and authority. This conflict was about more than just the territorial behavior of bureaucrats. The central administration and the *zemstva* had different conceptions of the role that self-government should play within the state, with activists within the *zemstva* seeing autonomous *zemstvo* activities as one step on the road to constitutionalism.[83]

Because the *zemstvo* system was instituted in the wake of the Polish uprising of 1863, the central administration declined to introduce self-government in nine of the western provinces, where the majority of the landowners were Polish. The government did, however, institute the *zemstvo* system in several Ukrainian provinces that contained large numbers of Jews.[84] Jews were barred from participating in the activities of the *zemstvo* but were nonetheless exposed to the potential of self-government, or *samoupravlenie*, a term that came to be widely used in the Jewish press. Educated Russian Jews who faced legal barriers to their full integration into the professions became the empire's third element par excellence. Furthermore, because Jews had fewer opportunities for participation in municipal and local self-government, a specifically Russian Jewish *obshchestvennost'* emerged that, like its Russian equivalent, strove to create institutions parallel to the state. More so than its Russian equivalent, however, the Jewish *obshchestvennost'* included participants from radical political elements in addition to liberal professionals. Because Russian Jewish institutions increasingly served both cultural and sociopolitical roles, these two missions became inextricably tied together. Some Jews, generally the liberal cohort, maintained a dual mission of building both Russian civil society and an autonomous Russian-Jewish equivalent. Others concentrated all their efforts on building autonomous Jewish cultural and political life in Russia.[85]

The builders of Russian *obshchestvennost'* balanced conflicting desires for individual consciousness on the one hand and collective identities—to the *narod* (the people) or the emerging nation—on the other.[86] Such questions of identity also afflicted the builders of Jewish *obshchestvennost'*, who faced the same personal dilemmas as Russians entering the public sphere. At least partly as a result of *obshchestvennost'* and the goal of creating institutions independent from the state, the very words *autonomous* (*avtonomnyi*) and *independent* (*samostoiatel'nyii*) became ubiquitous in Russian intellectual discourse.[87] Jewish adoption of the language of *obshchestvennost'*, most significantly the word *samoupravlenie*, further blurred the distinction between *obshchestvennost'* and the Jewish autonomist movement. For one example, the term *obshchestvennyi*, connoting something both social and public, was widely used by liberal Russian and Jewish thinkers. For another, the term *obshchestvo*, in addition to describing society (meaning both society at large and educated society), described the semi-official Jewish community after the abolition of the *kehila* and also denoted the Jews as a subgroup of Russian society.[88] Finally, as Jews began to envision a new or reformed institution of Jewish communal self-government, they adopted the term *obshchina* for it, meaning both community and commune, a concept that played a central role in the thinking of key nineteenth-century Russian liberal and radical thinkers, such as Konstantin Kavelin, Alexander Herzen, Nikolai Chernyshevskii, Mikhail Bakunin, and others.[89] Such ideas about communal self-government and the role of the "people" in their own self-improvement were also important concepts developed by the Russian populists, and we can see their influence on Jewish politics in the widespread use of the terms *narod* to describe the Jewish people and *samodeiatel'nost'* (self-action or self-reliance) to describe their affairs.[90] In sum, Jewish autonomist discourse mimicked and overlapped with the general Russian discussion about self-government and community reform that intensified beginning in the early 1890s.[91]

Participation in voluntary associations and engagement in *obshchestvennost'* did not begin as an exercise in ethnic particularism. Quite the opposite. These activities provided a nonsectarian setting for the development of new group identities based on profession, personal interest, and other factors.[92] Jews increasingly sought out shared spaces in civic life—literary and educational societies as well as professional and social associations—as an alternative to the shrinking opportunities available to them in municipal government, higher education, and the bar.[93] And parallel to Jewish participation in imperial civic life, Jews created their own voluntary associations. In some cases, especially in the bigger cities, growing secularization and conflicts within the Jewish community made voluntary associations attractive as an outlet for activism and a sense of community.[94] The creation of Jewish voluntary associations and the spirit of *obshchestvennost'* also served as a means of challenging the existing order and creating the basis for a new Jewish community: an *obshchina* based on national rather than religious identification.

Finally, Jews were not alone among nationalities in the Russian Empire in adapting the prevailing intellectual trends to their nascent national aspirations. Perhaps the best example can be seen in the nineteenth-century Ukrainian historian, folklorist, and political theorist Mykhailo Drahomanov (1841–95), who developed a program to decentralize the Russian Empire and create a Ukrainian federation of communities in which Ukrainians and non-Ukrainians equally would have the right to form national community organizations.[95] Drahomanov was a self-described autonomist, federalist, and pan-Slavist. He believed that each of the various Slavic groups living in the Russian and Austrian empires but without states of their own should develop first their cultural autonomy, then communal autonomy, then administrative local autonomy, and then finally national autonomy that could be joined in a federation.[96] He paid considerable attention to detailing the workings of his idealized levels of self-government and believed that the like-minded should seek election to the *zemstva* to press the case for Ukrainian autonomism.[97] What Drahomanov proposed in the 1870s— that Ukrainian intellectuals create their own *obshchestvennost'* to pave the way for autonomy—would be repeated, knowingly or not, by Jewish intellectuals thirty years later. Federalist ideas about pan-Slavism, as Drahomanov pointed out, originated with Slavs who lived as minorities without statehood and who hence felt the need for protection of their national rights. So summarized Drahomanov, "Thus it is more a defensive doctrine; above all it is dedicated to the idea of liberty."[98] Like Dubnov later, at the root of Drahomanov's autonomist political program was a John Stuart Mill–inspired commitment to the liberal ideals of political freedom and resistance to the tyranny of the state.[99] Drahomanov was labeled a separatist and forced out of his university appointment in Kiev.[100] But his ideas were later further developed by Mikola Porsh, who in 1907 argued for the decentralization of a future autonomous Ukraine and the establishment of local organs of self-government.[101] Mark von Hagen even makes the argument that pan-Slavic federalist thinking about the empire's distinctive nations is at the base of Eastern Europe's later national movements and other "pan-movements," including Zionism.[102]

It is impossible to separate the Jewish autonomist movement—or the autonomist movements of other nationalities in the empire—from Russian *obshchestvennost'*, because pan-Jewish institutions were created both to serve the Jewish public and to establish Jewish autonomy from the state. The idea that such institutions could serve the purpose of developing a nation separate from the Russian state echoed the belief of Russian liberal nationalists that national identity was something different from allegiance to the tsar. Russian Jews possessed regional identities, whether as Litvaks, Poles, or southern Jews. But just as Russian *obshchestvennost'* intrinsically tied public-mindedness and local autonomy to the spread of a universal pan-Russian national self-consciousness, Jewish *obshchestvennost'* engaged Jewish intellectuals in creating a particularly Russian-Jewish identity through publications, cultural organizations, and political activism. *Obshchestvennost'* was neither a political ideology nor a cohesive movement but rather a set of shared goals, often only implicitly assumed, among individuals from various backgrounds, many of whom saw their role in building Russian society as more of a social than a political task.[103] Still, the fact that Russian *obshchestvennost'* sought to modernize and enlighten autocratic Russia meant that a political agenda was never absent.[104] The Jewish third element was not any more ideologically homogeneous than its Russian equivalents, but in some sense Jewish *obshchestvennost'* was more overtly political because the Jewish autonomist movement included a struggle over who—individually and ideologically—might legitimately claim to represent Russian Jewry. Even so, the movement for Jewish autonomism paradoxically provided a common ground for Jewish parties in an era of ideological fragmentation.

Conclusion

The boundaries separating the various groups in the Russian Jewish nationalist movement were fluid, and individuals, even whole groups, often changed their ideological positions and moved between political parties. Yet considerable differences remained between socialist and liberal conceptions of Jewish autonomy. For many socialists the adoption of Jewish autonomist claims was about equal treatment within the broader socialist movement and stemmed from the practical challenges of creating a particularly Jewish socialist movement. These people were reluctant to put national concerns before those of the class struggle and accordingly limited their autonomist claims to the linguistic and cultural sphere. But some Jewish socialists did embrace a sociopolitical model of Jewish autonomy. Both socialist and liberal autonomism reflected the struggle of one nationality among many to find its place in a changing multiethnic empire. Jewish autonomism in its liberal forms stemmed from an attempt to create a Jewish equivalent to the general movement in imperial Russia to build a public life independent from the state. Jewish autonomism in its socialist forms stemmed from an attempt to create a proletarian Jewish national movement separate from Russian socialism. The ideas of Russian and other European socialists, especially those in the Austro-Hungarian Empire who saw solving national conflicts in heterogeneous areas as an essential step toward uniting the proletariat, influenced Jewish socialists in the Russian Empire, but different Jewish socialist movements and thinkers adopted differing principles of nonterritorial autonomy.

Jewish autonomists took the logic of *obshchestvennost'* a step further than propositions for local autonomy, estate autonomy, or professional autonomy, arguing for complete Jewish communal autonomy, cultural autonomy, and even national political autonomy. They used these ideas to develop their own theories of national sovereignty, decoupled from territory. The adaptation of these Russian ideas and the attempts to create a new Jewish communal framework seemed to provide a way for Jews to fulfill their national desires within the changing Russian Empire and, as we will see, enabled them to avoid having to choose between the competing nationalisms of the groups with whom they lived. This social movement to create a sphere of civil life autonomous from the state had a concrete connection to the claim to Jewish national rights and the development of Jewish nationalism. Moyshe Zilberfarb, one of the founders of both the Vozrozhdenie movement and SERP, considered "the most essential and the most cardinal question regarding national rights" to be "the question about the differentiation between the sphere of competence of the state and that of the nation."[105] Zilberfarb was correct, and the cardinal issue—from which all other issues stemmed—was determining what fell within the two spheres of state and nation and how to guarantee the legal rights of the nation within the state. In the Bund's more limited socialist autonomism the national sphere should be limited to rights over education, language, and culture. For the Sejmists, no less than the liberal nationalist followers of Dubnov, anything short of an elected assembly to represent the nation to the state, and that assembly's right to tax its membership, would fail to shield the national sphere from encroachment by the state. "Every nation has to be protected from the intrusion of a strange will into its inner life, and the main state law must recognize *droits de la nation* [national rights] on a par with *droits de l'homme* [the rights of man]."[106]

Three Revolution, Nationality Politics, and
the Legal Claim to Jewish Autonomy,
1905–7

Jewish intellectuals sought to use communal autonomy to fortify Russian Jews against the threat of assimilation (as they saw it), to reconnect themselves with "the people" or "folk" (again, as they saw them), and ironically (given this disconnection), to bring true emancipation to the people. Dubnov looked to history for justifications, precedents, and models for Jewish autonomy. Still, it is important to remember that Dubnov and the Jewish autonomists who followed him sought to create a completely new Jewish community. The new organ of self-government would be secular and democratic rather than religious and oligarchic, and in some ways it was intended to mimic the peasant *mir*. Jews could have autonomy over language, education, and key philanthropic institutions, and some even suggested a national assembly parallel to those demanded by other national groups in the Russian Empire. This was therefore a radical response to the challenges of integration. There was nothing novel in Jewish intellectuals, even the most acculturated among them, embracing national identification. In their customs, religion, language, and theology there is no doubt that Russian Jews saw themselves—and were seen—as intrinsically different from Russians or Poles. What was new was the idea that true integration for the Jews as a collective required a degree of legally defined separation.

In contrast to the intellectuals, the general Russian Jewish population focused most on the attainment of individual rights and full civil equality. Autonomists understood that the broader Jewish public cared more about individual equality than about national or collective rights. That is exactly why autonomists presented their mission—the creation of a new Jewish community—in such urgent terms, usually as the battle against assimilation. They believed that emancipation was going to come to Russian Jewry eventually. Their task was to restructure Russian Jewish communal life by creating a new secular and democratic Jewish community that would reinforce Jewish national sentiment and prevent what they believed to be a potential wholesale loss of identity, which is how they viewed the Jewish experience with emancipation in Western Europe. Liberal and socialist versions of autonomism developed and circulated at the very end of the nineteenth century and the beginning of the twentieth. But as I explore in this chapter, autonomism first moved from the realm of theory to practical politics, even if temporarily, during the revolutionary years of 1905–7. As such, Jewish autonomist ideas, in particular, demands in different forms for legally recognized national rights, played a central role in the birth of organized Jewish politics in the Russian Empire.

1897–1907: Anti-Jewish Violence, Nationalism, and the Promise of Reform

The years between 1897 and 1907 saw the creation and institutionalization of many of the key parties and organizations associated with modern Jewish political life. The World Zionist Congress met for the first time in 1897, and the Bund was founded in the same year. Dubnov also published the first of his letters in 1897, and in 1901, while living in Odessa, he established what he called a "nationalizing committee" of intellectuals for the purposes of launching an "Odessa *Kulturkampf*."[1] Many of the intellectuals involved in the "new Jewish politics" considered the pogroms in Kishinev in April 1903, at least retrospectively, to have been a formative moment on the journey to full-fledged national politics.[2] The shock of the violence in Kishinev—where mobs murdered nearly fifty people, maimed hundreds, and destroyed more than 1,000 homes—politically mobilized and reinforced the national sentiments of Dubnov and an entire generation of Jewish intellectuals, who fiercely criticized the traditional Jewish communal leadership for what they believed to be its passivity.[3] The Zionist leader Vladimir (Ze'ev) Jabotinsky (1880–1940), who was to become the ideological founder of the Revisionist Zionist movement, claimed in his memoirs "that the slaughter of Kishinev played an enormous role in our societal consciousness, because we then turned our attention to Jewish cowardice."[4] Although Jabotinsky underplayed the pogrom's significance as a turning point in his own personal worldview (or claimed that he did not remember it as such), the mobilization of Jewish political forces that followed it introduced him to the Russian Zionists living in Odessa.[5] The founding ideologue of spiritual Zionism, Ahad Ha'am, called the Jewish delegations to St. Petersburg "slaves" and released a public letter indicting the Russian Jewish leadership and population as a whole, saying they "stretch their necks to slaughter and cry for help, without as much as attempting to defend their own property, honor and lives."[6] Hayim Nahman Bialik's famous poem "Ba-'ir ha-hareiga" (In the City of Slaughter), written after Bialik traveled to Kishinev at Dubnov's request to personally investigate the circumstances of the pogrom, expressed much the same sentiment.[7] According to one contemporary, M. A. Krol', appeals published by Dubnov urging Jews not to wait for help from the enemy but to help themselves with their own hands "circulated in hundreds of copies in different Jewish communities, and it must be said, that these appeals worked on young Jews like an electric current."[8]

Dubnov's historiographic and political oeuvre reflects his understanding of the Jewish national movement's development as a natural reaction to anti-Jewish violence and focuses on several key crises, including the Kishinev pogroms of 1903 and the Russian revolutionary period of 1905–7, as representing formative moments in Jewish political life.[9] Dubnov's historical construction may have framed the transition among Jewish intellectuals from attempted integration to Jewish nationalism as stemming from anti-Jewish violence, but it is clear that many additional complex processes were at work. Still, this narrative took hold because it built on the simmering discontent with the Jews' legal status in the empire. And as we can see, other Jewish intellectuals at the time, especially those living in Odessa, such as Jabotinsky, Ahad Ha'am, and Bialik, directed their anger toward what they perceived as passivity on the part of the Jewish leadership in St. Petersburg. Indeed, the politicizing impact of the pogroms extended beyond Jewish intellectuals and became part of the history of the Russian "liberation" movement. Following the violence in Kishinev, a banquet in St. Petersburg held by Russian liberals to support victims of the pogrom helped to galvanize the general liberal opposition movement and proved to be an important step by the same people who would go on to found the Union of Liberation and the Union of Unions.[10]

It is difficult to ascertain exactly how passive the Jewish communal leadership really was during this crisis or what the leaders might have done differently. What seems clear is that the crisis of violence in 1903 and then again in 1905–7 provided an outlet for the increasingly assertive Jewish nationalist intelligentsia to lash out at the patrons of *shtadlanut* (Jewish intercession) and the politics of integration more generally. The year 1903 fueled the nationalists' preexisting perception of Jewish passivity and helplessness and, equally important, their belief that the existing Jewish communal leaders were inadequately representing Russian Jewry. This shift in Jewish communal power that began in the late nineteenth century rapidly sped up in 1903 and even more so after 1905. While the Kishinev pogroms may have made more urgent the question of who could best represent the interests of Russian Jews, as discussed in Chapter 1, profound societal changes had long affected the political consciousness of the Russian Empire's western subjects, not least the Jewish community.[11]

In the early years of the twentieth century, both Russian liberals (who favored a new constitutional arrangement) and revolutionary leftists (who sought radical societal reconstruction) were becoming more confident and determined, and discontent among national minorities helped to fuel revolutionary sentiment. The universities also became a focus of opposition to the regime, and as Samuel Kassow points out, the general public conflated the interests of Jews and those of student strikers (many of whom were Jews), leading to violence against both groups.[12] The most significant group pushing for a constitution, the Union of Liberation, was a broad political coalition that united individuals of many different ideologies in the collective goal of "national liberation" and presented its struggle as "class-less" and "all-national" (meaning not only for Russians).[13] Jewish liberals, lawyers, and students embraced the all-national character of the revolution, with many prominent Russians and Jews issuing statements jointly. But in seeing themselves as occupying a special space in Russian law (in the negative sense), Jews also understood the particular significance of the liberation movement to their community and did not seek to underplay the Jewish role in the revolutionary events.[14] Nicholas II believed the Jews to be at the core of all revolutionary activity in the empire, a view that was shared by many members of his government and in Russian right-wing political opinion as a whole.[15]

Wherever the Russian government might have placed blame for the growing opposition to autocratic rule, a combination of hubris, miscalculations, and bad luck between 1904 and 1905 undermined its authority. After the embarrassment of the Russo-Japanese War, the massacre of unarmed demonstrators in January 1905 known as Bloody Sunday, and the explosive strike movement that followed, the autocracy came to see its choices as being limited to concession and revolution. To create a safe outlet for discontent, Nicholas II initially created a consultative lower parliamentary chamber (the Bulygin Duma), but that tepid concession did nothing to temper the liberation movement, which dismissed the decree as meaningless and unfair without the corresponding freedoms of speech, assembly, and habeas corpus. Acceding to unrestrained liberal opposition, worker and national unrest, and pressure from Sergei Witte, whom the tsar had designated as premier, Nicholas promised sweeping new personal freedoms in his October Manifesto (issued on October 17, 1905, according to the Julian calendar) and endowed the Duma with legislative power.[16]

What might have been a hopeful period for Russian Jewry became instead a time of terror, as right-wing nationalists and monarchists whipped up anti-Jewish violence on a massive scale that rocked one Jewish community after another in the month following the manifesto's publication. Although not officially encouraged by the government, this anti-Jewish violence was inadequately repressed and the scale of it—more than 3,000 Jewish deaths—dwarfed any previous wave of pogroms.[17] It is undeniable that Nicholas felt personally vindicated by the violence. In a letter to his mother he explained that "the revolutionaries had angered the people once more; and because nine-tenths of the troublemakers are Jews, the people's whole anger turned against them.

That's how the pogroms happened. It is amazing how they took place simultaneously in the towns of Russia."[18]

Anti-Jewish violence and government blame contributed to Jewish disillusionment with the prospects for greater integration, but it also increased the desire among Jewish liberals for an improvement in their legal status and their inclination to demand collective rights. Between 1903 and 1905 both the general Jewish population and the many Jewish intellectuals who had previously taken part in the general *narodnik* (populist) and social democratic movements moved toward Jewish nationalism.[19] Still, until 1905, many politically active Russian Jews were in exile abroad, and the Bund and the Zionist movements were forced to conduct their activities underground. The 1905 revolution thus led to the open organization and mobilization of new Jewish political groups and the further radicalization of existing parties. Anti-Jewish violence, especially in 1903 and 1905, may have prompted some politically active Jews previously disinclined to nationalism to conclude that civil equality alone would not be enough to protect Russian Jewry, but widespread Jewish conviction of the need for national rights and the growth of autonomism as an ideology, which gained momentum before the revolution, fully took root only when the various Jewish political parties, factions, and umbrella groups established platforms to compete in the first parliamentary elections to be held in the Russian Empire. The spread of autonomism and the opportunity for a voice in government combined to create a sentiment of Jewish national affiliation, if not nationalism, among even the most integrationist groups.

Federalism on the March

The years leading up to the 1905 revolution were a time of general discontent among many of the empire's non-Russian nationalities, especially in Poland, the Baltic provinces, and Finland as well as Georgia and the Belorussian and Ukrainian provinces. When revolutionary steam began to gather, it was on the periphery (the northwest in particular), where national parties formed and mobilized for greater democracy and autonomy and where protests and strikes shook the government into harsh reaction and, ultimately, some concessions. Andreas Kappeler has called the 1905 revolution the "Springtime of the Peoples," alluding to the national revolutions that swept Europe, but not Russia, in 1848.[20] Kappeler points out that until the fall of 1905, incidents of strikes and revolutionary violence occurred disproportionately in the western provinces and Transcaucasia—to the point of imminent civil war—and had a national character that has been underappreciated by historians. Bloody protests and terrorism in Polish cities such as Łodz and Warsaw, agrarian revolts in Ukraine, the destruction of hundreds of Baltic German landowners' estates in Latvian and Estonian areas, declarations of a revolutionary republic in Guria in Georgia—for all these acts of rebellion the government response was considerably more brutal and violent than its attempts to quell Russian strikers, suggesting its particular fear of the national forces tugging apart the empire. The discontent for many national minorities was fueled by both economic grievances and resentment over suppression of their languages and religions. When these factors came together and state authority wavered, the result was newly voiced national and political aspirations.[21]

To varying degrees, the development of nationalism accompanied the process of politicization among all the empire's nationalities, including Russians. The brief political liberalization resulting from the 1905 revolution led to an atmosphere that was newly conducive to the voicing of national demands, and it created a venue for doing so: the Duma. All those groups developing aspirations for autonomy or federalism in the period before the revolution based their claims on a belief that Russia would become a free, constitutional or revolutionary socialist state. For example, the Lithuanian-Polish Irredentist Circle, established in December 1904 as a conglomerate of Polish and Lithuanian democrats based in Vilna, demanded "that the Russian constitution be based on a free federation of those countries (in their ethnographic boundaries), a population of which declare the individuality of their nation and require autonomy (Lithuania, Poland, Finland, and Ukraine)."[22] Interestingly, the Poles who participated in this group accepted that Vilna would form part of "ethnographic" Lithuania because they believed that their rights would be constitutionally safeguarded through an autonomous Poland.[23]

Both of the first two Lithuanian parties—the Lithuanian Social Democratic Party (LSDP, founded in 1896) and the Lithuanian Democratic Party (LDP, founded in 1902)—aimed for autonomy and eventual political independence.[24] At the initiative of the so-called national democrats, in November 1905 the Lithuanian parties held a Lithuanian congress in Vilna, attended by Lithuanians from everywhere in the Russian Empire and supported by Lithuanian Americans. All the parties at the congress agreed on the need for Lithuanian autonomy (though they disagreed on how it might be achieved), understood by many as the first stage leading to the eventual goal of independence.[25] The LDP (reconstituted after the congress as the liberal National Lithuanian Democratic Party) even made provision in its 1906 platform for Jews to use Yiddish as an official language and receive a proportional allocation of public educational funds.[26] In November 1905 Latvians and Estonians also held congresses and moved toward the idea of cultural and political autonomy.[27] Both of the major Polish parties founded in the 1890s, Roman Dmowski's National Democratic Party and Jozef Pilsudski's Polish Socialist Party, called for Polish autonomy as a first step to gaining independence, and in 1905 some Russian liberals and socialists also came to support Polish autonomy.[28] In addition to provincial, local, and village self-government, the Polish Social Democrats' 1905 program demanded "equality for all nationalities living under the Russian government, with guarantees for their freedom and cultural development, including national schools and free use of native languages, and governmental autonomy for Poland."[29] Ukrainian autonomists in 1905 faced the most significant obstacles, because even the most liberal Russian nationalists opposed any perceived threat to the territorial integrity of lands they considered Russian. Still, despite a campaign in the Russian-language Kiev press against any talk of separatism and a continued legal ban on publishing in Ukrainian, in 1905 Ukrainians in the Russian Empire started several Ukrainian-language newspapers and founded the Prosvita (enlightenment) Society to create and spread Ukrainian culture.[30]

Muslims also used the revolutionary opening in 1905 to demand full equality and collective rights. In 1905 the Muslim press (in several languages) experienced a tremendous expansion, and pan-Islamic politics emerged, especially among the Tatar and Transcaucasian elite. Three Muslim congresses were held in 1905 and 1906, and the Union of Muslims was created to represent Muslim interests politically. Even though, given the minimal participation from Central Asian Muslims, pan-Islamic politics in the Russian Empire was initially more theoretical than real, the rise of nonterritorial modern Muslim politics seeking cultural and religious renewal was enough to concern both the state and conservative Muslims.[31]

Even the general Russian parties forming to compete in the Duma elections had to acknowledge the demands of the empire's national minorities or be content with the support of Russian voters only. The 1905 program of the liberal Constitutional Democratic Party (known popularly as the Kadets) called for more powerful local self-government and autonomy for Poland and Finland.[32] The Socialist Revolutionary Party took the most federalist approach of any party; its members hoped to decentralize Russia radically by granting considerable autonomy not only to regions but also to municipalities and villages.[33]

Because most of the empire's Jews lived in its western borderlands and because of the correlation between revolutionary upheaval and national grievance in those provinces, Dubnov, his followers, Zionists, and a growing number of Jewish socialists became concerned in 1905–7 that they would be forced to take up the national demands of other minorities in place of their own national aspirations. Although Dubnov's arguments for the necessity of Jewish autonomy tended to relate to the spiritual health of the Jewish people, after 1905 he was increasingly sure that if the Jews did not create a program for nonterritorial Jewish autonomy, they would be left without the autonomous rights of the other national minorities. Even worse, in Dubnov's "Lessons of the Terrible Days," a letter written in response to the wave of pogroms that followed the October Manifesto, he reflected that despite their unique victimization, Russian Jews were not learning from the empire's other national groups and instead were willingly subordinating their own national struggle to the general goals of the liberation movement. In reference to October 1905, Dubnov wrote: "At a time when all oppressed nationalities in Russia—Poles, Armenians, Finns— conducted a revolutionary struggle under their national flags, Jewish revolutionary forces, with rare exceptions, struggled under the general Russian or Polish flags, and if and when a Jewish coloration existed, that exception was class and not nationality."[34] He also expressed profound disillusionment in this article, claiming that the violence of the previous month had convinced him that the Russian people would never agree to Jewish integration, that anti-Jewish violence was sure to return, and that therefore Russian Jewry must organize itself for national struggle.[35]

Dubnov extolled, and certainly exaggerated, the level of unity among other nationalities in the empire, the Poles chief among them. Contrary to Dubnov's exhortations of Polish political unity in favor of the national cause, Polish socialists in two rival parties (the Polish Socialist Party and the Social Democrats of the Kingdom of Poland and Lithuania) and the National Democrats were fighting between themselves, sometimes bloodily, for control of the revolution.[36] The Polish autonomist group, known as Koło and made up primarily of Poles from the Kingdom of Poland and the western provinces of the Russian Empire, formed the third largest political group in the First Duma.[37] The Koło faction was composed entirely of members of the Polish National Democratic Party, who often used antisemitism for political gain, and as such Koło proved rather ironically to be not just a model for how the Jews might conduct a campaign for their national rights in the Duma but also proof positive that the Poles did indeed see Jewish national claims as incompatible with their own. Despite heightened antisemitism among nationalist Poles, the experiment in electoral politics caused Russian right-wing parties and xenophobes to conflate the interests of the two groups. For example, Poles and Jews were lumped together by the conservative Octobrist Party, which attempted to smear the Kadets in the Duma as lovers of *inorodtsy*, or aliens, both Polish and Jewish.[38] Even the Duma itself was frequently denounced as a "Jewish institution," for example, in leaflets distributed by the antisemitic group known as the Black Hundreds before the pogroms in Bialystok.[39] Part of the reason that conservative Russians saw the interests of the Jews and other national minorities as the same related to concerns about the continued physical integrity and Russianness of the empire, leading to Russians' overall resistance to any autonomist aspirations, even educational or linguistic aspirations, among the empire's minorities. But the fact that the problem of anti-Jewish violence overshadowed the agenda of the short-lived Kadet-controlled First Duma may well have added to the impression that handing the Jews any victory at all might only embolden liberals and nationalists of all sorts.

The First Duma was the high-water mark for federalist thinking in the Russian Empire because it seemed to be the one moment before the spring of 1917 when the nationalities believed they had a genuine voice in the empire's transformation. The Duma's composition proved too radical for the tsar's cabinet though, and the transformative power of the empire's elected representatives turned out to be illusory. Nevertheless, during its two-month existence, the First Duma was a forum for debate about cultural autonomy, decentralization, and federalism, and it would have been surprising if at this moment—at the birth of mass party politics in Russia—Jewish parties did not also seek to find a separate space in whatever new political framework would emerge. Jews naturally followed the evolving national demands of other groups, because all national groups examined each others' programs in a mutually reinforcing process. When the Russian Zionists met in Helsinki (Helsingfors in Swedish) in November 1906 to determine their program for the Second Duma elections and their demands from the Russian state, the leading Finnish- and Swedish-language newspapers covered their proceedings and noted the extent of debate about Jewish demands for national rights in the Russian Empire.[40] The reestablishment of Finnish autonomy was, after all, the raison d'être of Finnish politics at the time, and Jewish national demands in no way threatened the Finns' claims. In sum, the Jews' demand for legal recognition as a nationality, and with it Jewish national rights and autonomy, fell naturally within the framework of the empire's decentralization as envisioned by many of its nationalities.

The Advent of Jewish Autonomist Politics

The 1905 revolution resulted from an accumulation of political pressures on the Russian government, and the general political mobilization preceding the revolution created a united Jewish liberal opposition that drew its inspiration from the general Russian liberation movement. One of the founders of the Union of Liberation, A. V. Peshekhonov, stated that "the liberal organization . . . combines not a class but various people, and then not in the name of class interest but in the name of the responsibilities of the intelligentsia to assist our oppressed people."[41] In March 1905 a union of liberal and moderately socialist Jewish parties known as the Union for the Attainment of Full Rights for the Jewish People in Russia (Soiuz dlia Dostizheniia Polnopraviia Evreiskogo Naroda v Rossii; also known as the Union for Full Rights) met for the first time in Vilna.[42] Although this unified Jewish political organization lasted just a short time, it played a vital role in organizing Jewish voters in Russia for the elections to the First Duma and held debates over exactly what the Jews of the empire should demand from the state. The tsar had the prerogative to dissolve the Duma and also to issue emergency decrees, but the franchise for the First Duma was, with a number of significant exceptions, relatively broad.[43] A curial system of elections loosely adapted the existing *zemstvo* electoral system, with the addition that workers elected their own representatives. After voters cast ballots for electors, the winning electors met to vote for a smaller number of deputies to the Duma. Despite the First Duma's short life, the opportunity to organize politically and participate in the elections with the rest of the empire's subjects catalyzed the Jews' political consciousness and, with it, the demand for Jewish national rights in the empire.

More than simply a means of electing Jewish Duma members, the Union for Full Rights was the first multiparty initiative for Jewish individual and collective rights. The group was also the first attempt by Jewish political activists and the Jewish intelligentsia to apply to the Jewish situation ideas about federalism and autonomy that were circulating among other national activists. In fact, the perception that the empire's Jews were more politically fragmented than other minorities drove the creation of the Union for Full Rights. Whether or not the empire's other minorities had actually unified to present their demands, most of the members of the Union and its Central Committee believed that they had.

The Union for Full Rights began with an illegal meeting organized in Vilna by two wealthy Jewish lawyers and liberals, Maksim Vinaver

(1862–1926) and Genrikh Sliozberg (1863–1937). They aimed to create a union of Jewish political groups to participate in the Union of Unions (Soiuz Soiuzov), the umbrella group of opposition movements dominated by Russian liberals. In response to the announcement of the Union for Full Rights' founding, sixty-seven prominent Russian Jews representing thirty-one cities came to Vilna.[44] Because of the timing of its formation on the cusp of revolution and the prominent positions of Dubnov and other autonomists in its Central Committee, the Union for Full Rights became the main vehicle for establishing the principles of autonomism in the Jewish political mainstream.[45] In addition to Dubnov's autonomist faction, known at the time as Dubnovists, the participants included the Zionists led by Jabotinsky, socialist but mostly non-Marxist members of Leontii Bramson's (1869–1941) Jewish Democratic Group, and liberals such as Vinaver, who would soon become important in the Kadet Party.

Despite the liberal and pan-national origins of the Union for Full Rights, the nationalists who participated were uncompromising in demanding that Jewish national rights be included in the group's Vilna platform. Shortly before the meeting, twenty-six Jewish communities issued a declaration to the government, stating: "As a cultural nation we demand the right to national-cultural self-determination, which must be granted to all incoming nationalities composing the Russian government."[46] The controversy over the wording of this declaration, signed by more than 7,000 Jews, raged in Vilna between nationalists and non-nationalists before and during the first meetings of the Union for Full Rights.[47] The term *cultural nation* might seem ambiguous enough to merit support from all quarters, as does the demand for "national-cultural" rights, with its implied emphasis on education and language. After all, no claim was being made that the Jews were a political or territorial nation. Yet the discussions in Vilna made clear to the liberal integrationists who had initiated the Union for Full Rights that there was considerable public support for a political and legal definition of the Jews as a separate nationality on a par with the empire's other nationalities. At stake was the legal foundation for Jewish emancipation. Because all Jewish political groups agreed that the Jews must achieve full civil equality, the debate that began with the Vilna declaration and persisted throughout the existence of the Union for Full Rights revolved around the extent to which the Jews should pursue their demands for national rights and autonomy—in essence, their legal right to self-determination and national equality. From the outset Dubnov and his supporters successfully imposed their position, insisting that the Union for Full Rights demand not only civil rights but also national rights, in the form of communal, linguistic, and educational autonomy.[48]

Dubnov had long argued that the best response to the virulent and intolerant nationalism then raging in Europe was an ethical Jewish nationalism secured by a legal framework for Jewish autonomy.[49] According to Dubnov, the limits to the legal autonomy of each individual nationality must be set at the point where one nationality's autonomy begins to curtail the autonomy of others.[50] Dubnov and his followers hoped that such a legal framework enabling Jewish autonomy might come into existence in the not-too-distant future. If it did, then Jewish political institutions like the Union for Full Rights were needed to prepare the way; if it did not, then such institutions would at least be useful in fighting against the infringement on Jewish autonomy by other national minorities.

Many other Jewish nationalists, including Zionists by this time, were also pushing for collective Jewish national rights in the empire, but Dubnov's personal influence on the program of the Union for Full Rights is undeniable. The organizational platform established in Vilna—which called for national-cultural self-determination in the form of linguistic and educational autonomy and which more specifically demanded that Jewish autonomy be based on the reintroduction of the *kehila* as a secular Jewish communal government—was, in effect, a reiteration of the tenets of autonomism promulgated in Dubnov's letters.[51] The Vilna platform was also, however, a reflection of the broad reception of Dubnov's vision of Jewish national autonomism within the many Jewish nationalist movements. By 1905 Dubnov's historical vision had seeped into the political sphere; self-government and the *kehilot* had become accepted as historically significant and a key demand for the future. Nonetheless, although Dubnov had as much influence over the platform as he could possibly have hoped for, the nationalists' victory in Vilna was temporary. Their insistence on including the demand for national rights in the platform resulted in the effective division of the Union for Full Rights into two blocks: on the one hand, the nationalists and Zionists; and on the other hand, the liberal nonnationalists and anyone else who gave civil equality a higher priority than any national considerations. Shortly after the meetings in Vilna, the Union for Full Rights joined the general Russian Union of Unions, despite opposition from Dubnov and other nationalists. This act foreshadowed the fact that nonnationalists such as Vinaver, Sliozberg, and Mikhail Kulisher, who had initiated the organization, would not back out of the struggle over the Union for Full Rights' priorities.[52]

Throughout the spring and summer Dubnov pressed the Central Committee of the Union for Full Rights to expand outreach to the Jewish public, to publish informational brochures, and to take an aggressive stance with the government, but his efforts were met with some trepidation about the potential risks.[53] Nonetheless, in the eight months between its founding and its second set of meetings in St. Petersburg in late November 1905, the Union for Full Rights established relations with 160 local organizations and grew to nearly 5,000 individual members.[54] The revolutionary events of the period no doubt boosted membership in the Union, with Jews participating in the student strikes and general strikes and in the Russian liberal campaign for a constitutional system. Less clear than the success of the Union for Full Rights in attracting members and organizing the Jewish electorate is whether its leaders truly represented the views of the Jewish general public. On the one hand, the Union was organized by highly acculturated liberals, and the decision to create a central committee with twenty-two members from St. Petersburg and the same number from the rest of the country ensured an overrepresentation of nonnationalists. On the other hand, the members of the Central Committee adhered to a variety of political ideologies, including not only Vinaver and Sliozberg but also Dubnov, Bramson (a socialist), Shmarya Levin (the Zionist publisher of *Dos yudishe folk*), and Mark Ratner (a Russian Socialist Revolutionary, a founder of SERP, and a fierce supporter of Jewish autonomism). What is clear is that the radical Jewish intelligentsia and professional political activists had carved out a sphere of influence in Jewish politics at a key moment.

Notably, the Union for Full Rights lacked participation from the Bund, the most significant force in Jewish socialist politics in the Russian Empire. Viewing the Duma as an instrument of the state, the Bund decided to boycott the elections and continued to advocate the revolutionary overthrow of the government.[55] The less revolutionarily inclined Jewish political groups represented by the Union for Full Rights, however, considered Jewish enfranchisement to be a good enough reason to participate in the elections.[56] Furthermore, the decision to boycott by the Bund, which was until that point the most organized Jewish political group, by default delegated the task of organizing the Jewish electorate to the Union for Full Rights.

As a result of the elections, the Union for Full Rights took on a much different role in Jewish political life than its founders had originally intended, and thus certain issues that they probably never thought would fall within the organization's purview continually dominated its debates. For example, the conflicts over Dubnov's proposal for a Jewish parliamentary faction and Jabotinsky's call for a Jewish national assembly (supported by the Dubnovists) proved particularly divisive and persisted throughout the Union's four congresses.[57] Although the end result of Jabotinsky's proposal was a vote in favor of a national assembly, the Union lacked the logistical means required to convene such a parliamentary body. The question of whether to form a Jewish parliamentary faction in the Duma was more relevant and became a particularly contentious issue leading up to the elections to the First Duma. The Jewish political parties and groups that participated in the Union for Full Rights, and in particular the Zionists, made the decision to use the Union to campaign for Jewish candidates running on the lists of the Russian parties or independently rather than running their own candidates separately. Because the twelve Jewish members who were eventually elected to the First Duma were all members of the Union for Full Rights and were elected in no small part as a result of the Union's efforts at organizing the Jewish electorate, the issue of forming a parliamentary faction had ramifications for both the candidates' electoral prospects and their relations with their own parties (the Kadets and the Trudoviks) once elected.[58] In practice, because all the Jewish Duma members were either Kadets or Trudoviks and also members of the

Union for Full Rights, cooperation on Jewish issues would take place in any event and would be only marginally enhanced by a resolution binding members to a faction. Still, creating a parliamentary faction would have had more than a symbolic effect. To have the Jewish members in Russia's first elected parliament join together as a national faction, or parliamentary caucus, was one more way to claim a legal space for Jews as a separate nationality, alongside the other nationalities represented by their factions in the Duma.

Delegates to the Union for Full Rights' congresses in February and May 1906 did not go as far as requiring the formation of a "national parliamentary group," as proposed by Dubnov, Iulii Brutskus, and others, but they did decide that deputies elected to the Duma must conduct their parliamentary affairs relating to Jewish issues according to the program established in Vilna, press for constitutionally enshrined freedoms for Jews, and not join a non-Jewish parliamentary faction in the Duma.[59] In the end, the Jewish Duma members were held to a rather vague commitment to unify on Jewish issues "in distinction from their general party programs and in steadfast recognition of their national unity."[60] When the Duma opened on April 27, 1906, the twelve Jewish deputies—nine Kadets and three Trudoviks—officially represented only their constituents and not a Jewish national faction.[61] Even so, the Union's congresses put the demand for national rights front and center in Jewish politics; in the first parliamentary elections in Russian history, all Jewish candidates accepted in principle the fundamental components of Jewish autonomism as articulated by Dubnov in his letters and incorporated into the Vilna platform.[62] Dubnov told his close friend Ahad Ha'am that he saw the Vilna meetings as an adoption of the essence of his political views and the sidelining of their opponents, both among utopian populists and nonnationalist liberals. Dubnov sardonically reported to Ahad Ha'am that after considerable debate the Union decided to include in its program "such terrible phrases as 'national law,' 'autonomy of communities,' the school, the freedom of the Jews. Instead of 'national representation' we agreed on a compromise: 'minority representation.'"[63]

The Union for Full Rights met in St. Petersburg just ten days after the Duma's opening to clarify the role of the Union in guiding the twelve elected Jewish parliamentarians.[64] Unsurprisingly, those members most opposed to the strong autonomist elements of the Vilna platform once again opposed a Jewish parliamentary group. After raucous deliberations the nationalists were able to pass a resolution in favor of a parliamentary faction, but the victory proved pyrrhic when a number of those opposed to the resolution—who would have had to sit in such a faction—quit the Union for Full Rights altogether.[65] The debate over whether to form a parliamentary faction in the Duma was more than a simple disagreement between nationalists and nonnationalists. Rather, because any Jewish parliamentary faction would be bound to the Vilna platform, it was a debate about whether the Jews should use their newly attained political representation to demand autonomy.

The driving force behind the creation of the Union for Full Rights was the perception among its founders, whether accurate or not, that Jews were more politically fragmented than the empire's other minorities.[66] In truth, the Jewish political leadership was fragmented, and the Jewish general public remained largely unpoliticized. The participants at the Vilna meetings represented not even the Jewish middle class but rather Russia's most intellectually and politically engaged Jews—its *obshchestvennost'*—and they were battling to shape the political consciousness of Russian Jews. Yet interestingly the acculturated Jewish elite in the Union perceived Jewish national demands to hold an intrinsic appeal to the Jewish public. It is notable that Sliozberg himself believed that the issue of national rights became a source of conflict in the Union because nonnationalists at the Vilna congress felt pressured by the "demagoguery of the Jewish street" to accept national rights.[67] According to Sliozberg, "Slogans thrown out were instinctively adopted by the Jewish masses who were unaware of the significance of these slogans."[68] His frustration stemmed from a sense of having lost control of an organization that he had helped to create, one that opened the door for new Jewish political parties to participate in Russian politics.[69] But in fact the Union worked equally as a conduit for the Jewish liberals—broadly, those who identified with the Russian liberal political movement—to participate in Jewish politics. Some members of the Union sought to tame its nationalist impulses, and others sought to strengthen them, but the creation of the Union must be viewed as a key moment in the democratization of Jewish national life in Russia.

The Birth of Jewish Nationalist Party Politics in the Russian Empire

Nicholas II agreed to a form of representative government only to save his regime, and he began to scale back its powers nearly as soon as it was created. The tsar enacted Russia's Fundamental Laws in April 1906, just days before the opening of the Duma, and among the 124 articles the tsar held the right to dismiss the Duma and veto its legislation. The First Duma was dominated by liberal Kadets and moderately socialist Trudoviks, and because the tsar's Council of Ministers refused to work with the legislators, they instead attacked the legality of the government's actions until the tsar dismissed the Duma after just ten weeks. The government was no more willing to cooperate with the Second Duma (which was more socialist in composition) than the first, and when the tsar dismissed it as well after just a few months in session (March–June 1907), Prime Minister Petr Stolypin rewrote the electoral laws to ensure a more conservative—and more Russian—Third Duma.

When the dissolution of the First Duma caused further ideological conflicts among the individuals and groups forming the Union for Full Rights and in the Jewish political sphere in general, the idea of an umbrella organization representing Jewish interests came to be seen as increasingly untenable. Dubnov claimed that by the time the Central Committee of the Union for Full Rights began preparing for the elections to the Second Duma, the dissolution of the organization seemed inevitable. Certainly by the fall of 1906, when the Central Committee openly expressed frustration with the organization's inability to agree on a program, it was apparent that the Union's constituent elements would experience ever greater difficulty in reaching a consensus.[70] But Dubnov refused to see the ideological differences as irreconcilable, despite being unwilling to yield any ground himself. Instead, he specifically blamed the Zionists' increasing independence for setting off a chain reaction that led to the Union's complete fragmentation.[71]

At the end of March 1907 the Union for Full Rights split into four separate organizations—the Jewish People's Group, the Russian Zionist Organization, the Jewish People's Party, and the Jewish Democratic Group—plus a fifth, nonparty group, but the members did not yet agree to abolish the Union.[72] The new form of the organization, essentially a loose coalition of Jewish parties, proved unsustainable, and in April the Central Committee admitted that the Union had become paralyzed by the different strategies and goals of its constituent groups, making it difficult for the organization to carry out its mandate of raising Jewish political consciousness and defending Jewish interests.[73] On May 16, 1907, the different factions within the Union agreed to continue to cooperate, but without the framework of a union. As Dubnov put it, the Union for Full Rights "was burned out after two years of existence: one year of blossoming, and one year of decay."[74]

At their Helsinki conference in 1906, the Russian Zionists had developed a plan for *Gegenwartsarbeit*, or work in the present, and decided to contest the elections to the Second Duma under their own flag. Dubnov blamed the rapid disintegration of the Union for Full Rights on the Zionists—he believed that they had appropriated his autonomist platform and his demand for national autonomy in the Diaspora—but his own campaign for a Jewish parliamentary faction in the Duma exposed the cracks in the Union that would eventually doom the organization. A liberal Kadet leader such as Maksim Vinaver, or other nonnationalists elected to the Duma, such as the journalist Grigorii Iollos or the lawyer Moisei Ostrogorskii, might accept a demand for national autonomy in the program of the Union for Full Rights, but to sit in a nationalist parliamentary faction with socialists and Zionists and demand Jewish national rights with the same urgency as civil rights was a step such staunch integrationists were unlikely to take.[75] Furthermore, it seems that Dubnov wanted the Union to serve a purpose that all its constituent factions would never endorse: to act as a united nationalist party to represent Jewish interests. Even before the organization's official end, nationalist members floated the idea of forming a new, nonpartisan group called the Jewish National (People's) Union (Evreiskii Natsional'nyi [Narodnyi] Soiuz), with the attainment of Jewish civil rights and national autonomy as its primary goals.[76] With the exception of Dubnov's faction, however, the other groups ultimately proved more committed to their own ideologies than to the idea of a multiparty union. The idea of a single political group representing the whole of the diverse spectrum of Jewish politics was one better suited to propaganda and lobbying (to Jews and the government, respectively) than to electoral politics.

After the demise of the Union for Full Rights, Dubnov, the communal activist Meir Kreinin (1866–1939), and a group of other autonomists decided to form their own party, the Evreiskaia Narodnaia Partiia, or Yidishe Folkspartey (Jewish People's Party), to advocate for the recognition of Jewish national and civil equality within the framework of a constitutional state. The founders of the Folkspartey (the Dubnovists, who became known as folkists thereafter) had been more reluctant to dissolve the Union for Full Rights than members of the other factions had been, as they were the least equipped organizationally to enter into the general political fray, and Dubnov had in any event managed to impose the fundamental components of his political ideology on the Union's program. In fact, the failure of the Union for Full Rights brought certain benefits to its other members. Although the liberals such as Vinaver and Sliozberg had initially formed the organization, they had become frustrated and drowned out by its nationalist members.[77] In contrast, many Zionists believed that their message was more appealing to the Jewish public than the Union's. Even though Dubnov hoped that the newly created Folkspartey would attract supporters searching for the ideological middle ground, he had long realized that his political program would come closer to implementation under a united Jewish party. Since November 1901, Dubnov had been calling for a united nationalist Jewish political front, including both Zionists and non-Zionists. In this he took the lead from other national minorities in the empire (especially Poles, Finns, and the Baltic groups), whom he perceived as more willing to put aside ideological differences to advance their respective national causes.[78]

The Folkspartey modeled its general platform on that of the left wing of the Kadet Party (in favor of a liberal, constitutionally based government guaranteeing a range of civil rights) and used the Union's Vilna program as the basis for its Jewish national demands.[79] But the founders of the Folkspartey took Dubnov's letters as their ideological foundation and saw the publication of the letters in book form in 1907 to be, in essence, their party's manifesto (though they did publish a separate itemized platform).[80] On this base the party established three initial goals: (1) a democratic Russian government with "complete equality of rights for all peoples of the empire"; (2) the legal recognition of Jewish nationality "as a single whole, with rights to national self-government in all realms of internal life"; and (3) the convocation of an all-Russian Jewish national assembly, "for the purpose of establishing the principles of national organization."[81]

We can see in the terminology used here the legal argument constructed by the folkists. Equality of rights means the right to Jewish self-government, and the right to Jewish self-government means the right to a national assembly. There is a rational, deductive logic for Jewish national equality and autonomy, in which recognizing the legal claims of the Jews as a nationality and instituting autonomy go hand in hand. It is for this reason that Dubnov emphasized in the platform's introduction that the principle of communal organization and self-government should be "national" and not "religious."[82] Only a few years later, when all the Jewish parties had accepted the necessity of reinstituting the *kehila* and were debating its form and purpose, the most significant point of contention between parties was whether the *kehilot* should serve a religious purpose in addition to their secular duties. At that point, Dubnov came out strongly against a purely secular Jewish communal structure, but what was important to him in 1906 was that the Jews should be considered a nationality and that their legal right to self-government should rest on that fact.[83] Hence the new party envisaged a Jewish community defined strictly by nationality and therefore discussed Jewish "national" representation rather than "religious" representation, with membership in the national community not defined by religion.[84] As its platform explained, the organs of Jewish self-government—namely, the *kehila* and the Jewish assembly—would have far-reaching rights, such as the right to send representatives to petition the central government and, perhaps most important, the authority to tax the Jewish population. The founding party platform explicitly linked the right of institutions of Jewish self-government to "forced taxation of the Jewish population" to the Jews' entitlement to "all the rights of a *legal* entity."[85]

In the party manifesto Dubnov explained the historical basis for Jewish autonomy in Russian and Polish lands and described how the new Jewish self-governing entities, unlike the *kahal* of the past, would be democratic rather than oligarchic, and secular rather than religious. In short, he claimed that the Folkspartey's approach to the Jewish struggle would be based on "a complete synthesis of Jewish life in the past and its practical needs in the present."[86] Of course, such a synthesis was impossible, and in fact the responsibilities of the new "institutions of national self-government" proposed by the folkists, such as "national education" and "workers' aid," bore little resemblance to anything that had existed before the *kahal*'s abolition in 1844.[87] What the folkists sought was to transform the philanthropic and cultural organizations established in the second half of the nineteenth century into legally recognized institutions of Jewish self-government. The folkist contingent of the Union for Full Rights, both during and after the organization's existence, assumed an increasing role in Jewish communal organizations such as the Society for Handicraft and Agricultural Work Among the Jews of Russia (ORT) and the Society for the Spread of Enlightenment Among the Jews in Russia (OPE). In fact, the Folkspartey was founded by a small group of professionals who embodied the professionalization of communal activism. In addition to Dubnov, the four other signatories to the Folkspartey's original platform were Meir Kreinin, a veteran activist with the OPE; A. V. Zalkind, a doctor; and two lawyers, V. S. Mandel' and S. I. Khoronzhitskii. Of the five, Kreinin was the most active in the Folkspartey, as is evident from both Dubnov's memoirs and the fact that Kreinin became the party's primary spokesperson in the press.[88] Like Dubnov, Kreinin had been born in a small town (Bykhov) in the Belorussian part of the Pale of Settlement and later became active in civic affairs, in particular the OPE and the Central Committee of the Union for Full Rights.[89] Kreinin gained experience in communal activities as one of the younger generation of Jews from the Pale who forcibly took control of the OPE in the 1880s and 1890s from the St. Petersburg–based financial elite, such as the Gintsburgs.[90] As Brian Horowitz argues, these new activists in the OPE were concerned not only with philanthropy but also with using the organization to establish Jewish national institutions (most notably a national school) intended to lead to greater cultural autonomy.[91] In fact, in 1905 and 1906 the conflict between the democratizing activists in the OPE led by Kreinin and the OPE's Executive Committee came to a head over the question of Yiddish education in OPE-run schools (a battle that the reformers lost, for the time being).[92]

The Folkspartey was created both in imitation of and in competition with the nationalist parties of other minorities that were forming in the new political atmosphere of the empire, and it was motivated by its founders' belief that Jewish parties were missing their chance to demand autonomy from the government. The legal basis for such demands was the notion that the Jews should be considered one of the Russian Empire's nationalities and therefore were entitled to national rights. The folkists justified the creation of their new party on the grounds that "the Jewish nation must pursue its own policy in the liberation movement" and that in every place in the empire where the Jews constitute a national minority, "they [should] obtain a guarantee of free existence, not subject to the social and cultural yoke of the surrounding national majority in either the general imperial or autonomous national territories."[93] In other words, in founding the party, the folkists adamantly rejected assimilating Jewish national or cultural demands with those of the Russians, Poles, or any other group.

Dubnov believed that because all the resulting parties made at least a token acknowledgment of autonomism, the Folkspartey could eventually bring the other factions formerly in the Union for Full Rights under its banner. The folkists did indeed eventually absorb a number of autonomists from the other Jewish political groups, but the Folkspartey's single-minded concentration on the attainment of autonomy was also its greatest weakness. All the parties that succeeded the Union for Full Rights—including Vinaver's liberal Jewish People's Group, Bramson's left-wing Jewish Democratic Group, and the Zionists—as well as the Bund, which had boycotted the Union, included in their platforms a demand for some form of Jewish autonomism, thereby lessening the need for a party organized around this single ideal.[94]

It is nonetheless important to emphasize just how influential Dubnov's ideas about national rights were to the development of Jewish nationalism in the Russian Empire—to Zionism in particular—and it is perhaps easiest to trace this influence between 1905 and 1907, at the birth of party politics in Russia. In 1906 Jabotinsky was among autonomism's most vociferous proponents in Zionist circles, and unlike Dubnov's other "forgetful imitators," as Jabotinsky put it, he duly credited Dubnov for originating the idea of autonomism in the letters and boldly developing the idea to its fullest.[95] Jabotinsky also argued that anyone could easily see the difference between the autonomism of the letters and the Bundists' more limited vision of it.[96] What is perhaps most astonishing in Jabotinsky's writings on Jewish national rights in Russia is his assumption that his readers had in-depth knowledge of the tenets of autonomism as articulated by Dubnov. Some Russian Zionists, such as the writer M. Shvartsman, even more explicitly called on their party to take up the slogans of "national self-government" and the "recreation of the Jewish community," and in explaining why Jews should adopt autonomism, he repeated Dubnov's historical explanation of autonomy's role in preserving Jewish nationality in the Diaspora.[97] Shmarya Levin (1867–1935), an important member of the coterie of new Zionists devoted to national rights in the Diaspora, attested to the personal influence of Dubnov during these years. In his memoirs Levin claimed: "In our intellectual world, which was not Zionist throughout, the first place was taken by Simon Dubnow. . . . He believed in the possibility of independent cultural evolution in the Diaspora, and he carried the principle of Jewish minority rights to its logical extreme."[98]

Dubnov, it should be noted, cultivated his influence among Zionists. In the summer of 1906 he chose to publish a new edition of his first and perhaps most influential letter, with the title "Osnovnyi nachala evreiskogo natsionalizma" (The Fundamental Principles of Jewish Nationalism), in the Zionist periodical *Evreiskaia zhizn'*. A footnote by Dubnov explained that his "concise theoretical synthesis . . . is brought to the attention of readers here as a general basis for Jewish nationalism," which, with modifications, can admit both "pure nationalists and nationalist-Zionists."[99] The Zionists, unsurprisingly, rejected Dubnov's hyphenated term (the editor added this note: "Not sharing the opinions

of the respected author, the editor gives a current place for his work like
the full and completed expression of his theory of spiritual nationalism"").
Nonetheless, the Zionists did essentially accept the idea that Jews must
be legally recognized as a nationality in the Russian Empire and accorded
the corresponding rights. In their journalistic writings, Jabotinsky, Abraham Idelson (1865–1921), and Yitshak Grinbaum (1879–1970) advocated
Jewish autonomy and *samoupravlenie* (self-government) and won over
many Russian Zionists to their ideas between 1905 and 1907.[100] During
this time, Zionist publications such as *Dos yudishe folk*, *Evreiskii narod*,
Evreiskaia zhizn', *Glos zydowski*, and *Evreiskaia mysl'* began to argue that
the Jews must not be the only minority failing to make national claims
on the government, and their editors moderated the general Zionist position that all Jewish national politics in Russia must serve a Zionist goal.[101]

The editors of these newspapers met somewhat regularly beginning
in the summer of 1906 to discuss how to incorporate *Gegenwartsarbeit*
into Zionism, and they were the crucial figures in establishing the so-
called Helsingfors Program (using the Swedish name for the city of
Helsinki, where the Russian Zionists met for the first time to decide on
their platform).[102] *Gegenwartsarbeit* was a program first proposed in 1901
by Martin Buber, the Viennese philosopher and editor of the Zionist
weekly *Die Welt*. Buber's concept of *Gegenwartsarbeit*, like the idea of
a Jewish renaissance that he put forward the same year, suggested that
educational and cultural development in the Diaspora could serve the
purpose of unifying the Jewish people, thereby preparing them for
Zionism and life in Palestine.[103] But the Russian Zionists, though they
used the term *Gegenwartsarbeit*, proposed more than just educational
and cultural work. The Russian Zionist Organization's Helsingfors Program came out in favor of a Jewish national assembly and some form
of democratically elected communal council with the right of taxation
and financial support from the government.[104] Also like Dubnov's party,
the Zionists demanded autonomy over emigration, aid, and the use of
Jewish languages. The Russian Zionists formalized their platform only
weeks before the official founding of the Folkspartey, but as the Zionists' demands for national autonomy had come to be almost identical to
those in the Vilna program of the Union for Full Rights, they were in
effect a reiteration of Dubnov's conception of autonomy.

Figure 3 Studio photo taken at the conference of the Russian Zionists in Helsinki, 1906. Yitshak Grinbaum stands second from left, Vladimir Jabotinsky fourth from left, and Boris Brutskus fifth from left. Abraham Idelson sits second from right (with elbow on the table). Courtesy of the Jabotinsky Institute in Israel, Tel Aviv.

The program established at the Helsinki conference showed that the Zionists knew the diaspora nationalists to be forming a new party of their own. The platform that the Zionists crafted in Helsinki responded to their expectations of the folkist program and stressed the still unresolved question of whether to form a united nationalist party. The conference was even extended by a day because of the length of debate on the question of whether to enter the Russian political arena as a Zionist party or as a nationalist party that could attract non-Zionists as well. A consensus eventually emerged in favor of maintaining the Zionist name, orientation, and program, but the Russian Zionists adopted into their official party platform the demand that Jews be legally recognized as a nationality and receive the rights to local and national self-government, with the corresponding rights to choose their form of local organization, language, and Sabbath observance.[105] Alexander

Goldstein (1884–1949), one of the architects of the Helsingfors Program, claimed that the national program of the Folkspartey "corresponds to the mood of the broad national masses" and even suggested that Zionists join together in coalition with or as a subgroup within this new party.[106] Shvartsman similarly argued in *Evreiskaia mysl'* that under a framework of "national democracy," the Zionists should come together with the nascent Folkspartey to create a joint movement, a suggestion that unleashed contentious debate in that publication.[107] In explaining why it was necessary to refute such an idea, Moisei Galinskii stated: "This opinion does not, as it would seem, belong to one or two Zionists, but rather expresses the attitude of a more or less noticeable portion of Russian Zionists."[108]

Some Zionists feared that the masses would prove more sympathetic to Dubnov's message than to Zionism. Hence Zionist proponents of a united party believed that if the Zionists joined the Folkspartey, they could play a leading role as the largest group inside a national "People's Party."[109] That way Zionists could support Jewish national rights in both Russia and Palestine without contradiction. Tellingly, Zionists who rejected a united party did so because they believed that if they formed a single party with diaspora nationalists, the Zionists would have to acknowledge the possibility of national rights without the goal of Zion, which would be fatal to the Zionist cause. For instance, Galinskii believed that if Zionists joined a united Folkspartey, it would achieve only one thing: "Zionism will wholly disappear from Russian Jewry's political picture. I underscore 'disappear,' as the 'Folkspartey' tactic will lead not to Zionism's partial extinction as the accumulator of Jewish politics, nor even to being pushed into the background by 'Dubnovism,' but will lead straight to its destruction."[110] According to Galinskii, the Zionists had to instead face the autonomists and let history, and the people, choose between them: "I dare to think that we must not take steps backward, and must not hide behind others' flags, but rather bravely and daringly go before the Jewish masses and explain to them who we are, what our goals are, and what we are trying to achieve in Russia."[111] Another Zionist, A. M. Borukhov, while likening the formation of a united party to "drinking wine to get rid of alcoholic drinks," lay some of the blame for the current predicament on the

Zionists themselves for having been too slow to accept Dubnov's prin-ciples.[112] According to Borukhov, "At the time when the Dubnovists—not to mention the activists of other specific parties—were fighting to organize Jews in the hopes of their own national initiatives, official Zionism included only the quintessential ideal of rebirth [in Palestine] as the last goal of national politics. Zionists at that time, for absolutely understandable psychological reasons, ignored, or even contradicted, all kinds of popular politics in the Diaspora."[113]

In an interesting parallel, a similar discussion took place among Aus-trian Zionists, who were at the same moment wading into electoral politics, finding their place among the other nationalities, and consider-ing the possibility of Jewish autonomy in Galicia and Bukovina (where most Jews in the Austrian Empire lived).[114] In Galicia even before 1905 Zionists attempted to wrest control of local communal leadership from the Polonized yet traditional Jewish leadership.[115] Nathan Birnbaum (1864–1937), who coined the term *Zionism*, argued in 1906 that all Jew-ish nationalists should join in an alliance to fight for national autonomy in Galicia and Bukovina and for the legal recognition of the Jews as a nationality in Austria. Birnbaum had earlier borrowed from Buber to propose a Jewish renaissance movement that would envelop all Jews (not just Zionists) in its cultural activities.[116] Birnbaum even sug-gested that the Jewish struggle for national rights in Austria was part of a broader movement encompassing all the Jews of Eastern Europe, because the question of autonomy "does not concern only the Jews of Galicia and Bukovina, but the entirety of Russian Jewry for whom the question of autonomy has long been raised."[117]

Russian Zionism developed within the context of the broader Jew-ish national movement in Russia and even perhaps, as Birnbaum sug-gested, Eastern Europe in general, a fact demonstrated in the debate about whether the Zionist movement should join in creating the Folks-partey. Within the Russian Empire it is easy to understand why many Zionists would embrace a platform for Jewish national autonomy in the Diaspora (and could do so without joining with the Folkspartey). Incorporating autonomism into their platform was a way for the Zion-ists to justify their participation in Russian politics, itself a new oppor-tunity resulting from the 1905 revolution. The Zionists could also use autonomism to rebut the frequent accusation that they were insensitive to the pressing needs of Russian Jewry, and they could argue that they had instead adapted to the new political landscape in Russia. After 1905 Russian Zionists increasingly argued that Jewish national autonomy and, in general, greater democracy in Russia could actually help facilitate emigration to Palestine.[118] Finally, what Zionist and non-Zionist nationalists shared was a view of the Jews in the Russian Empire as a nationality, and the legal ramification of such a view, established in the Vilna program of the Union for Full Rights, was equal entitlement to the rights of a nationality if and when the empire's legal system was transformed.

In viewing the struggle for autonomism in national terms, the folkists and the Zionists were therefore natural allies, even though Dubnov blamed the Zionists for the dissolution of the Union for Full Rights and obviously resented their appropriation of his ideological construction. The gulf, however, between the Zionists and the folkists was by no means small. The Zionists viewed national autonomy in Russia as a temporary solution to a problem that in the long term would be solved by emigration; the folkists saw emigration as a temporary balm and national autonomy in Russia as the permanent solution and the ultimate goal of Jewish political activity among the Jews of the Russian Empire. Dubnov supported emigration, especially to America, and to a lesser extent to a spiritual center in Palestine, until such a time when Jewish emancipation in Russia would be achieved, and he even suggested that organizing Jews for emigration could become the principal task of the folkists if the liberation movement failed.[119] In particular, Dubnov believed that America's political freedom and its high concentration of Jews uniquely positioned it for Jewish national and cultural autonomy, if proper steps were taken to protect immigrants from the temptations of assimilation. Dubnov argued that economic forces pulled people to America from all over Europe and that economic competition from Jews in industry and commerce would only increase Russian and Polish antisemitism in the near future.[120] But economic reasoning was not Dubnov's primary justification for supporting emigration, and his critics claimed that he presented all the Zionists' pessimism about Jewish life in Russia without their hope of a utopian alternative.

Dubnov's pessimism in favor of continued emigration was multilayered, and one layer—his argument that Russian Jewry might be strengthened if those individuals not strong enough to meet the challenges of forging a new society would leave—seemed to mirror the spiritual Zionist call for a Jewish avant-garde in Palestine.[121] Finally, Dubnov believed that the fierce criticism he met on the emigration issue was symptomatic of a more serious problem afflicting Jewish politics: the search for utopian answers—liberal, socialist, or Zionist—for all the problems afflicting Russian Jewry. Thus he argued that emigration should essentially be reserved as a contingency plan. He coldly observed: "If those who now pin all their hopes on the liberation now bury the emigration movement, they will be forced to exhume it later."[122]

Ultimately, diaspora nationalism and Zionism proved irreconcilable in 1905–7 because of the simple matter of ideology, despite the similarity of their platforms and immediate goals for Russian Jewry. Even Shvartsman in *Evreiskaia mysl'* acknowledged that an ideological gap between it and the Zionists could never fully be bridged, even in a united party:[123] "We think that our protracted disease demands an energetic and climactic treatment, and even then, not simply an entire change of climate will do, but only the mountainous climate of Palestine. In the atmosphere of the Diaspora, our lungs do not develop and cannot breathe freely."[124] The leaders of the Zionists and the folkists had differing views of both Jewish history and Jewish future—the disease and the cure.

Autonomism and Liberal Jewish Politics

Through bodies such as the Union for Full Rights, Jewish liberals influenced Russian Jewish politics by forcing all Jewish parties, including the Zionists and the Bund, to confront the question of whether and how to participate in Russian parliamentary politics. In the process, however, as Benjamin Nathans explains, Jewish liberals in the Russian Empire also became sympathetic to notions of national rights and autonomism: "In this they distinguished themselves from their counterparts in the [German] *Central-Verein* and the [French] *Alliance Israélite Universelle*, for whom national rights were virtually meaningless."[125]

In choosing to contest the Second Duma elections independently, rather than as Zionist members of Russian parties such as the Kadets, Russian Zionists sought to sharpen the distinction between Jewish nationalism and liberalism. And in a step with significant implications for the future, the Zionists decided in Helsinki to bar members of the Russian Zionist Organization from belonging to other Russian parties. Thus, simultaneously with their move to autonomism, the Zionists closed the door on a united nationalist party and broke away from Russian liberalism and, specifically, the Kadet Party.[126]

When the breakup of the Union for Full Rights and the independent course set by the Zionists forced Jewish liberals and moderate socialists to decide whether or not to continue to participate in a particularly Jewish politics, the answer was a resounding yes. As one of the founders of the Trudovik Party and a moderate socialist in the First Duma, Leontii Bramson exemplified the many leaders in the Jewish liberation movement who also played important roles in the general Russian liberation movement.[127] In addition to leading the Trudoviks, Bramson founded the moderately socialist Evreiskaia Demokraticheskaia Gruppa (Jewish Democratic Group), which sought to guarantee personal freedoms, a democratic and representative system of government, and the freedom of national-cultural and religious self-determination, in that order.[128] Bramson balanced his two roles as the leader of a party in the general Russian liberation movement and the leader of a Jewish political faction, and perhaps for that reason the priorities of his Jewish Democratic Group tended to be more universal than particular. In practice, however, Bramson was one of the small group of Jewish lawyers who became the most active professional Jewish communal activists in the empire—the core of Jewish *obshchestvennost'*—working in Jewish education, vocational training, and emigration.[129] He was described by a contemporary as almost a prototype for members of the emerging Russian-Jewish intelligentsia. Jewish issues defined his life work, but "on his path of development and self-realization, Jewish sources intersected with no less powerful influences, which emanated from Russian culture and the idealistic principles of the Russian liberation movement."[130] What concerned Bramson primarily was that Jews should embrace the ethos of self-help and create a Jewish *obshchestvennost'* that would improve Jews independently of any actions by the state.[131]

Only fairly minor differences separated Bramson from Jewish liberals such as Mikhail Sheftel' (1858–1922), the prominent lawyer and Duma member for Ekaterinoslav, and Lev Shternberg (1861–1927), the ethnographer and former *narodnik*, who joined together to form the Evreiskaia Narodnaia Gruppa (Jewish People's Group, or Folksgruppe) under the Kadet leader Vinaver.[132] The new Folksgruppe presented itself as the liberal alternative to Zionism and called for all those who did not view the Jews as foreigners in their own land of Russia to support its candidates for the Second Duma.[133] The Folksgruppe appealed to voters for the Second Duma not to be taken in by the fantasy of Zionism, which would lead only to Jewish isolation in Russia, and it also waged a heated war of words with the folkists about whether the attainment of civil or national rights was a higher priority for Jews in the empire.[134] However, the Folksgruppe felt compelled to acknowledge autonomists' demands and even vowed to "follow consistently the aims of the Union's Vilna program," demonstrating once again the breadth of acceptance of Jewish national demands.[135] Russian Jewish liberals clearly felt compelled to demonstrate their commitment to Jewish national rights while attempting to shift the argument about national rights to what Jewish political priorities should be in the current environment. The fact that Dubnov's group attacked the liberals' commitment to national rights immediately after both groups formed and that the liberals responded vociferously further kept the focus of Jewish politics on the issue of autonomy and national equality.[136]

If Jewish liberal, Zionist, and folkist parties shared any common ground, it was the sense that while the Jews argued among themselves, their subjugation by other nationalities would replace their subjugation by Russians. During the debates in the Union for Full Rights over a parliamentary faction, nonnationalists argued that the Jews must not create an equivalent to the Polish autonomist faction in the Duma, whereas autonomists and Zionists held up Kolo as exactly the model that the Jewish parliamentarians should follow, and this difference became especially evident in the campaign for the Second Duma.[137] But all groups felt equally threatened by the prospect of Polish autonomy without guaranteed rights for the Jews, and when it came to the Polish provinces of the Russian Empire, even the most liberal elements of the Jewish intelligentsia saw the need to create a legal space for Jewish autonomy. The liberal journal *Svoboda i ravenstvo* argued that Duma delegates should advocate democratic autonomy for all national groups, as opposed to the Poles alone, and worried that the Poles were completely ignoring the interests of their own large Jewish minority, because Koło proposed to guarantee language rights for Russians, Belorussians, Ukrainians, and Lithuanians but specifically excluded Jews from their autonomist formula.[138] Furthermore, Koło's strength reflected Jewish weakness; Jews made up 14 percent of the Kingdom of Poland's population but failed to elect a single Jewish delegate.[139] Despite the interest of the members of the Union for Full Rights in the politics on the ground in Poland, the Union's presence there was limited because Jewish community leaders had been wary of its association with Russian rather than Polish liberal movements (one member of the Union who went to Warsaw and was surprised by the unwilling response of the Jewish leadership there to cooperate with their political initiative claimed that these Jews were so Polish that they saw Russia as a foreign place[140]). The Jews in the Kingdom of Poland, like elsewhere, nonetheless went through a process of mass politicization as a result of revolution and elections. But in contrast to the other western provinces where liberal Russians and Jews frequently cooperated to elect mutually agreeable candidates, in the Kingdom of Poland the Jewish elite and intelligentsia who attempted to make common cause with Polish liberals and mobilize the Jewish electorate could not overcome the strength of the National Democrats.[141]

Members of the Union for Full Rights paid close attention to Polish autonomist politics, despite the organization's limited presence in the Kingdom of Poland. For example, the short-lived newsletter of the Union for Full Rights, *Evreiskii izbiratel'*, reported on the formation of Koło and devoted much space (especially considering the thinness of the publication) to the tactics of Koło and its position on Jewish questions.[142] Koło provided a test case for how a nationalist and autonomist faction in the Duma might function and also whether other nationalist groups would see Jewish autonomist claims as competing or complementary to their own. Some, such as the editors of *Svoboda i ravenstvo*, wanted to believe that the Jews in Poland would no less adamantly challenge attempted Polonization than the Poles challenged Russification.[143] Nonetheless, as the dissolution of the Union proved, the Koło model was not realistic for Russian Jewry. In 1905 nonterritorial autonomy failed to bridge other, more glaring ideological fissures within the Jewish political sphere. Still, for all the concerns of the Zionists and the autonomists about creating a Jewish faction in the Duma, the Jewish Duma members continually argued there that the achievement of Jewish legal equality, albeit not national autonomy, must take precedence over all other issues facing the empire.[144]

Autonomism and Class Warfare

Although a number of different ideological factions jointly formed the Union for Full Rights, all the participants were committed to constitutionalism. But, of course, Jews also participated in the general Russian revolutionary movement, and over time socialist parties came to command the support of an increasingly vocal and revolutionary, though proportionally small, segment of Russian Jewry.[145] With more than 30,000 members in 1906, the Bund was a formidably large party; it was also well organized. But the success of the Union at organizing voters for the elections to the First Duma suggests that, at least between 1905 and 1907, most of the empire's Jews were inclined to ignore the Bund's and other socialists' calls to boycott the elections and instead exercised their new right to participate in bourgeois politics.[146] For that reason the Jewish socialist parties changed their tactics and contested the elections to the Second Duma.

There had been good reasons for the socialists to boycott the Union for Full Rights and the previous elections to the Duma. For one, the requirement that factory workers be employed in establishments with at least fifty workers in order to vote (for representatives who would chose the electors) meant that if Jewish workers could not vote in the city curia, they could not vote at all.[147] Nonetheless, the Bund's boycott of the Union predated the plans for the Duma elections and had less to do with standing up for the Jewish proletariat than the reality that few members of the Bund—many of whom were out organizing strikes and collecting arms—could comprehend, or sympathize with, the worldview of people like Maksim Vinaver or Genrikh Sliozberg (and the lack of comprehension was mutual). Members of the revolutionary left who boycotted the Union were generally much younger than the liberals who organized the group, and thus a generation divide contributed to the difference in tactics between radicals and liberals. As Jonathan Frankel points out, "All the anger of the front-line troops for those living comfortably in the rear now came to divide the socialists of all denominations from the Union for Equal Rights."[148] Members of the Jewish socialist parties, such as the Bund and Poalei Zion, had become increasingly radicalized because of the constant danger of being arrested by the authorities, and the parties could see no benefit in demanding a Jewish national assembly that would in all likelihood strengthen the position of the liberals. Nonetheless, Jewish socialist groups needed to remain relevant to Russian Jewry, especially at a time when the legalized status of their competition placed them at an organizational disadvantage. One means of doing so was to adopt certain autonomist ideas that resonated more with the Jewish public than calls for international socialist solidarity.

The Bund crept gradually toward autonomism, beginning with its fourth congress in 1901. The resolutions produced there led to a heated conflict between it and Lenin's newspaper, *Iskra*, which ultimately resulted in the Bund's withdrawal from the Second Congress of the Russian Social Democratic Labor Party in August 1903.[149] In 1904 the Bund formally demanded cultural autonomy for the Jews of Eastern Europe, but it was not until after the 1905 revolution that the Bund's leaders claimed to lead a national as well as a proletarian movement.[150] The Bund's change in attitude in favor of Jewish cultural (but not national) autonomy was in part due to the Polish Socialist Party (PPS) also demanding national rights for Poland by this time. Another reason for the Bund's change in policy was its recognition of competition from new socialist Jewish political groups that included the demand for Jewish autonomy in their programs. Finally, and perhaps most important, the Bund also could not ignore the popular support for autonomism among its constituents. As one Bundist claimed in 1905, "A veritable wave of public opinion has come out for 'Bundist' national-cultural autonomy in one form or another, more or less explicit. Today it has become a topical question, a fashionable slogan."[151] Yet even as public opinion, competition, and the PPS platform forced the Bund to alter its stance in favor of cultural autonomy, the organization still refused to embrace full-fledged national autonomy or a sociopolitical model in which local self-government extended beyond education and language rights. The Bund adopted cultural autonomy quite simply because in the atmosphere of 1905 it could not afford to be the only Jewish party that did not favor some kind of autonomous arrangement for the Jews in the empire.

The Jewish proletarian parties' reluctance to embrace sociopolitical Jewish autonomism in the Russian Empire contributed to the creation of the Sejmist movement, Vozrozhdenie, and the socialist autonomist party SERP by repelling nationalists such as Zhitlowsky and failing to take in disaffected socialist Zionists. The Sejmists and SERP boycotted both the Union for Full Rights and the elections to the First Duma along with the Bund and other social democratic parties. But in the elections to the Second Duma, Zhitlowsky won a position as an elector in Vitebsk as a SERP representative under the list of the Socialist Revolutionary Party (Zhitlowsky's victory was annulled by the authorities). In the Second Duma elections the Zionists even supported the Sejmists in a number of places because of their shared national aims, such as in Volynia, where Jabotinsky renounced his candidacy to throw his support behind the socialist autonomist Mark Ratner.[152] Yet despite the fact that creating a Jewish national assembly—the supposed raison d'être of the Sejmists—consumed the deliberations of the Union for Full Rights, the Sejmists made socialist solidarity a higher priority and stayed out of the debate.[153] As was the case with Vozrozhdenie, proletarian victory was the primary driver of Sejmist ideology, and so its leaders consequently believed that a national assembly organized by groups aiming for constitutionalism would only serve the ends of the bourgeoisie. Zhitlowsky personally attacked Dubnov's call for the Jewish proletarian parties to abandon class struggle and concentrate on building spiritual nationalism, simultaneously questioning how, in Dubnov's conception, extraterritorial nationalities could conceive of organizing their communal autonomy without national autonomy in a *sejm*.[154] Zhitlowsky called such a position and Dubnov's embrace of the Kadets' general program "national-Jewish Kadetism."[155]

The events of 1905 and the feeling that change was imminent in Russia hastened the division of the socialist Zionists into Sejmist, Palestinophile, and territorialist camps, and the increased freedoms combined with the return of political exiles also led to new organizations, new publications, and new debates. Unlike the nonsocialist Zionists, the socialist autonomists could not be accused of incorporating autonomism into their ideology for political gain alone or to avoid appearing insensitive to the needs of Russian Jewry. Full national nonterritorial political autonomy for Russian Jewry lay at the heart of Vozrozhdenie and SERP. Like the Zionists, however, the socialist autonomists saw the adoption of national rights primarily as a means to an end. Whereas the Zionists justified the adoption of Dubnov's principles on the basis that guaranteeing national rights and representation would help facilitate Zionism, the socialist autonomists sought to use national rights to bring about the victory of the proletariat and the peasantry and, hopefully, the overthrow of the tsar. Thus, if the Sejmists in 1905–7 were maximalist in their demands for Jewish autonomy and critical of the Bund for its lack of earnestness in addressing Jewish national demands, it should not be forgotten that they were equally adamant about the primacy of the socialist struggle. By 1917 many socialist autonomists had changed their priorities, but the *vozrozhdentsy* and then the Sejmists considered themselves first and foremost "socialist-Jews," and it was the acceptance of this hyphenation that was their primary goal.[156]

The socialist and nonsocialist parties remained chiefly divided by the issue of class struggle. The leadership of the Union for Full Rights in fact published a circular accusing the socialists who refused to participate of dividing the Jewish body politic and prioritizing their narrow interests over the national struggle and even the basic issue of Jewish legal equality. Jewish equality before the law and communal autonomy came first, claimed the Union's Central Committee: "When this national goal will be achieved, the time will come for splitting affairs into economic and national-cultural factions."[157] Yet despite the continued divisions between socialists, liberals, and others, one can see in the flowering of Jewish politics that took place in 1905–7 that the difference between cosmopolitan and nationalist views of Jewish identity steadily receded into the background. Paradoxically, even as the Russian Jewish political world reached its apex of fractiousness, the socialist and nonsocialist groups narrowed many of their differences on the issue of autonomism.

Conclusion

The revolutionary period between 1905 and 1907 witnessed the general politicization of Russian Jewry. However brief, it was also a period of relative political cooperation between Jewish political groups (except the radical socialists). Though the deliberations of the Union for Full Rights were often stormy, the Union played an important role in organizing the Jewish electorate for the first popular elections in Russian history. In addition to aiding in the election of a number of Jewish representatives to the First Duma, the Union was also a forum for aspiring Jewish political activists to debate Jewish demands on the Russian government. To the surprise of the liberals, who had formed the Union as a way to participate in the general Russian liberation movement, the group's proceedings were consumed by debates about the necessity for a Jewish national assembly and whether or not Jewish members of the Duma should form a national faction. Although the members of the Union fought bitterly over the specifics of Jewish autonomy, most had come to accept a minimum program for Jewish civil rights and national recognition in the Russian Empire (embodied in the Vilna program), based loosely on Dubnov's writings on Jewish autonomism, not least because of pressure from the Jewish public. The experience with electoral politics changed the nature of Jewish political debate: Jewish politics had decidedly shifted in favor of increasing Jewish collective rights.

In the introduction to his letters that came out in 1907, Dubnov attempted to capture the significance of the changes in Russian Jewish political culture during the previous few years.

In these last few years, certain slogans which even recently seemed "terrifying" and heretical, catchphrases such as "natural rights," "autonomism," "cultural autonomy," "national school," etc. have come into common use in Jewish social life. If these slogans are today established in the programs of Jewish parties and affiliated organizations, side by side with the demand for political and civil emancipation, one may presume that, along with other influences, [these slogans] did not fail to influence our national evolutionary synthesis, which called for an internal renaissance in the Diaspora. However, I am still far from celebrating the victory of the national-cultural renaissance in Jewish life. Parts of our society were moved by the current of this renaissance more because of national mood than nationalist convictions, and a sizable part of our society is altogether unaffected by these new currents and still remains in the stage of assimilationist antithesis [to nationalism] or near this position. A systematic national philosophy is only just beginning to be worked out.[158]

Dubnov was correct that the revolutionary years had introduced a common language of national rights and autonomy into the empire's Jewish political discourse. He was also correct that not everyone viewed the purpose of Jewish autonomism in Russia as he did. Dubnov may have agreed with the Zionists' demand for full national rights for the Jews in Russia and supported the convocation of a Jewish national assembly, but because of their vastly differing long-term objectives, the gap between the folkists and the Zionists was much greater than that between the folkists and the liberals of the Folksgruppe. Vinaver made efforts to bring the folkists into the ranks of his organization and, according to Dubnov, even offered to incorporate aspects of the Folkspartey platform into that of the Folksgruppe if Dubnov would agree to run in his place for the Second Duma.[159] Dubnov supposedly refused because of the presence of "assimilationists" in the ranks of the Folksgruppe, an act that proved the hollowness of his many calls for *klal yisroel* (Jewish unity).[160]

For all of Dubnov's talk of the necessity of Jewish political unity, what he really meant was unity under his own political ideology. Despite his claim in the introduction to the Folkspartey's platform that the party "serves potentially as the *nucleus of the organized nation*," it would be an understatement to call such high-mindedness wishful thinking.[161] Neither was he entirely correct to state in his memoirs: "My ideology occupied the place between the extreme currents and shared the fate of all middle positions: it was attacked by the right and the left."[162] In fact, Dubnov's principled and unyielding stance on prioritizing Jewish autonomism above all else alienated him from the moderate liberal nationalists in the Folksgruppe, and his equally fierce opposition to both class warfare and the negation of the Diaspora provided little room for cooperation with either socialists or Zionists. It is not surprising, then, that other political groups chose instead to adopt the aspects of his theories that best served their own purposes.

Dubnov's diaspora-nationalist interpretation of history emphasized the importance of periods of acute crisis in bringing about Jewish societal change. Like others at the time, anti-Jewish violence also deeply affected his views about the prospects of integration, and he viewed the Jewish transition to nationalism as ever more natural and necessary in its wake. Yet we can see in the activities of the Union for Full Rights that Jewish political mobilization and the turn to Jewish national rights were more complex than merely an intuitive response to violence. The period 1905–7 was at the time viewed as a moment of both crisis and opportunity. Jews were simultaneously given the chance to play a greater role in shaping their own future and threatened physically by forces that sought to reject their inclusion in the body politic. Although the government capitulated to a number of liberal demands in order to stem the revolutionary tide, many powerful people—not least the tsar—blamed the Jews for the empire's turbulence and instability. It is fair to say that by 1905 antisemitism in official Russian circles had become obsessive and conspiratorial.[163] Most important, national rights became the watchword and slogan among the other nationalities among whom most Jews lived. This was a moment when Dubnov's earlier writings could only have seemed prophetic, as the concepts of national autonomy and communal self-government became widely adopted as fundamental Jewish political demands, and belief in the need to take advantage of all opportunities to construct a bulwark for Jewish autonomy became widespread.

Four Jewish Culture and Autonomy in Reform and Retrenchment, 1907–14

Almost as quickly as the 1905 revolution opened the door to the possibility of some form of representative government, that door closed again with the tsar's dissolution of the First Duma. After dismissing the Second Duma in 1907, the government further narrowed the electoral franchise, resulting in the election of only two Jewish members to the Third Duma. Furthermore, the Stolypin era that followed the end of the Second Duma, so called for Prime Minister Petr Arkadevich Stolypin (1862–1911), ushered in an era that mixed political repression with the maintenance of certain freedoms granted in the October Manifesto of 1905 and the Fundamental Laws of 1906, such as the freedoms of speech and assembly (however curtailed). During several years of the Third Duma, which sat its full term from 1907 to 1912, the Russian government was willing to allow the empire's national minorities to establish new nationally oriented cultural institutions. Government policies, especially between 1908 and 1911, led to the strengthening of minority nationalism everywhere in the empire. For the Jews, St. Petersburg between the revolutions of 1905 and 1917 became a place for intense political debate and cultural productivity, strengthening the forces of Jewish nationalism and autonomism.

Even though the revolution failed to bring about genuine constitutional democracy in Russia and despite the Jewish attempt at a unified liberation movement having splintered, the revolutionary years imprinted the aspiration for national rights on the Jewish intelligentsia and *obshchestvennost'*. The demand for national rights in Russia that swept Jewish politics between 1905 and 1907 did not go dormant when opportunities for political participation narrowed; rather, national rights became part of Jewish political discourse, and arguably its central concern, between 1907 and 1914. During this period, attention turned to determining the ideal form of Jewish communal organization and the meaning of Jewish nationalism in Russia. The differences of opinion between the various Jewish parties and factions remained vast, but the topics of "community" and the "national idea" served as a common ground for debate among them. The establishment of new cultural and communal organizations and the democratization of others reflected a new spirit of cooperative efforts to build the foundation of Jewish autonomy by whatever means the state granted. With the Bund in decline, Jewish political initiatives, both theoretical and practical, came from many of the prominent leaders of the Union for Full Rights and from a new cohort of young Jewish activists with socialist backgrounds who had moved to the capital. The 1905 revolution had ended, but St. Petersburg became ever more populated by the many Jewish political activists who had returned from exile or moved to the capital from other parts of the empire, and despite continued residential restrictions on Jews, the city became the empire's primary center of Jewish political activity.

A number of internal and external factors fueled the debate among Jewish intellectuals over the parameters of the Russian Jewish community and how such a community should govern itself. Externally, the Russian government's attempts at reform revolved around different aspects of the collective rights of its subjects, so the urgency of establishing specifically Jewish demands never disappeared. Government efforts to introduce *zemstva* into the western provinces, to officially recognize the rights of certain religious minorities, and to curb the autonomy of troublesome groups, such as the Finns, ensured that legal and political questions about self-government and community would continue to transfix all the empire's religious and national minorities. Furthermore, as Russian intellectuals became imbued with a new sense of *obshchestvennost'*, Jewish intellectuals similarly became increasingly involved in communal politics and sought to expand existing communal organizations so that they could take on greater responsibilities within the community.

Internally, as this chapter explores, the debate over Jewish autonomy and community after 1907 both reflected and exacerbated existing divisions, not least those between secular and religious definitions of the Jewish community and those between Yiddishists and their opponents. As we will see, the language question—which language, or languages, Russian Jews should adopt, revive, or maintain—became central to both the self-definition of Jewish intellectuals and the way various Jewish political ideologies presented the future of the Jews in Russia. The sociopolitical model of Jewish autonomy became fully developed through these debates, partly as a result of the efforts of liberals who hoped to tame two beasts—the religious and the nationalist—at once. Most important, autonomist projects of the period came to be based on the belief among highly Russified Jewish intellectuals that autonomy should be constructed as a bulwark against the pressures of assimilation on the Jewish public as a whole. Whether such pressures were real or imagined remained irrelevant to Jewish intellectuals, whose frustration with their inability to effect real change in the Jewish community led them to feel estranged from the people they claimed to serve and propelled them to attempt to reestablish their own authenticity.

Stolypin, Reform, and Jewish Political Rights

The short-lived Second Duma, which lasted only from February to June 1907, reduced Jewish representation from twelve to four members and led to the exclusion from politics of all the Kadets and Trudoviks who, following the First Duma's dismissal, had signed a statement, known as the Vyborg Appeal, that called for passive civil disobedience. Among the issues debated in the Second Duma's brief session was a bill intended to remove all legal discrimination based on religion (after initially excluding the Jews this bill was altered to include them in the new law). Nonetheless, the effort came to naught as the tsar dissolved the Duma. The Manifesto and Electoral Law of June 3, 1907, aimed to replace the first two Dumas with one in which the majority of representatives would share the worldview of the government, thus minimizing the representation of supposedly untrustworthy elements. Prime Minister Stolypin engineered the new electoral law to guarantee that a majority of voters and deputies would be rural Russian landowners (and, to a lesser extent, wealthy urbanites), and he aimed practically to eliminate the representation of non-Russian nationalities (the inhabitants of vast stretches of Central Asia were disenfranchised on the basis of their supposed backwardness).[1] Stolypin decided he could work most effectively with the Octobrists, a party whose representatives were primarily drawn from the nobility, landowners, and *zemstvo* activists. Although the Octobrists came into the Third Duma as only the second largest faction, after the group known as the Rights, the Octobrists' leader, Alexander Guchkov, managed to enlist enough moderates and Rights to give the newly named Union of 17 October a plurality of votes.[2] That only two Jewish candidates were elected reflected the generally difficult situation of the Kadet and Trudovik Parties under the new electoral system.

Stolypin believed that the Jews' precarious economic and legal situation could be improved through modest steps, beginning with the elimination of some of the most unreasonable residential restrictions on Jews in the cities and within the Pale of Settlement, to place them "on a nearly equal footing with other Russians."[3] But he ran up against determined opposition from Nicholas II to any legal concessions to the Jewish population. As Abraham Ascher observes in his biography of Stolypin, "Strangely, the prime minister seems not to have been aware of the depths of Nicholas's hostility toward the Jews. Or perhaps Stolypin assumed that while the tsar profoundly disliked the Jews, he would nevertheless rise above his personal feelings and approve the reforms for reasons of state—that is, to remove a source of political instability."[4]

In its treatment of the Jews, the Third Duma period is less remarkable for the introduction of new anti-Jewish legislation than the Duma's and the government's new zeal for fortifying or enforcing existing legislation. Instead of abolishing the Pale of Settlement, the Third Duma sought in 1908 to legally enshrine its status in perpetuity by explicitly mentioning the Pale as an exception to new laws on freedom of movement. During this period, 1,200 Jewish families were expelled from Kiev under the pretense that they had been living there illegally. Similarly, in the realm of education, existing statutes on quotas for Jewish students in secondary and postsecondary education were applied with new vigor in educational areas where such quotas, known as the *numerus clausus*, had previously been ignored.[5] When Count I. I. Tolstoi, who was appointed minister of education in October 1905, worked to eliminate the *numerus clausus* restricting Jewish admissions to the universities, he was opposed by the minister of the interior, P. N. Durnovo, and ultimately overridden (and fired) by the tsar.[6] In fact, in 1908 the *numerus clausus*—previously only a rule guiding educational institutions—was made into a law. Equally devastating to the growing number of educated Jewish professionals was the government's extension of the quotas to students returning with degrees from abroad who wanted to sit for examinations in Russia. This action effectively disqualified Jews who sought higher education elsewhere (to avoid the quotas) from practicing their profession in Russia.[7]

Although Stolypin's dismissal of the Second Duma came to be widely called a coup and ushered in a period of political repression, his policies and wrangling with the Third Duma were the autocracy's last major attempt at substantial reform.[8] Until his assassination in 1911, Stolypin attempted to pass agricultural and land-reform bills that the noble-dominated Octobrists, who were supposed to be Stolypin's supporters, opposed as against their interests. As a result, to gain support for his policies, Stolypin increasingly turned to the nationalists and tolerated their antisemitism when it was directed at his liberal opponents.[9] The period from June 1907 until the outbreak of war in 1914 was thus characterized by both relative freedom for Jews, such as in the press, and new frustrations, such as increased difficulties in obtaining degrees. The many inconsistencies of the Jews' legal status were apparent in all aspects of life, but Jewish rights during the interrevolutionary period generally followed the pattern of repression, relaxation, and then repression again that characterized the government's approach to all national minorities. So, concerned about the Zionists' independent politics, the government banned Zionism in 1907; the ban was easy to avert (through clever semantics) and ironically served to focus Russian Zionism on the national struggle at home rather than in Palestine.[10] Then in a bid to placate frustrated nationalities in 1908, the government allowed Jews (and others) to establish new cultural institutions. But by 1911 nationalists in the Duma were pressing the government to reverse course and squelch the growing autonomy of national minorities. The government needed little prodding to discourage Jewish nationalism and autonomist institutions. As early as March 1910 the general-major of the St. Petersburg police drew up a detailed report on the Union for Full Rights, using a transcript of their March 1905 meeting to determine who should be questioned for their "revolutionary speeches" of five years before.[11]

Few Jews viewed Stolypin positively, but even before his assassination it became apparent that the prime minister was in fact a moderating influence on both the tsar and the Third Duma. Stolypin understood that the revolutionary years had dissolved the state's authority, and thus the most important task ahead, as Francis Wcislo suggests, "was the reconstitution of a reformed autocratic order that possessed legitimacy in strata of society stable enough to uphold it."[12] Unfortunately for Stolypin, the Duma he had engineered was actually less conducive to reform than the two earlier Dumas, because the noble landowners were the group most resistant to any change that might diminish either their financial or social status.[13] To protect these interests, the Octobrists became great proponents of constitutionalism, as Stolypin increasingly sought to enact reform without the Duma.

Even though Jews, like most of the empire's population, possessed only a limited ability to influence the Stolypin government and the Third Duma, the issues of reform affected Jews' perception of their need for autonomy and of how it could best be achieved. For example, one issue occupying Stolypin and the Third Duma was the task of reforming the Russian *zemstvo* system and introducing the *zemstvo* to nine of the empire's western provinces that lacked it. When he began to plan this reform in 1907, Stolypin envisioned Jewish participation in the municipal Dumas and allowing Jews to hold posts on the government-appointed district *zemstvo* management boards.[14] Yet Stolypin also hoped to appeal to the Octobrists, whose representatives were drawn mainly from *zemstvo* activists, and at the same time to ensure that local government in the heterogeneous western provinces would be dominated by Russians (rather than Poles). To do this, he devised a complicated electoral system combining curiae by nationality and property so that most of the representatives in the new *zemstva* would be Russian but not peasants. And to lessen the opposition from conservatives and nationalists, the bills considered by the Duma and indeed the final Western Zemstvo Bill explicitly prohibited Jews from participating in the entire *zemstvo* system. After getting the bill through the Duma but failing to gain the cooperation of the State Council (the parliament's upper chamber), Stolypin promulgated it in March 1911 through extra-parliamentary means, using emergency powers.[15]

The Jews did not lose any privilege in the Western Zemstvo Bill as they had not previously participated in the *zemstvo* system. Still, the Jews' final and official exclusion from the very structure of self-government in the Russian Empire, even as it was expanding, only increased the sense among Jews that they lived as a legal anomaly. The exclusion also made final the distinction between Russian and Jewish *obshchestvennost'*, a division that became acute during World War I. The Third Duma was an era of what one scholar has called constitutional nationalism, when constitutionalism advanced only when it was seen to serve the Russian "people," itself a new source of political authority.[16] The state had long avoided introducing the *zemstvo* in the western provinces because the *zemstvo* electoral system, based on property and estate, would empower Polish landowners. But to engineer the desired result (Russian control), Stolypin shifted the legal framework for self-government from estate to nationality, and the Jews were still on the outside. At that same moment Jewish lawyers, communal activists, and cultural and intellectual figures—the Jewish *obshchestvennost'* and intelligentsia—were expanding and creating new Jewish communal organizations, cultural institutions, press, and political life. Jewish exclusion from a key element of imperial political life and the gathering steam of a separate Jewish national life were therefore mutually reinforcing. Even hopeful integrationists in this context looked to build parallel institutions of Jewish self-government.

Building a Community, Part I: Politics

Liberals, monarchists, and revolutionaries all disagreed on how to interpret the relevance of the revolutionary events of 1905–7. The tsar decided that those years represented less of a revolution than an aberration in Russian history, and he largely blamed his own weakness in not resisting the reformers; many Russians agreed with him. What became clear in the years between 1907 and 1914 was that the public's appetite for revolution dissipated, as evidenced by the end of strikes and disorders in the cities and countryside (a peace that lasted until 1912), the rapid decline in membership and influence of the Social Democratic Party, and the moderation of rhetoric and demands across the liberal and revolutionary spectrum. As Hans Rogger puts it, "The very idea of revolution, so long embraced or approved by the intelligentsia, seemed to have fallen into disrepute."[17]

Nonetheless, the debates over Jewish autonomism did not recede. In fact, the Union for Full Rights and its adoption of the Vilna platform set Russian Jewish politics down an irreversibly autonomist path. Thus, despite seeming to be no closer to achieving civil or national rights, Russian Jewish political and intellectual figures occupied themselves with discussing the ideal form of Jewish communal autonomy, the meaning of "nation," and the boundaries of the Jewish community. Such debates were conducted explicitly (e.g., in the pages of *Evreiskii mir*) and implicitly (e.g., in the activities of cultural institutions such as the Jewish Historical-Ethnographic Society). Furthermore, despite the Union's dissolution, intraparty cooperation was soon restored, and the political situation after 1907 still allowed Jews to hope that they might at least improve their communal structure, even if they would not have full civil and national equality soon. Once again, the initiators of the Union for Full Rights, the liberals of Vinaver and Sliozberg's Folksgruppe, sought a conference of notables to discuss some of the pressing issues of the day. This time the reason for the conference was a Duma bill in its preliminary stages that would potentially liberalize all religious denominational societies and communities. At the same time, the two Jewish Kadet Duma members, Naftali Fridman (1863–1921) and Lazar (Leopold) Nisselovich (1856–1914), were preparing a bill for the official legal recognition of the Jewish community and were important in organizing the conference as a means of soliciting a cross-section of Jewish political opinion. Some saw the potential in such a law for Jews to reform their existing communal structure and introduce the *kehila* as a true and democratic Jewish communal government. But questions remained about how and whom such a *kehila* (or *kehile* in Yiddish; or *obshchina* in Russian, the most common term) should govern.

One of the defining characteristics of individual and collective relations with a given state is the collective's ability to tax the individuals. It is no surprise, then, that one of the basic demands of Jewish autonomists, voiced in the December 1906 platform of the Folkspartey, was the Jewish communal authority's right to tax the Jewish population. Aside from the obvious benefit of providing the envisioned new organ of Jewish communal government with funding for its activities, the right to tax would also formally define its members as part of the Jewish community, binding them to it, and create (or, more accurately, maintain) a sphere of authority separate from that of the Russian government. Theoretically, being compelled to pay taxes to a *kehila* would also provide a tangible sense of belonging to the community and an awareness of the resulting individual rights and obligations.

Toward the end of the nineteenth century and in the early twentieth century, the government moved away from all forms of taxation by estate and toward individual taxation of income.[18] To its advocates an income tax had the added benefit of increasing personal integration into the state in a way not possible through collective taxation.[19] Furthermore, after the creation of a tax inspectorate in 1885, inspectors in local treasury offices were empowered not merely to assess taxes and determine tax rates but also to oversee local spending on health and education in the countryside.[20] In reality, however, the peasantry, whom the changes in the tax code most directly targeted, continued to be taxed collectively, even after 1910, when the government explicitly declared that peasants would be taxed on a per household basis. Jews also were taxed collectively well after the *kahal* had been abolished, as the government continued to require each Jewish community to provide it with a collective tax, which was usually achieved through the *korobka*, or tax on kosher meat.

If one considers how taxes and self-government define relations with the state, the new model for Jewish communal autonomy arose more from the abolition of serfdom than from the abolition of the *kahal*. When determining the form of social organization that would replace serfdom, the government attempted to create new governing institutions that would both satisfy the peasants' desire for some form of self-government and reinforce (or at least not diminish) the power of the state. *Zemstva*, municipal dumas, villages, townships, and other institutions were created to answer the demands of intellectuals for greater self-government and at the same time to replace the administrative functions of serfdom while giving up as little centralized authority as possible.[21] Thus in the mid-nineteenth century the idea of localized political autonomy throughout Russia—a major genesis of Alexander II's reforms—occurred nearly simultaneously with the dramatic curtailment (at least de jure) of Jewish autonomy in Russia. Although the government retracted legal recognition of the *kahal*, it continued to deal with the Jews as a collectivity because the community remained responsible for providing the government with military recruits and indirect taxes.[22] After the abolition of the *kahal*, Jews paid collective taxes to municipal governments but preserved ad hoc forms of communal and religious self-government that varied from place to place.[23] No one doubted that if the Jewish community was once again given a legal framework for its activities, communal self-government would need to be reformed and to have specific responsibilities assigned to it.

Following the revolutionary years of 1905–7 and the demands for collective rights by the Union for Full Rights, Jewish intellectuals and communal activists became increasingly concerned with how Jewish self-government might be organized. Much as Jewish liberals had taken the lead in organizing the Union, in 1909 Sliozberg and other prominent Jewish lawyers and communal activists in St. Petersburg invited influential Jews from all the major parties to Kovno for a conference on Jewish communal affairs. The idea was to have a broad discussion with the hope of determining the fundamentals of Jewish communal self-government in Russia before the legal reform that would make such self-government possible could be enacted.[24] Some participants were upset by the process of choosing delegates by invitation rather than by some form of election, but in the end all the Jewish parties participated.[25] In addition to the main organizers and Russian Jewish grandees such as L. I. Brodskii (from Kiev) and Baron V. G. Gintsburg (from St. Petersburg), delegates came from throughout the western Russian provinces.[26] The socialist parties, including the Bund and SERP, also participated in the conference, marking a dramatic departure from their refusal to join the Union for Full Rights and reflecting their recognition of the extent to which the popularity of revolutionary socialism was in decline after 1907.

The congress, or "conference on Jewish communal affairs," opened in the Klio Theater in Kovno on the morning of November 11, 1909. It was attended by 120 representatives from 46 locales.[27] In a speech opening the conference, I. B. Wolf stated: "Our wise King Solomon said, 'Help appears after carefully sought out advice.' His great parent answered, 'Help is in the hand of God.' Yes, this dictum will be fulfilled for the benefit of our people, who have long waited for relief from their difficult lot."[28] Wolf's words were portentous. Two related questions dominated the proceedings at Kovno: how to define membership in the Jewish community; and whether this community, the *obshchina*, should serve both secular and religious functions.[29] As Aron Perel'man (1876–1954) stated, "The question of the *character* of the community stood in the center of all of the conference and invoked the most impassioned debates."[30]

Speaking for the moderate and cautious reformers, Sliozberg argued that the composition of the community should be determined by requiring all Jews (observant or not) to register at a synagogue, whereas the leftists desired a complete secularization of Jewish communal life and the relegation of rabbis to religious roles only. Much of the debate centered on competing views of community expressed by Sliozberg and Leontii Bramson (beginning with the question of whether the attendees even had the right to speak for Russian Jewry[31]). Early in the conference, Sliozberg recounted the history of the *kahal*, including the function of *meshchanskie upravy* (management boards for townspeople) and Jewish participation in municipal self-government, before going on to the question of the *korobka*. Sliozberg's intentions were clear: to demonstrate that the *kahal* and the *kehila* had always been religious in nature. Stressing the historically religious basis of Jewish self-government allowed him to argue that membership in the Jewish community should be established by the synagogues, that new ideas about secular Jewish autonomy shared little in common with the religious responsibilities of the historic *kahal*, and that the Jewish *intelligenty*, in their removal from the synagogue and religious community, did not share the communal interests of traditionally religious Russian Jews.[32] Sliozberg was cautiously supported by some in the audience but vigorously opposed by those inclined to a national definition of the Jewish community. In debating Sliozberg, Bramson took exactly the opposite position on the religious or secular nature of community.

> Sliozberg's speech is based on erroneous principles: creating the obshchina by making use of the ready apparatus authorized by the prayer house. No, there is nowhere any need—not in the national, not in the historical, not in the religious point of view is there a tiny opening in the prayer house for the future obshchina. Even from the Orthodox point of view, deliberately summoning all to the synagogue must appear undesirable and able to evoke only conflict.[33]

Two competing definitions of Jewish community thereby emerged from the Kovno conference: one that maintained the essential character of Jewish self-government as a religious and community body; and the secular version, which aimed to replace the religious community with national identification and secular self-government.[34] Hence some suggested that the communal government should avoid issues of faith, because inevitably such questions would lead to the more vexing issue of membership and identity.[35] Bramson argued that synagogues and prayer houses could maintain their internal autonomy but that the new *obshchina* should be a municipal institution and therefore could not be the supreme religious authority.[36] Still others took a more emphatically national secular position. As M. N. Ezerskii stated, "Our *obshchina* must pursue its well-known national-cultural goals" because Jews are "not only a religion, but a nation and a people."[37]

One historian, Christoph Gassenschmidt, has argued that Kovno's proponents of modest reform and the maintenance of the religious basis of the Jewish community were motivated by their desire to retain their disproportionate influence as representatives in and of the community, whereas the more radical reformers were motivated by just the opposite: "For the reformers, secularization implied democratization which in turn meant the break from traditional leadership."[38] Whereas the radical reformers did equate secularization with democratization, it is less clear that Sliozberg and other liberals, the main organizers of the conference, argued for maintaining the religious definition of community out of a desire to keep their standing in the community. After their experience with the Union for Full Rights, Jewish liberals no doubt understood that the other Jewish parties would not meekly endorse their initiatives.[39] More accurately, it seems the liberals were attempting to control, or at least contain, the practical effects of the increasing nationalization of Russian Jewry. By calling a conference on Jewish communal affairs under his own leadership, Sliozberg attempted to prevent the use of possible future laws enacted by the Duma for nationalist purposes—in particular, the creation of comprehensive and separate Jewish self-government. Sliozberg said so plainly when he warned of the "great danger" in utilizing any future law granting the right of religious communities to organize: "If the *obshchina* will mean separation, we are threatened by complete bankruptcy."[40]

Sliozberg may have called for all parties to unite in the task of organizing Jewish communal life, but as a highly acculturated Jewish liberal, he clearly feared the growing separatism of the Jewish intelligentsia. Furthermore, the liberals realized that such *intelligenty* were already unapologetically asserting their right to a role in representing and leading Russian Jewry, and within certain limits the liberals acknowledged the need to democratize Jewish communal life. I. D. Romm, an important left-Kadet from Vilna (of the famous Romm publishing house, coincidentally sold to Baron David Gintsburg in 1910), conceded that *intelligenty* who were already participating in religious government would eventually assume communal leadership roles, but he warned of the danger of entrusting all popular education to people who might move the community in an irreversibly secular direction. Even Sliozberg sought to formalize some form of Jewish tax and its redistribution by the official community, and, as he stated retrospectively, "In this I supposed the *obshchina* must be given the right of complete self-government."[41] Interestingly, the liberals did not seek a narrowly religious definition of the Jewish community, despite eschewing separatism and attempting to create or preserve a *kehila* run through the synagogues.[42]

Sliozberg and the traditional leadership were intent on reform. Such reform was, in fact, the purpose of the conference, and Sliozberg argued that the communal leadership must salvage Jewish communal life before political factionalization made such a task impossible. To Sliozberg, "Reform of the *obshchina* is timely in the political sense, timely practically, and timely from the point of view of the spiritual idea [*ideino-dukhovnoi*]. I fear that in a few years it will be too late to reform, for [if] not united [the community] disintegrates into many parts."[43] Furthermore, the liberals were clearly attempting to work within the realm of possibility granted by the proposed law on religious communities. As the Duma member Naftali Fridman pointed out, the law before the Duma was to legalize religious communal authorities, and for the time being, therefore, that legalization alone should concern the conference.[44]

At the end of three days, the conference actually reached a surprising degree of agreement on the vague outline of the future Jewish self-government (presented as a virtual certainty). The communal governments were to gain "the status of a juridical person with the right of acquiring property by all legal means."[45] A Jew was determined to be anyone born Jewish, with the important exception of converts to Christianity.[46] All Jews over the age of 18 who had lived in a given town for more than a year had the right to run for office and vote and to directly elect members to a community council, who would then elect an executive. The exact system of taxes was to be determined by individual communities, but they were to be based on the principles of progressive and compulsory taxation. The finances of the *obshchiny* were to be transparent and subject to audit. Yet the very reason for reconstituting the legal community was left intentionally vague and open to further interpretation. According to the delegates, "The purpose of the community is to care for the religious institutions, welfare, and spiritual-cultural well-being of those from whom it is constituted."[47]

Despite Sliozberg's later claim that everyone agreed with his suggestions on compulsory Jewish membership in the community and the redistribution of taxes, of greater significance was the fact that the conference overwhelmingly rejected his key demands that the *obshchina* remain within the bounds of the synagogue and that membership in the Jewish community be determined by registering in a synagogue.[48] The rabbis in attendance accepted the conference's proposals, but it must be remembered that most of these were secularly educated state rabbis, several of whom, such as Rabbi Iakov Maze, were nationalists and active in the Zionist movement. The traditionally Orthodox rabbinic authorities, on the other hand, did not sit idly by and watch the Jewish intelligentsia challenge their authority. Rather, they chose to fight their battles in a different forum, the Rabbinic Commission, which was authorized by the state and initially dominated by *maskilim*. Between the 1870s and 1910, power in the realm of religious politics had shifted from reformers and modernizers to religious conservatives, as they had assumed control of the Rabbinic Commission and with it, as ChaeRan Freeze observes, "the ability to influence the state."[49] It is important to note that parallel to the debates over self-government by Jewish political and communal activists, the most conservative and traditionally religious leaders gained ground in practical terms through the state-sponsored Rabbinic Commission, what Freeze calls "the one institution with the authority to address a broad range of issues, especially those pertaining to the family."[50] While the Jewish political leadership debated the religious and secular responsibilities of a still theoretical Jewish communal authority of the future, the Orthodox leadership sought to extend their power with and within the state.[51] In closing the Kovno conference, Vinaver presented the findings almost as a new set of commandments, stating: "We received here the fundamentals of the Jewish *obshchina*."[52] What caused such (eventual) unanimity and optimism, especially compared to the proceedings of the Union for Full Rights? Without the imminence of revolutionary change, the stakes were much lower. In addition, with the most contentious issues absent from the debate (the transcript demonstrates that the status of the proletariat or Palestine, or for that matter Yiddish, never came up), the delegates could concentrate on the single issue the conference was devoted to: Jewish communal self-government. Despite the open-ended nature of its final declaration, the conference demonstrated the extent to which the gap in worldview between the more ardent nationalists and the so-called liberals had narrowed, and not just in terms of communal self-government. Liberals such as Vinaver spoke in strikingly nationalist

terms about the significance of their efforts and, by completely adopting the rhetoric of nationalism, attempted to co-opt the increasingly
separatist Jewish *intelligenty* into their own projects. Vinaver summarized the importance of the conference as follows:

> We spoke here a great deal about the Jewish spirit. . . . We can
> announce that Russian Jewry constitutes a separate national whole: the
> nation assembled here. And if we are planning to create a united Jew-
> ish community, then this proves that we feel the necessity for general
> national work. It is small work, but let it be the first step. The current
> conference proves that the nation is reborn. (prolonged applause)[53]

Many Zionists were naturally uncomfortable with the Kovno conference, because any successful sociopolitical reorganization of the Jewish community in Russia might divert Jewish national aspirations and
potentially undermine the settlement of Palestine.[54] By 1909 Russian
Zionists such as Abraham Idelson and the editors of *Rassvet* were
already finding the promises made in the Helsingfors Program inconvenient and were becoming increasingly critical of efforts to establish
Jewish autonomy in Russia. Many prominent Zionists were notably
absent from Kovno, indicating that without the prospect of participating in electoral politics (with a broad franchise), even the architects of
Gegenwartsarbeit and the Helsingfors Program were moving away from
efforts to boost communal autonomy. The impact of the Kovno conference on the Zionist movement bears some resemblance to the impact
of the Helsingfors Program on the Union for Full Rights. By adopting
the Vilna program at their congress in Helsinki, the Zionists sought to
satisfy those who might be inclined to Zionism but who were for the
time being more concerned with an improvement in Jewish life and
self-determination in Russia. In Kovno the liberals completely adopted
the rhetoric of nationalism, thereby deflating Zionist and folkist accusations of assimilationism. In 1910, in the first issue of its journal, *Evreiskaia nedelia*, a group of St. Petersburg liberals listed their two objectives
as "the struggle for our civil and national rights, unifying the power
of all Russian Jewry for the higher calling of the internal material and
spiritual renaissance of our people."[55] The expansion of Jewish self-government was presented as the key to achieving such goals, especially as

discussed in the series "The Organization of the Jewish *Obshchiny*" by the lawyer Mikhail Morgulis. In this series of articles, Morgulis outlined the tasks of the Jewish organs of self-government as "improvement of the spiritual and moral condition, charity, material prosperity, and the prevention and elimination of communal distress."[56] For those who advocated a separate Jewish politics, the major division was no longer between nationalists and nonnationalists but rather whether efforts to construct Jewish national life should be concentrated in Russia or Palestine.

To a certain extent, the gap was even narrowing between socialist and nonsocialist conceptions of Jewish national goals. The Kovno conference was the first significant example of political participation by radical socialist parties, such as the Bund and the Sejmists, and in a liberal Jewish initiative.[57] The Sejmists and former *vozrozhdentsy*, led by Zilberfarb, continued to advocate complete Jewish communal and national autonomy, more or less adhering to the Socialist Revolutionary Party's federalist model of national self-determination through national parliaments. Although the organizers of the Kovno conference did not accept the Sejmists' socialist and adamantly secular vision of Jewish autonomy, the fact that socialist autonomists, liberals, Zionists, and folkists met together to discuss the past, present, and future structures of Jewish autonomy marked these divergent groups' common interest. Even before the Kovno conference, Zilberfarb had written articles attacking the unreformed structure of the existing *obshchina*, particularly the unfair burden of the *korobka* on the working masses (and his disagreements with Sliozberg also predate Kovno).[58] Zilberfarb's argument for strengthening Jewish communal autonomy was based on the idea that it would be the first step toward the national autonomy that every minority in the empire was entitled to have. Furthermore, Zilberfarb argued, Jewish autonomy should be secular and completely separated from the synagogue. Although he suggested that a primary responsibility of the *obshchina* should be "to raise the economic and cultural level of the working masses," not unlike the so-called bourgeois parties, he also stressed the preparatory stage needed to strengthen Jewish communal organizations.[59] According to Zilberfarb:

We have already learned in our time to see our obshchina not only as a remnant of historical times, but as the basic organ of our future national-autonomous organization. It would be naïve to imagine a transition from our contemporary situation to autonomous national life as a jump from tsarist national slavery into tsarist national freedom. The essential prior conditions for this transition are raising and strengthening the foundation, to be based on some kind of national union. This foundation exists for national minorities in the national community [obshchina], composed as a constricted circle with revolving personal and national rights and responsibilities: the strengthening of our communal organizations, expanding and uniting their existing activities. In this way, one moves from the premise of historical necessity to that of our future national achievements.[60]

Throughout the debates on the organization and reform of the *obshchina*, the Bund resisted the idea of complete Jewish autonomy, continuing to advocate a more linguistic and educational-based model and thereby limiting the scope of the *obshchina*'s powers. Over the course of 1909, Vladimir Medem moderated the Bund's opposition to full communal self-government and convinced the group to enter into the debates about the parameters of communal authority. Earlier, as David Fishman observes, Medem and others in the Bund avoided the terms *kehila/kehile* and *obshchina*, "and it seems that they had in mind something much narrower—a kind of Jewish educational-cultural association."[61] But in 1910, articles by Medem and A. Litvak appeared in the Bundist publication *Tsayt-fragen* that discussed the Bundist position on the responsibilities of the *obshchina* and how to determine its membership.[62] Such tactical adjustments acknowledged the reality of the decline in the Bund's popularity, along with shrinking membership in the social democratic parties in general. Medem himself considered the years 1908–9 to be the nadir of the Bundist movement, referring to his contributions to certain nonpartisan publications as necessary for money (he was living in Geneva at the time).[63] According to Medem, during those years, "scores of people had left the movement. A mass of workers had departed for America. The intelligentsia fled the movement virtually in toto."[64] Indeed, repression, emigration, and disillusionment exacted a heavy toll on the Bund, reducing its membership from 33,890 people in 274 local chapters in 1906 to approximately 2,000 people in 10 chapters by 1910.[65] As Litvak stated, "Already in 1908 there was nearly no one with whom to talk about the crises. One after another, the organizations had either crumbled or fallen into a deep winter sleep."[66] Thus, at the Bund's poorly attended 1908 conference, the so-called *legalistn* (members of the party's Central Committee who favored prioritizing legal rather than underground activism) managed to win over their opponents and forced the conference to resolve to participate in all forms of communal activity as a means for the Bund to regain its lost political influence.[67] Yet as Vladimir Levin points out, despite their many justifications, in endeavoring to participate in communal government and communal reform, the socialists inadvertently joined the bourgeois mainstream.[68]

The precipitous decline in Bund membership led some members of the group, such as Litvak, to attack Medem's "neutralism," the guiding Bundist theory on Jewish nationalism. Medem himself clarified his theory in 1910 to make room for greater "national-cultural" activism (but not nationalism).[69] Still, the Bund continued to approach Jewish nationalism and autonomism cautiously and from a pragmatic point of view. Medem warned that even a "purely cultural" community (Medem used the German term *Kulturgemeinschaft*) would not always remain within the framework of an organized Jewish community. Mostly he was concerned by any attempt to internationalize Jewish political nationalism in the name of a united worldwide Jewry, an idea he repeatedly called a fetish of Jewish nationalists.[70]

With the exception of perhaps the Bund, both the radical and moderate reformers of the Jewish *obshchina* attempted to demonstrate continuity with existing Jewish communal structures. Part of this attitude resulted from the desire to embed the idea of Jewish communal self-government in the public mind, and part resulted from efforts to encourage activists to build Jewish communal structures even before they were legalized. For example, in 1913 a few prominent advocates of Jewish communal self-government founded a journal, *Vestnik evreiskoi obshchiny*, for public discussion of the Jewish *obshchina*. The journal, established by Dubnov, Zilberfarb, and other, more radical autonomists, but supported by Sliozberg, stressed both the continuity of

Jewish communal self-government and the need for further reform. The editors of this journal presented the turn to communal self-government as both a historical continuity and a novel idea. On the one hand, as they observed in their statement called "Our Tasks," the embrace of Jewish communal government by the Jewish intelligentsia was a new phenomenon: "For a long time our intelligentsia—partly under the influence of what has been degenerating the community for the past forty years, partly under the influence of the idea of a sense of civic duty, wrongly opposing the idea of communal self-determination—completely disavowed themselves from the community."[71] Now, they continued, "Among representatives of different communal groups and a variety of ideologies the call is frequently and loudly heard: back to the *obschina*! Back to the organization that since ancient times served as our shield against our enemies and as a roof over our cultural creativity."[72] On the other hand, the editors also stressed that even if the intelligentsia might have spurned it, Jewish communal self-government had never subsided. Jews continually worked within the available legal framework and, according to the editors, they should continue to do so.

> We aim to reorganize the Jewish obshchina in a legislative way in a new beginning, and we want to expand its now constricted rights and functions. But still, until the time when it will be possible to carry out its partial reorganization, we must lead and be guided by functioning legislation and, as far as it allows us, build up and revitalize the existing Jewish community (obshchina), for the Jewish obshchina did not cease to exist.[73]

In fact, Dubnov examined the modern crises in Jewish self-government from Western to Eastern Europe in the first article in the new journal. According to Dubnov, in the West "the crisis was related to the adaptation of autonomy to a new formation: *emancipation*."[74] Emancipation led to the curtailment of the scope of self-government, its incorporation into synagogue congregations, and the contraction of the official community's authority as civil institutions took over its responsibilities.[75] In Dubnov's view, however, the lack of emancipation in Russia created special conditions for Jewish self-government, even without a legal framework: "We saw something else in the Russian Jewish center. Here the *obshchina* had to become adjusted to the prevailing regime of civil *non-rights*."[76] Dubnov saw the idea of autonomism spreading, even to the communities that had adjusted fully to emancipation, such as Berlin, whose Jewish residents would over time strive to regain their national rights: "Sooner or later, the question of expanding Jewish communal autonomy will arrive on stage. In Russia for the moment we are faced with different tasks, such as the struggle against the disintegration of the *obshchina*, which began a long time ago and was caused not only by destruction from without but also by the indifference of the Jewish intelligentsia to the general needs of Jewish life."[77]

Both the Kovno conference and the journal *Vestnik evreiskoi obshchiny* can be seen as parts of a highly theoretical debate that presumed the near-term transformation of Russian empire and society. Yet the debate at the Kovno conference over how to structure Jewish communal self-government was only theoretical in the sense that the delegates awaited the legalization of many of their already existing activities. Jewish communal activists were not waiting for Russian government approval to expand their responsibilities. In *Vestnik*, activists (most notably Zilberfarb) reported weekly on the activities and new initiatives of communal governments and organizations in both Western and Eastern Europe.[78]

Throughout the Russian Empire Jewish religious authorities independently took the initiative to expand and transform their structures, often, as the organizers of Kovno recognized, because of the increased participation of the Jewish intelligentsia in communal politics. Thus, more than creating new bodies for Jewish self-government, the law before the Duma on religious denominations, if passed, would result in the legal recognition of existing bodies and a legal framework for their activities. At the Kovno conference many delegates spoke about the local conditions in their cities and towns and described the significant responsibilities of existing communal authorities, especially in running schools and hospitals, which led to the necessity of finding a way to raise significant funds. The resulting debates over Jewish taxation and the *korobka* thereby reflected the extent of the existing communal activities, because everyone spoke of the need to maintain a steady flow of income. The acceptance of L. G. Rabinovich's proposals to improve the economic situation of Jewish artisans through the expansion and improved coordination of existing educational and financial institutions as well as self-help organizations similarly reflected the Kovno delegates' equal concern for both immediate and future action.[79]

The fact that the reconstitution of self-government, specifically by reinstituting the *kehila*, had become a priority for Jewish liberals and some socialists attests to the influence of this particular Dubnovian idea. The debates at the Kovno conference and in the publications that came out of it support David Fishman's observation that after Dubnov's plan to reinstitute the *kehila* was widely adopted—as were his broad plans for communal and national autonomy—the ambiguities of its formulation spurred others to attempt to solve the question of how autonomy might be practically executed.[80] The question at hand related to the extent of continuity: whether the new *kehila* or *obshchina* should be a truly new form of Jewish self-government or rather should merely give a legal basis to what generally already existed. In sum, the conference reflected the triumph of the idea of Jewish *samoupravlenie*—self-government—and represented the broad political embrace of Jewish *obshchestvennost'*, reflected in the language of the attendees, who spoke in terms of the ethical obligations of the Jewish people. More than theoretical debate, the conference reflected the efforts of all the Jewish parties to engage with the populace in a manner similar to the Union for Full Rights, advancing the process of the national democratization of the Jewish political sphere.

Building a Community, Part II: Language

The Kovno conference's atmosphere of cooperation, disagreement, and ultimately compromise resulted from several years of growing collaboration between Jewish political activists and intellectuals. Such goodwill, however, did not immediately follow the end of revolution in 1907, when grievances associated with the failure of the Union for Full Rights still lingered. Nonetheless, one issue, the language question, brought Jewish activists into conversation with one another again because it pervaded so many other issues relating to communal self-government in the Russian Empire (and no less in the Austrian Empire, where the legal recognition of national rights was tied to language). One publication, *Evreiskii mir*, a nonpartisan journal of culture and politics, became a forum for discussion of this and other Jewish national and autonomist issues.

The breakup of the Union for Full Rights, Russian Jewry's first empirewide political organization, was in effect a multiparty divorce that seemingly ended broad Jewish political cooperation in Russia, or at least in the capital, St. Petersburg. With the possible exception of the Zionists, the political groups that formed in the wake of the Union's dissolution were essentially cadres of Jewish intellectuals, who for the most part lived in the capital; many of them were participants in one of the liberal or socialist general Russian political movements. Unsurprisingly, all the Jewish political groups used the greater press freedoms resulting from the 1905 revolution to attack and blame one another for the collapse of the Union and, more generally, for the erosion of Jewish unity. Thus the Zionists, through *Rassvet*, and the liberals, through *Svoboda i ravenstvo*, attacked one another, and both attacked the folkists of Dubnov's party. *Voskhod*, the tribune of liberal Russian Jewry, closed only weeks before the opening of the First Duma, and although its editors intended to transform the publication into a daily newspaper, ideological bickering sunk the entire project. As the editors of *Novyi voskhod* reflected in its first issue in 1910, "At that time we lived under the influence of disunity: the fracturing into many parties led to a level of discord between them which broke the outer limits."[81]

By 1908, with the revolution unquestionably over and Russian Jews facing new challenges, such as the increased enforcement of the *numerus clausus* in secondary and postsecondary education, political currents in the Jewish press shifted back toward cooperation. A group of Jewish intellectuals began to collaborate on founding a new journal of Jewish literature and political commentary. The initiative for the new publication came from three journalists at *Rassvet*, chiefly Aron Perel'man but also Aleksandr Braudo (1864–1924) and Grigorii Portugalov; all of whom were unhappy with the combative approach of Abraham Idelson, the editor of *Rassvet*, to Russian Jewish cultural projects.[82] Perel'man then recruited Dubnov and others to join the project. Dubnov, who had been hoping to create a party organ for the Folkspartey, saw the opportunity to run instead what seemed to be a reincarnation of *Voskhod* as too attractive to turn down. The initial editorial team included representatives from all the factions that had participated in the Union for Full Rights, with Dubnov—who, according to his own account, suggested the name *Evreiskii mir* (Jewish World)—serving as editor-in-chief and Semyon An-sky heading the literary section.[83] The journal, the first issue of which appeared in January 1909, was particularly concerned with discussion of the Jewish national idea and the prospects for Jewish autonomy in the Russian Empire. The editors sought to create an intra-ideological forum for debate about Jewish nationalism and autonomy, and they received contributions from across the ideological spectrum. For instance, Nathan Birnbaum, Mark Ratner, Vladimir Medem, and Ben-Adir (Avrom Rozin) all represented quite different Jewish national visions: Zionist autonomism, populism, social democracy, and socialist autonomism, respectively. The editors claimed unity only in the "struggle for civil and national rights for the Jewish people."[84] Most of all, the founders of *Evreiskii mir* considered themselves to be on the forefront of the fight against what they deemed "Jewish assimilationism," in both its socialist and liberal forms. As Avrom Rozin, a founder of the Vozrozhdenie group, stated in *Evreiskii mir*, "There is no doubt that on the Jewish street, at least in Russia, assimilationist ideology at the current time is morally discredited."[85]

Discussing the meaning and implications of Jewish nationalism and the ideal form of internal communal organization provided an outlet for different ideological opinions and united the various groups in the battle against assimilation and for what Perel'man called the "nationalization of the diaspora." Perel'man even recruited several liberals in Vinaver's Folksgruppe, who only a year before had savaged Dubnov as a neo-Zionist in their publication *Svoboda i ravenstvo*, to sit on the editorial board. Thus Zionists, socialists, liberals, and folkists all met regularly at Dubnov's apartment to discuss the issues of the day. In the close personal daily interaction of the Jewish intellectual class across political lines, *Evreiskii mir* as a project was characteristic of the Jewish intellectual environment in St. Petersburg between the revolutions of 1905 and 1917, where political opponents remained on close personal terms.[86] Furthermore, though the editors by no means agreed on the relative merits of various Jewish literary figures, all agreed, for the time being, on the necessity of a venue to publish Jewish literature in Russian, reflecting the St. Petersburg intellectuals' shared interest in translating Jewish literature into the imperial language.

The editors of *Evreiskii mir* clearly sought to turn autonomism into a common ground for Jewish political parties (even the book review section focused on examining relevant works of Bauer, Springer, and the Zionist theorist Daniel Pasmanik).[87] By creating a forum for intellectuals to debate the meaning of Jewish nationality and the ideal formulation of autonomism, the editors accomplished two goals. First, they kept the question of Jewish national rights in the political spotlight, and, second, they increased the public sense of autonomism's inevitability, leaving only the question of its form unresolved. To underscore this point, in 1911 (soon after *Evreiskii mir* closed), the editors published a separate anthology of essays under the title *Theoretical and Practical Questions of Jewish Life*. In this book Jewish theorists from different political parties debated the meaning and relevance of Jewish nationhood to Russian Jewry. The editors framed this debate within the particular circumstances of multinational Russia, where, unlike Western Europe, "the acknowledgement of a distinct Jewish nation is currently arising, as [increased national consciousness] is predominant not only among ourselves, but is also appearing in leading circles in the peoples around us."[88] The collection was notable for its breadth of opinion, including contributions from the Bundist Medem, the leftist liberal Grigorii Landau, the folkist Perel'man, the Zionist-turned-Yiddishist Nathan Birnbaum, and the fierce anti-Zionist Iosif Bikerman.

Planning for *Evreiskii mir* took place during the summer and fall of 1908, simultaneous with the Czernowitz conference on the Yiddish language, and its first issue came out only weeks after the founding of the Jewish Literary Society in St. Petersburg. Consequently, the language question was a significant component of discussion in *Evreiskii mir*. The Czernowitz conference was held in Austrian Bukovina in the city of Czernowitz (today Chernivtsy, Ukraine) from August 30 to September 3, 1908. The idea for a conference on the Yiddish language arose out of discussions in New York in 1907 between Birnbaum, Zhitlowsky, and the Yiddish novelist and playwright Dovid Pinski.[89] The three conference planners, at Pinski's insistence, intended the conference to avoid political issues and "resolutions on behalf of Yiddish" and to focus instead on creating a "practical agenda."[90] The conference's agenda mostly contemplated a discussion of Yiddish vocabulary, grammar, and orthography, as well as the Yiddish press, Jewish cultural issues, and the livelihood of Yiddish cultural and literary figures.[91] The conference was held in Czernowitz because of the greater freedom in Austria than in the Russian Empire, because of the city's convenient location near the Russian border, and, most of all, because Birnbaum's students from Vienna who hailed from Czernowitz had convinced him both to move to the city and to hold the event there.[92] Birnbaum was an advocate of Jewish autonomy in Austria and in 1907 had run for a seat (and lost) in the Reichsrat on a platform of national autonomy and Jewish renaissance.[93] His turn to Yiddish culture and language was in part a response to that failure.[94]

The invitation to attend the conference, written by Zhitlowsky, stated: "A fence needs to be established, some sort of protection for our precious mother tongue so that it [need] not wander about aimlessly as [it has] until now, so that it [need] not become chaotic, tattered and divided. All who are involved with the language—writers, poets, linguists, and those who simply love it—must confer and find the appropriate means and methods of establishing an authority to which all will have to and want to defer."[95] Only the final item on the agenda referred to "recognition for the Yiddish language."[96] Nonetheless, the goal of raising the stature of Yiddish became the conference's raison d'être. Besides Zhitlowsky and Birnbaum, many famous Jewish writers and intellectuals of the day attended (including I. L. Peretz, Sholem Asch, Moyshe-Leyb Halpern, H. D. Nomberg, Avrom Reyzen, Noyekh Prilutski, Matthias Mieses, and Esther Frumkin). The invited delegates not in attendance included literary luminaries such as Sholem Abramovich (Mendele) and Sholem Rabinovich (Sholem Aleichem), who as bilingual authors might have been reluctant to associate themselves with a potentially anti-Hebraist conference.[97] The fact that only about forty voting delegates were present reflected the degree to which interest in Yiddish as anything other than a popular vernacular was still limited to a small circle. Still, the Czernowitz conference not only boosted the efforts of Yiddish writers struggling to have their work taken seriously by a Jewish audience but also tied Yiddish to the issue of Jewish national rights (and the location in multinational Czernowitz was particularly appropriate). Peretz clearly articulated this sentiment when he claimed, "We already stand in the ranks beneath our own flag and in the name of our own cultural interests. . . . We proclaim to the world: we are a Jewish people and Yiddish is our language."[98]

It was not clear, even at the time, exactly what goals the delegates hoped to reach in the future. The great debate over the role of Yiddish in Jewish national life was resolved, for the purposes of the conference, by compromise. In its final declaration the conference recognized "Yiddish as *a* national language of the Jewish people," calling for "its political, social and cultural rights."[99] Furthermore, the conference granted each participant "the freedom to regard the Hebrew language according to his personal convictions."[100] Naturally, such declarations created a backlash, both from those who believed that Yiddish should have been declared *the* Jewish national language and from Hebraists unhappy with the implication that Yiddish was a Jewish national language at all.

Organizationally, nothing came of the conference (even the original minutes were lost). Its most significant product was the formal initiation of the Jewish language question as part of the broader national question, as clearly expressed in the pages of *Evreiskii mir* and in the Jewish political debates of 1907–14. The fact that many of these intellectuals experienced their conversion to Yiddishism in the living rooms of St. Petersburg and elsewhere and debated the question with one another in the pages of the Russian-language Jewish press at first seems ironic, but it speaks volumes about an important transition occurring in Jewish intellectual life in the Russian Empire. The Jewish intellectuals of the younger generation were in the process of consciously refashioning themselves from essentially Russian intellectuals into a new phenomenon: Yiddishist intellectuals. Of course, the most well-known Yiddish literary figures, such as I. L. Peretz, Mendele, and Sholem Aleichem, had taken up Yiddish as a literary language years earlier. But the adoption of Yiddish as the political language of professional activists was still something new in Russia, though it had begun earlier in London and New York. Even Zhitlowsky, an early advocate

Figure 4 Postcard from the Czernowitz conference, 1908, showing Chaim Zhitlowsky with prominent Yiddish literary figures. From right to left, H. D. Nomberg, Chaim Zhitlowsky, Sholem Asch, I. L. Peretz, and Avrom Reyzen. Courtesy of the YIVO Institute for Jewish Research, New York.

of political Yiddishism, wrote nearly all his political tracts before the Czernowitz conference in Russian (with the important exception of the essay "Why Only Yiddish?" which was published in New York's *Forverts* in 1900).[101] In fact, Zhitlowsky's acclaim in New York resulted from lectures he delivered in Russian on the Yiddish language, nationalism, and socialism. Yet at the time this use of Russian seemed not to matter. As one observer wrote, "Even those who did not understand what he had to say ran to hear him. When he held a lecture in Russian you could find individuals in the packed hall who did not understand a single word of Russian."[102] As Tony Michels points out, it was considered revolutionary enough that Zhitlowsky used Yiddish in his speeches at all.[103]

Another person who exemplified the transition from Russian to Yiddish intellectual was Nokhem (Nahum) Shtif (1879–1933), who became engrossed in Yiddish literary studies in, of all places, the library of the Asiatic Museum in St. Petersburg. Shtif underwent a self-described transformation between 1908 and 1912, devoting himself to two objectives: Yiddish literary study and "the struggle against Russification, against Russified banality and its influences, [a struggle] strengthened with a national-mystical element."[104] For others the conversion from Russian to Yiddish was less of an epiphany and more of a process. Aron Perel'man argued in his essay "On the Question of Language," published in *Evreiskii mir* in 1909, that although the language debate was quickly becoming the central question of Jewish cultural life, it was for the time being neither possible nor desirable for the Jews to choose only one language. Perel'man questioned the claims of those who saw Yiddish as uniquely positioned to resist external assimilatory pressure and believed that despite the new Yiddishist spirit, Russian was the adopted language of "the majority of our intellectuals," resulting in an inevitable linguistic eclecticism. To Perel'man everything did not rest on language, as the new Yiddishists suggested. Quite the contrary, he thought that the only realm of Jewish life in which the question of language had pressing relevance was the schools.[105]

One year later, however, Perel'man had become more of a diaspora nationalist and in the process had converted to the cause of Yiddish. In "The Jewish Language in the Diaspora," published in *Evreiskii mir* in 1910, Perel'man claimed that Yiddish originated "from a higher form of the people's distinctive character, on which the nation now depends. It is not only an instrument of the people's life; it is the slogan of national unity."[106] Most important, he came to agree with individuals, such as the journalist and Yiddish philologist Matthias (Matisyohu) Mieses, who equated the Russian language with assimilation and connected the Zionists to Russification.[107] According to Perel'man, the Zionists' "violent campaign against the hated *zhargon* and their overt preference for the Russian language mark the movement's complete repudiation of the nationalization of the Diaspora and their return to the principle of 'negation of exile.'"[108] In effect, Perel'man claimed that diaspora nationalists must move away from Russian precisely because of the perception (not accurate in all cases) that Zionists presented Russian Jewry with the false choice between adopting the language of the state or the language of the Zionist movement. Perel'man continued: "Those who put the question: Hebrew or Russian—this is the same as declaring: Palestine or assimilation. . . . National-democratic Jewry must with equal force fight against Russifiers cloaking themselves in the mantle of Hebraism, as against Hebraists playing into the hands of Russifiers."[109] In countering the Zionists, Perel'man thereby attempted to align "national-democratic Jewry"—by this time a signifier for autonomist intellectuals—with Yiddish and hence also with the masses.

The transition from Russian to Yiddish among Jewish intellectuals could produce results that were equally awkward and ironic. Dubnov tirelessly pointed out the artificiality of both the Yiddishist and Hebraist promotions of their respective languages as the national language of the Jews. In reference to the first meeting of the Jewish Literary Society, Dubnov remarked in his memoirs: "Here, in a meeting of Petersburg intelligentsia, where everyone spoke Russian, is where the current turned to purely Jewish literature, and against [all things] Russian-Jewish, that is to say, against the use of the Russian language. At the time I recorded in my notes 'A sign of the times! It was not long ago that Russian-Jewish literature was all considered *batlonus* (useless exercises)!'"[110] When in 1911 the famous Yiddish literary figure I. L. Peretz came from Warsaw to visit St. Petersburg, Dubnov's and Peretz's dislike for one another reached the boiling point. Dubnov insisted on delivering a speech in Peretz's honor in Russian instead of Yiddish—despite An-sky's entreaties—and when Peretz protested, Dubnov stormed out of the banquet in anger.[111] Dubnov claimed that An-sky, for his part, spoke *yevonishe Yiddish* (like a Jewish veteran of the Russian army), a claim supported by Iulii Engel, the composer and founder of the Jewish Folk Music Society.[112] Engel once described an incident on his ethnographic expedition with An-sky in 1912 when a Jewish coachman in Ruzhin would answer them only in Ukrainian and Russian, taking their Yiddish for a joke.[113]

Dubnov saw Russian, Yiddish, and Hebrew as all playing different but equally important roles in Jewish life. As a result, he defended each language from its detractors. In the wake of the Czernowitz conference, Dubnov passionately supported the value of Russian. Against the Bund and converted Yiddishists like Shtif, he defended Hebrew as the "national" (*natsional'nyi*) Jewish language, in contrast to Yiddish, the "popular" (*narodnyi*) language.[114] And soon after the Czernowitz conference, in the pages of *Evreiskii mir*, Dubnov defended Yiddish against the Zionists. Like Perel'man, Dubnov saw the Zionist battle against Yiddish as a betrayal of the mutual interest between Zionists and diaspora nationalists in developing the national consciousness of Russian Jewry. In his famous essay "The Affirmation of the Diaspora"— addressed to Ahad Ha'am, his close friend and the founder of spiritual Zionism—Dubnov suggested that only two issues prevented an "amalgamation of thought" between his folkists and the spiritual Zionists: the "negation of the Diaspora" and the Zionist attack on Yiddish, the second being a reflection of the first. Dubnov referred to Yiddish "as a part of the foundation of our people's unity" and said:

> To abandon it at this time, when the languages of the surrounding nations are tearing away from our people tens of thousands of "children," who will not have the ability to converse with their "fathers," to abandon strengthening the ability of zhargon [Yiddish] to compete with foreign languages—this would be insane. Since there is not much hope in the transformation of our old national language [Hebrew] into the language of daily life for all the Diaspora, we would be committing a national crime if in the struggle with assimilation we did not use all the strength of resistance given to us by our popular language [narodnyi iazyk].[115]

Dubnov, like others, saw Yiddish as a tool in what he viewed as the struggle against assimilation, and he acknowledged its advantages over Hebrew as a unifying (Ashkenazic) diasporic language. Yet it is difficult to understand how he could write without even a hint of irony in this Russian-language journal, which was supposedly devoted to fighting "Jewish assimilationism," that "foreign" languages in fact lead to assimilation, when by such a definition, he himself was an assimilated Jew serving as editor-in-chief of an assimilationist journal. Dubnov began his career with a typically dismissive view of Yiddish literature, but his views evolved, and in the late 1880s Dubnov played a significant role in giving Yiddish literature respectability simply by reviewing Yiddish works in the Russian-language Jewish press (Sholem Aleichem claimed that the few lines Dubnov wrote about his first work, "Dos meserl," in *Voskhod* gave him the necessary affirmation and strength to continue his literary career).[116] Although Dubnov made room for Yiddish literature, he was not one of those Jewish intellectuals who converted to Yiddishism. In contrast to many Yiddishists, he continued to defend the Jewish use of the language of the state, a norm he considered to have long historical precedent.[117] Even so, his equating the abandonment of Yiddish with "insanity" reflected how even the most Russian of Jewish intellectuals could begin to fear the bogeyman of assimilation in their adopted political and social language.

Despite the promotion of Yiddish by intellectuals, in reality few of these intellectuals chose it for their daily language. The Bundists' use of Russian became particularly difficult to justify, as it clearly marked them as separate from the Jewish proletariat.[118] The Bund was at that moment struggling to stay relevant and searching for a means to reestablish its influence. Thus, at the Bund's eighth party conference, held in the Galician city of Lemberg (Lvov) in 1910, Yiddish was used as the conference language for the first time. The twenty-five delegates, all prominent Bundists despite their small number, sought to enter the language war on the side of Yiddish while maintaining the organization's internationalist leanings. While claiming to have "reservations about those nationalist trends which turn the struggle for Yiddish into an instrument with which to blunt the class consciousness of the proletariat," the Bund nonetheless devoted itself to the promotion of Yiddish in public life and to the struggle against assimilationists and Hebraists.[119]

In theory the Bund's endorsement of both Yiddish and autonomism remained cautious, and the Bund still prioritized class consciousness over national consciousness. On the question of language, however, the Bundists shifted decisively toward a Yiddishist position. Medem took particular exception to the distinction that Dubnov, Peretz, and others made between Jewish "national" and "folk" or "popular" languages, and he castigated the way that "national" and "folk" became dichotomous in these disputes in general (he colorfully depicted the folk in the background, or otherwise kneeling reverently to the nation). Medem granted that titles can have symbolic meaning but urged people not to be distracted by such distinctions: "This dualism eats away at the core of the national movement, paralyzes its strength, kills its resolve. It creates a cult of fossils, it extends abominable hypocrisy, on account of which unbelieving freethinking people don the mask of the churchgoer;

it brings the living language to sacrifice to the dead one; it needs for this living language not to be able to get out of the swamp of disdain into which it was trampled."[120] In his attack on mask-donning secular Hebraists (read Zionists), Medem went beyond the Bundist embrace of Yiddish as the language of the Jewish proletariat, arguing that the impossibility of separating Hebrew from Judaism negated any possible function that Hebrew might serve as a national language.

Benjamin Harshav has argued that the language wars and the development of trilingual Jewish literature were collectively one of three "prongs"—along with the creation of Jewish political ideologies and the rise of Jewish social organizations—that marked a revolutionary turn by Jews to "new cultural modes modeled on European secular culture."[121] Most important, as Harshav points out, the new trilingual Jewish literature reflected the real trilingualism of Jewish society during the period. Hebrew could serve as a secular yet distinctly Jewish means of participating in European culture, Yiddish "embodied the new populism," and Russian (like German) served as "a bridge to the culture and science of the dominant society and to the Jewish youth who were rapidly assimilating and coming back from assimilation."[122] Yet this trilingualism also resulted in personal contradictions—contradictions in identity—that many Russian Jewish intellectuals struggled to resolve. Furthermore, the way in which linguistic acculturation and even multilingualism came to be associated with assimilation reveals the extent to which assimilation was more of an amorphous threat than a meaningful process.

Eventually *Evreiskii mir* buckled under the weight of these contradictions. It folded not because of political conflict but because of financial difficulties resulting from a lack of public interest. The publication was evidently in financial trouble, with its continued existence in question, as early as October 1909, when its editors began to contemplate reorganizing both its format and its finances. The editors sought to enlist the help of intellectuals in St. Petersburg and other cities, including Moscow, Kiev, Odessa, and Riga, and sent letters to prominent Jews seeking both guidance and financial contributions.[123] The publication also changed its format after its first year from a thick monthly journal in two parts to a much thinner periodical appearing three times per month and devoting a greater percentage of its pages to political issues.[124] The new format attempted to shift the journal from theoretical debate to more practical concerns of communal organization. But one has to wonder how long and effectively the battle against assimilation could be waged by a Russian-language publication read only by a small group of intellectuals who themselves were increasingly coming to equate the Russian language with the forces of assimilation. Jews, like everyone else, were more interested in tabloids such as *Gazeta-Kopeika* and other general audience publications founded by Mikhail Gorodetskii, a Jewish businessman who built a newspaper empire between 1908 and 1910.[125] Compared to the success of Gorodetskii's ventures, the failure of *Evreiskii mir* reflects the public lack of interest, Jewish and otherwise, in politics after 1907.

Soon after *Evreiskii mir* folded, a group of young Yiddishists—Perel'man, Shtif, Shmuel Niger (1883–1955), Yisroel (Sergei) Tsinberg (1873–1939), and Yisroel Efroikin—and the somewhat older An-sky and H. D. Horovits (the former editor of *Der fraynd* who had previously sparred with Dubnov over the emigration question) created a new journal: *Di yidishe velt*. Abandoning the pretense of nonpartisanship, the new journal's editorial board reflected a particular folkist and diaspora-nationalist worldview. An-sky, Perel'man, Horovits, and Efroikin reconstituted the party in 1912, and thus *Di yidishe velt* was intended as a semi-official party organ.[126] The new publication catered rather explicitly to "der yidisher inteligents," with the aim of building a bridge between modern culture and the culture of the folk.[127] The editors were aware of the difficulties of conducting such a task in St. Petersburg, a city they described as "aloft from the new Yiddish house, remote from every Jewish tradition, dry in daily Jewish life, and only in the least bit aware of the noise of the true poetry that surrounds folk-life and folk-custom."[128] Along with other high-culture intellectual efforts, such as the Yiddish literary journal *Di literarishe monatsshriften*, founded in Vilna in 1908 by Niger, the reconstitution of *Evreiskii mir* in the form of *Di yidishe velt* can be seen as emblematic of the rise of Yiddish high culture.[129] Certainly the Jewish intelligentsia became less interested in publishing Jewish literature in Russian than in publishing Yiddish literature in the original. However, the failure of a *Jewish World* in Russian and its replacement by a *Jewish*

World in Yiddish can also be seen as symbolic of the reconstruction of Jewish intellectual life from Russian into the vernacular of the majority of Eastern European Jewry. The return to Yiddish was further cast in the most populist language, and as an acknowledgment, at least in the mind of the intellectuals, that linguistic and geographic separation had led to a deep gulf between them and the people.

Whether Yiddishist, Hebraist, or Russifier, "language loyalists," in Eli Lederhendler's words, "need not necessarily use the particular language in all circumstances; but one *must* use it whenever *not* to do so would violate ideological norms."[130] Those Jewish intellectuals who transformed themselves into language loyalists of one kind or another did so out of a combination of personal and political reasons. Balancing ideological consistency and intellectual life became increasingly difficult, to the point where using Russian at all seemed to violate ideological norms, a situation particularly uncomfortable for those only fully at ease in that language. When Jewish political groups began talking to one another again after the disappointing conclusion of the 1905 revolution, they focused on both the future of Jewish autonomy and the question of language. These two issues were connected not merely by practical matters, such as the language of Jewish education and the language of Jewish communal government, but because both served as archetypes for debating the larger question of Russian Jewry's future. The short life of *Evreiskii mir* reflected growing cooperation among various Jewish political groups and parties, even if the articles in its pages foreshadowed coming conflicts. By drawing Bundists and socialist autonomists into the discussion of national organization, the publication, like the Kovno conference, succeeded where the Union for Full Rights failed. Despite disagreements, *Evreiskii mir* also demonstrated that autonomists of all stripes were beginning to view themselves as part of a movement. But as this movement coalesced, in no small part around opposition to assimilationism, conducting its activities in Russian seemed less tenable, and the transformation of the individual participants from Russian intellectuals to Yiddishists seemed an ideological and political necessity.

Many ideas about community, self-government, language, and the role of the intelligentsia became intertwined in the broader issue of how the folk might simultaneously be made self-consciously political and protected from the unspecified forces of assimilation. As the two-year anniversary of the Kovno conference approached, Yisroel Efroikin wrote a scathing critique of the Jewish intelligentsia's passivity since the conference. To Efroikin the Jewish intellectual was completely alienated from the people he claimed to serve, estranged from the folk and from its daily life. All that remained between the intellectuals and the folk was a shared sense of oppression.[131] Echoing the sentiments of Russian populists, Efroikin suggested that Jewish intellectuals attempt to learn from the masses, who always struggled against their oppressors to maintain their "true democratic forms of self-government."[132] Until they understood the Jews themselves, the intellectuals could not hope to remake Jewish communal life and achieve Jewish autonomy. Yet belatedly, in Efroikin's view, the intelligentsia (in particular, the "national democratic" intelligentsia) was beginning to understand its estrangement for what it was, and at the same time as infusing "a secular culture into the folk masses," it had begun the process of "Judaizing" itself.[133] Whether the intelligentsia could find its way home and become a real "folks' intelligentsia" remained to be seen, but to Efroikin and many others, without an elemental reconnection with the masses, conferences, programs, and plans for Jewish autonomy would remain meaningless.

Building a Community, Part III: Culture

Theorists of national development in Europe have suggested that among national minorities, efforts by activists to curtail assimilation and win back members of the group who had already assimilated mark a key step in the formation of "national elites."[134] The transformation of the Jewish language of politics from Russian to Yiddish worked in parallel to developments among other national movements in the Russian Empire whose "national elites" experienced similar transformations. For example, the intellectual and activist leaders of the Finnish national movement (who spoke Swedish), the Lithuanian national movement (who spoke Polish), and the Georgian and Ukrainian national movements (who spoke Russian) all changed their spoken language, literary language, and even their own names as popular vernaculars became national languages. Furthermore, the literary societies of many different national groups played a role in cultivating linguistic nationalism throughout the empire during this period, and for this reason the government, after briefly tolerating their existence, attempted to shut them all down. In 1910 Stolypin issued a circular urging the closure in particular of all Ukrainian and Jewish national organizations "promoting the rise of national self-consciousness."[135] The Jewish, Ukrainian, and Polish literary societies all had their permission to operate revoked in the summer of 1911. Yet in contrast to their growing opposition to the imperial government, Jewish intellectuals and those of other national minorities were still in sync with the spirit of the times among the Russian intelligentsia. In fact, the entire process in which Jewish political activists debated ideal modes of communal organization followed the general Russian intellectual movement after the 1905 revolution to build *obshchestvennost'*, especially in its second meaning of social and public responsibility.[136]

As political disillusionment set in with the revolution's failure, some Jews nonetheless hoped that the government would allow more substantial cultural work than it had permitted previously. The Jewish Literary Society was established in St. Petersburg in 1908 for the purpose of discussing questions of Jewish literature, culture, and communal affairs, and by 1910 it had 850 members.[137] Although the society conducted its business in Russian, its goal was to foster the creation of Jewish literature in Yiddish. Branches of the society sprang up across the empire, with 120 established within three years. Also in 1908, some of St. Petersburg's leading composers and Jewish intellectuals established the Society for Jewish Folk Music, and they held regular, often wildly popular, concerts that mixed the genres of liturgical music, Yiddish folk songs, and Hasidic and klezmer melodies with modern orchestral arrangements.[138] The Society for Jewish Folk Music's early membership and audience for its events was made up of the city's Jewish communal, commercial, and political leadership, who even before its establishment were attending "concert-balls" and "literary-musical evenings" where figures such as An-sky and the poet Semyon (Shimen) Frug (1860–1916) gave public readings.[139] Perhaps most important, the

Russian government also permitted the establishment of the Jewish Historical-Ethnographic Society in 1908, an institution that would survive the government's closure of minorities' cultural institutions (and, indeed, outlive the government itself). Finally, the same individuals who established these three societies also engaged in a massive encyclopedia project between 1908 and 1913, creating a multivolume reference work that reinforced, for Christians and Jews, the notion of Russian Jews as a distinct and unified group.[140] When it was published, the *Evreiskaia entsiklopediia*, which began with the modest intention of creating an improved Russian version of the American *Jewish Encyclopedia*, claimed no less an objective than to demonstrate how "the fate of the Jewish people's cultural creativity relates to the civilization of nearly all peoples."[141]

Like other European nationalists, Dubnov believed that historical study could reveal the Jews' ever-present national consciousness and repair that national consciousness among those Jews for whom it had weakened: "The Jewish national idea and the national feeling connected with it have their origin primarily in the historical consciousness, in a certain complex of ideas and predispositions. . . . Upon the knowledge of history, then, depends the strength of the national consciousness."[142] In 1888 Dubnov had famously published an article in *Voskhod* titled "On Studying the History of the Russian Jews and the Creation of a Russian-Jewish Historical Society," prompting a group of Jewish lawyers and Moscow University students to establish the Jewish Historical-Ethnographic Committee as part of the existing OPE.[143] The OPE's interest in promoting Jewish historical study predated even Dubnov's call to arms, as from its beginning the organization sought to encourage more publishing in Hebrew and Russian on Jewish historical questions.[144] Not until 1908, however, did the government accede to Maksim Vinaver's requests for permission to establish an independent society (meetings were held in Vinaver's apartment).[145] Lawyers still predominated among the new historical society's membership. In addition to Vinaver, Bramson, and Sliozberg, historian lawyers such as Aleksandr Isaievich Braudo (1864–1924), Grigorii Krasnii-Admoni (1881–1970), M. G. Syrkin, and L. A. Sev attended the first meeting, which was held on November 16, 1908, in the Aleksandrovskii Room of

St. Petersburg's Choral Synagogue.[146] Jewish lawyers turned to history in the late imperial period to create a cogent legal argument for Jewish emancipation, and in doing so they produced many volumes analyzing the historical record of tsarist legislation relating to the Jews for the dual purpose of influencing tsarist bureaucrats and aiding Jewish advocates.[147] Source books of Russian Jewish history collected by these lawyers, the most important of which was *Regesty i nadpisi* (Digests and Inscriptions), were used, for instance, by Vinaver in the First Duma to demonstrate the lengthy Jewish presence in Russia and the raft of discriminatory legislation imposed on the Jews.[148]

However, the membership of the Jewish Historical-Ethnographic Society extended beyond the legal profession, and the group's primary purpose was not the collection of tsarist legal documents. Instead, the society was one result of a move toward nationalism among liberals such as Vinaver, in which historical study played the role of both cause and effect: Immersion in Jewish history led them to nationalism, and nationalism fueled their interest in Jewish history. Thus the founders of the Jewish Historical-Ethnographic Society (none of whom, other than Dubnov, identified politically as particularly nationalistic) accepted and supported a nationalist mission for the group from its inception.[149] The purpose of the Jewish Historical-Ethnographic Society was to initiate a Jewish cultural revival by creating a historical foundation for Jewish national self-consciousness in Russia and Eastern Europe, and its key participants stated so rather explicitly.[150] In a speech at the Society's second meeting, titled "Processes of Humanization and Nationalization in the Recent History of the Jews," Dubnov traced the emergence of national consciousness and its opponents in Western and Eastern Europe, making both implicit and explicit arguments for diaspora nationalism.[151] Acknowledging the reversals of the promising 1905 revolution, Dubnov stated: "At any rate, these tremendously important facts cannot be erased from history: that half of the entire Diaspora proclaimed itself a nation and is engaged in a practical struggle for its personal and civil rights, on an equal footing with the other national groups of the Russian empire."[152] But it was in a speech at the Society's inaugural meeting that Dubnov most unambiguously linked the new group both to the spirit of *obshchestvennost'* and to the spread of national

consciousness while arguing that national salvation lay in such public work. Dubnov urged the attendees to reflect on the impact of the
failed revolution, asking, "Where are we now, when political reaction
has wreaked its worst havoc, when after devoting our people's energy
to the liberation movement of our age we experienced a moment of
despondency bordering on desperation?" He continued:

> Remember, gentlemen, one historical truth: in the life of a healthy
> people, an era of political reaction always leads to an era of greater
> strength. In this dark interval we accumulate the spiritual energy that
> will be expended in the coming era of liberation. . . . After all, we
> call not on a dead science, not on a sleep-inducing history, but rather
> one which will become idea and conscience, which raises and incites
> consciousness in daily affairs. . . . Arising under such auspices, our
> Historical-Ethnographic Society has a right to take up a special place
> in the heterogeneous public [obshchestvennykh] strata. And such is
> my ardent desire—in order for our new Society to really be "histori-
> cal," in order for it to be destined to play a historical role in the life of
> our people.[153]

Not only Dubnov but also all the founders viewed the Jewish Historical-Ethnographic Society as both an exercise in raising public historical
consciousness and a means of fighting repression through public activity. The Jewish Historical-Ethnographic Society thus became an important example of the cooperation, especially between diaspora nationalists
and liberals, in cultural and communal projects that marked the period
beginning in 1908, a cooperation that ended up blurring the differences
between the two groups.[154] Dubnov headed the historical section, and the
lawyer Mikhail Kulisher (1847–1919) headed the ethnographic section,
with both sitting as vice-chairs of the Society (the two had previously
worked against each other in the Union for Full Rights and with each
other, albeit stormily, on the *Evreiskaia entsiklopediia*). Vinaver served as
the entire organization's chair. Members of his Folksgruppe, such as Lev
Shternberg and M. L. Trivus-Shmi, played important roles in the Jewish Historical-Ethnographic Society, as did Perel'man, An-sky, and Tsinberg, who were already members of the Folkspartey or would soon join
it. Other prominent activists, such as Aleksandr Braudo and the historian
Iulii Gessen, were also involved.[155]

The new group immediately set to work, establishing a journal to publish academic studies of Jewish historical and ethnographic research.[156] Some believed that this journal, *Evreiskaia starina*, should be published in Hebrew, but Dubnov, as its editor and head of the Society's historical section, reaffirmed the need for a scientific journal in Russian (he also claimed that he was at the time attempting to extract himself from the language war between the Hebraists and Yiddishists).[157] Dubnov always believed in the interconnectedness of his political and historical work, and, as Jeffrey Veidlinger points out, Dubnov's seminal works presenting his autonomist interpretation of Jewish history were first serialized in *Evreiskaia starina*.[158] Albeit against some opposition, Dubnov chose to publish in *Evreiskaia starina* historical documents such as *pinkasim* (Jewish communal records), thereby emphasizing the historical basis for Jewish political autonomy. Although Vinaver disagreed with Dubnov's selection of materials for publication in *Evreiskaia starina*, he eventually acceded to Dubnov's editorial direction.[159] And regardless of its ideological underpinnings, *Evreiskaia starina* became the premier journal of Jewish historical studies in Russian, with subscribers from all over the Russian Empire and Europe, including France, England, Germany, and Austria. The publication received letters from Jewish literary societies and libraries throughout Russia and from political exiles in Ust'-Sylosk.[160] Judging from requests for copies from the libraries of the Psycho-Neurological Institute, the Ethnographic Section of the Russian Museum, and the State Duma, *Evreiskaia starina* reached far beyond a strictly Jewish audience.[161]

The Jewish Historical-Ethnographic Society also served more than a merely academic purpose. Between its founding and the 1917 revolutions, the society became increasingly involved in preserving the Jewish cultural heritage of Russia and Eastern Europe. The Society's origins lay in the desire to collect and preserve Jewish historical documents, but the scope of its collection and preservation efforts expanded dramatically with An-sky's organization of a series of ethnographic expeditions under its sponsorship. In his famous article "Jewish Ethnopoetics," published in the inaugural edition of *Perezhitoe* in 1908, An-sky called on the Jewish people (or at least the Jewish intelligentsia) to rediscover their folklore under the framework of a nationalist agenda that resembled both Dubnov's call for Jews to rediscover their past and similar attempts by intellectuals among other national groups to rediscover the voices and oral literature of their people.[162] An-sky first proposed the idea of an expedition through the Pale of Settlement to collect folk songs along with historical and ethnographic materials at a Jewish Historical-Ethnographic Society meeting on October 11, 1909.[163] Despite the fact that An-sky privately complained to his close friend Shmuel Niger about the difficulty of enticing St. Petersburg's wealthy Jews to contribute financially, the expeditions of the Jewish Historical-Ethnographic Society are perhaps the best example of how St. Petersburg Jewish intellectuals of varying ideological stripes were supported by the financial patronage of the Jewish elite in order to conduct nationalistically oriented cultural projects.[164] Beginning in the fall of 1907, An-sky was able to devote his efforts entirely to ethnographic research, thanks to the financial support of the oil magnate Samuel Moiseevich Shryro, who helped pay for the launching of *Perezhitoe*, and of the Gintsburg family, who directly funded An-sky's ethnographic expeditions.[165] Vladimir Gintsburg donated 10,000 rubles (the single largest contribution) to the ethnographic expedition, which he had named after his deceased father, Baron Naftali Horace Gintsburg.[166]

An-sky led two expeditions, first through Kiev and Volynia Provinces in the summer and fall of 1912 and then through Volynia and Podolia Provinces in the summer and fall of 1913 (a third expedition in 1914, in progress but without An-sky, was cut short by the war). An-sky was primarily concerned with recording Jewish music and folklore, and in addition to the anthropologists, folklorists, and historians who assisted his preparations in St. Petersburg, he compiled an expedition team that included the musicologist and composer Iulii (Yoel) Engel, the artist and photographer (and An-sky's nephew) Solomon (Shlomo) Iudovin, and a specialist in folklore, Zinovii (Zusman) Kiselgof and several of his students (who joined the second expedition).[167] What An-sky sought was nothing less than a vast ethnographic record of traditional Jewish life—recorded through sounds, images, stories, data, and material culture—that would help "estranged intellectuals" like him maintain a connection to their people and perhaps even help with national regeneration.[168]

The goal of preserving Jewish cultural artifacts became urgent with the outbreak of war in the summer of 1914. A little more than a year later, in November 1915, An-sky created a committee to organize a special ethnographic section within the Jewish Historical-Ethnographic Society for the purpose of mounting a new expedition as quickly as possible.[169] The materials collected would be stored, and some displayed, for the time being in the library of the Jewish Historical-Ethnographic Society, but the intention was eventually to create a museum for them.[170] In what might have been an acknowledgment of the questionable future of Russian Jewry or an indication of the growing allure of Zionism, or both, the Ethnographic Committee considered the possibility of establishing this museum in Palestine.[171]

The goal of the Jewish Historical-Ethnographic Society was not Jewish communal self-government but rather Jewish historical and contemporary self-knowledge (as An-sky phrased it, *samopoznanie*). Still, like *Evreiskii mir* and the Kovno conference, St. Petersburg's new Jewish cultural projects resulted from the efforts of a growing body of Jewish intellectuals in the imperial capital who aspired to lead Russian Jewry's transition to a politicized and self-conscious national group. The significance of all the Jewish cultural, communal, and journalistic projects of the period lies in their representing a bridge between discussing the Jewish national idea and fostering Jewish national self-consciousness in Russia. If Jews understood the historical roots of their right to national equality in the Russian Empire, they would be more likely to support demands for Jewish autonomy. Nonetheless, the fact that such projects were based in St. Petersburg and conducted in Russian created its own impetus to both cultural production and communal reorganization. Representatives of diverse political groups created new Jewish publications and cultural and communal institutions to serve in their struggle against assimilation. Yet by virtue of the St. Petersburg Jewish *intelligenty*'s constant awareness of their physical and linguistic separation from those whom they sought to imbue with national self-consciousness, the struggle itself became a surrogate for genuine political mobilization.

Conclusion

In a poem written to Dubnov and published in the first issue of *Evre-iskii mir*, Semyon Frug captured much of the essence of the Jewish political and cultural climate in St. Petersburg in the years following the 1905 revolution, especially the dissonance between the outlooks of the older and younger generations that resulted from the latter's inclination to reject Russian as the language of politics and, in doing so, increasingly isolate themselves from Russian culture.[172] Frug wrote Russian, Yiddish, and Hebrew poetry, and he never perceived that one of these languages must culturally or politically triumph over the other, a fact that contributed to his widespread popularity.[173] The poem to Dubnov was titled "Molodniak," the Russian term for saplings that also has the additional meaning of "younger generation."

> Here stands the old apple tree in its garden, dear;
> Here the willow by the stream. In its babbling hiss
> I hear the echo of my first kiss
> Of first rhythms—the powers to appear. . . .
>
> Past trails augur a sprig of imagination,
> Outlining them like a living chronicle,
> And strong saplings grow in every direction,
> Buzzing as joy, and light, and dark encounter all together.
>
> Oh, who will replace us, old friend?
> In the clear morning, and in the dark hour of stormy tryst,
> About what do they rustle, our saplings around,
> Bringing which fruit and awaiting what happiness?
>
> We, the old roots, crowded together in darkened gloom,
> We lived it all; what a cluster of days.
> Our strength we give to you, our youth you now assume
> Grow tall, my dears, and blossom under godly rays! . . .
>
> Have they yet grown strong enough on their still young roots?
> Oh, leaves of June! In fog and frost
> We nurtured your rise in torment and tears,
> And yet appearing to us strange and dark, your noise is lost! . . .[174]

Both Dubnov and Frug exemplified the *maskil*-turned-nationalist. In 1883, before his full embrace of nationalism, Dubnov brought attention to the generational shift to argue against the Palestinophile auto-emancipation proposed by Lev Pinsker and for internal Jewish religious reform that would allow greater integration.[175] In that essay Dubnov used the metaphor of fathers and sons, suggesting that fathers stood for traditional Judaism and sons for a radical break with religion. Dubnov claimed that he, unlike the fathers or the sons, interpreted "self-emancipation" (*samoemantsipatsiia*) as organic communal religious reforms, self-help (*samopomoshch*), and cultural work that would allow for the transformation of Russia's Jews into *Russian* Jews.[176] In their move to nationalism—more evolution than conversion for Dubnov and Frug—both writers had challenged the older generation of Jewish leaders: in the 1880s for their passivity and, after the 1903 pogroms, for their supposed willful appeasement of Russian authorities. In 1909 Frug understood correctly that the next generation of Jewish intellectuals would soon be challenging them.

St. Petersburg in this period should be viewed as the key place and time when the members of the Russian-Jewish intelligentsia (and this hyphenated form came into use at the time) consciously transformed themselves into Yiddishist or Hebraist political activists. Many of the battles of the Jewish language war were fought in the Russian-language Jewish press because Russian was still, for the time being, the language of Jewish politics in the Russian Empire. *Evreiskii mir*, therefore, was representative of the many contradictions inherent in the intertwined cultural and political battles of the period, and the publication's end also demonstrated that a particular form of Jewish nationalism in Russia that balanced Jewish national demands and cultural activities with participation in the Russian political world was failing to appeal to the younger generation of Jewish political activists. Nowhere did generational differences appear more pronounced than over the question of language. With some notable exceptions, the generation born in the 1880s found it far easier to adapt to the politics of Yiddish than the generation born twenty years earlier. For example, aside from a contribution to its first issue, Dubnov had little to do with *Di yidishe velt*, and it is clear that he was never as comfortable writing in Yiddish as he was in Russian.[177] The end of *Evreiskii mir* also accelerated Dubnov's move away from Jewish politics, and he increasingly became more of a figurehead than an active participant in his party.

The period between the end of the 1905 revolution and the beginning of World War I was, in essence, Russian Jewry's *Fathers and Sons* moment. In Ivan Turgenev's novel *Fathers and Sons* (*Otsy i deti*, literally "fathers and children"), published in 1862, the radical and nihilistic views of the younger generation returning from the city shock the espoused "progressive" fathers, who nonetheless feel obliged to defer to their sons while not changing their own opinions. The essence of the sons' critique of the fathers is the fathers' presumed passivity; the younger generation accuses the older of speaking of change but failing to act.[178] For the Jews the more liberal older generation reluctantly stepped aside to allow the younger and more radical generation to take up the struggle it had begun. One participant at the Kovno conference, Iakov Maze, even made the analogy explicit, comparing the moderate reformers to the fathers and the adamant secularists to the sons. He claimed that the debates over self-government and community had come to replace the old disputes over how to infuse Jewish principles into daily life, disputes that he said had died: "This dead world is enclosed between 'Fathers and Sons,' with both sides granting the other rights, such as the freedom to keep the old prayer house with all its outmoded procedures, or the right to stand outside any kind of prayer house at all and outside any kind of understanding of Jewry."[179] Although Maze's subsequent lambasting of supposed "non-Jewish Jews" met with applause, his familiarity with Turgenev (and the presumed familiarity of the attendees) demonstrated the complex situation that Russified Jewish intellectuals faced as they tried to create a form of Jewish national self-consciousness that they could use to navigate around the rocky waters of assimilation, while remaining part of the Russian body politic.

The challenge for many of these individuals, who also debated Jewish nationalism, autonomism, and communal self-government at the Kovno conference or in the pages of *Evreiskii mir*, was to move from a theoretical discussion of Jewish needs to practical steps to meet them. Many were aware of the difficulties they faced. The editors of one journal, established by the OPE in St. Petersburg and devoted to discussing problems of Jewish education in Russia, argued that "Jews must have communal self-government and self-help in order to secure educational institutions and financial means for the younger generation."[180] According to the editors, the educational and financial security of future generations rested in "the appreciable shift from the realm of theoretical argument and disagreement to the sphere of real practical transformation of [communal] duties," a process requiring careful thought and detailed planning.[181]

Both the creation of new cultural institutions and the debate over the national idea and community helped to narrow the gap between the different Jewish political visions.[182] In a sense, the Kovno conference, the establishment of *Evreiskii mir*, and even the creation of the Jewish Historical-Ethnographic Society represented a return to the ethos of the Union for Full Rights. By drawing Bundists and socialist Zionists into discussions of Jewish autonomy, these projects also succeeded where the Union had failed, thereby sowing the seeds for full participation in Jewish politics in 1917. The Bund and the Zionists even had to invent new terms to justify their participation in bourgeois and Diaspora politics, respectively, but whatever one named the new spirit of Jewish *obshchestvennost'* in the Russian Empire—even *kultur-arbeyt* (cultural work) as the Bund did, or *Gegenwartsarbeit* (work in the present) as the Zionists did—Jewish autonomism became the calling of the day.

In his 1912 article "The Survival of the Jewish People," notably written in
Hebrew for *He-ʿAtid*, Simon Dubnov used militaristic terms to describe
the historical struggle for Jewish autonomy in the Diaspora, portraying
autonomy as a kind of armor protecting the community from hostile
surrounding armies. Dubnov clearly borrowed his language, message,
and means from the Zionists in order to counter their Palestine-based
national vision. He described autonomy, realized through the *kahal*, as
a surrogate for the state and each community as a soldier united as an
army in dispersion. Dubnov even placed a new emphasis on the role of
religious laws in acting as the weapon that historically defended Jewish
autonomy.[1] Within a couple of years, this metaphor proved more apt
than even Dubnov might have perceived. The onset of war in 1914 was
as unexpected to Russian Jewry as their subsequent persecution during
the conflict. The war's eastern front fluctuated in ripples through the
areas of Europe's densest Jewish population. And despite hundreds of
thousands of Jews serving in the Russian imperial army, Jewish civilians came to be labeled as spies and blamed by the Russian military
for all its failures. Evacuations became mass expulsions accompanied by
violence and the confiscation of property. In the most generous assessment, during World War I the Russian state failed its Jewish population; at worst, the state victimized it. Yet in creating a refugee crisis, the
state also created space for Jewish organizations to provide care in its
place. The need to provide immediate relief, permanent resettlement,   167
and occupational retraining to a large segment of the population led to
a massive expansion of Jewish communal work. In failing to provide
for Jewish refugees adequately, the Russian government had no choice

but to allow Jewish organizations greater autonomy to do so them-selves. While Dubnov spoke metaphorically about the battle for Jewish autonomy, because of the war, Jewish communal organizations did in fact become a surrogate for the state and, in turn, created the edifice of Jewish communal and legal autonomy.

Like Jews elsewhere in Europe, some Russian Jews, mostly urban and liberal ones, initially believed that the war might bring Jewry new freedoms and greater acceptance.[2] It was not long, however, before such hopes were dashed in Russia. Not only did the military and certain civilian sources spread false accusations against the Jews, but the censor would not even allow the capital's progressive press to report positively on Jewish contributions to the war effort. Because Jewish expulsions from areas at risk of German conquest began in earnest in January and February of 1915, the Russian military and government's policies turned hundreds of thousands of Jews into homeless and destitute refugees. As a result, a significant proportion of the Jewish population as a whole came to rely for their material, educational, and spiritual needs on Jew-ish communal institutions.

During World War I, professional Jewish relief workers expanded the responsibilities of Jewish communal organizations for the general well-being of the Jewish population. Although, as we have seen, the Jewish intelligentsia's involvement in communal affairs began earlier, Jewish communal work became professionalized during the war.[3] In this period Jewish activists accelerated their communal efforts and put into practice many of the theories of self-government developed between 1907 and 1914, and at the same time they continued to work hand in hand with key figures of the Jewish financial elite. The war created the need for relief on a massive scale, and the organization of such relief dramatically expanded the scope of activities undertaken by Jewish communal organizations. The war also provided both the gov-ernmental leeway and urgent crisis necessary to centralize Jewish com-munal organizations under a single body in St. Petersburg, controlled by a mix of the Jewish financial elite—the same Jewish lawyers who participated in the Jewish cultural projects—and professional activists.

In this chapter I trace how World War I led to a form of proto-auton-omism that laid the foundation for genuine Jewish political autonomy.

Recent assessments of how Russia fought and managed the war—how its government, military, and civil society responded to such enormous challenges as food supply and the resettlement of refugees and people fleeing the conflict—have emphasized the extent to which the communal infrastructure mobilized by various national groups stepped into the breech left, or created, by the Russian government.[4] Peter Holquist in particular has tried to reshape how we understand the Russian revolutionary period as a "continuum of crisis" beginning in 1914 and ending only in 1921 or 1922 with the victory of the Bolsheviks in the civil war.[5] Holquist's point is that Russia's political classes used the opportunity and tools of wartime mobilization to advance their own political goals, which was a situation that continued until fighting ended. As Holquist also suggests, "The resulting network of semipublic, semistate structures was less a public sphere autonomous of the state than a 'parastatal complex' in which society and state were tightly intertwined."[6] Such a description perfectly fits the wartime activities of the Russian Jewish political class as well, with the important difference that the political projects constructed by Russian Jews, though partly funded by the government, existed completely independently of state structures. Jewish organizations essentially took on all responsibilities forfeited by the state, and they raised much of the funds necessary to do so through foreign support and Jewish taxation.

Corresponding with anti-Jewish violence and the massive relief efforts on the part of Jewish organizations, the war brought many more Jews into the net of Jewish communal organizations, a process that likely bolstered Jewish national identification. Yet one also has to consider the fading hopes for Jewish civil equality, let alone integration, in a Russian Empire that was rapidly unraveling. As Jews became scapegoats, the perception (whether accurate or not) that few, even among the most strident liberal opponents of the regime, were willing to challenge the rumors or to defend Russian Jewry from its government, even symbolically, contributed to the declining appeal of Russian liberalism among Jews. As the Kadets and liberals lost credibility by failing to defend even Jewish individual rights, Jews increasingly came to believe that the outcome of the war should secure their national rights. Finally, the war forced all Jewish political parties to participate in what amounted to a centralized Jewish proto-governmental organization, thus completing the centralization of Russian Jewish political life and organization in St. Petersburg and pushing Jewish public opinion inexorably closer to favoring full Jewish autonomy. All these changes set the stage for Jewish demands for guaranteed national rights, both at Versailles at the end of the war and under the eventual new order in Russia. The international links between Jewish political groups and the persistent reliance on networks of the global Jewish elite intensified even as Jews fought against each other in the armies of Europe. The question of who spoke for the Jews would become ever more urgent over the course of the world war and even more so in the efforts to end it. For Russian Jewry, World War I was a period of suffering, wide-scale dislocation, intense communal need, and, finally, an opening for transformative communal change.

The Jews as Scapegoats

The consequences of World War I for the Russian Empire are well-known: The empire, and Romanov rule, came to an end while the war was still raging. The destruction wrought upon Russian Jewry during the war is less known.[7] The most immediate consequence of the outbreak of war for Russian Jewry was the massive evacuation of Jews from the front and adjacent areas. Because Jews were densely populated in the westernmost regions of the empire, they were particularly adversely affected by the outbreak of war (nearly the entire Pale of Settlement was placed under military rule when the fighting began). In addition, almost immediately after the war began, the Russian army launched a massive campaign against spying, targeting mainly ethnic Germans and Jews. Army headquarters, known as Stavka, was made responsible for the coordination of civilian affairs and invested with tremendous authority (the Council of Ministers required the tsar's personal intervention to overrule Stavka), and it took frequent advantage of its right to deport suspected groups and individuals without trial.[8] Even though the army was authorized to expel only individuals, and therefore mass deportations were

technically illegal, in reality the total expulsion of various populations began in the fall of 1914.[9]

Deportations were based on the army's belief that Jewish populations near the front were unreliable and evolved into the practice of
taking hostages (*zalozhniki*) as a preventive measure against spying
and sabotage through the enforcement of collective responsibility.
Throughout the war the military's objectives in deporting both the Jewish and German populations from the front shifted from being about
security to the goal of transferring those groups' property to Russians,
on both nationalist and socioeconomic grounds.[10] Even before the
war, Russian generals widely believed that as "enemies of Russia" Jews
should not serve in the military and Stavka developed preexisting antisemitic stereotypes into wartime propaganda in order to tar the entire
Jewish population as traitors.[11] Suspicions of the Jews during a violent
and chaotic time served to put them outside the law, and Jewish civilians became victims of widespread anti-Jewish violence, often directed
and carried out by the military. Some Jews, such as An-sky, blamed lies
spread by Polish antisemites for almost all the accusations of treason.
In An-sky's opinion, "The Poles hoped not only to achieve the goal of
ridding themselves of Jews but also to exploit the idea of Jewish treason
to cover up their own sin of Austrian leanings."[12] But An-sky possessed
a cognitive dissonance about the possibility that Russian peasants and
soldiers could act so violently toward Jews, and he consequently sought
to blame Poles, Russian officers, and the effects of rumors instead.[13] An-
sky's sentiments notwithstanding, Stavka was motivated to deport the
Jewish population less by specific accusations of treason than by preexisting hostility toward the Jewish and German population, made worse
by the army's poor performance in the early stage of the war.

For the most part both the Council of Ministers and the Duma
opposed the military's actions against the Jews. But because of the
scope of the military commanders' authority to prosecute the war as
they saw fit, the military did little to address the civilian governments'
concerns about the deportations.[14] This was a period of extreme geographic displacement and anti-Jewish violence, for which the army's
brutal expulsions were largely responsible.[15] Pogroms, initiated by soldiers and enthusiastically embraced by locals, accompanied the mass

deportation of Jews, resulting in thousands of rapes, murders, and the wide-scale confiscation of Jewish property.[16] Such violence was especially grave during the Russian invasion of Galicia (in that case the violence was directed toward Jewish subjects of Austria) and only increased with the chaos of the Russian retreat of 1915, as Cossack divisions of the army frequently extorted money and property from Jewish populations.[17] The Jews in Galicia were stuck in the middle of a multiethnic conflict where they faced violence and hostility from all sides; in particular, the Russians hoped to "liberate" the Ukrainians and join Galicia to the empire, and the Poles hoped Galicia would become part of an independent Poland (the Austrians simply sought to hold onto the territory). As the Austrians first withdrew, Jews suffered violence at the hands of Poles for being "pro-government" and hoped the Russians would restore order, only to be faced with violence at the hands of Cossacks, who claimed to be freeing the local Poles and Ukrainians from the supposed "Jewish yoke."[18]

In the capital many Jewish liberals and even Zionists were at first eager to demonstrate their loyalty to the state, and they viewed the war and the Russian alliance with democratic France and Britain as likely to bring greater freedom for Russian Jews. In a speech to the Duma the Jewish Kadet Naftali Markovich Fridman (1863–1921) stated: "We have lived, and still live, under particularly difficult legal restrictions; nonetheless, we have always felt ourselves to be Russian citizens and have always been faithful sons of our motherland, and no power on earth will sever us from our Russian motherland, from the land to which we are bound by the bonds of generations."[19] Maksim Vinaver called the beginning of the war a moment of patriotic élan for the empire's Jewish population.[20] Indeed, early in the war, liberal Jewish publications such as *Novy voskhod* regularly exhorted Russian Jews to volunteer to defend Russia from her enemies and argued that Jewish sacrifice would be rewarded like that of other national minorities.[21]

In feeling from the outset great trepidation about the bloody war that was certain to be fought in Jewish towns and villages, Dubnov may have been exceptional, but it was not long into the war before Jewish leaders lost all hope that the war would improve the Jews' situation in Russia.[22] Not only were false accusations against the Jews spread by the military and certain civilian sources, but the censor would not even allow Petrograd's progressive journals (such as *Rech'*, *Den'*, *Birzhevye vedomosti*, and *Petrogradskii kur'er*) to report positively on Jewish contributions to the war effort or even about individual Jews decorated with the Cross of Saint George.[23] As Fridman commented in a speech to the Duma in August 1915, "In a long war lucky events alternate with unlucky ones, and in any case it is naturally useful to have scapegoats in reserve. For this purpose there exists the old firm: the Jew."[24] Fridman outlined the false accusations against the Jews, their mistreatment through forced expulsions (along with the shameful waste of valuable transport), and the unprecedented taking of Jewish hostages from among the empire's own subjects.[25] Fridman himself, despite being the elected representative from Kovno, was expelled as a Jew from his constituency. Particularly galling to Fridman and others was the government's refusal to acknowledge the enormous Jewish contributions to the war effort, especially in terms of soldiers, and its failure to make use of what he perceived to be the obvious patriotism of the Jewish population.[26] At the same time that Jewish civilians faced violence and dispossession, hundreds of thousands of Jews continued to serve loyally (and in some cases fervently) in the military, and Jewish journalists struggled mightily to evade the censors and publish about Jewish heroism.[27]

The most pressing issue faced by Jewish leaders was that of the Jewish refugees. At first, Jewish refugees were resettled in already crowded areas of the Pale of Settlement farther east. Yet an added complication was that parts of Poltava and Ekaterinoslav Provinces were the only districts left within the Pale that were not under military rule, and therefore they were the only legally valid destinations for Jewish deportees, a situation that the civilian government found greatly disturbing because of the resulting dense Jewish population there. By August 1915 the government, having run out of options, granted Jews permission to settle in any towns (but not rural villages) in the empire except St. Petersburg (now called by a new Slavicized name, Petrograd), Moscow, and Cossack areas. The refusal to allow Jewish settlement in villages, despite terrible overcrowding in the towns, stemmed from the government's continued belief in the need to protect the peasantry from supposedly rapacious and exploitative Jews. The government also made clear that it took such measures to ease residential restrictions only "because of the exigencies of the military situation";[28] in other words, Jewish settlement in these areas would not be permanent and therefore Jews were forbidden from buying land or property in their new residences.

The minister of internal affairs, Prince N. B. Shcherbatov, criticized the army for using the Jews as scapegoats for its own failures, creating the refugee crisis, and thereby stirring up revolutionary sentiment. Shcherbatov was also the most outspoken supporter of eliminating Jewish residential restrictions.[29] Yet the primary motivation for all the ministers who favored removing the residential restrictions was not humanitarian. Rather, it stemmed from their desire to be seen as making an effort to relieve Jewish suffering in order to secure credit from Jewish financiers in both Russia and America—the ministers more or less equated Jewish capital and American capital—and to get the Jewish leaders to do their part in influencing the Jewish masses and "quieting them down."[30] In Shcherbatov's words, "If the evil influence of the Jews is undebatable, the necessity for money with which to conduct the war is equally undebatable."[31] The Jews thereby won the relaxation of residential restrictions only because of the government's cynical pragmatism, itself based on certain fundamentally antisemitic assumptions. And in fact, the exaggerated sense of American Jewry's power to influence its government was tactically encouraged by highly placed British Jews. When Russian minister of finance P. L. Bark came to meet in London with Anglo-Jewry's wealthiest and most influential representatives, Claude Montefiore, Leopold de Rothschild, and David Alexander emphasized that because, unlike them, American Jewry was unrestrained by their country's neutrality, they were free to discourage financial assistance to the allies and, in particular, Russia. For that reason, according to these Jewish eminences, the Russian government would do well to consider making a number of concessions to its Jewish population.[32]

World War I marked a key moment in the politicization of Russian Jewry. Whatever positions were being advocated on Russian Jewry's behalf, faced with the military's deportations, the government's impotence, and the press's willingness to accept and spread anti-Jewish accusations, Jews found it increasingly difficult to identify with the Russian polity as the war progressed. Events during the war spurred the

Jewish move away from Russian liberalism, a process that was to have an impact on Jewish political opinion during the revolutionary year of 1917. Jewish disaffection with Russian liberalism during the war originated to a large extent with the Kadet Party's own actions in the Duma. Before the war Russian liberals at least symbolically advocated for Jewish civil equality. For example, as a result of Vinaver's personal advocacy with the Kadet parliamentary leadership, a statement proposing Jewish emancipation was read into the official record in 1909. With the support of some other representatives, the Kadets also introduced a bill in 1910 calling for the abolition of the Pale of Settlement. The 165 members who voted to table the bill did so to make a public statement of liberal support for the Jews, because they knew the legislation would not pass.[33] In theory, Russian and Jewish liberalism, represented politically by the Kadet Party, was naturally more appealing to Jews than other ideologies and parties. The Kadets favored full Jewish equality and, unlike the socialist parties, both Jewish and non-Jewish, they defended Jewish economic interests and the right to practice traditional Judaism. Furthermore, the fact that there were Jewish Kadet members in all four Dumas indicated that at least Jews could participate in government as members of the Kadet Party (though from the Second Duma onward few options existed for elected Jewish members other than joining with the Kadets). Even the Russian Zionists began their political activities within the confines of the Kadet Party.

During World War I, however, even though the program of the majority coalition of liberal and centrist conservatives known as the Progressive Bloc called on the government to abolish incrementally a number of anti-Jewish restrictions, in reality the progressives and liberals turned a blind eye to the military's abuse of the Jews and in some cases accepted the accusations of Jewish treason.[34] In the eyes of the Jewish public, the Kadets (including the Jewish representatives) consistently failed to defend Jewish interests for the sake of preserving their coalition with the Octobrists and other parties that included unreformed antisemites in their ranks.[35] Officially, the Kadet Party defended the Jews against collective punishment and antisemitic demagoguery for "isolated cases of espionage."[36] But it is no surprise that many Jews saw such a defense as inadequate.

The turning point leading to deep Jewish disillusionment with the Kadets was the so-called circulars affair, when two of the party's Jewish Duma deputies, Naftali Fridman and Meir Bomash, drew up an interpellation requiring the government to disclose whether two circulars accusing the Jews of hoarding, exacerbating the food crisis, and fomenting revolution had been withdrawn or were still guiding policy.[37] The Kafafov circular, signed by the acting director of the Department of Police (within the Ministry of Internal Affairs), detailed the ways in which Jews supposedly subverted the Russian war effort through economic warfare, including currency manipulation, hoarding, and artificially creating a food crisis. A second circular issued by the Ministry of Finance instructed rural tax collectors to be aware of a possible German plan to have spies and Jews burn Russian crops and to pass on any relevant suspicions or information. The circulars were directly responsible for the arrest of hundreds of Jews, but Fridman and Bomash were forced under pressure from their own party to withdraw their interpellation.[38] Jews felt rebuffed in their expectation of support at the highest echelons of Russian liberal influence. For example, the Kadet leader Pavel Miliukov, in response to English Jews' urging to be more forceful with the Russian government, reportedly claimed that, while sympathetic, the problem as he saw it was that Russian Jews and their supporters elsewhere would not at this point be satisfied with anything less than complete emancipation, an exceedingly difficult outcome to achieve.[39] The result was that resentment grew against what some perceived as the passivity or helplessness of the Jews' most visible public representatives, a resentment borne by Jewish Kadets and expressed in eroding Jewish support for Russian liberalism.

According to Iakov Frumkin, a prominent Jewish liberal and lawyer, the circulars affair "had a highly disconcerting effect on the Jewish community."[40] Frumkin was sympathetic to the Jewish Duma members and other Jewish liberals (e.g., Maksim Vinaver), whom he saw as doing what they could under the circumstances. But in one recollection of an informal social gathering at someone's home in St. Petersburg in 1915 where both Petr Struve and Pavel Miliukov, two founders of the Kadet Party, were present, Frumkin also rather vividly depicted the breakdown of trust between Russian and Jewish liberals. When Struve pressed Miliukov on why his newspaper *Rech'* did not do more to condemn the deportations and other mistreatments of the Jews, Miliukov supposedly replied that he "had no wish to please Berlin." In Frumkin's telling, Iosif Bikerman, the only other Jew in the room, responded that Miliukov "has no wish to please Berlin, but his tactics surely will. They may, in fact, help Berlin win the war."[41] In Frumkin's account Bikerman sought to make clear to Miliukov that the liberal failure to stand with the Jews could have unintended consequences for the Russian liberals, the moral standing of the government, and the war effort (though Frumkin was writing later, with the knowledge of the full course of events, and hence may be telling us more about his own interpretation than Bikerman's).

Michael Hamm observes that during the war the Jewish question became "untimely" for the Kadets, who came to view its divisiveness as a liability outweighing the benefits of Jewish support.[42] Yet the Kadets' policy with respect to the Jews reflected their generally poor grasp of political realities throughout the war. The Kadets continually deluded themselves about the prospect of winning the war and maintaining the territorial integrity of the empire (and about the supposed weakness of the Bolsheviks).[43] Reporting on a conference of the Kadets' Duma faction in June 1915, *Evreiskaia nedelia* commented that, despite the party's standing for civil equality and self-determination for all the peoples of Russia, it was failing to address the tragedy inflicted on the Jews and the new wave of horrible antisemitism, assuming instead that in the future the Jewish question would be dealt with justly. As the paper observed, "It is a pity there were no pessimists at the conference."[44] Individual liberals and Russian intellectuals in general did become more sympathetic to the plight of the Jews as the military's brutality intensified between mid-1915 and mid-1916.[45] During that time some Kadets and Russian liberals came to see the need to hold the line against ever more virulent antisemitism and lawlessness, as did a number of non-Jewish intellectuals from different political viewpoints.[46] Yet the loudest and most persistent voices among the Russian liberals defending the Jews remained the Jews among them, especially Maksim Vinaver, who had to simultaneously assert the loyalty of the Jewish public and defend the Kadets against accusations from antisemites of being a "Jewish Party."[47] Nonetheless, the Kadets, though occasionally critical of the government for its anti-Jewish policies, consistently refused to place any blame on the general public, the masses, or even the military for anti-Jewish violence. In the face of compelling evidence of wide-scale antisemitism through the ranks in the army, the Kadets continued to blame only the government, accusing it of directing the pogroms to distract people from its failures.[48]

The Jewish groups whose members still remained committed to Russian liberalism—the Folksgruppe, the Folkspartey, and the liberal Zionists—as well as some socialists met during the war as the Political Bureau of Jewish communal activists, for the main purpose of guiding the Jewish representatives in the Duma.[49] The transcripts of the Political Bureau's Executive Committee meetings during the circulars affair reveal a deep sense of betrayal among all the attendees, both those who had been among the Kadets' most consistent supporters and those who had only pragmatically put their faith in the party. One debate, which lasted until 4 in the morning, revolved around whether the Jewish deputies should withdraw from the Kadets' parliamentary faction (as opposed to whether the Jewish Kadet members should independently withdraw from the Progressive Bloc, for which there was by this time near-universal agreement). In this debate those who defended the deputies' right to stay with the Kadets were ironically the ones whose arguments most clearly showed the extent of disillusionment with Russian liberalism. As Genrikh Sliozberg phrased the issue, we "can and must curse at the Kadets, but it is as necessary as before to do its deeds."[50] Surprisingly, the socialist autonomist Yisroel Efroikin also opposed pressuring the Jewish Duma members to leave the Kadets, but as he said, he came to the same position from a different angle, that of the general political struggle against the regime. Efroikin suggested of Sliozberg, "You see in all of these questions only the Jewish perspective and you forget all the rest. You repudiate the general political struggle." Efroikin continued, "Where is the basis for independent Jewish politics? As long as we live under someone else's government, we will have no possibility for independent politics."[51]

In essence, according to Efroikin, the committee expected too much from the Jewish Duma members and, in fact, the whole parliamentary system. Sliozberg believed that the Jewish representatives should stay with the Kadets in order to work to improve the Jews' situation from the inside, whereas Efroikin simply believed that a committee

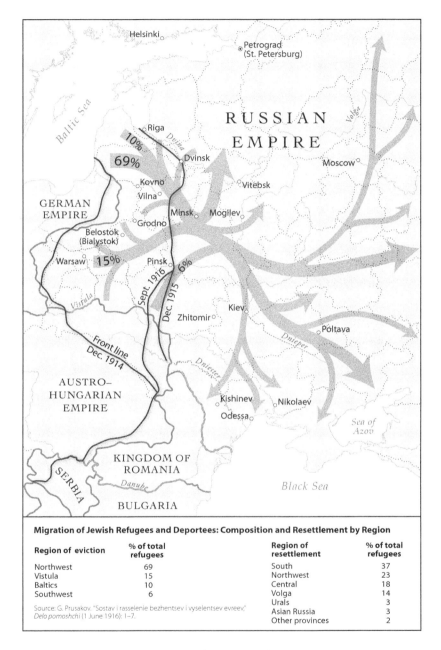

Migration of Jewish Refugees and Deportees: Composition and Resettlement by Region			
Region of eviction	**% of total refugees**	**Region of resettlement**	**% of total refugees**
Northwest	69	South	37
Vistula	15	Northwest	23
Baltics	10	Central	18
Southwest	6	Volga	14
		Urals	3
		Asian Russia	3
		Other provinces	2

Source: G. Prusakov. "Sostav i rasselenie bezhentsev i vyselentsev evreev," *Delo pomoshchi* (1 June 1916): 1–7.

Figure 5 World War I and Jewish displacement in the Russian Empire.

of notables and intellectuals had no place dictating party affiliation to Jews, including Jewish Duma members. To Efroikin the committee and Duma members should give up the pretense of independence in the Duma and concentrate on the general political struggle and Jewish autonomy. The chaos of war, the faltering Russian government, and the refugee crisis provided enough opportunity for both.

War Relief and Jewish Autonomy

By August 1916 the Jewish Committee to Aid Victims of War, known by its Russian acronym EKOPO, was directly responsible for the care of 200,000 registered Jewish refugees and indirectly responsible for another 200,000.[52] At the same time the Russian government began to subsidize EKOPO directly with enough funds to allow for its massive organizational expansion. The government's first grant to EKOPO came in May 1915, and between then and June 1917 government subsidies to EKOPO came to more than 17 million rubles, over half of EKOPO's total income.[53] Vast numbers of refugees came to rely on Jewish communal organizations for their material, educational, and spiritual needs, leading to the establishment of a Jewish governing bureaucracy that existed completely outside of, in place of, and yet substantially funded by the imperial government. Jews followed the example of Russian local self-governmental organizations that were simultaneously carving out an important sphere of political influence in providing war relief. Early in the war, the Union of Zemstvos (Zemskii Soiuz) and the Union of Towns (Soiuz Gorodov), which later combined into a single organization known as Zemgor, took on the responsibility of war relief for the general population, including Jews. To the Jewish communal leadership, however, it was apparent that special organizations coordinating assistance to Jews would be necessary. A group of communal workers and the trustees of Petrograd's Choral Synagogue formed EKOPO to provide immediate assistance to Russian Jewry.[54] The new organization initially intended to focus its activities on helping the families of Jewish injured and dead soldiers, but with the massive relocations of Jews from the front, EKOPO also took on the responsibilities of wide-scale relief.[55] The organizing committee, chaired first by the banker Mark Varshavskii and then by Baron Aleksandr Gintsburg, was composed of sitting and former Jewish Duma members such as Meir Bomash, Ezekiel Gurevich, Naftali Fridman, Lazar Nisselovich, Mikhail Sheftel', and Lazar Rabinovich; St. Petersburg rabbis such as the city's crown rabbi Moisei Aizenshtadt and its *dukhovnyi ravvin* (spiritual rabbi) David Katzenelenbogen; and Maksim Vinaver, Leontii Bramson, and Meir Kreinin, all of whom by this point were included in the leadership of every Jewish communal project based in the capital.

The effective abolition of the Pale of Settlement during the war alleviated Jewish overcrowding but also greatly complicated resettlement and the provision of relief, which led in turn to greatly expanded responsibilities for EKOPO.[56] The Russian government's mobilization of civilian society for the war effort and relief also provided EKOPO with operational freedom impossible for a Jewish organization before the war, and its activists intended to take full advantage of the opportunity. Like EKOPO, at the beginning of the war the Russian organizations limited their activities to providing medical assistance to the wounded and sick, before massively expanding their responsibilities into realms previously controlled by the government. In particular, the Union of Zemstvos took over distributing and regulating the food supply, and it did so with government acquiescence because the government itself was not able to do the job.[57] Furthermore, Russian liberals such as Petr Struve and Prince Lvov gained organizational experience at the head of these organizations. They worked throughout the war to preserve formal separation from the government and *zemstvo* autonomy, even at the cost of failing to coordinate with the government to improve Russia's food supply.[58] As Lvov's power increased, he even went so far as to describe *zemstvo* activities as "state" (*gosudarstvo*) activities.

Like its Armenian, Lithuanian, and Latvian counterparts, EKOPO became a centralized national committee—in essence a governing agency that worked parallel to the Russian state. Zemgor's success in organizing relief and its assumption of responsibilities ordinarily held by the Russian government led to a rapid expansion of Russian civil society, and EKOPO's role echoed Zemgor's in catalyzing (not

creating) Jewish civil society. EKOPO came into being out of necessity, but it quickly began to use its budget and activists to manage other
Jewish communal organizations and to create something approaching
a national autonomous institution. Because of how funds were received
and disbursed, the organization remained centralized in Petrograd, but
activists throughout Russia created local EKOPO committees that, for
the most part, worked completely separately from those of Zemgor.[59]
EKOPO established 142 local Jewish committees and employed agents
in 160 other locales. Its agents included rabbis, attorneys, druggists,
dentists, doctors, medical dispensers, and engineers.[60] Yet, according to
EKOPO, non-Jewish rural and urban organizations assisted the Jewish
aid committees "only in very rare instances."[61] Through their actions
both Zemgor and the government also encouraged the creation of a
separate and centralized Jewish war relief organization. Immediately
following the first government grant to EKOPO, the Ministry of the
Interior's Department of Police sent out a circular instructing gover-
nors throughout the empire not to distribute funds and food to Jewish refugees but rather to refer all Jews to the Petrograd Committee of
EKOPO.[62]

Wartime journals such as *Pomoshch* (Help) and *Vestnik trudovoi
pomoshchi sredi evreev* (Journal of Labor Assistance for Jews)—both
founded in Petrograd in December 1915—illustrate the enormity of the
refugee problem and its contribution to centralizing Jewish communal
leadership in Petrograd under EKOPO. *Pomoshch*, which was "dedicated to the questions of helping Jewish victims of war," included such
information as the number of evacuees relocated and where they were
moved to and when; a breakdown of what food was shipped where;
and what loans were made to which professionals in different locations.
It also contained a legal section that published the laws relating to refugees, a section on Jewish mercantile and professional rights, and, in
each issue, a list of individual donors to EKOPO. The different divisions of EKOPO published informative sections in *Pomoshch* and *Delo
pomoshchi* (Aid Affairs, which succeeded *Pomoshch* in June 1916) about
their activities, and correspondents on the ground reported the most
basic details of life in the centers where Jewish refugees were concentrated. *Pomoshch* also included limited reporting on how Jews on the

other side of the front were faring. *Pomoshch* functioned almost like a chronicle, and its contents constitute a narrative of Jewish life during the war: massive displacement, followed by efforts to rebuild a new society, with the intellectuals and activists in the center attempting to guide the process. As *Pomoshch* explained in its first issue, in addition to helping the refugees create new lives for themselves, the publication intended also to "put forward the *national-cultural* questions, the questions of the internal cultural and communal life of the refugees."[63] In fact, the journal's format put little emphasis on so-called national-cultural questions. Each issue consisted of a short editorial, followed by statistics and reporting. The second task laid out by the editors— "to inform the Jewish population about obtaining the different kinds of help from *government and civic institutions*, which requires considerable *practical guidance and advice*"—certainly took precedence over the first.[64] Although editorials explicitly linked work with refugees to communal reconstruction and Jewish national life, the vast volume of statistics the journal published, in showing both the extent of problems and EKOPO's role in the solutions, seems intended to prove the necessity and usefulness of EKOPO to all aspects of Jewish life.[65]

It is clear that the war provided both the necessary impetus and government compliance to create a centralized Jewish political structure responsible for the material, educational, and spiritual needs of not just the refugees but also much of the rest of Russian Jewry. All the prewar communal institutions—the Society for the Spread of Enlightenment Among the Jews of Russia (OPE), the Society for Handicraft and Agricultural Work Among the Jews of Russia (ORT), the Jewish Colonization Association (ICA), and the Society for the Protection of Health of the Jewish Population (OZE)—essentially became divisions of EKOPO through a series of conferences in 1915 and 1916 that delineated the specific responsibilities of each body. ORT concentrated on the creation of labor bureaus, OZE on medical work and orphaned children, and the OPE on education, and many of the responsibilities of the ICA were suspended or absorbed by the other divisions.[66] In addition to becoming the administrative parent of the other Jewish communal organizations, in August 1916 EKOPO established three levels of self-governance: the Assembly of Delegates, the Society Council,

Table 1 Number of Refugees Registered with EKOPO in November 1916, by Province (Guberniia or Oblast)

Province	Number	Province	Number
Akmola	554	Poltava	14,374
Arkhangelsk	29	Riazan	1,004
Astrakhan	2,591	Rostov-on-Don	1,500
Bessarabia	3,557	Samara	5,048
Chernigov	1,778	Samarkand Oblast	28
Ekaterinoslav	17,021	Saratov	9,173
Iaroslav	3,562	Semipalatinsk Oblast	33
Irkutsk	346	Simbirsk	1,287
Kaluga	414	Smolensk	842
Kazan	2,256	Stavropol	280
Kharkov	9,711	Tambov	8,121
Kherson	4,926	Tauride	10,146
Kiev	5,540	Tobolsk	25
Kostroma	770	Tomsk	825
Kursk	3,149	Tula	1,496
Livland	2,866	Tver	1,016
Minsk	30,018	Ufa	1,586
Mogilev	11,245	Viatka	468
Moscow	2,230	Vilna	4,139
Nizhnii Novgorod	12,670	Vitebsk	13,827
Novgorod	456	Vladimir	1,408
Odessa	6,250	Vologda	1,311
Orenburg	1,565	Volynia	14,594
Orel	3,835	Voronezh	5,943
Penza	5,233	Zabaikal	74
Perm	2,891		
Podolia	3,000	Total*	237,011

Source: *Delo pomoshchi* 12 (20 November 1916): 49–54.
*Calculates to 1,000 less than indicated in the source.

and the Central Committee. The new society's leadership structure was engineered to ensure a leading role for Petrograd (its rules required that twenty of the sixty-two members of the Assembly of Delegates be residents of Petrograd). Furthermore, fifteen of the sixty-two Central Committee members were from EKOPO's existing Petrograd Committee, and twenty of the thirty-five members of the Executive Committee were Central Committee members permanently residing in Petrograd.[67] One representative each from the OPE, ORT, OZE, ICA, and the Varshavskii Banking House, as well as the Jewish members of the Duma and the State Council (Gosudarstvennyi Sovet) and, seemingly as an afterthought, a representative of the refugees, would also participate in the Central Committee.[68] Perhaps most important for Jewish autonomy, those present at the August 1916 conference envisioned that the structure would remain intact in the postwar period, and they agreed on the principle of funding EKOPO's long-term operations by self-taxation of the Jewish population for expressly communal reasons—as the Central Committee put it, "recognizing the extraordinary importance of gradually strengthening the idea of self-taxation in Jewish civil life [*obshchestvennost'*]."[69] By any assessment, this conference created an important precedent for Jewish self-government and, in fact, marked the formation of a Jewish proto-government—or at the least a parastatal complex—in the capital.

Although not an elected national assembly, EKOPO nevertheless constituted a pan-Jewish political body that collected funds from the government and the Jewish population and dispensed it to departments with specific communal responsibilities—acting, in fact, just like a governmental ministry. The organization also attempted to set a precedent for taxing the Jewish population, even if on a voluntary basis, and urged all Russian Jews to become members. When the Jewish relief and communal committees formally merged in August 1916, they collectively took the important step of opening membership in the central organization to anyone willing to pay an annual fee of 3 rubles. Finally, EKOPO decided in 1916 that its difficult financial situation required it to become involved in organizing local *obshchiny* in order to have these self-governing institutions take over some of its responsibilities. The new urgency in solving the "*obshchina* question," as EKOPO saw it, stemmed directly from the refugees, who dramatically swelled the Jewish population of certain localities and had seen the destruction of their old communal life.[70] Thus, in advocating the "creation of *self-governing obshchiny*" to engage local Jewish populations to participate in communal institutions, EKOPO and its subsidiaries actively sought to promote a kind of self-generated de facto Jewish autonomism.[71]

Jewish communal activists in Petrograd and their representatives and agents in the field understood that self-help and self-government by Jewish civilians was about more than simply care; rather, it was about establishing Jewish rights for the postwar settlement. For that reason the same activists also devoted tremendous effort to documenting and archiving anti-Jewish violence during the war. This was done by collecting testimony from Jewish and non-Jewish soldiers, civilians, and refugees and also, where possible, acquiring official records of government and military edicts. The Jewish Political Bureau in Petrograd created an information bureau for exactly such a purpose, and Dubnov and associates spent late nights sorting through the material at Naftali Fridman's apartment.[72] Detailed directions were sent from the Information Bureau to EKOPO's agents in the field about whom to interview, how to conduct interviews (e.g., without applying one's own preconceptions and paying attention to the attitude of the interviewee), and what information to record on topics ranging from the details of anti-Jewish violence, to the response of the Jewish and non-Jewish population, to what factors might have contributed to the historical and immediate causes of anti-Jewish violence or mistreatment.[73] These interviewers were also instructed to record details about the situation on the ground in terms of the physical state of the given town and its Jewish community and to collect, where possible, materials related to Jewish patriotic support for the war, military service, and heroism.[74] As such, every EKOPO agent became a demographer, statistician, and historian and, in doing so, helped with the connected tasks of managing the immediate needs of the Jewish population, establishing Jewish self-government, and creating the historical record that was intended to ensure its preservation.

Polly Zavadivker has suggested that two key figures in particular, Dubnov and An-sky, saw their attempts to document and chronicle the atrocities as part of a conscious effort to create a particularly Jewish narrative of wartime experience.[75] An-sky, through his work as an agent in the field for EKOPO and in an office of the Unions of Towns and Zemstvos (despite the law against the latter employing Jews) traversed the front and shuttled between Moscow and Petrograd, doling out financial assistance, recording accounts of anti-Jewish violence, and salvaging Jewish ritual items and artifacts.[76] An-sky also published, along with the writers I. L. Peretz and Yankev Dinezon, an appeal in the Warsaw Yiddish daily *Haynt* (while Warsaw was still under Russian control and publishing in Yiddish was still possible) for every member of the Jewish public to understand the importance of the moment, to become a historian, and to collect material evidence and send it to the Jewish Historical-Ethnographic Society in Petrograd.[77] In his writings, especially those published in Yiddish after the war (based on his Russian diaries), An-sky tried to give meaning to Jewish suffering. Dubnov, on the other hand, was more concerned that the record of wartime violence and displacement be used in the argument for Jewish rights for the postwar period in a new Russia and independent Poland. Yet the very act of collecting, chronicling, and transcribing, as Zavadivker explains, represented a continuity with earlier efforts to defend Jews by documenting violence and set a precedent for later Jewish war writing (such as during World War II).[78] Above all, the task to collect and record—not only by An-sky and Dubnov but by all Jewish communal activists—was consistent with the ongoing project to use history as a pillar for Jewish national self-consciousness and as a premise for Jewish autonomy.

Jewish Relief and National Rights as International Issues

EKOPO collected funds from the Jewish population and was also subsidized by the Council of Ministers (specifically, the Ministry of Interior), the Special Conference on Refugees, and the Committee of Grand Duchess Tatiana. But one-third of its total income came from abroad.[79] Most important, EKOPO received extensive funding from the American Joint Distribution Committee, an organization founded specifically to provide assistance to Jews in the war zones. During the war, the Joint, as it has since become known, managed to channel a huge amount of money to the Petrograd Committee through the American Embassy in Petrograd, thanks to the assistance of U.S. ambassador David R. Francis, and became Russian Jewry's lifeline.[80] Francis raised the issue of the freedom of Jewish American citizens to travel in Russia immediately after taking his post and was rebuffed, a fact that probably encouraged him to go around the authorities in assisting Russian Jews.[81]

The American Joint Distribution Committee formed as a federation of American Jewish relief organizations established at the outbreak of the war by the (nonnationalist) American Jewish Committee, the Central Relief Committee created by Orthodox U.S. Jews, and the socialist Zionist People's Relief Committee. Although the last two organizations understood that by joining the federation, they were giving up some influence to an organization with a different worldview from their own, they considered the importance of Jewish unity in overseas relief and the possibility of guiding this relief to be worth the sacrifice.[82] Each wing of the Joint had a different public that could be asked for funds, and collectively the members of the Joint raised more than $16.5 million between 1915 and 1917—an enormous amount of money for the time—and $27.4 million in the two years immediately after the war.[83] The Joint also needed and attracted young professionals to raise money, develop plans, engage in advocacy and lobbying, and even send fieldworkers and specialists to Europe to assist in providing relief.[84] The Joint thereby represented a transformation in American Jewry parallel to that indicated by EKOPO in Russia; the U.S. organization rose to prominence as a secular agency uniting communal institutions and committed Jewish activists in a period of crisis.

The Joint's funding of EKOPO reflected a dramatic shift in priorities among the American Jewish public toward national rights for Jews around the world. The war and the need to advocate for the interests of European Jewry finally led to the creation of the American Jewish Congress, which had long been talked about as a possibility. Jewish nationalists and Zionists in the United States believed that it would be imperative during the war—and, even more important, in the peace talks that were sure to follow it—to properly use American Jewish economic and political clout. This effort to democratize American Jewish communal life by expanding public participation and communal leadership to a broader segment of the Jewish population was feared by many in the elite leadership of the American Jewish Committee, who resisted creating the American Jewish Congress because it would dilute their power. In part stemming from the broadening of public participation among the leaders of American Jewry, the differences of opinion that came to a head during the war in the American Jewish Congress centered on whether to define Jews as a nation, and if so, whether they were entitled to national rights in Europe, Palestine, and even the United States.[85]

The more nationalist American Jews fully understood that the ultimate mission of relief work was to attain national rights for Jews in Eastern Europe. In contrast, the nonnationalists could only try to moderate this aspect of Jewish relief work and attempt to prevent the Congress from making demands for Jewish national rights in the United States and Palestine. The best that the older generation of American Jewish communal leaders could do was to impose a semantic compromise on the mission of the American Jewish Congress: substituting the nationalists' use of the term *national rights* with the phrase *group rights* and replacing the word *nationalities* with *peoples*. The agreement to establish the American Jewish Congress, which was ratified at a preliminary conference in Philadelphia in 1916, called for Jews to have their collective rights recognized wherever such legal rights were possessed by other groups but denied to Jews.[86] The desire to create a unified American Jewish organization to aid in the relief of Russian Jewry extended back to the nineteenth century, but by 1915 the political consensus among American Jews, both liberal and socialist, had shifted toward a more clearly defined sense of Jewish nationalism.[87] Furthermore, this shift and the development of the American Jewish Congress movement were closely followed by Russian and Eastern European Jewry.[88]

In addition to funds from the United States, British contributions also made their way to EKOPO through the contacts of Aleksandr Gintsburg at the Conjoint Committee of the Board of Deputies of British Jews and the Anglo-Jewish Association (known commonly as the Conjoint).[89] Throughout the war years, the Conjoint collected copies of army telegrams and circulars (memos or bulletins) through its correspondents as well as transcripts of meetings between Russian Jewish leaders and government officials. In particular, through David Mowshowitch, the Conjoint's correspondent in Stockholm, British Jewry's leadership regularly received extensive reports on the Jewish situation in wartime Russia that they then used to guide the Conjoint's policies.[90] Initially the Conjoint trod carefully, both to appear loyal to Great Britain by not damaging relations with its Russian ally and to avoid appearing overly concerned with "denominational interests."[91] The members of the Conjoint felt constrained in their advocacy by their government's wartime alliance with Russia and even felt threatened by the freedom with which the American Jewish community could act because of their country's neutrality.[92] For example, when in January 1915 a group of prominent Russian Zionists that included Yekhiel Tchlenov and Nahum Sokolov appealed to the Conjoint's unofficial foreign secretary, Lucien Wolf (1857–1930), to take action on Russian Jewry's behalf, Wolf indicated that the Conjoint would take only an informational approach, emphasizing Russian Jewish loyalty and contribution to the war effort, in order to prevent damaging Anglo-Russian relations.[93]

Indeed, the British government was loath to press their ally on deportations that were framed as a military necessity and, at least in some cases, fully accepted the Russian government's justifications. In March 1915 the British ambassador to Petrograd reported back: "There cannot be the slightest doubt that a very large number of Jews have been in German pay and have acted as spies during the campaign in Poland."[94] In fact, Wolf attempted to intervene diplomatically with the Foreign Office, presenting documents to the foreign secretary, Sir Edward Grey, regarding anti-Jewish violence and the expulsion of Jews from the front, but he found no success. Grey consulted the British ambassador in Petrograd as well as "an experienced British military Officer recently attached to the Russian Armies" and passed on their assessment that such actions were "justified" and "natural" given "that the whole German spy system is said to have been carried out by Jews" and "in view of the pro-German attitude of the Jewish population."[95]

As the Conjoint received data pertaining to pogroms and the taking of Jewish hostages, its leaders became more willing to voice their concerns to the British government, as Wolf did, but, despite repeated negotiations, the Conjoint refused to cooperate with the Russian Zionist Organization, deeming their form of nationalism dangerous.[96] Rumors even circulated that the Conjoint was considering a secret campaign against, or possibly a formal denunciation of, Zionism.[97] Still, Wolf and the Conjoint were forced by events to recognize that in the new states of Eastern Europe, civil emancipation would not be enough to ensure Jewish safety and prosperity. In 1916 Wolf reluctantly became involved in the creation of an advocacy group initially called the Union for Jewish Rights, but when the new organization attempted to call itself the Jewish National Union, Wolf objected to this "exceedingly mischievous" implication of a separate Jewish nationality. He was willing to accept only a reference to "national rights" in the Union's program "if it is understood that by these rights is meant autonomy for Eastern Jewish communities in religious and educational matters. . . . In the great majority of cases we cannot well ask for greater privileges than are enjoyed by Jews of this country."[98] Soon thereafter, however, David Mowshowitch seems to have persuaded Wolf of the necessity for a more comprehensive and indeed national understanding of Jewish autonomy in Eastern Europe.[99] In fact as the war progressed and the dismemberment of the Russian Empire became more likely, the Conjoint became a vocal advocate of national rights for the Jews of Russia and its successor states, demanding guaranteed rights for the Jewish minority in any eventual postwar treaty.[100]

When Cyrus Adler (1863–1940), an orientalist scholar who was a prominent figure in American Jewish life, wrote to Wolf in 1915 for more information about how to represent the interests of European Jewry among Jewish organizations in the United States, Wolf wrote back addressing the diplomatic issues he believed should be addressed at a peace conference, whenever it should come, but dismissed what could be done politically while the war was being fought.[101] According to Wolf, "So far as the present situation is concerned, the task, though heavy, is not one of great complexity. It is essentially philanthropic, and resolves itself chiefly into the relief of the necessities of the Jewish victims of the war in Russia."[102] In contrast to Wolf's perception, however, providing the necessities of life to hundreds of thousands of uprooted people was anything but simple. As EKOPO's Central Committee reported to the American Joint Distribution Committee in March 1916, dire necessity had compelled it to completely set aside many of its initial goals, such as aiding the families of Jewish soldiers and helping the wounded, in order to organize new lives for refugees and all of those displaced or affected by the war: "expenditures too heavy for a philanthropic organization."[103] The EKOPO Central Committee hoped to convey to the Joint the magnitude of its relief activities and financial need. Yet it is clear that the activists and organizers in EKOPO also had greater ambitions. More than philanthropy, in fact, the organization sought societal transformation.

Democracy and Politics in Wartime Jewish Communal Affairs

During the war, funds were funneled from the United States and England directly to EKOPO, which then supplied the other Jewish communal organizations with the bulk of their operating budgets, with the result that EKOPO became a centralized umbrella organization.[104] All information flowed through Petrograd, with the Petrograd Committee coordinating the distribution of evacuees and their place of resettlement. EKOPO established local branches (at first illegally) and held conferences in Kiev and Vilna in addition to Petrograd, but the organization was nonetheless centrally controlled by the Petrograd Committee, thereby speeding the centralization of Russian Jewish political life in St. Petersburg that had begun in earnest in 1905 and would reach its peak in 1917. As the Joint recognized, EKOPO's Central Committee and the Petrograd Committee were one and the same, acting as a "unifying center" for all other local branches and in most cases serving as the only source of funds for those local committees.[105] As a result, the Petrograd Committee worked in the provinces almost entirely through its own agents. Various committees in Petrograd also ran each of the other Jewish communal organizations, now EKOPO's subdivisions. OZE's committee in Petrograd, for example, established 40 medical feeding divisions in 1915–16 with 140 doctors, doctors' assistants, and other employees providing medicine and food to 60,000 refugees.[106]

Although the Russian government, the American Joint Distribution Committee, and other international funders subsidized the Petrograd Committee, these funds were not nearly enough to meet the needs of Jewish refugees throughout the empire. To make up the difference, EKOPO instituted a voluntary self-taxation of the Jewish population, with contributions and taxation in Petrograd accounting for a disproportionate one-third of all revenue coming from Russian Jewry.[107] One of the EKOPO organizers' first tasks was to divide Petrograd into ten zones, each with a committee responsible for collecting monthly and irregular contributions.[108] The Petrograd Committee even devised a formula on which taxation was based: 5 percent of (self-assessed) individual income.[109] The Petrograd Committee's financial responsibilities only increased as the war dragged on, and the ability of its Russia-wide agents and organizations to raise money locally, where needed, decreased.[110] By July 1916 funds raised in Petrograd through various means came to two-thirds of all Russian individual contributions.[111]

According to the Petrograd Committee's own account, it became the entire organization's central committee and the epicenter of Jewish relief and aid activities because of the breadth of the committee's activities and its location in the country's administrative and political center.[112] Aleksandr Gintsburg, on the other hand, explained the centralization in a letter to the American Jewish Relief Committee as stemming also from the Petrograd Committee's high standing with the government and role as the conduit of funds.[113] While true, these facts obscure another key reason for the Petrograd Committee's role as the central governing body of a massive organization that delivered essential services to hundreds of thousands of Jews throughout the empire. From the Union for Full Rights, through the Kovno conference, and continuing with the founding of EKOPO, the initiative for such large pan-Russian-Jewish projects came from a small coterie of activists who after 1905 increasingly lived in the capital. These people—Vinaver, Bramson, Kreinin, and Sliozberg, to name a few—gained not only organizational skills through their activities but also credibility, at least in their own minds, as the representatives of Russian Jewry.

Whatever hopes the Russian government might have had about the temporary nature of Jewish wartime displacement, the military's role in transferring the property of Jews to others made it likely that Jewish emigration to different parts of Russia would be permanent.[114] This is certainly how Jewish relief workers saw the situation. Furthermore, the institutions of war relief explicitly linked the tragedy of the refugees to an opportunity to establish a new communal reality.[115] EKOPO's massive budget and the equally massive need created an army of professional relief workers.[116] Pointing to political figures such as Bramson, Boris and Iulii (Julius) Brutskus, and Iosif Bikerman, Steven Zipperstein suggests that individuals who had worked for years for institutional change achieved real leadership only during the war years, when radical societal transformation seemed inevitable.[117] Mikhail Beizer makes a similar observation: "Although at first glance EKOPO was another 'Baronskii' institution managed by the Gintsburgs and a narrow circle of Petrograd oligarchs, from the very beginning, the scale of the task facing it compelled the EKOPO Central Committee to cooperate with the general strata of the population and make use of their initiative and enthusiasm."[118] Such factors as voluntary taxation and the refugees' demands for a say in Jewish communal life also likely contributed to greater accountability in EKOPO.[119]

Yet, looking at the process of Jewish communal activism and organizing during the war, we can see as much evidence of continuity with prewar trends as of dramatic change. During the war the Jewish elite by no means relinquished control of such organizations. For example, although Bramson and Kreinin were joint secretaries of the Petrograd Committee, contacts with the government remained firmly in the hands of the elite; the lawyers Sliozberg and Sheftel' represented the Petrograd Committee on the Government Commission for Relief of Refugees, and Baron Gintsburg represented it on the Committee of Grand Duchess Tatiana.[120] Furthermore, as we have already seen, the Jewish communal organizations broadened their leadership before the war. Although there is no doubt that the war sped up the process of Jewish communal democratization, at least since 1905 and in some cases earlier, communal organizations previously run by the St. Petersburg financial elite had increasingly been challenged by younger professional activists to change their leadership and their focus. All the attendees at the Kovno conference in 1909 recognized the growing role of the intelligentsia in Jewish communal life and the need for greater democratization, by which they meant primarily expanding leadership roles outside the financial elite. One good example can be seen in how the Society for the Spread of Enlightenment (the OPE) shifted from an organization primarily devoted to helping Jewish students to pay for university education to what Brian Horowitz describes as "a vibrant institution committed to Jewish cultural renaissance."[121] Horowitz argues that although young activists and intellectuals, most notably Bramson, Kreinin, and Vinaver, helped to guide this shift, in fact the Gintsburgs and others continued to underwrite the organization and appeared devoted to change.[122] Horowitz goes so far as to describe the OPE, as it existed between 1893 and 1905, as "a rare instance of a kind of national parliament without political power, a training ground for democratic rule and political organization."[123] Whether or not the OPE was a paragon of democratization, it is a good example of how the wartime changes in Jewish communal leadership were largely a continuation of prewar trends, as the activities of a core of communal activists pulled power away from the financial elite while continuing to use their connections and capital.

Nowhere was the success of prewar democratizing efforts clearer than in the case of ORT, perhaps the most important organization under EKOPO during the war. The Society for Handicraft and Agricultural Work Among the Jews of Russia (known by its Russian acronym, ORT) was created in 1880 by Russia's great Jewish financiers. By the 1890s liberal activists were already attempting to change ORT's organizational framework and assume greater control of decision making and the distribution of funds. But they were unable to do so, not the least because connections between wealthy Jewish families and the authorities were essential to keeping ORT operational.[124] In the first twenty years of ORT's existence, 75 percent of regular contributions came from its members in St. Petersburg, but after the 1905 revolution the organization sought a larger membership to take on an expanded role in the organization's governance, and the organization's membership indeed rose significantly between 1907 and 1914.[125] Furthermore, in 1908–9 so-called progressives within the organization worked to shift its focus from small-scale philanthropic work to the creation of self-help

organizations, vocational training initiatives, and producer cooperatives, with an open dispute arising in 1909 over whether ORT's mission was to help individuals or groups.[126] The reformers were for the
most part successful in these disputes, winning a majority of seats on
the Executive Committee. Chief among them was Leontii Bramson,
who served as ORT's spokesman at the Kovno conference and was its
chief executive between 1911 and 1914.

Before the war ORT conducted social surveys, subsidized producer
cooperatives, opened local offices, and helped Jews settle in the interior
of the empire. Still, even though ORT assisted thousands of Jews in
the Pale of Settlement and beyond with training and credit for tools,
machinery, and materials, it had a great deal of difficulty opening local
branches, and only a small minority of Jewish artisans in 1914 were
aware of the organization.[127] The structural changes to the organization
initiated by Bramson and others, such as Boris Brutskus and Genrikh
Sliozberg, in the three years or so preceding the war, allowed ORT to
take on the massive responsibility of education and vocational training
for refugees during the war. In particular, the organization's purpose
shifted from helping Jews to integrate into the Russian economy to,
according to Gennady Estraikh, "building semi-autonomous pockets
of Jewish economy."[128] During the war, under the direction of Boris
Brutskus, Jacob Latskii-Bertoldi, and Jacob Lestchinskii, ORT collected
information on the status of Jewish refugees and attempted to create
a program that provided relief through work. The work involved pro-
ducing materials vital to the war effort in the hope of winning the support of the Russian government—a well-meaning but inevitably impossible task—and ORT refocused its efforts on the establishment of labor
bureaus to find gainful employment for refugees. EKOPO reported
that the need for food rations declined in 1916, as refugees found work
in their places of resettlement; this seems to indicate at least a degree
of effectiveness of ORT's programs, including the labor bureaus (altogether, ORT established forty-seven employment agencies and fifteen
reference bureaus in thirty-two towns).[129]

Similarly, much of the work done by the Jewish Colonization Association—the ICA—in the years immediately preceding the war helped
to lay the groundwork for its activities, and those of EKOPO, with

refugees during the war. Although the ICA was ostensibly committed to Jewish colonization anywhere and facilitated emigration and settlement in Canada, Argentina, and Palestine, a huge proportion of its efforts and budget went to improving Jewish life in the Russian Empire through funding activities unconnected to colonization or emigration. In fact, in the ICA's 1914 budget, prepared before the outbreak of war, the Russian chapter was the single largest recipient of funds, accounting for more than 20 percent of the organization's expenditures (and this figure did not include funding to aid emigration from there).[130] The ICA funded Jewish professional schools, trade schools, agricultural schools, women's professional schools, credit and cooperative societies, and almost anything else that would promote Jewish self-sufficiency in the Russian Empire. At the ICA's headquarters in Paris, meetings were regularly attended by the council members belonging to the Montefiore, Hirsch, Rothschild, and other wealthy families, and their activities were coordinated with those of the Gintsburgs in St. Petersburg. The St. Petersburg Central Committee of the ICA oversaw a huge funding enterprise and apparatus, and it redistributed funds from the ICA to other organizations controlled by the Gintsburgs, including the OPE as well as cooperative banks, professional schools, agricultural schools, and girls' schools.[131] Yet it seems that the ICA's central administration in Paris knew little of the changes in communal life in Russia that went on during the war. The Paris staff heard nothing from the ICA's Petrograd Central Committee for eighteen months over the course of 1916 and 1917, until the Russian committee responded to an inquiring telegram with a request for funding.[132]

There was always an underlying tension between the philanthropic aims of the *shtadlonim*—the grandees who represented Jews to governments, whether in Russia or abroad—and the political aims of Jewish *obshchestvennost'*. For the *shtadlonim* the purpose of philanthropy and Jewish self-help was fundamentally integrative: to make Jews more Russian and more modern. Although this integrative impulse existed with the Jewish communal activists as well, Dubnov's ideas about Jewish autonomy, national rights, and self-government fully penetrated the ethos of Jewish communal activism between 1905 and 1914, and the war presented the opportunity, some might say the necessity, to initiate a permanent change in Jewish society. In particular, Dubnov's idea that Russian Jews could not achieve genuine emancipation without legally recognized Jewish national rights and Jewish national institutions was strengthened by the circumstances of the war. Even though wide disagreement separated the political aims of various groups—liberals, socialists, Zionists (liberal and socialist), and autonomists—and even though they continued to disagree on, for instance, the proper language for Jewish education, the old elite seemed to grasp that their vision of Jewish integration was waning.[133] The war did not change the government's perspective that relations should be conducted through certain reliable Jewish individuals—if anything, it reinforced this opinion—and the Jewish financial elite was still needed for its connections to the wealthiest Jews in other countries. Nonetheless, during the course of the war the old elite lost whatever remaining ability it possessed to shape, moderate, or mediate the demands of the Jews. Aleksandr Gintsburg complained bitterly in a letter to Felix Warburg that the efforts of various activists to control EKOPO and the wartime persecution and suffering had brought about a "decided revival of separatism" conducive to the "national aims" of Yiddishists and Zionists.[134] Besides Gintsburg's deep hatred for "Yiddishists," he also stressed an even greater resistance to the politicization of Jewish communal life and, in fact, the politicization of Jewish life in general. Gintsburg told Warburg that his family and associates assiduously avoided all forms of politics and "are before everything else Russian citizens," and, astonishingly, he argued that "nobody has a right to compromise the tranquility of Jews by joining for purposes a political party of any kind."[135] At the root of Gintsburg's critique of Jewish politicization lies his belief in individual rather than collective rights. Of the radicals he opposed Gintsburg stated: "They are preparing a generation of *Yiddish atheists* instead of Judao[*sic*]-Russian citizens which they expect to conquer new rights in our autocratic Russia."[136]

When Gintsburg eventually stepped down from the Petrograd Committee after the February Revolution of 1917, he sent a letter to the Conjoint urging Anglo Jewry to stop funding EKOPO, because the money would be used to suppress religious practice.[137] David Mowshowitch's long internal memo prepared for the Conjoint in response openly mocked Gintsburg's claims. Despite Gintsburg's suggestion that EKOPO could not function without him, Mowshowitch sarcastically put forward the possibility that some work, at least, was done by the Committee's 58 other members with the 26 million rubles spent in 340 localities. To make his case for continued funding, Mowshowitch outlined the qualifications of a dozen other leading members of the Petrograd Committee, EKOPO's representatives in Moscow and Kiev, and the process for electing leadership in the provinces. He cataloged the creation of a secular national Jewish education system since 1914 (something Mowshowitch clearly favored over religious education), the expansion of communal welfare and medical work, and the "irresistible" democratization of Jewish communal governance. Mowshowitch argued pointedly that if Gintsburg was out of touch with the Jewish public before the war, the conflict had made him an anachronism, or worse, a reactionary.[138]

EKOPO had some successes and some failures in its war relief activities. Providing adequate clothing and housing for all the hundreds of thousands of refugees proved difficult, even impossible. Despite special medical expeditions organized by OZE, during which dozens of Jewish doctors, nurses, and dietitians ministered to thousands of refugees, sanitary and medical conditions among the Jewish refugees remained terrible.[139] The Jewish newspapers and journals were filled daily with stories of starving, freezing, and sick refugees searching for basic needs such as food and shelter. Still, considering the circumstances, EKOPO's response to the war was rapid and far-reaching.[140] What can be said, at the least, is that EKOPO oversaw the massive geographic and occupational transformation of a significant number of Russian Jews. As of November 1915, out of nearly 160,000 refugees almost 65,000 had been resettled in the internal provinces; as of September 1916, well over 200,000 refugees originating from nearly 1,900 locations had been resettled throughout what remained of the Russian Empire, and as of November 1916, at least 237,011 refugees were receiving help from EKOPO.[141] Furthermore, EKOPO and its subsidiaries kept careful track of refugee and evictee reemployment, beginning immediately with the onset of the crisis. Their collection of data relating to profession, gender, literacy, and dependents assisted the relief workers on the ground in finding work for the resettled refugees and hopefully in making the resettlement permanent. Throughout 1915 ORT and EKOPO managed to find employment for approximately 40 percent of those seeking it in more than thirty cities. In many cities the number was closer to 60 percent (and in Moscow nearly 90 percent).[142] In these data we can see the enormous geographic change in terms of where Jews came to live by the end of the war, especially moving from the northwestern, Baltic, and Polish provinces into a few key cities in the northwest, such as Gomel and Minsk, but mainly to the southern provinces, central Russia, the Volga region, and even the Urals, Siberia, and Central and East Asian provinces.[143] Finally, although the war and the enormous task of assisting Jewish refugees might have created an army of professional Jewish relief workers, on the whole what existed of the Jewish middle class fared the worst in the upheaval. Whereas uprooted Jewish clothing and leather workers, tradespeople, and unskilled laborers overwhelmingly found new employment in their professions, office and commercial workers, people in trade, and educated professionals did so in starkly lower numbers (at least initially).[144]

Perhaps most important, EKOPO's goal, as its organizers saw it, was for Jews to become responsible for themselves. The first necessity, as determined at the Vilna conference in January 1915, was "to supply a basis for *self-help* and *self-action*," two concepts much discussed in the previous ten years.[145] EKOPO became increasingly involved in organizing local communal governments to take on some of its responsibilities and urged the "creation of *self-governing* communities." It is worth recalling the unanimity reached at the Kovno conference regarding the vague outline of the future of Jewish self-government, as a "juridical person," with the right of compulsory taxation and the responsibility to care for both spiritual-cultural matters and the physical well-being of everyone born Jewish. Solving the question of communal reorganization was no doubt made more urgent by the needs of refugees, who dramatically swelled the Jewish population in certain localities and saw the destruction of their old communal life; however, we can also see how some saw an opportunity to bring into practice elements of self-government discussed at the Kovno conference and in the pages of *Evreiskii mir* and other prewar publications. One activist made exactly

Figure 6 Studio portrait taken at a conference held by EKOPO in the town of Melitopol for OPE educators working in schools for Jewish refugees, January 1916. Courtesy of the YIVO Institute for Jewish Research, New York.

this point: "Despite the severity of wartime conditions, in the midst of destruction we developed further as a society, and Jewish democracy was founded as an institution capable of stimulating our emerging initiatives, curing the sick atmosphere of the day, and showing the masses not just material, but also moral support."[146]

Conclusion

Despite Jewish war deaths, anti-Jewish violence, and the disastrous consequences to Jews who became refugees, the Jewish intelligentsia in St. Petersburg, who for a decade had been debating and planning the parameters of Jewish autonomy, were acutely conscious that the war and the progressive disintegration of the empire also provided an opportunity for Jewish societal reconstruction. The war was a moment for self-help, self-action, and self-government. No one knew how the conflict would end, but the possibility once again emerged that the regime could fall, and hence the Jews continued to imagine the moment of Jewish emancipation and what Jews should demand from the state in its wake. Although beyond the scope of this study, Austrian Jews in the imperial capital of Vienna also had to deal with a massive refugee crisis, and the challenge of organizing refugee relief there also politicized Jewish communal work, utilized funds from the American Joint Distribution Committee, and brought the question of Jewish autonomy and national rights in the east to the center of Jewish politics.[147] In fact, at the same time that EKOPO worked to establish a framework for Jewish autonomy among the Jews in Russian territory, the Jews who came under German and Austrian occupation used the comparative freedom to establish greater autonomy than they had ever had under Russian rule, especially in the realm of education.[148]

In explaining the evolution of Russian Jewish political life during World War I, this chapter has traced two separate but connected developments: in essence, how the war affected Jews and how they responded. The first development relates to how the Jews were treated by the state, the military, and even political allies during the war. In sum, Jews were suspect at best and enemies at worst, and they suffered violence, robbery, and physical displacement when their protection was put outside the bounds of the law. For many Jewish civilians, whatever patriotism they might have felt at the beginning of the war was short-lived, and in any event few had much faith in the military or the tsar's bureaucracy to begin with (Jewish soldiers, on the other hand, overwhelmingly remained patriotic throughout the war). In contrast to Jews' expectations of the tsar and army, Jews did expect to be defended by Russian liberals, and the impact of Duma politics on the Jewish masses, though difficult to measure, was considerable. As censorship increased during the war, the government came to prevent all publishing in the Hebrew alphabet (suspecting that it was being used to pass information to the enemy), which resulted in the closure of the Yiddish and Hebrew presses. Nonetheless, the Russian-language Jewish press covered the debates of the Duma and the circulars affair extensively.

Throughout the empire the general population was acutely aware of the Duma's wartime deliberations because of the heightened desire for information under difficult circumstances, a desire met by pamphleteering, touring Duma members, and information spread by word of mouth. Influential Jewish liberals such as Maksim Vinaver may have ultimately remained with the Kadets, but the importance of Jewish intellectual disillusionment with Russia's only liberal party—a party that supposedly represented *obshchestvennost'*, progress, and the liberation movement—should not be underestimated, as it pushed many influential Jews to become increasingly sympathetic to the aims of the Jewish national movement. Most significant, Russian Jews became increasingly convinced that their future lay with parties advocating Jewish self-government and national rights rather than Jewish emancipation as individuals.

The second development—how Jews responded to the crisis—relates to autonomism, organization, and ultimately power. In the midst of violent chaos, a generally liberal Jewish leadership in Petrograd mobilized a massive relief effort. Out of necessity these leaders extended EKOPO's activities beyond mere philanthropy, but EKOPO's leaders—in many cases the same people who participated in the Kovno conference—did not waste the opportunity to establish a Russia-wide, Jewish, self-governing body with far-reaching responsibilities, firmly anchored in the capital. In general, massive civilian displacements during the war and interethnic relations in the cities populated by refugees served to bolster group identity among minorities, and Jews were no exception.[149] For such Russian Jewish liberals as Sliozberg, who earlier favored Jewish community work but feared the separatism it promoted, the war made such concerns moot. Not only did the Russian government see little room for integration at this time, but it also willingly labeled the Jews traitors.

These two developments merge in any analysis of the remaining gap between the *obshchestvo* (the Jewish political elite, intellectuals, and communal activists) and the bulk of the Jewish population. EKOPO was not quite a project in national democratization; its purpose was not to stir national consciousness. Nonetheless, one of its stated goals was to prepare Jews both to help and to govern themselves. Furthermore, its leaders clearly felt the need to bridge the gap between themselves and the masses. And Jewish intellectuals grappled directly with the issue of their separation from the Jewish masses at this critical juncture. Discussion about the unknown future, and the role of the Jewish intelligentsia in it, did not subside during the conflict. For example, in a lecture to the Jewish Historical-Ethnographic Society in February 1915, Dubnov once again spoke about the issue of the Jewish national question in Poland and Russia, both historically and in the present. Dubnov repeated his political and historical theory of the need to create a synthesis between the medieval period's national autonomy without any individual rights and the Western model of emancipation entailing the sacrifice of all national rights for civil emancipation. In the debate about Dubnov's lecture that followed, Vinaver took up the issue of the Polish Jewish leadership's nineteenth-century assimilation. According to him, the Polish Jewish intelligentsia's denial of Jewish peoplehood in the nineteenth century left Polish Jewry leaderless in the twentieth century. Vinaver (who was born in Warsaw) argued that Polish Jewish intellectuals' continued denial of Jewish nationality was "inconsistent with history and ethnography" and resulted in an "intelligentsia unnaturally torn from the masses."[150] Apparently Vinaver, Russia's leading Jewish Kadet, had come to employ the anti-assimilationist rhetoric previously used by nationalists to describe him and his colleagues. Although Vinaver believed that a constitutional state in Russia could emancipate Russian Jewry and preserve its national and spiritual culture, it remained unclear to him "which form the national-cultural self-determination of the Jewish people would take."[151]

 The Jewish Autonomist Movement
and the Revolutions of 1917

Between February 23 and 27, 1917, workers' demonstrations in Petro-grad and the mutiny by the military units responsible for suppressing the disorder led to the breakdown of governmental authority in the capital. When Nicholas II dissolved the Duma on February 27, the Rus-sian Empire appeared to be without any government at all, immediately leading to a battle among various political groups to fill the vacuum.[1] On March 2 Nicholas II abdicated and refused to allow his son to take his place as tsar. The throne then passed to Nicholas's brother Michael, who was willing to take up the position only if asked to do so by an elected constituent assembly. By that point, two competing seats of authority had been established in Petrograd: the reformist liberal Tem-porary Committee of the State Duma and the socialist Petrograd Soviet of Workers' and Soldiers' Deputies. Because the Duma committee (later reconstituted as the Provisional Government) could not main-tain legitimacy without the support of the revolutionary parties and the general population, it was forced to seek legitimacy from the Petrograd Soviet. Nonetheless, socialist support for a liberal or bourgeois gov-ernment proved qualified and ephemeral, especially among the mass of workers, peasants, soldiers, and members of national minority groups. Between the February Revolution and the Bolshevik seizure of power in October, the Provisional Government and the Soviets (along with political parties and groups) competed, debated, and clashed violently over the social and political form of the new state.[2] Meanwhile, the war raged on, and the need to settle key social and organizational questions only became more acute. In the midst of this anarchy most national minorities in the empire pressed their demands for greater autonomy, and Jews were no exception.

The euphoria among Russian Jews after the tsar's overthrow was matched by an equal concern about their future in the successor state or states. Semyon An-sky, who was in war-ravaged Galicia at the time, first heard of the tsar's abdication from an army doctor, who shouted "Mazel tov! Mazel tov!" But An-sky noted terror among Jews about what might come next.[3] Like other minorities, the Jews immediately sought to establish national institutions independent of the government that would be responsible for protecting, representing, and even governing their own people.[4] Even though an obstacle to Jewish equality had been removed, nothing guaranteed that the tsarist regime would be replaced by a government any more sympathetic to Jewish aspirations, both civil and national.

As the Russian Empire disintegrated during World War I, the Jews, like the empire's other national minorities, asserted their claim to autonomous national rights. The fact that most of Russia's Jews lived among other national groups vying for territorial independence or autonomy within a federal state bolstered the determination of Jewish autonomists to secure similar rights for Jews. Although during the war EKOPO was transformed into something resembling a proto-government, 1917 presented the first opportunity to fully implement Jewish autonomy in Russia. Taking advantage of new political freedoms, a multiparty Jewish national council was established to convoke an all-Russian Jewish congress that would be responsible for determining the specifics of Jewish national demands and the form of Jewish autonomy in Russia. At the same time, Jewish communal activists founded local self-governing bodies—*kehilot* or *obshchiny*—throughout Russia and Ukraine, with the Petrograd Jewish community taking the lead in defining the responsibilities of Jewish self-government at the local level.

As fractured as Jewish political leadership was during these anarchic years, the one common aspiration of all Jewish political parties was autonomy, in one form or another, in the new state. The February Revolution wiped clean the slate of Russian social and political life, and, like every other group, the Jews were divided about what model of government should replace the autocratic regime. This chapter examines the institutional and political construction of Jewish autonomy in Russia between the February and October Revolutions of 1917 and assesses the significance of the dramatic changes in Russian society to the political views of the broader Jewish public. A constitutional or a revolutionary state, socialism or liberalism, individual civil rights versus national self-determination—all of these were questions that turned organizing for the All-Russian Jewish Congress, the general elections to the All-Russian Constituent Assembly, and the local Jewish self-governments into battlegrounds between conflicting ideological visions of the future. Along the way the historical processes that led to the eventual failure of Jewish autonomy in revolutionary Russia reflected broader ideological conflicts in Russia's transition to a new order.

Autonomy Realized

With restrictions lifted against organizing politically, Jews focused their political energies on creating the mechanisms of Jewish national autonomy that had been discussed in theory in the Jewish press since Simon Dubnov's articulation of autonomism between 1897 and 1907. During that time, a near total consensus developed among Jewish parties in favor of some form of autonomous arrangement for Russian Jewry. When opportunities for political action were greatly reduced after 1907, the Jewish parties debated with great intensity how Jewish autonomism could be implemented in the future and, in the meantime, sought to create the secular Jewish cultural, educational, and philanthropic institutions intended to eventually form the core of Jewish autonomy in Russia. In the midst of war Jewish activists created a vast, centralized communal organization that would not only provide necessary relief to Jewish refugees but also create the institutional framework for Russia-wide Jewish autonomy. When the Provisional Government proclaimed formal Jewish emancipation in March 1917, it conferred freedom of the press and freedom of political association in addition to the right for Jews to live where they desired, precipitating widespread Jewish political mobilization, with dozens of newspapers and political organizations opening (or reopening).

Immediately following the February Revolution, Jewish political parties began organizing their own congresses to clarify their platforms ahead of the campaign for the All-Russian Constituent Assembly, the representative body that was to replace the Provisional Government, draft a new constitution, and create a new state structure. An intraparty Jewish political council established formal contacts among the Jewish parties and began to plan the path to a Jewish national assembly. Parallel to the general Russian process, a national assembly was the ultimate goal, but it would be convened only after the All-Russian Jewish Congress determined the framework of Jewish autonomous self-government. The demand for a Jewish congress or national assembly dated to the organization of the Union for Full Rights, and the question of whether to demand some form of Jewish parliament from the Russian government had persisted throughout most of the Union's existence—splitting apart nationalists and nonnationalists—and subsequently became a major demand of the Russian Zionists, socialist Zionists, Sejmists, and Dubnov's folkists. Once again, Jewish activists and intellectuals revived the idea of a Jewish national assembly or congress. On this occasion, however, the Jewish parties and their representatives believed that they would be able to meet unhampered by government authorities. Their goals were to determine the basis for Jewish self-government and, perhaps most important, to present a united Jewish front in dealing with the future All-Russian Constituent Assembly.

The movement for Jewish autonomy was galvanized by the fact that the social democratic (primarily Menshevik) parties of the various national minorities met throughout 1917 to press for territorial autonomy, and the Socialist Revolutionary Party began to lean toward federalism again. At their first congress in 1906, the Socialist Revolutionaries declared the "unconditional right" of national self-determination, but as they came closer to taking power, they moved further away from embracing that ideal.[5] During and after the February Revolution, minority affiliates of the Socialist Revolutionary Party, especially the Jewish Sejmists, pushed the party (despite the resistance of its Russian membership) toward favoring extraterritorial autonomy as a means of keeping the economically important western regions within a future republic.[6] By mid-1917 the Socialist Revolutionaries had more or less agreed on a decentralized federation that would remain a single state.[7] The Kadet Party, while continuing to defend "Russia, One and Indivisible" and fighting to halt the territorial disintegration of the empire, considered the possibility of nonterritorial autonomy for all the former empire's minorities a more acceptable alternative to territorial fractionalization.[8] It is clear, however, that the question of federalism versus centralization became a major issue that divided the Petrograd Soviet from the Provisional Government. As a telling portent of the future, the Bolsheviks, though firmly in favor of territorial self-determination, continued—as part of their rivalry with the Bund—to adamantly oppose any form of nonterritorial autonomy.[9]

The Folkspartey Reborn

It is no coincidence that Jewish political parties in 1917 centered their autonomist demands on Dubnovian concepts such as an all-Russian Jewish congress and local *kehilot* or *obshchiny*. In Petrograd especially, Dubnov's followers and intellectual descendants were instrumental in pressing other parties to cooperate in the creation of these autonomist institutions. By 1917 a large number of Jewish intellectuals accepted the basic tenets of the Folkspartey's original 1906 platform, including the demand for a comprehensive autonomous arrangement for Russian Jewry, and the Folkspartey reorganized, consolidating a number of Jewish autonomist groups into a single party. Immediately after the February Revolution, several diaspora-nationalist Jewish political organizations were established in Petrograd and Moscow (as the Jewish Democratic Union) and in Odessa (as the Jewish National Democratic Party). These independent folkist-oriented organizations formed the new Folkspartey in 1917 by officially consecrating themselves as wings of a larger Folkspartey and recruiting individuals from other parties to join the new party leadership. Through this process the Folkspartey came to resemble an autonomist umbrella group. The party had not become the large, united nationalist group that Dubnov consistently hoped for, but the folkists had won over some of their greatest skeptics. And in its commitment to national rights, its mix of liberalism and moderate socialism, and its formation as an umbrella group, the new Folkspartey in some ways resembled the Union for Full Rights of 1905–7. In absorbing a number of prominent socialists and former socialists, the new folkist coalition was more inclined to socialism than the original Folkspartey, but the attainment of Jewish national autonomy continued to be its highest priority.

The leadership of the Folkspartey sought Dubnov's participation as a figurehead who could unite the new party's disparate groups and lend his stature to the party's leadership. Dubnov wavered on whether or not to participate actively in politics in 1917, but it is clear that by that point his ideology had taken on a life of its own and that the Folkspartey would be reorganized with or without his help. On an almost daily basis, Dubnov threw himself into politics, only to pull himself out once again. He vociferously criticized the many Jewish parties for failing to unite while leaving the Folkspartey each time its new leadership compromised any of his principles. As early as April 1917, Dubnov, Yisroel Efroikin, and Aron Perel'man had begun planning to transform their diaspora-nationalist association, the National Group, into a new Folkspartey. Yet An-sky, A. V. Zalkind, and a few others left the group over "linguistic" differences, as the battles of the Jewish language war continued. In contrast to 1911, An-sky no longer pleaded with Dubnov to use Yiddish but rather criticized other folkists for taking Yiddishism too far at the expense of Hebrew. Dubnov accused An-sky and Zalkind of going the way of the Zionists for arguing that the Folkspartey should include in its platform an article on the primacy of the Hebrew language, especially because the party's plans for cultural autonomy already included a commitment to Yiddish as the language of public life for Russian Jewry.[10] For An-sky, however, the pull to participate in the general political struggle with the Socialist Revolutionary Party—a party he had helped found—probably far outweighed the push of the language issue in the Folkspartey.[11]

By May 1917 all energy for political activities had left Dubnov. He seems to have been weary of the political wrangling, and he was also stubbornly unwilling to compromise ideologically.[12] The secretary of the Petrograd branch of the Folkspartey, Yudel Mark, wrote several letters to Dubnov pleading with him to come to meetings, in particular to help plan a national council meant to organize a Jewish congress and eventually a national assembly, and to represent the folkists in negotiations with the Bund and Zionists over the composition of this council.[13] Dubnov was also invited to Moscow for the organizational conference of the Jewish Democratic Union, which took place from June 24 to July 4, 1917, but Dubnov repeatedly rebuffed these requests.[14] Despite his absence, the Democratic Union that emerged from this conference proved close to Dubnov ideologically, discussing such issues as the reinstitution of the *kehila*, the creation of the Jewish congress, work in Jewish schools, and of course the economic health and well-being of Jews in the empire (with no direct references to socialism).[15] Although Meir Kreinin had successfully forged a compromise between the leftist diaspora-nationalist Jewish Democratic Union and the new Folkspartey, Dubnov refused to lend his support to a joint program when it was finally established. He later wrote: "I didn't join with them as a program of compromises I cannot tolerate. I will remain alone in my ideology and will develop it in literature like [I did] during the era of the 'Letters on Judaism.'"[16]

The new Folkspartey's organizational committee met in Petrograd in August, with representatives from that city, Kharkov, Moscow, and Vitebsk.[17] In that same month, the Moscow-based Jewish Democratic Union also decided to adopt the program of the Folkspartey, and it appeared the new folkist party was beginning to take on a truly national character. Once the various folkist and national-democratic groups had united into a nationally organized Folkspartey, the new united party's leaders, Kreinin and Perel'man, visited Dubnov to try to convince him to become politically active again, in particular, to help organize for the All-Russian Constituent Assembly. Dubnov agreed to participate, though according to him, he intended to do so only nominally: "I explained to them that I had decided to abandon all political activity but that my conscience commanded me to accept normal entry to the committee; in essence, a refusal on my part would have cast a shadow over the objectives of the renovated party."[18] Although Dubnov's obstinacy eventually subsided and he returned to the party, the incident reflected the fact that his insistence on ideological purity was a continued obstacle to a large, pro-autonomist Jewish organization. It also demonstrated that the Folkspartey could be organized without its ideological mentor.

Nearly every Jewish publication and political party now demanded some form of national rights for the Jews, and although the folkists could to some extent claim to be the pioneers of the autonomist movement, they still needed to forge a new, coherent platform that distinguished them from the other parties. The Petrograd branch of the Jewish Democratic Union considered itself the left wing of the Folkspartey, because the Union was made up primarily of former labor Zionists and actively advocated socialism in Russia.[19] Its leaders included the St. Petersburg folkists who had founded *Di yidishe velt*, including Yisroel Efroikin and Nokhem Shtif; members of the Vozrozhdenie group, such as Jacob (Ze'ev Wolf) Latskii-Bertoldi (1881–1940); and Max Laserson (1887–1951), who was deputy director of national minorities in the Interior Ministry of Alexander Kerenskii's government (Kerenskii, a member of the Trudoviks, was the Provisional Government's second prime minister).[20] Having begun as a separate entity, the Union published its own platform, stating that the guiding principle of its organization was "defending the beginnings of democracy, socialism, and self-determination of nationalities in political and economic areas and international relations."[21] Despite the nod to socialism in its introduction, the Union's platform was primarily concerned with Jewish national autonomy and self-government and did not diverge appreciably from the original platform of the Folkspartey in 1906. Reflecting the political realities of 1917, the new platform also called for the "decentralization" of all of Russia and the devolution of powers through regional and national autonomy and local self-government.[22]

In Odessa the Jewish National Democratic Party became the centrist wing of the Folkspartey and took on organizational responsibility for the party's activities in all of southern Russia. Eschewing socialist objectives and placing primary importance on building Jewish cultural institutions, the Odessa branch came closest to Dubnov's own autonomist vision.[23] Dubinskii and Latskii-Bertoldi also established a Kiev branch of the Folkspartey, naming it the Jewish Democratic People's Party.

When Dubnov and Kreinin founded the Folkspartey in December 1906, they divided its platform into two parts: general Russian demands, which closely followed the positions of the Kadet Party; and specifically Jewish demands for nonterritorial autonomy. Thus the Folkspartey at that time appealed essentially to liberal Jews of diaspora-nationalist sentiment. Dubnov, for his part, adamantly opposed all forms of class struggle, though he was not against improving conditions for the masses. In contrast, in 1917 the basic strategy of the Folkspartey was to appeal to all Jews who felt unrepresented by other Jewish parties—which, in the folkists' opinion, was the vast majority of the Jewish public. Unlike the original founders such as Kreinin and V. S. Mandel', many leaders of the new Folkspartey joined it because of disillusionment with party politics, whether socialist, Zionist, or liberal. Because the larger umbrella party had been established by a number of smaller diaspora-nationalist organizations, local affiliates were given discretion to craft their own platforms and make alliances with candidates who ran as independents. In addition, because many of the new leaders came from socialist movements, folkism in 1917 became more concerned with the welfare of Jewish working people. Even so, folkists across the board considered the socialist parties obsessed with the small Jewish proletariat at the expense of the vast majority of working Jews, who were employed as artisans and petty merchants. The Folkspartey thus welcomed local groups of artisans to form nonparty committees that could be added to the party's list of candidates in elections.[24] The party also took up Dubnov's argument that the Bund and the proletarian socialist Zionists in Poalei Zion were working against Russian Jewry's economic interests, whereas the Folkspartey promised to protect "artisans, working intellectuals, petty tradesmen and all toiling Jews!" In the opinion of its leaders, this "party of the people" would "care for the needs of the common people."[25]

Perhaps most important, in its efforts to reach out to all Jews, the Folkspartey promoted its ideology as one of Jewish democracy. The folkists claimed: "Hand-in-hand with democrats of other peoples, we will protect the rights of the Jewish people and the economic and spiritual interests of all of its social strata."[26] Although arguably this commitment to the "democracy of the common people" was rooted in an attempt to distinguish the folkists from the Zionist and socialist parties that also advocated autonomism and to appeal to the majority of the

Jewish population still unaffiliated with any party, the idea of Jewish national democracy had appeared in liberal nationalist circles much earlier. The folkists' attempt to depict themselves as true democrats and to appeal to all Jews is evident in the names of the party wings (which all included "Democratic" in their titles) and in their slogans, such as "The Yidishe Folkspartey is a party for the common Jews, for the majority of the folk."[27] Not unlike *Evreiskii mir*, folkist literature scorned "assimilationists" for not understanding "Jewish democracy." As one poster stated (in Russian), "They [assimilationists] are incomprehensible, alien, and in essence hostile to the new aspiration for Jewish democracy."[28] In contrast, the Folkspartey stated: "We call on the Jewish intelligentsia, we call upon its energy in the struggle for new Jewish culture, for democratic Jewish community, for free national life."[29] While casting itself as the party of Jewish democracy, the Folkspartey also, with no sense of contradiction, perceived and presented itself as the party of the intelligentsia. In fact, the belief that the intelligentsia was responsible for developing the institutional framework for Jewish popular representation—the masses' understanding of democracy—was perhaps the most important tenet uniting the ideologically diverse folkist leaders.

Despite the absorption of socialist organizations into the Folkspartey, the umbrella party continued to disavow class warfare and claimed to protect the economic interests of all Jews. Especially in the provinces and small towns, the Folkspartey attempted to set itself apart from the Bund, whose members traditionally viewed with disdain the petty merchants and artisans who made up the majority of Jews in Eastern Europe. The Folkspartey confidently asserted that it was "the party of the Jewish working masses," representing the interests of "ALL Jewish workers: laborers, petty artisans, petty merchants, farmers, and intellectual workers."[30] Outside Petrograd this strategy appears to have met with some success. On a party membership list for the city of Poltava, a major center for Jewish refugees, approximately one-third of the members listed their profession as *torgovets*, meaning merchant or tradesman.[31] The balance of the membership was composed of students, hairdressers, tailors, office workers, and accountants—all common Jewish professions that stood to suffer economically under the Bund's (or the Bolsheviks') proletarian socialism.[32]

Perhaps the most graphic example of the Folkspartey's attempt to reach out to the common people and create an impression of Jewish democracy can be seen in a full-color election poster (discussed in the Introduction) for the All-Russian Jewish Congress. The poster was created by Shlomo (Solomon) Iudovin, An-sky's nephew and photographer on his ethnographic expeditions, and Iudovin seems quite clearly to have borrowed from his expedition photographs to create the graphic image in the poster. The huddled group surrounding a Folkspartey poster in an evidently small town is all that is necessary to convey the message that the party represents Jewish solidarity and communal autonomy, despite its limited presence in small towns. On the one hand, the message here stands in marked contrast to the posters and literature the party addressed, in Russian rather than Yiddish, "To the Jewish Intelligentsia."[33] But, on the other hand, not unlike An-sky's ethnographic work, the Folkspartey offered more of an opportunity for the intellectuals to reconnect to the folk, rather than to mass politics for the folk themselves. Unsurprisingly, this seems particularly to be the case with the Petrograd branch, which stated its aims in self-consciously more cerebral language than slogans of "Jewish democracy" or claims to represent "the people." For the elections to the Petrograd Jewish *obshchina*, for example, the six "special tasks of the Petrograd community," according to the Folkspartey, were entirely academic and cultural: to create an academy of higher Jewish knowledge, a library of literature and science, a Jewish museum, a Jewish theater and music institute, the collection of Jewish historical materials, and stipends for Jewish artists.[34]

Composed of both socialists and liberals, the Folkspartey of 1917 tried to establish itself as the ultimate builder of bridges between classes and parties. Its message, whether to small-town artisans or Petrograd intellectuals, stressed that Jewish parties at a time of crisis should not expend their energies on class conflict or partisanship but rather should build coalitions and construct the basis for Jewish autonomy. Furthermore, some folkists seemed concerned with controlling the revolutionary impulses of the masses, arguing that, at least for now, a bourgeois democracy was the best protector of the Jews' interests and would help foster the necessary democratic culture.[35] In October 1917 the folkists

Figure 7 "Vote for list 4." Folkspartey electoral poster for the All-Russian Jewish Congress, designed by Shlomo Iudovin. Courtesy of the YIVO Institute for Jewish Research, New York.

Figure 8 Photograph of the Shepetovka town square, with synagogue on the left, by Shlomo Iudovin. Courtesy of the Interdepartmental Center, "Petersburg Judaica," at the European University, St. Petersburg.

in Petrograd founded a newspaper devoted to discussing and promoting Jewish autonomism and the platform of the Folkspartey. *Dos yidishe folksblat* was edited by Nokhem Shtif, with Yisroel Efroikin and Shmuel Niger as two of its primary contributors.[36] In *Dos yidishe folksblat*, as in *Evreiskii mir* and *Di yidishe velt*, folkists debated the ideal structure of Jewish autonomy, the *kehila*, and the All-Russian Jewish Congress.[37] The new folkist publication perhaps best exemplified the party's democratic populism, as Shtif focused his and other articles on the topic of Jewish democracy. In particular, Shtif argued that the folkists should reach out to Orthodox Jews because that group was totally ignored by the proletarian parties and because the *kehilot* in the villages were in any event already operating as religious communities by providing education, funding to yeshivas, hospitals, and care for the elderly. In sum, according to Shtif, the religious *kehilot* performed mitzvot (commandments or, in this context, good deeds), "the principle of *yiddishkeit!*"

Shtif argued that by demanding a secular *obshchina* only, the proletarian parties were ignoring 90 percent of Russian Jewry and thereby negating the purpose of Jewish self-government.[38]

Although "Jewish democracy" became the slogan of the Folkspartey, Jewish *obshchestvennost'* remained its overriding mission. Efroikin spoke of the "construction of Jewish national life" and phrased the Folkspartey's central demand from the Provisional Government as "a legal basis for the creation everywhere of a democratic Jewish community [*obshchina*] granting it the right of forced taxation of its members to satisfy the national needs of the Jewish population."[39] Furthermore, the Folkspartey considered the reconstitution of the *obshchina* on a democratic basis as the best means of achieving both autonomist and democratic objectives and argued adamantly for the full democratization of Jewish communal life, starting in Petrograd.[40] As the party stated, "The *obshchina* is after all the cornerstone of our national autonomy, the guarantor of our future freedom of national life. Only by means of the democratic *obshchiny* can we transform from human dust and uncoordinated elements into an organic, whole, national collective."[41]

Even before the February Revolution, the lack of a proper Jewish communal self-government in the imperial capital appeared to Jewish activists to be incongruous with the city's role at the center of Jewish politics and communal work. Until that time the *obshchina* was made up of only the dues-paying membership of the city's main prayer house, the Choral Synagogue.[42] In 1916 only 780 out of 50,000 Jews in Petrograd were dues-paying full members in the *obshchina*,[43] and ballot lists for its general assembly in October 1916 and lists of candidates for active membership from the same year show that virtually none of the city's Jewish political activists were *obshchina* members at this time.[44] The high cost of dues restricted the *obshchina*'s membership to the capital's Jewish elite, and the fact that the *obshchina* drew much, if not most, of its budget from large private donations ensured that its leadership was composed of the city's (and, to a certain extent, thereby also the empire's) wealthiest Jews.[45] Although the prerevolutionary Petrograd *obshchina* possessed no official responsibilities outside of organizing Jewish religious affairs in the city, unofficially it acted as an organ of *shtadlanut* (intercession) advocating on behalf of all Russian Jewry.

Still, because its narrowly defined responsibilities prevented the *obshchina* from becoming involved in important communal activities, such as education and health, the Jewish communal organizations based in the capital (such as ORT, EKOPO, the OPE, and OZE) existed as completely separate entities from the *obshchina*. Before the war the secular Jewish political activists and intelligentsia shunned the religious-based *obshchina*. During the war, however, the necessity of coordinating financial assistance with the *obshchina* forced these activists, many of whom had taken over the running of the communal organizations, to cooperate with the *obshchina*, and they consequently increased the pressure to democratize Jewish communal government in the capital. Meir Kreinin was particularly concerned with reducing the sway of the OPE's Central Committee within the *obshchina* so that it did not outweigh the influence of the other communal organizations.[46] In 1916 Kreinin even led a group of democratizing autonomists who attempted unsuccessfully to have the fees lowered in order to broaden membership in the official Jewish community, but the initiative was blocked by the government (probably because the government saw no benefit from empowering a broader segment of the Jewish population in the capital).[47]

After the February Revolution Jews could organize their communal self-government however they liked, and the Petrograd Committee of the Folkspartey claimed that the new Petrograd *obshchina* would be charged with representing all of Russian Jewry and would be responsible for establishing new "national-cultural institutes" in the capital.[48] According to the folkists, the flood of new Jewish residents in the capital after the February Revolution made the city's Jews more representative of the professional makeup of Russian Jewry as a whole and would invigorate life in the city. However, the influx also made the need to democratize and reconstitute the *obshchina* all the more urgent.[49] Over the course of 1917, all the Jewish political parties came to view the democratization of the Petrograd *obshchina* as a prototype for Jewish autonomy at the local level. Though all purported to want the *obshchina* democratized, the fact that Jewish political activists of national stature sought to lead it suggests that they also accepted its role as Russian Jewry's preeminent intercessor with the government.[50] Following Petrograd's example, similar organs were established throughout Russia and Ukraine in 1917, but it is clear that the council in the capital, where most Jewish communal activists and leaders lived, represented itself as the voice of Russian Jewry until the expected creation of the All-Russian Jewish Congress.[51]

The circumstances in 1917 may have been different, but the essence of folkism had remained unchanged since 1906. To those associated with the autonomist movement and the new folkist and national democratic parties, the only way to ensure national democracy and thereby popular democracy was still through the institution of complete legal autonomy at the local and national level. Like Russian *obshchestvennost'*, these Jewish intellectuals clearly saw a special role for the intelligentsia—themselves—in bringing about their particular form of decentralization, self-government, and popular democracy. The composition of the Folkspartey leadership in 1917 reflected the fact that liberal and socialist autonomists had managed to bridge their differences at a crucial moment. In addition to socialists, the Folkspartey drew into its ranks a number of Jewish liberals who were unhappy with the Zionists, Kadets, and the Folksgruppe. For example, Oskar Osipovich Gruzenberg (1866–1940), one of Russia's most prominent Jewish lawyers, left the Kadet Party and became a leading figure in the new Folkspartey. Gruzenberg was invited by the party's Odessa branch (the Jewish National Democratic Party) to run as the Folkspartey's candidate either in the first position on the electoral list of a Jewish bloc with the Zionists or, failing that outcome, independently for the Folkspartey.[52] Gruzenberg rose to prominence in the Jewish world by defending first David Blondes of Vilna and then Mendel Beilis of Kiev against charges of obtaining Christian blood for ritual purposes and ritual murder, respectively (Gruzenberg also defended Gorky, Trotsky, Pavel Miliukov, and Vladimir Korolenko, among many others).[53] But Gruzenberg was an acculturated liberal and a Kadet of Vinaver and Sliozberg's ilk—he defended the signatories of the Vyborg Appeal and also ran and lost as a Kadet in the elections to the Second Duma—whose participation in Jewish communal affairs was limited to providing legal services before he suddenly joined the Folkspartey in 1917.[54] Gruzenberg's motivations for joining the Folkspartey and for his jump into communal politics are unknown, as are the reasons for his shift to Jewish nationalism, though his closest friend suggested that Gruzenberg had long been sympathetic to Zionism and was influenced by Lev Pinsker's *Autoemancipation*.[55] Whatever Gruzenberg's intentions, his joining the Folkspartey exemplified the steady move toward nationalism by the stalwarts of Jewish liberalism.

Leontii Bramson, the prominent Trudovik leader, lawyer, and OPE activist, also merged his Jewish Democratic Group with the Folkspartey over the course of 1917 and joined the folkist leadership.[56] The party's leaders also included other prominent lawyers, such as Jacob Teitel (1851–1939) and V. S. Mandel', one of the founders of the original Folkspartey and the president of the Jewish Folk Music Society. Historians (perhaps unsurprisingly) also flocked to the party, including Samuel Lozinskii (1874–1945), a historian and contributor to the *Evreiskaia entsiklopediia* who stayed in the Soviet Union and took over the editorship of *Evreiskaia starina*.[57] Literary figures were perhaps the most prominent members of the new Folkspartey. In addition to Shtif and Niger, Yisroel Tsinberg—editor of the Yiddish and Hebrew literature sections for the *Evreiskaia entsiklopediia*, one of the founders of *Di yidishe velt*, and the author of a comprehensive history of Yiddish literature—also ran for election on the party's slate. The Folkspartey fielded such varied candidates as the economists Kh. G. Korobkov and P. M. Klinchin and the philosopher Esther Eliasheva Gurliand.[58] Thus the Folkspartey was a collaborative enterprise between intellectuals involved in the cultural projects of 1907–14, such as the *Evreiskaia entsiklopediia*, *Evreiskii mir*, and *Di yidishe velt*, and the communal activists who led the Jewish communal organizations (Niger, Tsinberg, Efroikin, Perel'man, and others were involved in both); it was very clearly the party of Jewish *obshchestvennost'*. Not until 1917 did the Folkspartey become anything resembling a party in the conventional sense, with a central committee, conventions, and local party affiliates. With some notable exceptions, such as in Odessa, the Folkspartey failed to attract truly broad support among the Jewish masses. Yet popularity mattered less to the folkists than the creation of autonomist institutions such as local *obshchiny* and the All-Russian Jewish Congress. Through them Jewish democracy could be established, even if the Folkspartey did not become a mass movement.

„ИДИШЕ ФОЛКСПАРТЕЙ".

КЪ ЕВРЕЙСКОЙ ИНТЕЛЛИГЕНЦІИ.

Подъ гнетомъ царскаго режима, въ условіяхъ тяжкаго политическаго рабства, русское еврейство проявило удивительную духовную мощь—оно выработало основы гордаго свободнаго національнаго сознанія. Оно изжило ассимиляціонную идеологію, отвергло формы общественной жизни евреевъ въ Западной Европѣ и, находясь еще въ гетто, лишенное элементарныхъ человѣческихъ правъ, оно опредѣлило свои національныя требованія и стремилось къ автономіи, какъ къ необходимому условію для его нормальной, культурной, творческой жизни.

И вотъ нынѣ сбывается мечта поколѣній. Мы приступаемъ къ осуществленію нашихъ національныхъ чаяній.

Въ томъ самомъ Петроградѣ, гдѣ всего только годъ тому назадъ царское правительство отказало намъ въ пониженіи годового взноса въ общину съ 25 рублей до 3, мы организуемъ нашу новую общину на основѣ самой демократической избирательной системы. А община вѣдь краеугольный камень нашей національной автономіи, залогъ нашей будущей свободной національной жизни. Лишь при помощи демократической общины мы сможемъ изъ людской пыли, изъ разрозненныхъ элементовъ превратиться въ органическое цѣлое, въ національный коллективъ.

Десятками лѣтъ нуждъ и исканій передовая еврейская интеллигенція выработала основы своего національнаго міросозерцанія. Сознавъ себя органической частью нашего народа, почувствовавъ себя наслѣдницей и преемницей—нашего величественнаго прошлаго, передовая еврейская интеллигенція осознала и свою великую отвѣтственность передъ настоящимъ и будущимъ нашего народа. Она поняла что для жизни въ свободѣ, для полноты національнаго существованія требуется созданіе новыхъ формъ національной культуры и творчества, новыхъ національныхъ и вмѣстѣ съ тѣмъ еврейскихъ формъ нашей народной жизни.

Наше поколѣніе призвано заложить на фундаментѣ историческаго прошлаго основы этой новой жизни, въ исторіи еврейства суждено намъ дѣйственно начать новую эпоху.

Мы знаемъ, намъ предстоитъ еще тяжелая борьба.

Большія массы народа, крѣпко связанныя съ прошлымъ, не видятъ, не сознаютъ еще нашего будущаго; питомцы традиціонной культуры гетто, имъ дорогъ старый укладъ жизни, и имъ непонятна еще тоска передовыхъ слоевъ еврейства по новой свѣтской еврейской культурѣ.

Мы знаемъ также, что живы еще умѣлявшіе остатки нѣкогда гордой ассимиляціонной рати. Неуклюже и громко, какъ всѣ поверхностные неофиты, они въ послѣдніе годы не переставая пѣли національную „аллилуйю", отрекались торжественно отъ идей ассимиляціи. Но эти люди опаснѣе открытыхъ ассимиляторовъ. Духовно опустошенные, оторванные и отчужденные отъ еврейской жизни и еврейскаго прошлаго—они на все согласны, они готовы выступить подъ любымъ лозунгомъ, принять любой девизъ, потому что имъ ничто не дорого, имъ все одинаково чуждо.

Имъ непонятны, чужды и по существу враждебны новыя стремленія еврейской демократіи.

Еврейской интеллигенціи, національной и демократической, не замыкающейся въ тѣсныя классовыя границы, предстоитъ потому, большая борьба необходимо напрячь всѣ усилія.

Мы зовемъ еврейскую интеллигенцію, мы призываемъ ее къ энергичной борьбѣ за новую еврейскую культуру, за демократическую еврейскую общину, за свободную національную жизнь.

Въ предстоящихъ 29-го октября выборахъ въ петроградскую еврейскую общину мы ждемъ сочувствія, поддержки и активнаго содѣйствія петроградской еврейской интеллигенціи. Мы надѣемся, что она будетъ вѣрна знамени національной еврейской демократіи, которая призываетъ широкія народныя еврейскія массы и еврейскую интеллигенцію къ строительству свободной творческой, національной жизни.

Евреи интеллигенты! Помните о еврейской общинѣ, агитируйте и голосуйте за списокъ № 4, списокъ „Идише Фолкспартей".

Наши кандидаты.

1) С. Г. Дубновъ.
2) О. О. Грузенбергъ.
3) М. Н. Крейнинъ.
4) Л. М. Брамсонъ.
5) И. Р. Ефройкинъ.
6) г-жа М. Л. Бэръ.
7) Ш. Нигеръ.
8) В. С. Мандель.
9) С. Л. Цинбергъ.
10) Н. І. Штифъ.
(Баль-димйонъ).
11) А. Ф. Перельманъ.
12) И. Б. Штейнъ.
13) Я. Л. Тейтель.
14) В. М. Пумпянская.

15) С. Г. Лозинскій.
16) І. С. Черниховъ (Даніэли).
17) М. І. Гинзбургъ.
18) Я. Л. Пумпянскій.
19) П. М. Клячникъ.
20) И. И. Басевичъ.
21) Х. Г. Коробковъ.
22) М. Д. Сандомирскій.
23) г-жа С. Л. Шабадъ.
(изъ Вильны).
24) Г. С. Александровъ.
25) Э. З. Ельяшева-Гурлянда.
26) В. Н. Сольцъ.
27) З. Н. Бруннъ.
28) д-ръ А. Д. Корольникъ.

29) Б. Л. Гуревичъ.
30) Г. Я. Красный.
31) г-жа Т. І. Лурье.
32) М. І. Золотаревскій.
33) Я. М. Мерсонъ.
34) Н. Н. Ламъ.
35) д-ръ Г. С. Ландау.
36) г-жа Д. И. Зильберфарбъ-Штифъ.
37) Е. Р. Керкисъ.
38) Я. И. Зеликманъ.
39) Х.-И. Н. Гинзбургъ.
40) В. И. Лацкій (Бертольди).

Екатерининская типографія. Петроградъ. Звенигородская ул., с. д. № 30.

Figure 9 "To the Jewish Intelligentsia." Folkspartey electoral list and platform for the Petrograd obshchina. Courtesy of the YIVO Institute for Jewish Research, New York.

In the days following the February Revolution, as Boris Kolonitskii points out, "Democratization was seen as a universal means to solve any kind of problem."[59] Kolonitskii argues that democracy was understood in different ways by different parties, and the socialists tended to interpret it as mass participation in politics rather than as representative government. For the folkists Jewish democracy meant both. The democratization of the *obshchina/kehila* and other structures of Jewish self-government held the potential to engage the masses in the political process; equally, it could lead to a particularly Jewish form of representative government. In addition, the Folkspartey added its own Jewish autonomist corollary to the rhetoric of democratization: defense against assimilation. Despite the changed composition of the party, the folkists continued to equate national freedom with a rejection of assimilation, an idea developed in Dubnov's letters, on the pages of *Evreiskii mir*, and elsewhere. The purpose of autonomism had long been to reconstruct Jewish communal life in preparation for the moment of complete and final Jewish emancipation. Having finally arrived at that moment, or at least its possibility, the folkists desperately sought to reconstruct the Jewish community to avoid what they believed were the mistakes of Western European Jews during their process of emancipation. Thus, as the logical product of the earlier theoretical debates and cultural work and in an obvious nod to its mentor, the Folkspartey expressed the importance of rejecting assimilation at this historical moment and the expectation that the Jews would soon receive their long-sought national rights in Russia.

> Under the yoke of the tsarist regime, under conditions of severe political slavery, Russian Jewry developed remarkable spiritual power—it built the foundation of a proud and free national consciousness. It rid itself of assimilationist ideology, rejecting the form of communal life in Western Europe and finding another in the ghetto. Lacking elementary human rights, it formed its national demands and strove for autonomy, and for the necessary conditions for its normal, cultural, creative life.
>
> And now the dream of a generation is being realized. We are setting out to fulfill our national hopes.[60]

A Congress for All the Jews of Russia

Support for an all-Russian Jewish congress, the first step toward a Jewish national assembly, appears to have been a key ingredient linking all of those who joined together to form the new Folkspartey in 1917. Meetings of the organizational committee for the congress, covered in the newspaper *Evreiskaia nedelia*, were dominated by old folkists, such as Kreinin and Mandel', and by those who joined the party later, including Shtif, Niger, and Latskii-Bertoldi. Furthermore, Kreinin was president of the national council charged with planning a preliminary conference (which in turn would plan the final congress). These individuals saw an all-Russian Jewish congress as the ultimate expression of Jewish autonomy in Russia and as an important vehicle for the establishment of autonomous organs of Jewish self-government. Although both the Bund and the Zionists saw positive aspects resulting from establishing Jewish autonomy in Russia, these parties saw both the All-Russian Jewish Congress and Jewish autonomy itself as a means to an end. Therefore all three groups sought to co-opt not just the congress but also its very purpose: to spread socialism, to reinforce Russian Jewry's commitment to a homeland in Palestine, or to create viable institutions of Jewish autonomy so that the Jews could remain in Eastern Europe.

In March and April of 1917`, representatives of all the Jewish political parties, groups, and communal organizations convened in Petrograd for the purpose of organizing the All-Russian Jewish Congress. Initially, the Jewish communal and cultural organizations played as significant a role as the political parties in the Congress's organization. The organizers included representatives of the major Jewish cultural societies established in the previous ten years, such as the Jewish Literary Society (also called the I. L. Peretz Society), the Jewish Historical-Ethnographic Society, and the Jewish Folk Music Society, as well as representatives of the Jewish communal organizations such as ORT, OZE, EKOPO, and the Jewish Emigration Society.[61] In fact, twice as many cultural and communal organizations as political parties took part in planning the All-Russian Jewish Congress. The folkists, liberal autonomists, and moderate socialist autonomists had been working since the 1905 revolution to build an institutional framework for Jewish autonomy in Russia, and the All-Russian Jewish Congress was a natural extension of this communal work. Even though disputes between the Zionists and the Bund dominated later proceedings, at these early meetings the two parties sent just one representative each (Moshe Rafes [1883–1942] for the Bund and Yitshak Grinbaum for the Zionists), whereas the Folkspartey, the Jewish Democratic Union, and the Jewish Democratic Group (which had not yet merged at this point) together had six representatives, and Maksim Vinaver and Sliozberg's Folksgruppe had a further two representatives. Most of the representatives from the communal institutions were also members of either the Folksgruppe or the soon to be amalgamated Folkspartey. The Jewish socialist parties, not unlike the Russian socialist parties, had trouble deciding whether their involvement in bourgeois politics would advance or detract from their revolutionary agendas. The Bund, the United Jewish Socialist Workers' Party (known as the Fareynikte), and Poalei Zion all abandoned the initial negotiations over convening a preliminary conference and eventual congress, but these parties eventually decided that they had more to lose by not participating.[62]

The process of convening the All-Russian Jewish Congress, let alone implementing its goals, proved complicated, and, rather than narrowing differences between Jewish political parties, it exposed the deep fissures separating them. During the summer of 1917, the various Jewish parties held conventions to formulate their platforms and met together in an intraparty national committee to determine the makeup of the Congress and the process of holding elections to it. At their respective conventions and in their resulting platforms, all the major Jewish parties voiced support for some form of Jewish autonomy. The Bund continued to demand national and cultural autonomy, with an emphasis on education in the Jewish vernacular, whereas the Zionists, socialist Zionists, folkists, and a newly formed traditional religious Jewish political league envisioned a more comprehensive form of Jewish self-government. Believing that they had Jewish public opinion behind them, the Zionists planned to place Palestine at center stage in any future Jewish congress or national assembly in Russia and argued that Jewish claims to Palestine must be articulated at whatever representative body of Russian Jewry was established.[63]

Central though Palestine may have been in the Russian Zionist plat-form, debates among Russian Zionists in 1917 actually revolved far more around Jewish national rights in Russia than around Palestine. To win elections, the Zionists would have to present settlement in Pales-tine as a long-term aspiration (supported through fundraising among Russian Jewry) and Jewish national autonomy in the Russian Republic as an immediate and nonnegotiable demand. At the Seventh Congress of Russian Zionists, held in May 1917, the Helsingfors Program was confirmed as the basis for Jewish national autonomy in Russia, and *Gegenwartsarbeit*, or work in the present, returned to the fore.[64] In a continuation of earlier debates the Congress divided over the respon-sibilities of Jewish communal self-government, with one of Russian Zionism's leading figures, Yitshak Grinbaum, backing a purely secular *obshchina* but opposed by a significant group of delegates.[65] Nonethe-less, the debates over Jewish communal self-government at the Seventh Congress showed that the Russian Zionists had not merely pragmati-cally adopted autonomism; rather, Jewish autonomy in Russia had become as important (and certainly more pressing) to Russian Zion-ists as Jewish autonomy in Palestine. As *Evreiskaia zhizn'* put it, "equal rights and Palestine" (presumably in that order) would be the Zionist slogan for 1917.[66]

The prospects for unity through the All-Russian Jewish Congress might have seemed promising, but disputes between the two largest Jewish parties, the Bund and the Zionists, nearly sank the whole proj-ect of creating an autonomous representative body for Russian Jews. The Bundists, who had previously rejected the idea of a Jewish national assembly, agreed to participate in the All-Russian Jewish Congress, but they accepted the Congress only as a nonbinding advisory body, claiming that all decisions about national autonomy must ultimately lie with the All-Russian Constituent Assembly. Whereas folkists strug-gled to outline the responsibilities of the All-Russian Jewish Congress, Bundists and Zionists squabbled over the question of Palestine and its role in the future of Russian Jewry. Kreinin had to shuttle between the various parties—not just the Zionists and the Bundists but also Poa-lei Zion and smaller labor Zionist parties—in order to reach a consen-sus on how to organize the All-Russian Jewish Congress and even the preliminary conference charged with establishing the electoral rules and agenda for it.[67] During the summer, while Dubnov regularly threatened to leave politics forever, he nonetheless weighed in on the debate over the form of the All-Russian Jewish Congress, primarily blaming the Bund and the Zionists for their inability or unwillingness to cooperate with one another. Dubnov considered the problem of interparty fighting to be worsened by the fact that the parties, in his view, did not really represent the majority of Russian Jewry. He proposed instead what he considered a more democratic structure, that about three-fourths of the delegates to the All-Russian Jewish Congress be elected from non-party groups, or at least that they not be from the so-called intellectual parties.[68]

By June a group composed of the three Jewish members of the Fourth Duma, twenty-six representatives from various Jewish parties and organizations, and an executive committee primarily made up of members of the Folkspartey devised a formula for elections to a preliminary conference, whereby all cities with more than 50,000 Jews would select four delegates from Jewish parties and communal organizations, excluding the Bund and the Fareynikte.[69] Those two socialist parties were granted the right to send one delegate independently from each city where they had more than 300 members.[70] Despite reaching out to the provinces, the preliminary conference effectively disenfranchised nonsocialists from cities and towns with fewer than 50,000 Jewish residents, but it did so in order to convene the conference quickly (in less than a month). What is truly remarkable is that those charged with planning the preliminary conference managed to find a reasonable compromise allowing for representation for the socialist parties, who had little to do with the existing Jewish communal framework.

The proceedings of the Congress's preliminary conference, which began on July 18, 1917, suggest that the folkists and communal activists who put the project in motion were more committed to establishing the cooperative institutions of Jewish autonomy than were other groups, which preferred to use those institutions to conduct ideological battles in the public sphere. Kreinin made the opening speech, in which he expressed his hope that the conference would lay the foundation for the accomplishment of what he called "our national ideal, our national autonomy."[71] Kreinin claimed that the conference represented the majority of Jewish political groups and parties and hence the majority of the Jewish people, and he insisted that the program be broad in order to find a sympathetic response on the Jewish street.[72] Relations between the Zionists, the Bund, and the liberals led by Sliozberg were nonetheless acrimonious and threatened to derail the entire project of creating the All-Russian Jewish Congress. It is clear that all three had different perceptions of what the Jewish public really wanted, and the fact that Kreinin eventually moderated a compromise, again, was no small achievement.

Kreinin established four goals for the eventual All-Russian Jewish Congress that were subsequently accepted by the delegates to the preliminary conference: (1) to elaborate the principles and framework of Jewish autonomy and national self-government in Russia; (2) to specify the guarantees for the Jewish national minority to be demanded from the government; (3) to determine how the Jewish communities should be formed during the transition period; and (4) to discuss Jewish rights in other countries.[73] The four aims of the All-Russian Jewish Congress were relayed to Russian Jews in newspaper reports and in bulletins "to all of the Jews of Russia," along with the explanation that "the Congress must formulate its conception of national rights, the realization of which the Jewish nation will demand from the All-Russian Constituent Assembly."[74] The Congress's organizational committee stressed that the very purpose of the All-Russian Jewish Congress would be to establish Jewish autonomy on a firm legal footing: "The Congress must outline the legal norms which will regulate Jewish life in Russia and the organizational forms which are necessary for our national existence."[75] This last point was the final step in an incremental and cumulative movement for the legal recognition of Jewish national rights and an articulation of the specific legal parameters of Jewish autonomy.

The Bund resisted the Zionists' attempts to introduce the question of Jewish rights outside Russia, but the preliminary conference agreed to allow the All-Russian Jewish Congress to discuss the question of guaranteed autonomy for the Jewish minority in independent Poland, Palestine, and Romania as well.[76] Like any good compromise, this one did not entirely satisfy anyone. Palestine would be on the agenda, but it would be discussed only within the general context of Jews outside Russia. The fact that the Bund, which opposed discussing Jews outside Russia at all, agreed to this compromise must be considered a sign that it recognized the growing strength of the Zionists.[77] In the end, all the major parties ran slates in the All-Russian Jewish Congress elections, including the Fareynikte, the Orthodox Agudat Yisrael, the Folkspartey (in some places in a union with nonparty candidates), the Bund, the Zionists, and Poalei Zion, as well as the Folksgruppe in some districts.[78]

Once the structure of the Congress had been organized, a new and important role in the elections was played by Agudat Yisrael, known popularly in Russia as Akhdus.[79] Agudat Yisrael was founded in 1912 as an international organization for the preservation of Orthodox Judaism. On earlier occasions, Orthodox groups sought to co-opt Jewish politicization in order to protect traditional Judaism. Beginning in 1907, Russian and Polish rabbis, such as the Vilna Rabbi Khaim Ozer Grodzinski (1863–1940), argued for the necessity of an organized Orthodox public, not just individual rabbis, to promote and defend the interests of Orthodox Jewry.[80] Grodzinski created the Russian Empire's first Orthodox political organization, Knesset Yisrael, as an Orthodox answer to liberal Jewish politics, and though it failed, Knesset Yisrael served as a forerunner to the later Akhdus.[81] In some cases Orthodox Jewish politics involved battling against religious reformers. In other cases, as with the Orthodox Zionists, known as Mizrahim, a political movement with secular origins attempted to serve a religious purpose. Akhdus was a political party, but one that defied the need for a coherent platform. Its only goal was embodied in its slogan: "To solve all the problems of our time in accordance with the spirit of the Torah and tradition."[82] Although the amorphous nature of Akhdus limited its political efficacy, 1917 marked an important point in Orthodox Jewry's incorporation into the Jewish political world.

The elections to the All-Russian Jewish Congress took place in November 1917, in the immediate wake of the Bolshevik seizure of power, and the Zionists won an outright majority of the available seats, polling well above any other party.[83] The Bolsheviks, and in particular the party's central Jewish Commissariat (known as Evkom), were perfectly clear that they would not allow such a hostile congress to convene, and therefore the organizers had no choice but to postpone its convocation, first from December to January and then indefinitely. The All-Russian Jewish Congress was in fact Evkom's first target in its attack on autonomist Jewish communal institutions.[84] As a stopgap measure, the leaders of the different Jewish parties established the National Provisional Jewish Council, using the results of the elections as a basis for distributing votes.[85] But the results of the voting had already convinced the new Bolshevik government to seek alternatives to a hostile, Zionist-dominated Jewish congress, such as the All-Russian Congress of Jewish Soviets and the establishment of Jewish sections within the Communist Party.[86] The Bolsheviks underscored their intentions regarding any possible nonsocialist Jewish congress when they arrested Kreinin in April 1918 on charges of "aiding the bourgeoisie in its struggle against the Soviets."[87]

Even if the All-Russian Jewish Congress never convened, the results of the elections for it make it possible to compare the opinions of the voters with those of the Jewish parties. To begin with, low voter turnout, especially in the larger cities, indicated the disaffection or simply lack of interest in the internecine bickering of the Jewish leaders. The elections for a Jewish representative body whose sole purpose was to debate highly theoretical demands at a time when the political future of Russia was still uncertain did not succeed in bringing even a majority of Jewish voters to the polls. Mordechai Altshuler calculates that in Moscow less than 13 percent of eligible voters took part, whereas in both Petrograd and Odessa approximately one-third participated.[88] It appears that Dubnov was correct when he stated during negotiations about organizing the preliminary conference that most of Russia's Jews did not believe that any of the parties represented them.[89] The folkists tried to exploit this situation by welcoming nonparty candidates to their list, and there was even an unsuccessful attempt by a small group of folkists and independents to establish the nonparty Jewish People's Union (Evreiskii Narodnyi Soiuz), which would focus on Jewish self-government and provide a home for "all Jews without a place in different parties, groups and classes to join together."[90] But it seems that unaffiliated Jews were not as engaged in the project of Jewish self-government as the folkists might have hoped.

The leaders of Jewish *obshchestvennost'* who had dominated Jewish communal politics since the 1905 revolution were most responsible for the attempt to create the All-Russian Jewish Congress, yet they clearly failed to translate their leadership into anything resembling an electoral victory. Had the Congress actually met, it may not have mattered much because 40 of its 485 seats were reserved for members of the central committees of major Jewish organizations, thereby guaranteeing at least a continued presence for the leaders of Jewish *obshchestvennost'*.[91] Still, despite the fact that many of the activists in the Folksgruppe and the Folkspartey had wrested control of Jewish communal institutions from the traditional St. Petersburg financial elite, such as the Gintsburg family, ironically these activists failed to move from elite to popular politics, evident in the fact that both parties did not even run candidates in many districts.[92] Even though the Folkspartey and the Folksgruppe presented themselves, respectively, as the party and group "of the people," both failed to reach out considerably beyond their core intellectual constituencies.

The failure to adapt to electoral politics also stemmed from generational differences. The young guard of the 1890s and 1900s had become the old guard of 1917, and at that time universal truths proved more attractive than eclectic ideologies. As Jonathan Frankel observes, after 1917 there were two ideologies, Zionism and Communism—in effect, Jerusalem and Moscow—which "were in direct competition for the allegiance of the Jewish youth in Eastern Europe."[93] Even so, when we look at the general Jewish population in 1917 and how they voted in Russian elections, the story is one of a progressive and multifaceted transition in Jewish popular opinion rather than a sharp radicalization. Most important, as we will see, the declining appeal of Russian liberalism resulted in a significant political realignment among the majority of the Jewish population, a shift from support for Russian liberalism of a generally Jewish nationalist type to a Jewish nationalism of a generally liberal type.

Russian Liberalism and Jewish Public Opinion

It is only because of the 1905 revolution and the birth of electoral politics in Russia that Dubnov's vision of nonterritorial autonomy for

Russian Jewry moved out of the realm of political theory and became a concrete demand for Jewish national rights accepted by every major Jewish political party in Russia. The elections to the First Duma launched the Jewish autonomist movement as a consensus developed across Jewish party lines that their lack of territory should not be an obstacle to the Jews' obtaining the same national rights as the empire's other national minorities. The subsequent election campaign, for the Second Duma, forced each of the Jewish parties to clarify its vision of nonterritorial Jewish autonomy. In 1917 the autonomist movement was once again galvanized by revolution and also by Jewish participation in Russian elections. As in 1905, when given the chance, Jews sought to secure national rights by means of the ballot. Even though Jews had been granted civil equality in March 1917, the belief persisted that an improvement in civil status alone would not safeguard the collective legal rights of Russian Jewry. Once again the question of Jewish national rights became an issue absorbing the entire Jewish political world, this time even more urgently, because the former empire was in the process of dissolving into nation-states.

After the February Revolution the Provisional Government and the Petrograd Soviet were able to coexist for a while because of an agreement that all decisions relating to the political and social organization of the new state would be left until after the convocation of the All-Russian Constituent Assembly. This agreement created a framework that allowed the caretaker government to function on a day-to-day basis if it agreed to put off all important decisions until the convening of the new popularly elected body.[94] The desire for a popularly elected assembly to resolve Russia's problems long predated the February Revolution, but with the founding of the Provisional Government, the convocation of such an assembly became necessary for the establishment of a new legitimate state structure to replace the autocracy.[95] The Bolsheviks even justified their seizure of power in October 1917 on the basis that only they could ensure a fair and swift election to the Constituent Assembly. Although the agreement to leave all social, economic, and state structural questions to the future Constituent Assembly achieved an uneasy truce among the revolutionary, reformist, and even conservative parties, this deferment also tied the hands of the Provisional Government to such a degree that the Bolsheviks later argued against establishing yet one more ineffective chamber.[96] Whether or not the assembly might have effectively resolved the many problems that were postponed pending its convocation and thus set Russia along a constitutional, democratic, and, given the electoral results, moderately socialist path, will forever remain unclear. But because the voting took place (for the most part), the results allow for a rare glimpse into the public mood at the time.

The elections to the Constituent Assembly were until that point the largest elections in world history, in terms of both the geographic territory covered and the number of voters, and they were conducted in the context of ongoing war and increasing anarchy and civil strife.[97] Even given the circumstances in which the elections were held, the results provide a window into the political processes affecting Russian Jewry, both immediately in the fall of 1917 and in the longer term. First and foremost, it is evident that Jewish political leaders were far more factionalized than the Jewish population as a whole. Taking into account the fact that many Russian Jews evidently considered themselves unrepresented by any of the parties, the election results still demonstrate that the Jewish population was far less divided than the large number of parties might otherwise seem to indicate. The creation of Jewish national coalitions resolved a good deal of ideological hairsplitting, but the number of Jewish parties that fielded candidates in the various elections is astounding. In some districts in the elections to the All-Russian Constituent Assembly, more than one-third of the parties listed on the slate appealed only to Jewish voters. Examples include Zhitomir, where five out of thirteen parties were Jewish; Gomel, where four out of eleven parties were Jewish; and Poltava, where five out of fourteen parties were Jewish (Poltava's large population of Jewish refugees displaced from other areas of the Pale of Settlement during the war may partly account for its political diversity). Voters could chose between two or more Jewish parties in fourteen districts.[98] Nonetheless, when voting took place in November and December 1917, the Jewish electorate was fairly unified. At least 622,797 people voted for Jewish parties in the Constituent Assembly elections. Eighty percent of those votes were for Jewish national coalitions.[99] All the Jewish socialist parties—the

Fareynikte, Poalei Zion, and the Bund—together received less than 15 percent of the total vote for Jewish parties (though this figure excludes votes for Bund-Menshevik coalitions). Due to the difficulties of establishing Jewish population figures by city in 1917, it is impossible to know the percentage of Jewish votes that went to Jewish parties, but indisputably, the large majority of votes for Jewish parties went to the national coalitions.[100]

As the Constituent Assembly election results make clear, Jews (workers and otherwise) supported the Jewish national coalitions in far greater numbers than they did the Jewish workers' parties. Intuitively one might presume that support for the Jewish socialist parties would have been higher if not for the loss of Russia's Polish provinces and, with them, industrialized cities such as Warsaw and Lodz, with their large Jewish populations. Yet election results for the Polish Constituent Sejm in 1919 demonstrate that this was clearly not the case. Jews living in former Russian provinces in independent Poland voted overwhelmingly for a list dominated by Zionists known as the Temporary Jewish National Council, and to a lesser extent they also supported the Folkspartey (whose candidates in Poland ran separately from the Zionists) and non-Zionist Orthodox parties. The Bund and other Jewish socialist parties, on the other hand, proved exceptionally weak.[101] As Ezra Mendelsohn points out, the 1919 elections refuted Polish accusations of Jewish socialist and Bolshevik sympathies: "On the contrary, they demonstrated the moderate social views of a basically conservative population much more interested in protecting its civil and national rights than in promoting social change."[102] As a whole, when given the opportunity to participate in general elections, Jews living in the territories of the former Russian Empire expressed only marginal support for the Jewish socialist parties and instead voted for parties and coalitions that principally demanded Jewish collective rights within a liberal framework.

The results of the Constituent Assembly elections do reflect a change in Russian Jews' priorities. Because Jewish civil equality and the abolition of legal disadvantages had taken place swiftly, the implementation of national rights and autonomy—in Russia and in Palestine—became a means of physical and spiritual protection. In the months leading up to the elections, groups running under slogans of Jewish autonomy and national rights decided to reconcile their differences (which tended to be matters of emphasis rather than substance), and, as a result, the Zionists, Orthodox groups, and the Folkspartey ran as a coalition in most districts. The Folkspartey, given its diverse composition, was perhaps the foremost advocate of creating a Jewish national coalition to contest the All-Russian Constituent Assembly elections. As one folkist stated in *Dos yidishe folksblat*, "We must argue that we are one people, and reflect our national task in our name."[103] The Zionists stressed the importance of facilitating a national homeland in Palestine but, like the folkists, demanded full national and local self-government for the Jews in Russia. The emerging Orthodox groups (some of which were Zionist) that joined these coalitions were most concerned with religious autonomy but also acknowledged a secular role for communal self-government. These nonsocialist Jewish coalitions ran under such titles as the Jewish National Electoral Committee and the Jewish National Bloc, an extension of a practice that began in the Duma elections when Jews formed committees to represent the Jews of a given locality and to nominate Jews as electors.[104]

Jewish coalitions won the Jewish vote (at least for the Jewish parties) in elections to the All-Russian Constituent Assembly, and the Zionists were certainly the anchor of the coalitions in many districts, but there also is no doubt that the Zionists benefited from these strategic partnerships. Only three of the five representatives elected to the Constituent Assembly from these coalitions were affiliated with the Zionist movement: Iulii Brutskus in Minsk, Iakov Maze in Mogilev, and Moshe Nahum Syrkin in Kiev.[105] In Kherson, Oskar Gruzenberg won a seat as a member of the Folkspartey, running in the number one position on the electoral list of the Jewish National Bloc. In Mogilev, Naftali Fridman, a non-Zionist Kadet in the Fourth Duma, won a seat as a candidate from the Jewish National Electoral Committee. Also in Mogilev, An-sky, who had left the Folkspartey in April, chose to run as a candidate from the Socialist Revolutionary Party instead of the Jewish National Electoral Committee, and Jews no doubt played a role in his election there. Jewish voting behavior in 1917 evidently followed the pattern of the First and Second Dumas, when Jews also voted in large number: When Jews voted, they voted for prominent Jews, paying little attention to party affiliation.[106] As Vladimir Levin writes of the Duma elections, "The political views of candidates were of minor importance, while the fact of their being Jewish and their prominence and popularity in local or central Jewish affairs played a decisive role."[107] Similarly, in 1917, although Jews overwhelmingly supported Jewish national coalitions in the All-Russian Constituent Assembly elections, doing so did not necessarily represent a declaration of sympathy with Zionism, or even Jewish nationalism, but continued a long-standing pattern of voting for prominent Jews regardless of party affiliation.[108]

It may not seem surprising that most Jewish voters in 1917 supported Jewish nationalist parties, but the election results to the All-Russian Constituent Assembly were the culmination of a progressive move by Jewish political leaders away from Russian liberalism rather than a quick and dramatic shift in loyalties brought about by a single outside event, such as the Balfour Declaration issued on November 2 (in the declaration British foreign secretary Arthur Balfour declared Britain's support for a national home for the Jewish people in Palestine).[109] This move away from Russian liberalism began as early as elections to the Second Duma, when the Zionists first ran independently, and the trend accelerated during the war years, when Russian liberals consistently failed to defend the Jews or advocate for Jewish rights. After the February Revolution invalidated the ideology of the Octobrists (who believed that reform of the empire should be based on the tsar's October Manifesto of 1905), the Kadets effectively became the party of the right and more stridently sought to uphold the integrity of the empire. Ironically, before the outbreak of war, many Jewish nationalists were willing to support the Kadet Party, even though the Kadets looked far from positively on the possibility of Jewish national rights, but when they perceived that the party would not even consistently support Jewish civil rights, they threw their support en masse to Jewish national coalitions and parties.

As a result of an accumulation of Kadet decisions that caused ill will among Jewish supporters—such as the Kadet coalition with Octobrists in the Progressive Bloc, the circulars affair, and the Kadets' generally tepid defense of the Jews during the war—by 1917 and the election to the All-Russian Constituent Assembly, the appeal of Russian liberalism to Jews had all but ended. As Russian liberalism weakened, Jewish nationalism grew stronger, but of course Jews were not alone in their growing pessimism about the constitutional future of the Russian Republic. Under Bolshevik rule this public uncertainty only increased. In fact, despite the surprisingly high level of participation in the Constituent Assembly election, given such strenuous circumstances, one of the election's notable features was the urban intelligentsia's general abstention from voting. These people were the Kadets' natural base of support, especially in the provincial cities, where many Russians had come to see the Constituent Assembly elections as the legitimization of mob rule.[110] In contrast to the wide-scale abstention of the non-Jewish urban intelligentsia, Jewish voters shifted their loyalties (and in some provinces, the urban intelligentsia was almost entirely Jewish) directly from the Kadet Party to Jewish national coalitions, a process evident in any comparison between the elections to the First Duma and the elections to the Constituent Assembly in 1917.

Examining the Constituent Assembly electoral returns for the districts that elected Jewish representatives to the First Duma illustrates the extent to which Jewish support moved from the Kadets to the Jewish coalitions. In every district that elected a Jewish member of the Kadet Party in the elections to the First Duma and that was still geographically part of Russia in November 1917, the Kadet Party was outpolled by nonsocialist Jewish national coalitions by significant margins.[111] In Minsk, where the Kadet member elected to the First Duma, Semyon Rozenbaum, was an active Zionist, the Jewish National Electoral Committee received in the Constituent Assembly elections more than six times as many votes as the Kadets. Similarly in Vitebsk, where the Zionist Kadet Grigorii (Zvi Hirsh) Bruk was elected to the First Duma, Bruk ran in 1917 for the Jewish National Electoral Committee and received more than three times as many votes as the Kadets. It is understandable that areas with historically strong Zionist support that had previously elected Zionist representatives as Duma members would vote heavily in favor of Zionists and Jewish nationalists who had left the Kadet Party. But in districts such as Kiev, which in 1906 elected two Jewish Duma members (one Kadet and one Trudovik, both of whom were nonnationalists), more than 90,000 people voted for the Jewish Bloc in 1917.

Although Zionist criticism of the Kadets intensified with each Duma election, the Zionists could not fight the Kadets head on in the Pale of Settlement because, given the system of indirect elections, their support was needed in the assemblies of electors (who chose the Duma representatives) to elect any Jewish candidate at all.[112] The direct electoral system to the All-Russian Constituent Assembly, in contrast, freed the Zionists and all Jewish nationalists of this restraint.[113] Thus, in areas with large Jewish concentrations, the creation of a separate Jewish nationalist list led to what was essentially a split in the Kadet Party, and the Jews who left the party took their supporters with them. Results of municipal Duma elections demonstrate the same trend. In Minsk the Jewish nonsocialist bloc won sixteen seats in the city Duma compared to the Kadet Party's three.[114] For many Russians, Jews included, voting for the Kadets was a last effort to prevent social and political disintegration.[115] But for those Jews who voted for the Jewish national coalitions, the direct representation of their interests was of greater importance.

Looking at public opinion as a whole, the many various elections suggest the simultaneous triumph of two ideas: autonomism and Zionism. Zionists could succeed in campaigning for Jewish self-government without making any mention of Zionism because they were both Zionists and autonomists. Locally, the Zionists intentionally obscured the differences between themselves and the folkists. In the campaign for the new democratically elected Moscow *obshchina*, for example, the Zionists committed the party to diaspora nationalism using Dubnovian arguments for the historical basis of that nationalism. The first point in the Moscow Zionist program read: "The Zionists see in the *obshchina* the historical institute of Jewish self-government, embodying the idea of national unity in Diaspora life and the uniting of the nation's strength around its everyday life and its historical interests."[116] One Zionist, arguing in May 1917 for the need to organize *obshchiny* throughout Russia, even attempted to bolster the autonomist credentials of the Zionist movement by claiming that when others disdained the idea of Jewish self-government as "reaction" and "fantasy," the Zionists in contrast "recognized the *obshchiny* as the native affairs of the people, the vestige of our national independence, the transmitter of the idea of our distinctive national existence, putting it on a firm basis, on which we must stand in the struggle for national autonomy in the countries of the Diaspora."[117] Some Zionists had come not only to embrace autonomism, but also to extol their pedigree in its development.

Jewish Public Opinion in Multiethnic Cities

It is important to remember that the voting in 1917 took place after a period of dramatic dislocation for many Jews. The Jewish population of Russia was physically reshaped by war and the new freedom of movement that followed the February Revolution. In November 1917 the Kingdom of Poland lay beyond the front, as did much of what had been the Baltic provinces and part of the previous Pale of Settlement. Although at this time Russia had lost what amounted to Poland, Lithuania, and parts of Belorussia, a considerable portion of the Jewish population from these areas remained in Russia, having been previously deported from the front or having left during the Russian retreat from Poland and Galicia in 1915 (and similarly, many Austrian Jews fled westward when the Russians first took Galicia from Austria). The army forced Jews east out of Volynia and out of many Belorussian towns and much of the Baltic region. In some cases, such as Kaunas (Kovno) and much of the Kurland province, all the Jews were forced east. Thus, perhaps ironically, the loss of these provinces did not result in the loss of their whole Jewish population, especially given that two-fifths of Jews displaced in 1915 moved to Russian areas previously closed to them.[118] When all restrictions on Jewish residence were repealed by the Provisional Government in March 1917, Jews moved in even greater numbers into cities where their residence had previously been restricted.

The experience of war and the difficulties that all nationalities faced in caring for their civilian populations heightened national identity, especially among refugee populations and in multiethnic cities. Even before the war, Jews lived predominantly in places where occupational structure correlated closely with nationality (or perhaps more accurately, language). But the sudden burst of urbanization that occurred over just a few years during World War I—first because of the fighting and then as a result of new freedoms—further underlined the social and economic distinctions between national groups living together, and the very fact that the empire and autocracy were no more weakened the ties that bound the different nationalities to one another. These factors made voting along national lines more likely, and the elections themselves, when every individual could participate in the construction of new forms of government, could only have mutually reinforced national differences.

To take one example of how this process played out, western Ukraine was the region of the Russian Empire with the closest correlation between class and ethnicity, a fact reflected in the makeup of the political parties active in that area. In western Ukraine, Ukrainian speakers made up the peasantry and most of the overall population; Russian speakers dominated the small proletariat; Poles and Russians were landowners; and Jews were concentrated in the urban centers as merchants and artisans. Correspondingly, nationalist Ukrainian parties were either peasant-based populist parties or socialist parties, and in the Constituent Assembly elections they won the vast majority of the vote.[119] Bolshevik support was primarily Russian, as was support in the cities for the Kadet Party. Because the Kadets were outflanked on the left by the socialist parties and on the right by the Octobrists, from 1907 onward the Kadet Party was strong only among urban renters, small business owners, and small property owners (known under the Duma electoral system as the second curia), and in most western Ukrainian and Belorussian cities and towns this meant Jews.[120] In the Kiev and Volynia Provinces, for example, Jews made up 96 percent and 82 percent, respectively, of the merchant class.[121] Nonetheless, instead of the Kadets, in 1917 Jews voted for Jewish parties, coalitions, and lists of notables. Nowhere is this trend clearer than in the municipal duma elections. Jewish parties probably obtained somewhere around 3–4 percent of municipal duma seats in the European provinces. In the provincial capitals of European Russia, however, Jewish parties obtained more than one-third of all seats won by all national and religious parties, a number completely disproportionate to their share of the general population but consistent with their demographic representation in cities and towns.[122]

The victory by the Ukrainian nationalist agrarian socialist parties in the All-Russian Constituent Assembly elections has spurred a debate about whether the results indicate widespread Ukrainian national self-consciousness among the peasantry. Steven Guthier explains the massive success of the Ukrainian parties as resulting from the fact that "the major social issues commanding the attention of the peasantry could be readily forged into national issues as well," and he argues that the results of the Constituent Assembly elections suggest that a popular base of support for Ukrainian national consciousness was already well established in 1917.[123] On the other hand, Ronald Suny sees in the Ukrainian nationalist success "ethnic awareness" rather than "full-blown political nationalism."[124] According to Suny, the fact that Ukrainian peasants voted for Ukrainian parties reflects a preference for candidates who could speak Ukrainian and who promised to work for local interests, but in no way does the vote suggest that Ukrainian peasants accepted the national or nationalist aspects of those candidates' programs or even that the peasants saw Ukrainians as a nation.[125]

We cannot determine whether Jewish voting represented "ethnic awareness" or "political nationalism," but we must consider the possibility that the rise of Jewish national sentiment, at least as reflected in Jewish voting, similarly represented a simple preference by Jews in the cities and towns for candidates who could speak their own language and secure their local interests—a preference reinforced by the fact that other parties were closely identified with other national groups. One scholar has argued that the development of Jewish nationalism in late imperial Russia stemmed from discontent among Jewish workers with their declining economic situation compared to that of non-Jewish Russians, a process that fostered a sense of class and national consciousness that became one and the same.[126] Yet in 1917 Jews voted for Jewish parties, even when doing so was not necessarily in their best common interest. Poltava Province, for instance, was perhaps the most Ukrainian province in Ukraine and the stronghold of Ukrainian autonomism, and the city of Poltava was the only significantly sized Ukrainian city with a slim Ukrainian majority population (the rest was split approximately evenly between Russians and Jews).[127] In such a place the 20 percent of the population that was Jewish would benefit most from cooperating with the 20 percent that was Russian (as was done previously from within the Kadet Party). But in the elections Jews (and anyone else) could vote for one of five specifically Jewish parties plus a coalition of the Bund, Mensheviks, and Polish Social Democrats. The results are telling: In the province as a whole the Kadets on the one hand and a coalition between the Jewish National Electoral Committee and the Folkspartey on the other each received a number of votes equal to the respective number of Russian and Jewish residents of the city.[128] In short, Jews voted for the nonsocialist Jewish coalition, Russians voted for the Kadets, and neither group won a seat.

Again, the evidence points to an important continuity with the earlier Jewish electoral experience and to an important change. In the elections to the imperial Dumas, Jews could elect representatives only in areas where nationality, class, and party conflict coincided, because in those places Jews could cooperate with the Kadets and liberal Russian elements to defend their mutual interests.[129] In 1917, although this pattern for the most part held true, Jews were willing to forsake cooperation with the Kadets to at least attempt to elect representatives who would defend their civil and national rights more forcefully. Jewish voting therefore confounded even the expectations of contemporary observers. Abraham Revutsky, a prominent member of Poalei Zion who briefly served as minister for Jewish affairs in the independent Ukrainian National Republic, incorrectly claimed that the "Jewish urban bourgeoisie," along with the Jewish intelligentsia, "perceived the Ukrainian movement as a serious threat to their interests and as militantly opposed to all that they had achieved [in the February Revolution]. A real opportunity to assimilate into the dominant Russian culture was more important to them than abstract ideas."[130] In actual fact, nothing in how Jews voted in Ukraine, or elsewhere, suggests this was the case.

The elections to the Constituent Assembly turned out not to matter (as we will see in Chapter 7), but examining how Jews voted during the tempest of revolution is the best possible means to gauge Jewish popular opinion at the exact moment of the Bolshevik takeover and the Russian Republic's collapse. Contrary to Revutsky's perception of Jewish Russification or the prevailing perceptions of either intensified Zionism on the one hand or widespread sympathy with socialism on the other, the picture that emerges from the various election results in the provinces of European Russia suggests that Jewish voters behaved similar to Ukrainian peasants: They supported Jewish parties because the confluence of social, economic, and national interests led to a desire for some form of national autonomy. All these factors and the spread of Jewish autonomism as a political aim can be traced back at least to the revolution of 1905; at the same time, the war, the revolutionary tumult of 1917, and the experience of living in a state yet to define itself also undoubtedly affected the national self-consciousness of individual Jews. In Ukraine the relevance to Jews of being surrounded by another autonomist movement sympathetic, at least initially, to Jewish autonomist aims should also not be discounted. Some Ukrainian political groups advocated Jewish autonomy in the prerevolutionary period, even before some Jewish parties had done so, and the Ukrainian nationalist devotion to the general principle of Jewish autonomy impressed many Jews.[131] The Ukrainian nationalists who in March 1917 established the Central Rada (a large parliamentary assembly created without the authority of the Provisional Government) made efforts to include representatives of other nationalities and claimed only to want autonomy within a federated Russia.[132] Surrounded by an autonomist movement growing ever more strident in its demands, it would be surprising if Jews did not emphasize similar claims, especially given that Jewish politics had by then already been oriented toward autonomism for a dozen years. As the Poltova municipal Folkspartey warned, it was a mistake to believe that with formal civil equality the Jews had received everything they needed: "As a matter of fact, it still is not *complete rights*, it is only *equality*, and full rights will only be possible with the final blow; the right to be equal among equals."[133]

Conclusion

In the end, the Jewish public proved less enthusiastic about participating in Jewish communal politics than one might presume from the statements of the advocates for Jewish communal democratization. The fact that many more Jews voted for national coalitions in the

Constituent Assembly elections than voted at all in the Jewish Congress elections indicates that in 1917 Russian Jewry placed greater hope in securing their national rights through Russian rather than Jewish parliamentary institutions. Yet just as the general Russian public (Jews included) had little recourse open to them after the dismissal of the All-Russian Constituent Assembly, Russian Jews could do little to oppose the cancellation of their congress or the closure of their communal institutions.

The year 1917 thus turned out to be the pinnacle of Jewish national politics in Russia. In 1917 the various Jewish political parties and groups hoped to use the All-Russian Jewish Congress and the All-Russian Constituent Assembly to press Jewish demands for nonterritorial autonomy as an official nationality in the new republic and across Russia communal activists established organizational committees for elections to genuinely democratic self-governments. Jews were bombarded with political material about Jewish autonomy, the All-Russian Jewish Congress, local *obshchiny*, and the need to create new national institutions. As a result of the ongoing war, Jewish communal organizations had taken on a proto-governmental character and continued to touch the lives of hundreds of thousands of Jews by providing relief to refugees. In such a context an autonomist Jewish political life seemed natural to most Jews, especially when considered alongside the declining appeal of Russian liberalism and the growing nationalism of surrounding populations.

In assessing the impact of the February Revolution on Russian Jewry, Kenneth Moss observes that the Jewish nationalist intellectuals who converged on Moscow, Petrograd, and Kiev "all aspired to transform Russian Jewry according to the overlapping, intersecting, and at times conflicting logics of Jewish nationalism, socialism, secularism, and the Jewish cultural project. Caught up, moreover, in the revolutionary process, they not only pursued long-standing plans but articulated more encompassing and more radical visions of what Russian Jewry and Jewishness could be."[134] Moss suggests that for Jewish intellectuals, as for members of the broader revolutionary movement, the anarchic and desperate reality of daily life coexisted with a strong "belief in the malleability of social reality and in one's own capacity to play a role in its transformation."[135] In sum, February 1917 brought the opportunity to turn what had been theory into action. All the components of Jewish communal autonomy took shape in 1917: a framework and elections to the All-Russian Jewish Congress, a successful Jewish national coalition for representation in the Constituent Assembly, and a prototype for Jewish autonomy at the local level. Although these efforts may have ended in disappointment because of Bolshevik intervention, significantly all these institutions were planned with the broad participation of the Jewish communal organizations and of all the Jewish parties, including the biggest skeptics of Jewish sociopolitical autonomy (such as the Bund).

The folkists are a case in point, demonstrating how the self-described Jewish intelligentsia could and did effectively transform the sociopolitical organization of Jewish life, even if the influence of these particular intellectuals was not reflected in their political fortunes. The leadership of the Folkspartey included many cultural figures and communal activists but few politicians. Refashioning their movement into a party of Jewish national democracy, the folkists attempted to use the promise of self-government to reach out to the toiling masses. In 1917 the folkists hoped that their ideologically eclectic composition and strident antipartisanship would have broad appeal, but the question remains of how many members of the Folkspartey actually wanted power within the community rather than simply the adoption of their and Dubnov's ideas about Jewish autonomy. The fact that the folkists failed to rally popular support for their party may not have been relevant, even to them. When one looks at how much the structure of Jewish politics in 1917 reflected their vision, the ideology of autonomism looks rather more successful. That Russian Jewry was primarily concerned with establishing autonomy in 1917, and with doing so through the All-Russian Jewish Congress and a system of local Jewish communal governments, must be considered a vindication of the Dubnovian worldview.

It proved impossible to reconcile Jewish autonomy with Bolshevism, and perhaps it would even have proved difficult to achieve autonomy under constitutional-democratic liberalism. Until fairly late in 1917, however, the future seemed to lie with the Socialist Revolutionary Party, whose considerable popularity was confirmed by their receiving the most votes and seats in the Constituent Assembly elections. The Socialist Revolutionaries promoted the idea that each nationality should possess its own representative *sejm*, or parliament, and came to support the idea that national autonomy should be extraterritorial. When one considers the vast public support of the Socialist Revolutionaries in Russia in general, the hope that Jews would be treated like other nationalities in a new multinational Russia, albeit without a territory, was not altogether unreasonable. As *Evreiskaia nedelia* put it in September 1917, "A solution to Russia's national question seems to have been found in its nationalities' flowering while its unity is maintained, as achieved through the basis of [both] national-territorial and national-personal autonomy. The Jewish people in all parties and currents are striving to achieve the latter."[136] Even so, given that the Socialist Revolutionaries' support for national minority rights in general tended to weaken the closer they came to holding power (and grew after the Bolsheviks' coup), it is impossible to know the extent to which Jewish autonomy would in actuality have been able to flower under a Socialist Revolutionary government.

From the earliest days of widespread revolutionary disturbances at the beginning of 1917, just as in 1905, national discontent served as a catalyst to the empire's unraveling. As such, among the first demands of the Petrograd Soviet to the Provisional Government was that "a paragraph should be included in the programme of the Provisional Government giving cultural and national self-determination to all nationalities."[137] The Petrograd Soviet, composed at the time of a number of different socialist groups, sought to cast itself as the defender of national self-determination. Similarly, despite the fact that the All-Russian Constituent Assembly met for a mere two days before being dissolved by Lenin, the rights of national minorities was one of the first topics it brought up for discussion (though the assembly soon turned instead to the war, agrarian issues, and class struggle). Reflecting the extent of the Socialist Revolutionary Party's recognition—whether pragmatically or not—of the need to address national rights, Viktor Chernov, the chairman of the assembly's single session (and a close friend of both An-sky and Zhitlowsky), held January 5–6, 1918, resolved to settle the issue of autonomy, both territorial and nonterritorial, for all Russia's minorities and made a special point of calling for Jewish autonomy: "The Jewish people, who have no continuous territory available to them, will have in the territories of the Russian Republic, equally with all different peoples, the right to create national organs of self-government and to express through them their earned emancipation. The armed might of Russia will draw strength from the legions of different nationalities uniting from previous dispersion, in front of which, hereafter, no one will dare to place any obstacle."[138] As all of Russia's inhabitants soon discovered, Chernov could not have been more mistaken.[139]

Seven Independent States and Unfulfilled Expectations

As the Austro-Hungarian and Russian Empires came apart at the seams in the final years of World War I, the moment many nationalists and revolutionaries had long sought seemed to have finally arrived. Between 1917 and 1922 the entire map of east-central and eastern Europe would be redrawn. In drawing the borders of both independent states and new federations, the catchword of the moment was national rights. The principle that every nationality had the right to govern itself politically had become the dominant paradigm for state reorganization. That Jews in Eastern Europe should gain national minority rights and a measure of autonomy as an outcome of the diplomatic agreements ending the war became commonly accepted during the war itself. As the lawyer and American Zionist leader Louis Brandeis (1856–1941) wrote to Lucien Wolf regarding the creation of the American Jewish Congress in 1916, "The war now being waged involves the issue of the rights of the smaller nationalities and groups. We are hopeful that in the consideration of those rights, and in the general revision of international affairs which will ensue when the present war is concluded, the problem of the Jewish people will also be taken up. We American Jews have realized, however, that if the lot of our peoples is to be permanently improved and radically cured of its defects, we ourselves must effectively co-operate in the work of redemption, in person and directly."[1]

Before World War I ended, Zionists in England scored an enormous coup. Although the exact significance of the Balfour Declaration and of British intentions can be debated, at the time it appeared to Jews that the Zionists had won the backing—in writing and in public—of the British Empire to establish a Jewish homeland in Palestine. The

Balfour Declaration certainly represented the Zionists' victory over the Conjoint Committee in the competition waged between them throughout the war for the ear of the British foreign secretary.[2] Socialists and anti-Zionists could simply reject and oppose the Balfour Declaration. But what of diaspora nationalists like Dubnov and his associates, who claimed not to oppose either the nationalism of the Zionists or the building-up of Palestine but rather what they believed to be the unrealistic focus of Jewish nationalism in that direction and the negation of the Diaspora? Dubnov, for one, did not oppose the Balfour Declaration, but he worried that it was a distraction. After all, millions of Jews needed legal sanction for national autonomy in the Diaspora, and the world was instead focusing on a place with relatively few Jews.

As it turned out, the question of Jewish national rights in Eastern Europe became only more important as a result of the war's conclusion. By the time the war's victors came to Versailles to plan the peace, Jews from the Russian Empire and Austria-Hungary had been partitioned into two remarkably distinct political universes (though the frontier that divided them was still shifting because of the still unresolved wars in Eastern Europe). Much of the heart of the former Pale of Settlement was now part of a federally organized revolutionary socialist state. Much of the rest of the Jewish population found itself in the newly independent national states of Lithuania and Poland and a newly enlarged Romania. The Russian Empire's northwest region and its westernmost provinces, plus Austrian Galicia, were incorporated into independent Lithuanian and Polish states. Romania took Bukovina from Austria and Bessarabia from Russia. The diplomats at Versailles had no influence, or any interest, in how the Soviets approached its Jewish population. They were, however, acutely aware that the new nation-states created out of the remnants of the two empires were by no means homogeneous, and as such the leaders at Versailles sought to ensure the rights of minorities to prevent further conflict. Thus, by luck or circumstance, a Jew might find him- or herself either a citizen of the Soviet Union, a state hostile to religious traditionalism but eager to integrate Jews as individuals into the body politic, or a citizen of one of the nation-states, which were indifferent to religious traditionalism but reluctant to integrate Jews as full participants in national politics. Only in Lithuania and

Ukraine, and then only briefly, did Jews find themselves in states willing to grant Jews their national autonomy. For different reasons Jewish autonomy ran counter to the political objectives of the Soviet Union and the national states equally. As I explore in this chapter, all the states where Jews came to live in the post-Versailles era eventually squelched the one political aspiration that united the different strands of Jewish politics in Russia and Eastern Europe: autonomy.

Jewish Autonomy and the Consolidation of Bolshevik Power

As Yuri Slezkine observes, "On the eve of the revolution, Russia had census nationalities, nationalist parties and national 'questions,' but it had no official view of what constituted nationality."[3] The Bolsheviks embraced national rights and national self-determination in order to consolidate power and reconquer breakaway regions, but as they started to win the civil war and consolidate their rule, the debate about the form and structure of the new state intensified. Many within the Bolshevik party leadership were uncomfortable with the new emphasis on national rights, preferring instead to organize the new federative state along economic lines, but the civil war in the western borderlands, Ukraine, and the Caucasus was won by the Red Army and pro-Bolshevik forces in no small part on the basis of Bolshevik promises to respect national rights.[4] The civil war itself created the need for the Bolsheviks to co-opt and cultivate local allies, and they often recognized local autonomy after the fact as a matter of pragmatics. A number of legally recognized kinds of republics, regions, and communes existed in the early stages of Soviet federalism, based on different principles of organization and definitions of autonomy. Nonetheless, to quote Slezkine again, "Some autonomies appeared more autonomous than others but 'nationality' reigned supreme."[5] In 1919 the borders between Ukrainian, Belorussian, and Russian territories were demarcated on the basis of a linguistic definition of nationality. When the dust settled, the Union of Soviet Socialist Republics was formed in 1922 by an agreement between the Ukrainian and Belorussian Soviet Socialist Republics and

Figure 10 Eastern Europe, 1923.

the Russian and Transcaucasian Soviet Federative Socialist Republics. Against internal opposition and doubt, Lenin and Stalin effectively institutionalized the principle of ethnic self-determination at all levels. These policies were part of a struggle against "backwardness" that required efforts to develop all of Russia's oppressed nationalities. Stalin's "autonomization plan" called for extreme centralization in essential matters, in conjunction with an acceptance that nonessential matters—language and culture—would be left to the autonomous republics.[6]

So where did Jewish self-determination fit in Bolshevik ideology? All indications suggest that Lenin was sympathetic to the plight of Russian Jewry as an oppressed, if not the most oppressed, people. But Lenin saw assimilated Western Jewry, and especially Western Jewish socialists, as a positive example for Russian Jewry to follow. The Bund, he believed, was the only major obstacle to Russian Jewry's assimilation. The answer, to Lenin: "Beat the Jews out of the list of nations."[7] Between 1912 and 1914 Lenin and Stalin had modified much of their previous resistance to the supposed artificial boundaries between the proletariat in favor of national self-determination for the peoples of the former Russian Empire. But the two leaders took special pains to speak out against the concept of nonterritorial autonomy and the recognition of the Jews as a nationality, and after 1917 the Bolsheviks maintained their strict territorial definition of nationality. Stalin attempted in a 1913 pamphlet to prove that Jews were not a nation and came out strongly against the idea, then in vogue, of personal autonomy.[8] Besides supporting the use of the Yiddish language for propagandizing among the Jewish proletariat, Lenin had virtually no room in his ideology for any element of Jewish autonomy or national sentiment. He stated in the fall of 1913: "Whoever, directly or indirectly, puts forward the slogan of 'national culture' is (whatever his good intentions may be) an enemy of the proletariat, a supporter of all that is *outmoded* and connected with *caste* among the Jewish people; he is an accomplice of the rabbis and the bourgeoisie."[9]

Lenin also opposed endorsing any form of Jewish autonomism in the Bolshevik platform, or "cultural-national" autonomy in general as an acceptable principle, blaming the Bund for the spread of the idea: "Neither the Austrian nor the Russian Social-Democrats have incorporated 'cultural-national' autonomy in their programme. However the Jewish bourgeois parties in a most backward country [Russia], and a number of petty-bourgeois, so-called socialist groups *have adopted it* in order to spread ideas of bourgeois nationalism among the working class."[10] Yet even Stalin and Lenin recognized the need for a certain degree of pragmatism in dealing with the Jewish national question, just as they pragmatically addressed the national questions of other nationalities. This need was even more pressing considering the circumstances under which the Bolsheviks took power: not after a long period of capitalist transition and Jewish assimilation (as expected by the Bolsheviks before the revolution), but after a rapid revolution that left the Bolshevik government with a highly urbanized and overwhelmingly unassimilated Jewish population. Because the Bolshevik coup amounted to imposing the will of the cities on the countryside, the significance of the Jewish population—concentrated as it was in the cities and towns of Belorussia and Ukraine, where the Bolshevik Party was weakest—was out of proportion to its size.[11] When Lenin reluctantly agreed to create the Jewish Commissariat (Evkom) and recognized Jewish sections of the Communist Party (Evsektsiia), he in effect recognized the importance of Jewish support for the new government, but this pragmatism did not reflect a change in Bolshevik ideology.[12]

If the elections to the All-Russian Jewish Congress demonstrate that Jews believed they could achieve national rights in Russia and if the results of the election to the All-Russian Constituent Assembly explain the complexities of Jewish nationalism and national self-consciousness during the period, then the short life of the Jewish *obshchina* in Petrograd is emblematic of the process that crushed Jewish autonomist aspirations. Held in December 1917, the communal elections in Petrograd were a victory for the Zionists, who won thirty-five seats, or exactly half the total available on the council.[13] The remaining seats were split between the local Orthodox party (nine), the Folkspartey (eight), the Bund (eight), the Folksgruppe (five), the Fareynikte (two), and the Democratic Group, Poalei Zion, and a nonparty candidate (one seat each).[14] The Bolsheviks eventually eliminated all socialist opposition, so there was no outcome to these elections that would have satisfied them, but even so, the Petrograd elections brought forth a Jewish communal leadership deeply at odds with the goals of the October Revolution. The Bolsheviks' response to this challenge was to use the promise of community leadership as an incentive for Jewish communists to take the lead in squelching Jewish national aspirations.

The Soviet of People's Commissars (Sovnarkom) issued a directive titled "The Separation of Church and State" on January 20 that, while directed at the nationalization of church property, was intended to take the legal grounding from all religions and make religious practice more difficult. It also provided the framework for dismantling the authority of Jewish communal and religious figures, though this proved to be a more complicated process in the western borderlands of the former Pale than in the capital.[15] In Petrograd the Commissariat for Jewish Affairs actively worked to counter Jewish autonomy: holding the right to approve or prohibit all publications, clubs, and organizations; agitating among the Jewish masses for communism; and publishing and distributing party literature in Yiddish.[16] Lenin named Semyon Dimanshtein (1888–1937), a long-time Bolshevik (and former rabbi), Commissar for Jewish National Affairs in January 1918. Dimanshtein became the first editor of the Communist Yiddish newspaper *Der emes* (The Truth), from which he helped to gather the writers who would form the new Soviet Yiddish intelligentsia.[17]

As early as October 1918, at their first conference, the Jewish sections of the Communist Party and the Jewish commissariats decided to do away with the local *obshchiny* system established during the previous year and a half.[18] The Jewish Section in Petrograd required little coaching from Evkom to dismantle Jewish autonomy. In December 1918 the section wrote a series of requests to the Commissariat for Nationalities Affairs, stating simply that the Jewish *obshchina* "is engaged in work whose purpose is counterrevolutionary. The [Jewish] Section requests that the *obshchina* close and transfer its inventory to the Commissariat for Nationalities Affairs."[19] According to the Evsektsiia, "In surveying the activities of the Jewish *obshchina* in Petersburg, our colleagues arrived at a unanimous decision for the immediate liquidation of the *obshchina* with all of its departments and its activities, which are not only useless but also harmful."[20] The only reason the Evsektsiia gave for its request to close the *obshchina* related directly (and unashamedly) to the democratic choice of the city's Jews. Before urging the speedy closure of the *obshchina*, the secretary of the Evsektsiia explained: "The Jewish *obshchina* was elected on the basis of universal voting rights, the result of which rendered overt counterrevolutionary elements as the *obshchina*'s leadership, who are endeavoring to belittle the significance of the Soviet regime in the eyes of the Jewish people."[21] It is interesting that the Jewish Section in Petrograd felt particularly threatened by the election of Zionists (who themselves had replaced the old financial elite) to the leadership of the Petrograd community. But the existence of a competing center of authority in the Jewish community, whoever was at its head, would not have been tolerated by the Bolsheviks for long.[22]

Jewish Autonomy in Civil-War Ukraine

Following the February Revolution, Ukraine, though remaining part of the new Russian Republic, created its own Central Rada, parallel to the Provisional Government in Petrograd. To gain support from the Jewish, Russian, and Polish minorities for Ukrainian autonomy or independence, the Rada created first secretariats and then ministries to represent these nationalities. In January 1918 the Rada passed the Law on National and Personal Autonomy, granting Jews, Poles, and Russians the right to nonterritorial autonomy within Ukraine through their own elected constituent assemblies with the power to create an internal government with the right of taxation. The Law on National and Personal Autonomy was created nearly simultaneous with the Rada's declaration of independence from Russia. Although Jewish parties and the Jewish population ideally wanted a Ukrainian federation with Russia, after the Bolsheviks' dismissal of the Constituent Assembly in January 1918, the Russian Republic ceased to exist. Despite wariness of Ukrainian independence, the Jewish parties overwhelmingly supported the Ukrainian Central Rada against the Red Army invasion. In a first for any government, Moyshe Zilberfarb became minister for Jewish affairs.[23] Even from an early stage, the prospects for Jewish autonomy if the Soviets seized control of Ukraine looked bleak compared to Ukrainian independence. In his account of the period Zilberfarb claims that even during the Red Army's first occupation of Kiev, in January 1918, the Bolsheviks attempted to dismantle Jewish autonomy, seizing the quarters of the Ministry for Jewish Affairs along with their archive and portraying Jewish autonomy as a bourgeois plot.[24] Surprisingly, during the next year of civil war, anti-Jewish violence, and repeated changes of government, Jewish autonomy in Ukraine pressed ahead. Jewish intellectuals and political activists who fled the Bolshevik takeover in Petrograd congregated in Kiev, where they hoped, despite violence and anarchy, that Jewish autonomy might take root. Many were involved in the creation of the Kultur-Lige, which sought to create a new secular Jewish culture in Yiddish through new schools and artistic and publishing projects.[25]

Even so, one should not overstate the extent to which any government at all had authority over Ukraine before Bolshevik control. Outside of a few major urban centers, what existed there between 1919 and 1921 was, simply put, anarchy. This was a multidimensional civil war between socialist Ukrainian nationalists, counterrevolutionary White forces, the Red Army, anarchists, and most commonly, roaming bands of criminals. General Anton Denikin's Volunteer Army, composed mainly of Cossacks and former Russian army officers, took as a given the Jews' responsibility for Bolshevism and tied monarchic restoration to mass murder. This was an astonishingly violent and lawless period for all the area's inhabitants, but the Jews consistently bore the brunt of the worst outrages. In many places Jews fell victim to what appeared to be organized orgies of violence, rape, and pillaging.[26]

In Ukraine, where autonomy might have been possible in an autonomous Ukrainian republic federated with Russia, such hopes collapsed in the chaos of the civil war and, ultimately, Bolshevik victory. Jonathan Frankel observes that Jewish national autonomy, as briefly instituted in Ukraine, exposed inherent problems in both Jewish politics and the relationship between the Jews as a minority and the majority nation. Chief among the problems was partisanship and the growing distance between the different ideologies. As Frankel states, "The greater the polarization in the Jewish world and the greater the hope of one faction or another finding powerful allies outside the Jewish world, the less was the chance of autonomism becoming a reality."[27] Indeed, this seems to have been the case during the period of Jewish autonomy in Ukraine, when the various Jewish political parties jockeyed to position themselves for influence with whoever was, usually quite momentarily, in power.[28] But as Frankel also points out, the Ukrainian autonomist experiment was conducted in the midst of war, revolution, and an unstable political environment. Although Jewish political polarization would likely have impeded Jewish autonomy's implementation even under a stable government, it is possible that such obstacles could be overcome. Crucially, all parties had come to accept the necessity of Jewish autonomy and of participating in the process. If Ukraine's short-lived experiment with Jewish autonomy can teach us anything, it is that with government accommodation, the institutional foundations of Jewish autonomy could be established under almost any conditions.

The Versailles Treaty and Eastern Europe's New States

Jewish politics in the Russian Empire developed in concert with expectations for decentralization and federalism. The Dubnovian principle that Eastern European Jewish emancipation must include Jewish national rights or else it is not truly emancipation had by war's end come to dominate Jewish politics in the former Russian Empire. In essence, those Jews who did not demand some form of Jewish autonomy or national rights did not espouse a separate Jewish politics. As we have seen, autonomism incorporated more and more of the Jewish political sphere from 1905 onward, and the experience of war fully enforced the sense among Jews that civil equality in the new states would not adequately protect the Jews physically, legally, or spiritually. Nonetheless, by 1919 the new states that emerged to replace the Russian and Austrian Empires had little incentive or desire to acknowledge Jewish national rights. The federal entity that the Bolsheviks sought to craft (which was not yet the USSR) actively sought to repress Jewish autonomy, and Poland and Lithuania sought to construct new national states around their own languages and cultures. Furthermore, the key victorious powers—Great Britain, France, and the United States—went to Versailles with the affirmed belief that the war proved the benefits of national rather than imperial or federal states (at least where others were concerned).

The paradox of Jewish politics in the post–World War I era is that Jews in all the new states came to adhere to the idea that their rights would best be secured under a federal, decentralized model, at precisely the moment of victory in the international arena for the nation-state idea. The very purpose of autonomism had always been to prevent Jews from being forced to assimilate the national demands of the groups among whom they lived, and now, following the consolidation of Jewish autonomy on the ground, this battle seemed about to be lost in law. Jewish autonomism was also intended, as always, as a helpful form of neutrality in the competition between competing national groups who, like the Poles, Russians, Ukrainians, and Lithuanians, were at the time of the Paris Peace Conference involved in multisided military conflicts with one another. Yet, as feared by some, the Allied victory in the war, the dissolution of the Russian and Austrian Empires, and the creation of independent states out of the multiethnic borderlands created a situation in which new and aspiring political movements sought maximum sovereignty as they constructed their new states.

During the war various Jewish spokesmen gained the ears of powerful politicians because of the Allies' desperate desire to gain any advantage in the conflict and the exaggerated sense, among British leaders in particular, of Jewish influence in global affairs. The Balfour Declaration is perhaps the best known success of Jewish diplomatic efforts before the creation of Israel. At the Paris Peace Conference in 1919 the war's victors gathered to craft treaties that, it was hoped, would preserve the peace in Europe, and competing Jewish voices once again sought to have their views heard. All of the new states emerging from the wreckage of the Russian and Austrian Empires, plus enlarged states such as Romania, were linguistically and religiously heterogeneous. The Western European Allied victors, especially France, Great Britain, and the United States, faced the quandary of how to find a formula for peace in Eastern Europe that would recognize the new states but protect their minorities and dampen the prospects for military conflict. The leaders of the victor states somehow had to balance the demand for total sovereignty by the new states with the demand for protection by groups that would become minorities in these new states. There was precedent for such agreements, such as when the Treaty of Berlin in 1878 conditioned Great Power recognition of an independent Romania on religious equality for all, with the intention of gaining citizenship for Romanian Jews.[29] Given the continued legal inequality of Romanian Jewry in 1919, however, as far as European Jews were concerned, this precedent was not exactly heartening.

As an event, the Paris Peace Conference must be one of the better documented moments in Jewish political, and certainly diplomatic, history. All the Jewish institutions, delegations, and individuals present had a sense of the historical importance of the event and kept records to justify the incredibly divergent opinions that ultimately emerged. The documentary bounty has produced an enormous literature on the role of Jewish delegations at Versailles, both by participants and by historians.[30] With the important exception of German Jews, Jewish organizations from around Europe and North America set up diplomatic and lobbying outfits in Paris: the French Alliance Israélite Universelle, the Joint Foreign Committee of British Jews (the Conjoint's successor), the American Jewish Committee, and the Committee of the Jewish Delegations, or the Comité, as it was popularly known (taken from its French name Comité des Délégations Juives), which was mostly made up of representatives from the new states in Eastern Europe. All shared a common concern for the legal status and physical security of Eastern European Jewry, especially in Poland, which was certain to end up with the largest Jewish population among the new states. What the various groups did not share was any sort of consensus about what legal rights would best ensure the long-term safety and prosperity of Jews in the new states.

Jewish delegates may have had considerable access to high echelons of Allied leadership, but the Allied leaders favored guaranteed minority rights more as means of preventing hostilities than anything else. In particular, with the creation of considerable German minorities in new states such as Czechoslovakia and Poland, the Germans became the most enthusiastic supporter of minority rights and the Allies became concerned with not allowing Germany's protection of German minorities in other states to become a premise for backing out of the treaty (as indeed proved to be the case).[31] Despite the reality that protecting Jewish rights and interests was not the foremost purpose of the separate clauses and treaties outlining the rights of minorities in the new states, the perception of Jewish power and influence among the signatories, all of whom believed the minority treaties violated their sovereignty, contributed to the desire among the new states to forget or abrogate the terms as soon as possible.

As the leaders of the victors of World War I drafted the treaties that would create new states in Central and Eastern Europe, so too did their Jewish organizations send representatives—their own diplomats—to Paris to attempt to enshrine the legal rights of Jews in the treaties establishing the new states' sovereignty. After several years of suffering anti-Jewish violence and what seemed to be the hardening of antisemitic positions among Polish political groups, the Jewish delegations became Versaille's most vocal advocates of separate minority treaties for the new states. With reports of horrific anti-Jewish violence streaming in from Poland and Ukraine daily, even nonnationalist Western Jewish leaders were concerned that the Jews' physical security and legal equality should be put in writing in exchange for the powers assembled at Versailles ushering into being the new states, such as Poland. Considerable differences separated the various Jewish delegations at Versailles. The French, represented by the Alliance Israélite Universelle, spoke with more authority than perhaps was their due, owing to the conference's location, their ties to French political leadership, and their sense of the Alliance's historical mission in defending the rights of the Jews in the Diaspora.[32] Yet their insistence that Jewish demands for national rights in Eastern Europe put all of Diaspora Jewry in danger made the Alliance the antagonists of the delegates from Eastern Europe.

The Comité, dominated by Jewish nationalists, sought exactly what the French wanted to avoid: recognition from the international community that the Jews are a nation and hence entitled to the rights of other nations. The new political environment that Jews found themselves in effectively closed most of the remaining daylight between the positions of Palestine-oriented and Diaspora-oriented Jewish nationalist movements (with the notable exception of the Bund and other Jewish social democratic movements, which claimed anyway not to be nationalist in form). Autonomists could support a Jewish national home in Palestine so long as equal or greater efforts went to securing Jewish national rights in Eastern Europe. The Zionists, who could claim to be the only organized global Jewish political movement, felt no less passionately than autonomists about the need for legally guaranteed national rights in the new states. With the war nearing an end, in October 1918, the Zionists issued the so-called Copenhagen Manifesto (the Zionist Organization had moved its central office to Copenhagen to preserve neutrality), in which they made three claims: In addition to a national home in Palestine, the Zionists also demanded "full and real equal rights for the Jews in all countries" and "national autonomy in the cultural, social, and political sphere for the Jewish population of countries where Jews live in large numbers, [and] where necessary, other countries whose Jewish population demands it."[33]

The British and American delegations fell in a space in between the French and the Eastern Europeans. Both delegations had individual members who were sympathetic to Zionism, and both had members who were not. Both delegations broadly supported Jewish legal claims to some kind of autonomy in the new states. Both were careful to differentiate between the collective legal needs of the Jews in Eastern Europe and the adequate security of their individual legal equality at home. The American Jewish Congress met in December 1918 to decide on the position of the American Jewish delegation to Versailles. The nationalists and those favoring national rights in Eastern Europe, chief among them Chaim Zhitlowsky, prevailed in their demand for the Congress's representatives to advocate for national rights. They even drew up a Jewish "bill of rights."[34] The delegation of British Jews, headed by Lucien Wolf, had also come to the conclusion that Jewish national autonomy in Eastern Europe needed to be protected by law. The Joint Foreign Committee of British Jews presented a report to Arthur Balfour in December 1918 to update him on the position of the leading figures of Anglo Jewry ahead of a coming peace conference. The committee members explained that with the disintegration of the Russian Empire, national autonomy became a demand shared by the majority of Eastern Europe's Jews and was viewed favorably by "the best local statesmanship."[35] But in Poland and Romania the persecution Jews faced was so severe that added stipulations beyond guarantees for Jewish autonomy were believed necessary to ensure basic Jewish freedoms, such as the free return of refugee populations and freedom from economic boycott and restrictions on Sunday trading.[36]

In the heat of rivalry and intense debate in Paris, the American delegation was more inclined to accept the Eastern European formulation of their legal demands and allow the Comité to drive the process, whereas the British were closer in attitude to the French. What is notable is the unanimity in acceptance of the principle of legally enshrining Jewish autonomy in the treaties establishing the new states, and what is more, French minimalism in this regard made their delegation the outlier. As others have already observed, acrimonious debates between the Jewish delegations—in particular when the British and French took one side and the American and Eastern Europeans took the opposite—about whether or not Jewish legal demands should be phrased as "national" highlighted the fundamentally different worldview between the Jews who fell to the east and west of German-speaking lands.[37] One might also argue that the British and French Jewish delegations simply understood the purpose of the Paris Peace Conference best: The Great Powers were in Paris to make nation-states. In one interpretation of the negotiations over the minorities treaties, much of the process was driven by Lucien Wolf's single-minded drive to achieve compromise between the different Jewish positions in order to pressure the British into tying the Poles to the strongest provisions possible.[38] Wolf adopted Jewish national rights and nonterritorial autonomy based on the Renner principle (for personal autonomy) in April 1917, at a time when there was still hope that a peace treaty might bring into being a new, liberal, federated state in Eastern Europe to replace the Russian Empire.[39] Yet, whatever the new reality on the ground in 1919, the Eastern European nationalists in the Comité were ascendant, desperate, and determined not to be bullied by grandees they considered out of touch with their needs and probably even the needs of Western European Jews.

In contrast to the Jewish delegates at Versailles from Western Europe and the United States, for whom autonomy was an abstract idea, the delegates from Eastern Europe who made up the Comité were professional political activists devoted solely to attaining Jewish national rights in Eastern Europe and Palestine. These were people who believed that Jewish equality required a separate Jewish politics. Of course, during the war, the American Joint, the British Conjoint, and the Jewish

Colonization Association (ICA) in Paris thought primarily about assisting their suffering brethren in Eastern Europe with immediate relief, but
one of the consequences of the war and its outcome was the extent to
which Jews throughout Eastern Europe desperately sought to consolidate legally what they had built during the war. In the war, in the Russian revolutions of 1917, and in Versailles, the voices of the proponents of
the Jewish politics of integration became increasingly drowned out and
shouted over by the proponents of Jewish separation. Civil equality may
have been enough for the Jews in France, England, Germany, and the
United States, but in the Comité's perspective, it would not be enough in
Poland, Lithuania, or for that matter the new Soviet republics.

Collapse

Woodrow Wilson's statement of Fourteen Points in January 1918
famously brought the principle of national self-determination onto
the agenda of reorganizing Europe's states. This principle was clearest
when applied to the specific examples of Italy's borders, the independence of the Balkan states, the dismantling of the Ottoman Empire,
and the creation of Poland. But Wilson's position, and the final version
of his fourteen points, was hardly unequivocal on self-determination.
For example, on adjusting colonial claims and determining sovereignty,
he called only for the interests of the populations concerned to have
equal claims with the colonial government.[40] Perhaps most important,
in the Fourteen Points Wilson said nothing about the rights of the
populations who were not in the majority in any of the new states. New
borders needed to be drawn across east-central Europe, from the Baltic
to the Adriatic and Black Seas. To bring peace and stability to Europe,
Wilson determined that national groups should rule themselves. The
problem was that little ethnic homogeneity existed in east-central
Europe. However one drew the borders, substantial minorities would
remain. Furthermore, the leaders of the nascent nation-states showed
little indication of concern for the rights of their minority citizens. Wilson and the other victors dealt with this problem by forcing thirteen
states, beginning with Poland, to accept what came to be known as the

Minority Treaties in exchange for diplomatic recognition. Signing the Minorities Treaties was difficult for these states to swallow but proved easy for them to subsequently ignore.

The prospects for Jewish autonomism in an independent Poland began inauspiciously. During the spring of 1915 the Central Powers pushed the Russians out of Galicia, and in fact, conquered much of what had been the Kingdom of Poland. Although Germany and Austria initially divided Poland into zones and ruled their zones for more than a year, in November 1916 they suddenly declared the creation of "independent" Poland.[41] The war and the German and Austrian occupation greatly exacerbated Polish-Jewish tensions. The Polish political classes of all stripes rightly understood that the nature of the future Polish state hung in the balance of power. Popular antisemitism flourished, and the leaders of the two most significant Polish political movements, Jozef Pilsudski and Roman Dmowski, equally sought a state that was fully Polish in character. This is not to say that there were no differences between Pilsudski and Dmowski. Pilsudski's Polish nationalism was a civic nationalism that sought a federal connection to hoped-for independent states of Ukraine, Belorussia, and Lithuania. Dmowski's was a more ethnic nationalism willing to make do with smaller borders for a more homogeneously Polish state.[42] Dmowski opposed not only Jewish national rights but also Jewish civil rights, and even though he signed the Polish Minorities Treaty, he blamed Jewish influence for forcing him to do so. The Jews in interwar Poland nonetheless developed a lively, and often fractious, independent political, cultural, and communal life, though this had much less to do with the quickly disregarded provisions of the Minorities Treaty than the absence of Polish desire to integrate the Jews.[43]

Independent Lithuania was the only state recognized at Versailles to attempt, at least at first, a genuine experiment with Jewish autonomy. At Versailles the Lithuanian foreign minister, Augustas Voldemaras, came to an understanding with the Comité that Jews be granted the right to use the Yiddish language in public life and governmental institutions and to have autonomous control over matters of religion, social services, philanthropy, education, and cultural affairs through the reinstitution of *kehilot* with the power to issue binding governmental ordinances and impose taxes.[44] The Lithuanian government enacted the Law on Kehilot in March 1920. The minister for Jewish affairs, Max Soloveitchik, had been a colleague of Dubnov's at the Jewish Historical-Ethnographic Society, and in the spring of 1921 the Lithuanian government formally invited Dubnov to reside in Kaunas (previously Kovno) and requested that the Soviet government provide him with an exit visa.[45] By the time the Soviet government acquiesced in the autumn of 1922, the Lithuanian government had retreated from its enthusiasm for Jewish autonomy and Soloveitchik had resigned over the failure to guarantee Jewish autonomy constitutionally. Although the premise for Dubnov's move to Kaunas was for him to take up a chair in Jewish history at the university, disputes over creating the position, the fading of Jewish autonomy in Lithuania, and no doubt the small-town provincialism of Kaunas led him to move quickly on to Berlin, where he settled between 1922 and 1933.[46]

The physical vulnerability of Eastern Europe's Jewish population and the impossibility of meaningful League of Nations protection for minorities were clear enough to the Comité, and in particular to its representatives from Ukraine. At the time of the meetings in Paris and Versailles, the Jews in Poland faced intermittent violence, and the Jews in Ukraine were suffering a wave of violence unprecedented for its scale, chaos, and brutality.[47] The extent of the violence in Ukraine became known to the Jewish delegations only in bits and pieces, and many initially believed the survivor accounts to be exaggerated. Yet anti-Jewish violence, and with it a massive Jewish refugee crisis, substantially worsened as a result of the war's end. First, Poles, Ukrainians, and Russians were fighting one another to determine the independence and borders of new states. Jews in cities such as Lemberg (Lvov, or today's Lviv) that passed back and forth between Ukrainian and Polish hands suffered particularly grievously. Austrian and Hungarian Jewish subjects who had earlier fled west, mainly from Galicia, to avoid the Russian army's advance found themselves in states that wanted the refugees evicted from their capitals, Vienna and Budapest. Tens of thousands had fled Ukraine for Romania, and up to 100,000 refugees came to Poland, either returning to cities they had been forced to flee or fleeing the Red Army.[48]

The Comité claimed that the horror of the recently concluded war had the effect of numbing the sensitivities of world leaders, who additionally preferred not to tarnish the reputations of the new states, especially Poland, even though the press reported on much of the violence going on there.[49] In 1920, when overwhelming documentary evidence made clear the extent of the violence in Ukraine, the Comité lodged a memorandum with the League of Nations. Its delegates later described the timing of the memorandum, its futility, and their fear for the future.

> The struggles in Eastern Europe were not yet over: in several parts of the former Russian Empire blood was freely being shed, and amid the convulsions of a disappearing world the Jews lived as outlaws and in fear that their total extermination was a question of time only. The representation of Jewries of many countries then set up in Paris, filled as it was with grave anxiety for the further fate of millions of panic-stricken fellow Jews, cherished the firm belief that it would suffice to draw attention to the facts in order to induce that body which after the war assumed the task of speaking on behalf of humanity to take action which would put an end to the fatalistic progress of destruction and extermination. The hopes then entertained were doomed to disappointment, and for a long time the fears for the future became intensified. For the League of Nations paid scant attention to the memorandum.[50]

What is perhaps most interesting in these words is the equation of lawlessness with the fear of *total extermination*. Eastern Europe's Jews in 1920 lived, or were perceived to live, outside any state's protection, and hence their only hope lay in an outside guarantor. Ominous signs were present even before the Polish delegations left for Versailles. At a meeting in February 1919 between the Polish prime minister Ignacy Jan Paderewski and the leaders of the Jewish parliamentary factions recently elected to the Polish Constituent Sejm, Noah Prylucki, the leader of the Polish Folkspartey, and Yitshak Grinbaum, who became head of the Polish Zionist Federation in 1918, presented their respective platforms for Jewish national autonomy in Poland. Paderewski claimed that he supported the Western democratic model of civil equality based on citizenship, but he dismissed out of hand the Jewish national demands or even the idea of official recognition for Yiddish. Not only did Paderewski suggest that "no Polish government will agree to the Jewish nationalist program," but he also taunted Prylucki that a Pole in America would pay with his life for taking such a position.[51]

The Polish Sejm ratified the Minorities Treaty, or "little treaty of Versailles," only because it was tied inseparably to the "big" treaty granting recognition to independent Poland. The Polish Minorities Treaty held its government explicitly to the responsibility of civil equality for all citizens "without distinction as to race, language, or religion." It also had several stipulations intended to guarantee citizenship for repatriated refugees and two articles addressed to the Jews by name guaranteeing Jewish public education and banning elections on the Jewish sabbath.[52] From the start, however, the opposition to even the limited Jewish educational autonomy guaranteed by the treaty was intense among the two main Polish parties. Paderewski and other Polish political leaders in Paris were particularly incensed by the idea that Polish citizens should have the right to lodge complaints with the League of Nations against the state or appeal to external protection. And because Polish Jews were reluctant to confirm Polish suspicions or aggravate relations, they, unlike the German minority in Poland, almost never petitioned the League for redress of Polish failure to honor the Minorities Treaty.[53] Indeed, this was a sentiment shared by the political representatives of religious Jews. Agudat Yisrael, the strongest Jewish political organization in Poland, refused to participate in a conference organized in 1927 to protect Jewish minority rights in Eastern Europe on the premise that in most places the claim to equal rights and national rights provoked passions that religious claims did not.[54]

The 1927 interparty conference on Jewish rights held in Zurich appears to be the last, ultimately unsuccessful, attempt to hold the new states of Eastern Europe accountable for their obligations under the Minorities Treaties. The Conference for the Protection of Jewish Rights was organized by the Comité in Paris and the American Jewish Congress to create a single organization to represent the Jewish minority in the various states of Eastern Europe. Jewish nationalists in the Comité had pushed during treaty negotiations for Jews to be designated as a nation in the League, to the opposition of not only nonnationalist French and British Jews but, more important, Woodrow

Wilson, who determined that political sovereignty should be the benchmark for membership in the League of Nations. In 1927 the same Jewish political leaders who had pushed at Versailles for national rights and Jewish membership in the League of Nations had come to the conclusion, quite accurately, that even the limited guarantees for the Jewish minority gained at Versailles had been ignored and unenforced. The fact remained that so long as the League was the body responsible for protecting minority rights, nations without states lacked an effective advocate to petition for redress.

The failure of the Minorities Treaties erased any ideological differences that remained between Zionists and autonomists. All autonomists had become Zionists, supporting the national project in Palestine; and all Zionists had become autonomists, demanding Jewish national rights in Eastern Europe.[55] The battle lines of Jewish politics had simplified dramatically between those who believed in the Jews as a nation and the necessity of national rights and those who did not. Dubnov summarized the issue as follows:

> The problem is this: after the peace treaties formally recognized the East European Jewish communities as national minorities whose rights rest on the protection of the League of Nations, a territorial Jewish organization must be created to bring together all of the initiatives to protect these rights in various countries, such as Poland, Romania, Hungary, Lithuania, and Latvia. A German minority in Poland, Italy, or Czechoslovakia can appeal against an injustice done to them through Germany's representative in the League of Nations; the Jewish people have no such representative in the League of Nations. Therefore a collective must be created to function as a Jewish representative in instances where the internationally guaranteed Jewish minority rights are violated. This is the only path for Jewish politicians, if they don't wish to return to the old politics behind closed doors, to shtadlanut, to degraded supplication to ministers and diplomats who are at the helm today and disappear tomorrow.[56]

Once again, Dubnov was arguing for a unified political body (it is not clear what he meant by a "territorial" organization) to determine fundamental Jewish positions and represent them to the powers that be, only now those powers were international. One year later, Dubnov sought to address publicly the divide between Western and Eastern European Jews that appeared to have widened at the Zurich conference. The main institutions of French, British, and German Jewry had refused to send representatives to Zurich. In Dubnov's assessment the Jewish communal leadership in Western Europe was stuck in the mentality of assimilation and *shtadlanut*, terrified by both the nationalist and democratic tendencies of the 5 million Jewish citizens of Poland, the Baltic states, and the Balkans. And in making common cause with Agudat Yisrael and liberal rabbis in Eastern Europe, who anyway preferred the designation of "religious minority," Western leaders ignored the Jewish majority demanding their legally guaranteed civil and national equality. As Dubnov said of this strategy, the fight against the national concept is futile: "The national consciousness of the Jew will triumph and the branches which separate themselves from the main stem will whither away." To Dubnov the link between nationalism and autonomism in the movement for Jewish emancipation in Eastern Europe between 1905 and 1917 had already "proved to the world that the recital of the Kaddish after the Jewish nation was premature."[37] Soviet Jewry may be lost, but the rights of the Jews of Poland, Latvia, and Lithuania, he pointed out, remained under the protection of the League of Nations. And therein lay the problem, as Dubnov placed an almost desperate faith in the protection of the new internationalism. The League had little interest or capability in protecting Jewish legal rights, and few Jews sought its redress. Five prominent Jewish international lawyers wrote a detailed postmortem of the Minorities Treaties, titled *Were the Minorities Treaties a Failure?* and published in 1943. Their book provides the simplest and best explanation for why a system that required Jews to petition for League intervention was bound to fail: "Jewish groups were extremely reluctant to turn to Geneva. Long experience had taught them that winning a case against their government was often a Pyrrhic victory at best."[38]

As evident from both the Paris Peace Conference and the Zurich Conference on Jewish Rights, the issue of Jewish national rights had split the Jewish world in two. The American Jewish Congress continued its close alignment with the Comité and had fully taken up the position of the advocates of Jewish national rights in Eastern Europe. Few American Jews in the interwar period sought collective rights for themselves (at least explicitly) or legal separation for the Jews in the United States, but the development of American Zionism under Louis Brandeis and others reflected widespread and growing sympathy with the notion that Jewish nationalism, directed elsewhere, need not contradict American patriotism. While there was no single American position on Jewish nationalism, a kind of liberal Jewish nationalism that balanced the three pillars of Jewish autonomy in Eastern Europe, Zionism in Palestine, and integration in the United States evolved out of the country's mix of Jewish immigrant and American-born intellectuals.[59] The concept of an American Jewish Congress that might collectively represent American Jewry, and the political divisions within it, though a far cry from sociopolitical autonomy, suggested at least an overlap in worldview between Russian and American Jewries.

Meanwhile, the Jewish experience in the Soviet Union went in a completely different direction. Jews received full civil equality in the new state, yet there was no room for any independent political life outside communism. With educational opportunities and employment in the new state apparatus suddenly open to Jews, the new Soviet citizens, especially the young, rushed to acquire Russian fluency, degrees, and jobs. In the 1920s the number of Jews in the Communist Party was only slightly disproportionately higher than their percentage of the population, but for the first time in Russia's history many Jews (and people married to Jews) held prominent and highly visible roles in the government, in the security apparatus, and in popular and elite culture.[60] The regime was at once opposed to antisemitism and at the same time deeply antireligious. As was the case in Petrograd, the Evsektsiia throughout the Soviet Union was empowered not only to end Jewish autonomy and close Jewish communal institutions but also to lead a campaign against Judaism at its roots: synagogues, schools, holidays, and rituals. All these factors, combined with rapid urbanization and industrialization, contributed to create a wave of dramatic and sudden, albeit incomplete, Jewish assimilation. The one area where a separate Soviet Jewish cultural life and identity was possible (for a while) was through the socialist Yiddish press, school system, and literature, but this came at exactly the time when Jews stood to benefit the most from becoming part of the majority culture.[61] In order to make Jews a "normal" territorial nation and encourage Jewish agriculture colonization, in 1934 the government created an official Soviet Jewish homeland in the Far East, known as Birobidzhan, though the state quickly backed away from the project and the Great Purges of 1936–39 destroyed much of its political and cultural leadership.[62] Jews remained a nationality in the Soviet Union, and many maintained a distinct sense of Jewishness, but Jewish national rights or autonomy outside a narrow Soviet definition proved impossible under communism. For all the efforts of autonomists to build a fortress against assimilation, Soviet citizenship quickly breached those walls (and only after World War II would Soviet antisemitism eventually rebuild them).

Conclusion

Autonomism was based, fundamentally, on the expectation of the Russian Empire's transformation into a multinational state with greater personal and collective freedoms and the delineation of specified rights to its nationalities. The empire's disintegration into a proletarian dictatorship plus a number of national, though still ethnically heterogeneous, states did not figure into this vision. After the Bolshevik victory in the Civil War, the new regime sought to craft an unrivaled Soviet public sphere, eventually putting an end to all competing autonomous civic life.[63] The post–World War I period thus represented both the autonomist movement's climax and dénouement. Jewish political parties—folkist, Zionist, and socialist—attempted unsuccessfully to use the Minorities Treaties after the war to bind Poland and Lithuania to Jewish autonomy. The idea of nonterritorial Jewish autonomy was incompatible with the nation-states that emerged in the post–World War I era, the federation of Soviet republics that became the Soviet Union, and even less so the ethnically homogeneous states in the post–World War II era.

To return briefly to Versailles, during the attempt to unify the Jewish delegations to the Paris Peace Conference, a meeting was held at the offices of the French Consistory in April 1919. The point of contention preventing a unified delegation was the refusal of the French delegation to agree to the demand for national rights for Eastern European Jewry or even the use of the word *national* in the delegation's set of demands. Menahem Ussishkin, as a delegate of Ukraine's 3 million Jews, declared the absurdity of the antinationalist refusal to recognize the present reality. Ukraine's Jews had already organized a national community and achieved a governmentally recognized national autonomy. In Ussishkin's telling, he pointed to a painting of the Napoleonic Sanhedrin hanging on the wall and suggested that one day a painting of the First Zionist Congress in Basel would hang there instead.[64] It is unlikely this exchange happened quite this way (if it happened at all). Nonetheless, Ussishkin nicely boils down how Eastern European nationalists viewed their conflict with the nonnationalist leadership of Western Jewry. The decisions of the Sanhedrin held in Paris in 1807 at Napoleon's behest, Ussishkin sought to convey, had become anachronistic even to French Jews. The Jewish religious and communal figures in the Sanhedrin theatrically proclaimed their patriotism and obedience to the state, hoping to convince Napoleon that "we are no wise separated from the society of men."[65] Yet even in Paris, the epicenter of such a model of Jewish emancipation so attacked by Dubnov and others, the Consistory would eventually turn to that sense of separateness and embrace of national liberation that the Congress in Basel had come to represent.

In Europe, North America, Israel, and elsewhere, Jewish collective legal rights persist today, albeit in different forms than envisioned by autonomists in the early twentieth century. The right to judge religious matters before a religious court, to teach in one's own language, and to have institutions exempt from taxation, to give just a few examples, tend to be justified by laws protecting individual rights but can just as easily be seen as collective rights, and ones cautiously guarded by Jewish communities around the world. With the exception of those in Israel, these Jewish collective rights fall far short of the legal recognition of Jewish national rights demanded by the representatives of Eastern European Jews at Versailles and in Zurich. Ultimately, Jewish national rights in Eastern Europe were unattainable under the post–World War

I settlement and the Bolshevik one-party state. Jews could not envision the events that would eventually make viable the homogeneous nation-states that resulted from World War II, but many had a sense that their security rested on their protection by the law. The myth of Jewish power contrasted starkly with the Jewish self-perception of weakness.

Conclusion   The Fate of Jewish Autonomism

How did autonomism become the genesis of Jewish political culture in late imperial and revolutionary Russia? The first part of the answer is to understand Jewish autonomism as a form of *obshchestvennost'*. Autonomism was an attempt to carve out a Jewish public space autonomous from the Russian state, a process that steadily took on a more overtly nationalist agenda as the years progressed. Combining *obshchestvennost'* and Jewish nationalism resulted from a growing concern with combating assimilation among Jewish intellectuals. Many of these same intellectuals concluded that if assimilation was a negative quality to be avoided by secular Jews, then a path must be found to protect Jewish national self-consciousness in the Diaspora. The answer for many came in the form of autonomous Jewish self-government. Modern Jewish autonomism, however, required an engaged citizenry to meet the democratic ideals of its proponents, and so Jewish activists—*obshchestvennost'* and intelligentsia—across the political spectrum adopted national rights as well as national, or "all-Russian," Jewish institutions as a means of politicizing the broader Jewish public.

The question remains of how to measure Dubnov's influence on the development of Jewish nationalism, broadly speaking, and the assumption of Jewish demands for national rights and autonomy specifically. Dubnov thought that a direct line could be drawn from the publication of his theoretical writings, to the adoption of his formula for Jewish autonomy by the Union for Full Rights, to the eventual guarantees of minority rights in the Minorities Treaties following World War I.[1] In reality, Dubnov's participation in this process occurred in fits and bursts, and intensive engagement was often followed by withdrawal to

274

his historical studies, particularly when disagreements arose. Even so, many of his ideas, most notably instituting secular communal self-government based on the *kehila*, moved forward with their own momentum, and many acknowledged that these ideas originated in Dubnov's early writings. In essence, Dubnov's contribution was to foster a form of liberal nationalism based on building an autonomous Jewish society in Russia, an idea as influential among socialists as it was among liberals. He gave coherence to these ideas in his historical research, his theoretical writings, and his political party and by serving as a figurehead and living embodiment of autonomism's ideals.[2] In the end, Dubnov's party played a similar role to that predicted by *Evreiskaia mysl'* on the Folkspartey's founding. That journal, despite serious misgivings about a nationalist party that lacked a Zionist component, nonetheless saw one redeeming quality for which the party's creation should be hailed: "It will give a chance to a known contingency of our intelligentsia that is yet to join, for one reason or another, any kind of Jewish party, to work for the good of its people."[3] Many Jewish intellectuals without an ideological or political home indeed became folkists, but autonomism also developed its own ideological coherence—focused singularly on building an autonomous Jewish cultural and political life in Russia—that attracted the disillusioned from other parties as well. Most important, Dubnov gave impetus to both integrationists and Zionists to move toward a common ground of Jewish nationalism based on the Jews' legally recognized autonomy in Russia. From the Union for Full Rights to the Kovno conference, EKOPO to the plans for the All-Russian Jewish Congress, Dubnov's legacy was in the steady progression of Jewish political life, ideologically and practically, toward constructing autonomy.

In March 1923, Maksim Vinaver, then living in Paris, wrote a letter to Dubnov, in Berlin, with feedback on a chapter or article that Dubnov was writing about the period 1904–14. Vinaver's major concerns were with how Dubnov presented Russian Jewish liberalism and how Dubnov presented his own role in what Vinaver called the "beginning of the Jewish national awakening." Regarding Dubnov's views about Jewish liberalism, Vinaver was clearly concerned that Dubnov had judged it too harshly, especially in the First Duma. Dubnov apparently claimed in the work he sent to Vinaver that the Jewish liberals failed to create a shared purpose with the interests of Russian liberals. Vinaver suggested in response that Dubnov continued to perceive Russian liberalism too narrowly and did not appreciate the extent to which it was fluid and adapted to changing circumstances. He also emphasized the achievement of Russian Jewish liberals in creating national institutions. Vinaver pointed out that the Kovno conference in 1909 was the only conference attended by all the Jewish political groups, from the Orthodox to the Bund, and was therefore the closest they collectively ever came to the much discussed goal of a Jewish national assembly. The second closest was the Union for Full Rights. As for Dubnov's role in Jewish nationalism, Vinaver bluntly stated, "In particular, you underestimate the impact of your books about Russian Jewish history and thought, which played the role of a magnet, attracting a rush to a new single center, and found a new way for the Russian-Jewish intelligentsia."[4] Vinaver's metaphor of the magnet is perhaps the best assessment of Dubnov's role in the development of Jewish nationalism.

A final task is to consider autonomism's ultimate viability.[5] Whether autonomism and genuine national rights for Jews as a nonterritorial minority might have taken hold in Eastern Europe largely depends on how one views the historical prospects of the Austro-Hungarian and Russian Empires. The collapse of those empires, and the manner in which they collapsed, was by no means historically inevitable. Without going to extremes of counterfactual history, one can imagine a number of scenarios in which these empires might have federalized under new liberal or socialist constitutions. Indeed, as we have seen in the case of the brief Russian Republic that existed between March and October of 1917, Jewish and other national autonomy was instituted de facto and well positioned to be recognized de jure. The results of the Constituent Assembly elections showed the broadest support among the Russian public for the Socialist Revolutionaries, the political group most sympathetic to decentralization and federalism. Even in Ukraine, anti-Jewish violence did not end the experiment with Jewish autonomy; the Red Army's total victory in the civil war did. One can interpret Jewish autonomy in Ukraine as doomed by violence, anarchy, inter-Jewish fighting, and the lack of liberal institutions, or, on the other hand, one can suggest the surprising extent to which Jewish autonomy forged ahead even under such conditions. Thus, to accept the inevitability of Jewish autonomism's failure in the remnants of the Russian Empire is to a certain extent to accept the Bolshevik historical narrative of the inevitable triumph of proletarian socialism.

Of course, the new states were also shaped by the victors of the war. Because of the substantial German minorities in the Russian Empire's western borderlands, the new states that might have formed in the event of the Central Powers' victory in the east would have had a much more powerful guarantor of minority rights (though the experience of the Jewish minority during the period of German-occupied Poland was mixed at best). Yet the Treaty of Brest-Litovsk in 1918, which ended the war between the Central Powers and the new Bolshevik government, also eliminated the possibility of a negotiated end to the war with the remaining Allied powers, and this fact shaped the postwar peace.

Autonomism's greatest success was in the most unlikely of places: Palestine. Zionists did not establish a state overnight. For more than forty years preceding Israeli independence, the Jews in Palestine, as part of both the Ottoman and British Empires, formed a politically diverse minority population that built similar institutions of communal and national autonomy to what the Jewish autonomists in Eastern Europe envisioned for the Russian Empire. In the years when Jews made up a substantial minority, but not a majority, of the population in Palestine and statehood did not appear on the imminent horizon, the Zionists there considered many possibilities of how best in the meantime to create a workable structure of Jewish national autonomy. The construction of Jewish national and cultural institutions intended to build a "Hebrew" culture in Palestine—assemblies, educational institutions, language development, and communal activism—began during the Ottoman period and followed a remarkably similar script to that playing out simultaneously in Russia.[6] Under the British Mandate, Jewish lawyers attempted to create "Hebrew" law that would apply autonomously to the Jewish community of Palestine, Jewish socialists built up a massive autonomous labor federation, and Zionists of different stripes debated what kind of national autonomy would best suit their political circumstance.[7] Indeed, the ideas of Jewish nationalists such as Dubnov were no less influential in prestate Israel than in Europe.[8]

As the prospect for Jewish national autonomy in Eastern Europe receded in the 1920s and as the safety of European Jewry became the more pressing issue in the 1930s, Jewish politics came to focus on finding a refuge for a vulnerable population. State Zionists saw long-term Jewish security as possible only through territorial sovereignty and a Jewish majority, and for reasons beyond the scope of this book that vision succeeded. But the development of Jewish nationalism in the modern political sense—whether territorial or nonterritorial, whether socialist or liberal, and whether Zionist, autonomist, or national democratic—consistently revolved around the question of how to define the Jews' legal rights as a nation. The very idea of Jewish national rights emerged in response to changing ideas about minority rights in a fluctuating legal environment: In Europe, demanding recognition as a nationality was the key first rite of all nations.

Notes

A complete bibliography can be found at https://sites.google.com/site/jewishrightsnationalrites/bibliography.

Abbreviations Used in the Notes

CAHJP	Central Archive for the History of the Jewish People, Jerusalem
CZA	Central Zionist Archives, Jerusalem
GARF	State Archive of the Russian Federation, Moscow
IVRAN SPb	Institute of Oriental Studies of the Russian Academy of Science, St. Petersburg
JDC NY	Archives of the American Joint Distribution Committee, New York
JNUL	Jewish National and University Library, Archive and Manuscript Division, Jerusalem
RGIA	Russian State Historical Archive, St. Petersburg
TsGA SPb	Central State Archive of St. Petersburg
TsGAOO/TsDAHO	Central State Archive of Public Organizations of Ukraine, Kiev
TsGAVO/TsDAVO	Central State Archive of the Higher Organs of State Government Administration of Ukraine, Kiev
TsGIA SPb	Central State Historical Archive of St. Petersburg
TsGIA Ukraine	Central State Historical Archive of Ukraine, Kiev
YIVO	Archives of the YIVO Institute for Jewish Research, New York

Introduction

Epigraph source: Simon Dubnov, "Pis'mo pervoe: Teoriia evreiskogo natsionalizma," in *Pis'ma o starom i novom evreistve* (St. Petersburg, 1907), 5; emphasis in original. Unless otherwise noted, all translations are my own.

1. Simon Dubnov, "Autonomismus," *Jüdisches Lexikon* (Berlin, 1927), 1: 615.

2. All of Dubnov's "letters" first appeared in *Voskhod* between 1897 and 1906, with the exception of the fifth letter, which appeared in *Budushchnost'*. The letters

(along with Dubnov's essay "The Goals and Tasks of the Folkspartey") were edited and revised by Dubnov in 1906 and published collectively in 1907 as *Pis'ma o starom i novom evreistve (1897–1907)*. I primarily use this 1907 edition. In 1937 this collection (minus three of the letters) was published in Hebrew with Dubnov's collaboration (and including a number of his changes to the original) as *Mikhtavim 'al ha-Yahadut ha-yeshana veha-khadasha*, Avraham Levinson, trans. (Tel Aviv, 1937). An English edition of the letters (heavily edited and based primarily on the Hebrew edition), together with a number of Dubnov's other important essays, was published in *Nationalism and History: Essays on Old and New Judaism*, Koppel S. Pinson, ed. (Philadelphia, 1958; reprinted New York, 1970). The only complete translation of all the letters in a Western language is Simon Doubnov, *Lettres sur le judaïsm ancien et nouveau*, Renée Poznanski, trans. and ed. (Paris, 1989). An annotated new translation of Dubnov's second letter appears as "Jews as a Spiritual (Cultural-Historical) Nation Among Political Nations," in Simon Rabinovitch, ed., *Jews and Diaspora Nationalism: Writings on Jewish Peoplehood in Europe and the United States* (Waltham, Mass., 2012), 25–44.

3. Simon Dubnov, "Pis'mo chetvertoe: Avtonomism, kak osnova natsional'noi programmy," in Dubnov, *Pis'ma*, 82; emphasis in original.

4. Dubnov, "Autonomismus," 1: 615–16.

5. For a compelling assessment of how historians' view of Jewish assimilation in the West has changed over the past thirty to forty years, see Maud Mandel, "Assimilation and Cultural Exchange in Modern Jewish History," in Jeremy Cohen and Moshe Rosman, eds., *Rethinking European Jewish History* (Oxford, 2009), 72–92. Mandel argues for "cultural exchange"—a two-way process—rather than "assimilation" as a new lens for viewing the Jewish experience in the modern world.

6. See Benjamin Nathans, *Beyond the Pale: The Jewish Encounter with Late Imperial Russia* (Berkeley, Calif., 2002); and Olga Litvak, *Conscription and the Search for Modern Russian Jewry* (Bloomington, 2006).

7. Y. Efren [Yisroel Efroikin], "*Kehile*, folk un inteligentsie," *Di yidishe velt* 2 (April 1912): 49.

8. Efren, "*Kehile*," 49.

9. For biographical details, see *Leksikon fun der nayer yidisher literatur*, s.v. Efroikin, Yisroel (New York, 1968), 7: 30; and *The Encyclopedia of Russian Jewry*, s.v. Efroikin, Israel (Northvale, N.J., 1998), 1: 306. See also Joshua Karlip, "At the Crossroads Between War and Genocide: A Reassessment of Jewish Ideology in 1940," *Jewish Social Studies* 11.2 (2005): 171; and Joshua Karlip, "The Center That Could Not Hold: Afn Sheydveg and the Crisis of Diaspora Nationalism" (PhD diss., Jewish Theological Seminary, 2006), 28.

10. Most notably Benedict Anderson, Rogers Brubaker, Ernest Gellner, Liah Greenfeld, Eric Hobsbawm, Miroslav Hroch, and Anthony Smith.

11. Vladimir Medem, "The Worldwide Jewish Nation," in Rabinovitch, *Jews and Diaspora Nationalism*, 108.

12. Nathans, *Beyond the Pale*; Litvak, *Conscription*; Brian Horowitz, *Empire Jews: Jewish Nationalism and Acculturation in 19th- and Early 20th-Century Russia* (Bloomington, Ind., 2009); Brian Horowitz, *Jewish Philanthropy and Enlightenment in Late-Tsarist Russia* (Seattle, 2009); and Vladimir Levin, "Ha-Politika ha-Yehudit ba-Imperya ha-Rusit be-idan ha-re'aktsiya 1907–1914" (PhD diss., Hebrew University of Jerusalem, 2007), forthcoming as a book titled *Min ha-meitsar* (Jerusalem, 2014).

13. Nathaniel Deutsch, *The Jewish Dark Continent: Life and Death in the Russian Pale of Settlement* (Cambridge, Mass., 2011); James Loeffler, *The Most Musical Nation: Jews and Culture in the Late Russian Empire* (New Haven, Conn., 2010); Kenneth Moss, *Jewish Renaissance in the Russian Revolution* (Cambridge, Mass., 2009); Gabriella Safran, *Wandering Soul: The Dybbuk's Creator, S. An-Sky* (Cambridge, Mass., 2010); and Jeffrey Veidlinger, *Jewish Public Culture in the Late Russian Empire* (Bloomington, Ind., 2009). All these scholars have been influenced by the works of Steven Zipperstein and Michael Stanislawski. See also the review essay by Nathaniel Deutsch, "When Culture Became the New Torah: Late Imperial Russia and the Discovery of Jewish Culture," *Jewish Quarterly Review* 102.3 (2012): 455–73.

14. I use the term *Russian Jewry* to refer to the Jews of the Russian Empire, without making regional distinctions or a special exception for Poland. This is not to suggest that all the Jews of the empire defined themselves according to their membership in a collective Russian Jewish entity. However, by the early twentieth century, the empire's Jews unquestionably understood themselves to be Russian subjects. As Eli Lederhendler states: "The political 'nation' of Russia was being defined by territorial unity and unitary government. Jews 'belonging' to Russia were, in that sense, Russian" ("Did Russian Jewry Exist Prior to 1917?" in Yaacov Ro'i, ed., *Jews and Jewish Life in Russia and the Soviet Union* [Ilford, U.K., 1995], 24).

15. See, for example, David Biale, *Power and Powerlessness in Jewish History* (New York, 1986); and Ruth R. Wisse, *Jews and Power* (New York, 2007).

16. Michael Chabon, *The Yiddish Policemen's Union: A Novel* (New York, 2007).

17. Philip Roth's *Plot Against America* (Boston, 2004) is another commercially successful novel based on a counterfactual treatment of American and Jewish history in the mid-twentieth century.

18. The plan for Birobidzhan followed a number of important but less well-known efforts at Jewish regional representation in the Soviet Union, in particular in Crimea.

19. See Simon Rabinovitch, "Simon Dubnov," in David Biale ed., *Oxford Bibliographies in Jewish Studies* (New York, 2014), http://www.oxfordbibliographies.com.

20. Steven J. Zipperstein, "The Politics of Relief: The Transformation of Russian Jewish Communal Life During the First World War," *Studies in Contemporary Jewry* 4 (1988): 38.

Chapter 1

1. We now have a much more nuanced and complex view of the many and different integrative processes that Jews experienced throughout Europe. See, for example, Pierre Birnbaum and Ira Katznelson, eds., *Paths of Emancipation: Jews, States, and Citizenship* (Princeton, N.J., 1995); and Jonathan Frankel and Steven J. Zipperstein, eds., *Assimilation and Community: The Jews in Nineteenth-Century Europe* (Cambridge, U.K., 1992).

2. Recent reevaluations include Michael Brenner, *Prophets of the Past: Interpreters of Jewish History*, Steven Rendall, trans. (Princeton, N.J., 2010; originally published in 2006 as *Propheten des Vergangenen*), 93–106; Avraham Greenbaum, Israel Bartal, and Dan Haruv, eds., *Writer and Warrior: Simon Dubnov, Historian and Public Figure* (Jerusalem, 2010 [Hebrew and English]); Anke Hilbrenner, *Diaspora-Natsionalismus: Zur Geschichtkonstruktion Simon Dubnows* (Göttingen, 2007); V. E. Kel'ner, *Missioner istorii: Zhizn' i trudy Semena Markovicha Dubnova* (St. Petersburg, 2008); and Jeffrey Veidlinger, *Jewish Public Culture in the Late Russian Empire* (Bloomington, Ind., 2009), 229–82.

3. For biographical information on Simon Dubnov, see his memoirs, *Kniga zhizni: Vospominaniia i razmyshleniia, materialy dlia istorii moego vremeni* (St. Petersburg, 1998). A comprehensive annotated bibliography of works by and about Dubnov can be found in Simon Rabinovitch, "Simon Dubnov," in David Biale, ed., *Oxford Bibliographies in Jewish Studies* (New York, 2014), http://www.oxford-bibliographies.com. Also see Sophie Dubnov-Erlich, *The Life and Work of S. M. Dubnov: Diaspora Nationalism and Jewish History*, Judith Vowles, trans., and Jeffrey Shandler, ed. (New York, 1991); Kristi A. Groberg, "The Life and Influence of Simon Dubnov (1860–1941): An Appreciation," *Modern Judaism* 13 (1993): 71–93; Kel'ner, *Missioner istorii*; Renée Poznanski, "Introduction: S. Doubnov, l'homme et son époque," in Simon Doubnov, *Lettres sur le judaïsm ancien et nouveau*, Renée Poznanski, trans. and ed. (Paris, 1989), 11–70; Robert Seltzer, "Coming Home: The Personal Basis of Simon Dubnow's Ideology," *AJS Review* 1 (1976): 283–301; and Robert Seltzer, "Simon Dubnow: A Critical Biography of His Early Years" (PhD diss., Columbia University, 1970).

4. Robert Seltzer observes that "Dubnow's exodus from the shtetl was only partial: he broke with the family's way of life but never ran away" ("Coming Home," 287).

5. Jonathan Frankel, "S. M. Dubnov: Historian and Ideologist," in Dubnov-Ehrlich, *Life and Work of S. M. Dubnov*, 5.

6. S. M. Dubnov, "Pis'mo pervoe: Teoriia evreiskogo natsionalizma," in S. M. Dubnov, *Pis'ma o starom i novom evreistve (1897–1907)* (St. Petersburg, 1907), 1–28.

7. Dubnov, *Kniga zhizni*, 169–215. Also see Steven J. Zipperstein, *Elusive Prophet: Ahad Ha'am and the Origins of Zionism* (Berkeley, Calif., 1993), 68–75; and Robert M. Seltzer, "Ahad Ha-am and Dubnov: Friends and Adversaries," in

Jacques Kornberg, ed., *At the Crossroads: Essays on Ahad Ha-am* (Albany, N.Y., 1983), 60–73.

8. See Anke Hilbrenner, "Nationalization in Odessa: Simon Dubnow and the Society for the Dissemination of Enlightenment Among the Jews in Russia," *Simon Dubnow Institute Yearbook* 2 (2003): 223–39. Hilbrenner applies the theories of Pierre Bourdieu to argue that both Dubnov and the Odessa "Enlighteners," whom Dubnov resembled when he arrived, used the OPE as a "social space" to claim the superiority of their respective "cultural capital." In Hilbrenner's analysis, Dubnov was nationalized not by the opinions of his literary circle but by their shared marginalization with respect to the city's Jewish professional elite.

9. A large body of literature connects Dubnov's historical scholarship to his political philosophy. See in particular the collection of articles in Aaron Steinberg, ed., *Simon Dubnov, l'homme et son oeuvre: publié a l'occasion du centenaire de sa naissance (1860–1960)* (Paris, 1963); and Simon Rawidowicz, ed., *Sefer Shimon Dubnov* (London, 1954). More recent assessments include Anke Hilbrenner, "Simon Dubnov's Master Narrative and the Construction of a Jewish Collective Memory in the Russian Empire," *Ab Imperio* 4 (2003): 143–64; Hilbrenner, *Diaspora-Nationalismus*; and Simon Rabinovitch, "The Dawn of a New Diaspora: Simon Dubnov's Autonomism, from St. Petersburg to Berlin," *Leo Baeck Institute Year Book* 50 (2005): 268–70.

10. Dubnov, "Pis'mo pervoe," 2–3; and Dubnov, "Pis'mo chetvertoe: Avtonomizm, kak osnova natsional'noi programmy," in Dubnov, *Pis'ma*, 75.

11. Benjamin Nathans, "On Russian-Jewish Historiography," in Thomas Sanders, ed., *Historiography of Imperial Russia: The Profession and Writing of History in a Multinational State* (Armonk, N.Y., 1999), 415. See also *K kharakteristike evreiskogo studenchestva, po dannym ankety sredi evreiskogo studenchestva g. Kieva v noiabre 1910 g.* (Kiev, 1913), 28.

12. For an assessment of Dubnov's ideological influences, see Lionel Kochan, "The Apotheosis of History: Dubnow," in his *The Jew and His History* (New York, 1977), 88–98; and Seltzer, "Simon Dubnow." For a thorough investigation into the intellectual influences on Dubnov's historical theories, see Jeffrey Veidlinger, "Simon Dubnow Recontextualized: The Sociological Conception of Jewish History and the Russian Intellectual Legacy," *Simon Dubnow Institute Yearbook* 3 (2004): 411–27.

13. Veidlinger, "Simon Dubnow Recontextualized," 418–27.

14. Veidlinger, "Simon Dubnow Recontextualized," 425; and Simon Dubnov, "Pis'mo tret'e: Etika natsionalizma," in Dubnov, *Pis'ma*, 62–67.

15. Dubnov, "Pis'mo tret'e," 61.

16. Dubnov, "Pis'mo tret'e," 61.

17. Dubnov, "Pis'mo tret'e," 62.

18. Perets ben Moshe Smolenskin, "Am olam," in his *Ma'amarim* (Jerusalem, 1925), 1: 1–162. Relevant parts of this essay appear in an annotated translation in

Simon Rabinovitch, ed., *Jews and Diaspora Nationalism: Writings on Jewish Peoplehood in Europe and the United States* (Waltham, Mass., 2012), 5–22. See also Charles H. Freundlich, *Peretz Smolenskin, His Life and Thought: A Study of the Renascence of Jewish Nationalism* (New York, 1965).

19. See Peretz Smolenskin, "It is Time to Plant" (Et lata'at), in Arthur Hertzberg, ed., *The Zionist Idea: A Historical Analysis and Reader* (Philadelphia, 1997), 145–47.

20. Shmuel Feiner considers a striking feature in both "Am olam" and "Et lata'at" to be "the transformation of traditional and maskilic concepts, which acquired nationalistic significance through their secularization" (*Haskalah and History: The Emergence of a Modern Jewish Historical Consciousness* [Oxford, U.K., 2002], 318–19). Like Dubnov, Smolenskin admired English liberalism and was influenced by Henry Buckle (325–26).

21. Simon Dubnov, "Pis'mo vtoroe: Evreistvo, kak duhovnaia (kul'turno-istoricheskaia) natsiia sredi politicheskih natsii," in Dubnov, *Pis'ma*, 52.

22. See Dubnov, "Pis'mo chetvertoe."

23. Dubnov quotes Clermont-Tonnere in "Pis'mo vtoroe," 43.

24. Theodore R. Weeks, *Nation and State in Late Imperial Russia: Nationalism and Russification on the Western Frontier, 1863–1914* (DeKalb, Ill., 1996), 9.

25. Dubnov, "Pis'mo vtoroe," 43–44.

26. Dubnov, "Pis'mo chetvertoe," 79.

27. See Dubnov's call to arms in S. M. Dubnov, *Ob izuchenii istorii russkikh evreev i ob uchrezhdenii russko-evreiskogo istoricheskogo obshchestva* (St. Petersburg, 1891).

28. Dubnov and other autonomists also had to defend themselves against charges of utopianism. For example, the proto-Zionist Moshe Lieb Lilienblum, a formative influence on Dubnov's intellectual development, accused Dubnov of being a dreamer and denounced as ridiculous the idea that the Jews could achieve national freedom in the Diaspora. See Simon Dubnov, "Pis'mo sedmoe: Natsiia nastoiashchago i natsiia budushago," in Dubnov, *Pis'ma*, 194.

29. See the three-volume collection of essays on Jewish self-rule from the ancient period to the modern: *Kehal Yisrael: ha-shilton ha-'atsmi ha-Yehudi le-dorotav*, vol. 1, Isaiah Gafni, ed. (Jerusalem, 2001); vol. 2, Avraham Grossman and Yosef Kaplan, eds. (Jerusalem, 2004); and vol. 3, Israel Bartal, ed. (Jerusalem, 2004). See also Louis Finkelstein, *Jewish Self-Government in the Middle Ages* (New York, 1924); Michael Walzer, Menachem Lorderbaum, and Noam J. Zohar, eds., *The Jewish Political Tradition* (New Haven, Conn., 2000), 1: 379–429; and Salo Baron's eighteen-volume *Social and Religious History of the Jews*. Dubnov's own oeuvre of historical writings contains a thorough elucidation of Jewish autonomy and self-government from the Babylonian period until the twentieth century.

30. The distinction between the *kahal* and the *kehila* was not always clear to Jews themselves, and, according to John Klier, they had become semantically syn-

onymous by the time of the Polish partitions ("The *Kahal* in the Russian Empire," *Simon Dubnow Institute Yearbook* 5 [2006]: 33–36). For the sake of clarity for the reader, I have tried to maintain the distinction and use *kehila* to refer to the legal community and *kahal* for its institutional leadership.

31. Antony Polonsky, *The Jews in Poland and Russia*, vol. 1, *1350–1881* (Oxford, U.K., 2010), 40–41, 49–58; Michael Stanislawski, "Kahal," in *YIVO Encyclopedia of Jews in Eastern* Europe (New Haven, Conn., 2008), 1: 845–48.

32. Polonsky, *Jews in Poland and Russia*, 1: 42–48.

33. For a description of these activities, see Gershon David Hundert, *Jews in Poland-Lithuania in the Eighteenth Century: A Genealogy of Modernity* (Berkeley, Calif., 2004), 79–98.

34. For a helpful comparison of Jewish communal autonomy in Italian, Dutch, German, Ottoman, and Eastern European contexts, see David B. Ruderman, *Early Modern Jewry: A New Cultural History* (Princeton, N.J., 2010), 57–98.

35. On the bureaucratic structure and election process, see Polonsky, *Jews in Poland and Russia*, 1: 51–52.

36. Hundert observes: "Disobedience of a communal enactment was thus simultaneously a civil offense and a sin" (*Jews in Poland-Lithuania*, 80).

37. Eli Lederhendler, "The Decline of the Polish-Lithuanian *Kahal*," *Polin* 2 (1987): 151.

38. Klier, "The *Kahal* in the Russian Empire," 35.

39. Polonsky, *Jews in Poland and Russia*, 1: 58–61; Adam Teller, "Councils," in *YIVO Encyclopedia of Jews in Eastern Europe* (New Haven, Conn., 2008), 1: 352–57.

40. See Israel Bartal, "Dubnov's Image of Medieval Autonomy," in Kristi Groberg and Avraham Greenbaum, eds., *A Missionary for History: Essays in Honor of Simon Dubnov* (Minneapolis, 1998), 11–18.

41. Eli Lederhendler, *The Road to Modern Jewish Politics: Political Tradition and Political Reconstruction in the Jewish Community of Tsarist Russia* (New York, 1989), 12–13.

42. Jacob Katz, *Tradition and Crisis: Jewish Society at the End of the Middle Ages*, Bernard Dov Cooperman, trans. (Syracuse, N.Y., 2000), 217–18.

43. M. J. Rosman, *The Lord's Jews: Magnate-Jewish Relations in the Polish-Lithuanian Commonwealth During the 18th Century* (Cambridge, Mass., 1990), 187–205.

44. See S. M. Dubnow [Dubnov], *History of the Jews in Russia and Poland*, vol. 1, *From the Earliest Times Until the Present Day*, I. Friedlaender, trans. (Philadelphia, 1916); and S. M. Dubnov, *Toldot ha-Hasidut* (Tel Aviv, 1930).

45. Much of the debate over whether a communal crisis occurred in the eighteenth century stems from the attempt, beginning with Dubnov, to explain the emergence of Hasidism. To Dubnov, the intense suffering of Polish Jewry in the early eighteenth century was compounded by the oppressive nature of rabbinic religion, and Hasidism provided an alternative, popularized form of Judaism that addressed the emotional needs of common Jews. Benzion Dinur later saw the pe-

riod as one of primarily communal as opposed to religious conflict; he claimed that Hasidism emerged in protest to the socially oppressive powers of the *kehilot*. Jacob Katz interpreted the emergence of Hasidism as a direct result of a crisis in communal leadership. According to Katz, communal leadership across Eastern Europe became increasingly corrupt, and leaders held their positions with help from the non-Jewish authorities against the popular will of the people. Moshe Rosman and Gershon Hundert have since challenged the extent of Jewish suffering and communal crisis in the eighteenth century, arguing that the period was in fact one of both economic and demographic recovery for the Jews in Poland-Lithuania. While recognizing internal conflicts in some *kehilot*, Hundert also questions the claim of a general pattern of communal crisis in eighteenth-century Poland. See Hundert's chapter "Was There a Communal 'Crisis' in the Eighteenth Century?" in his *Jews in Poland-Lithuania*, 99–118. See also Dubnov, *Toldot ha-Hasidut*; Benzion Dinur, *Be-mifne ha-dorot: mehkarim ve-ʻiyunim be-reshitam shel ha-zemanim ha-hadashim be-toldot Yisrael* (Jerusalem, 1955); and Katz, *Tradition and Crisis*. For recent revisions, see Gershon Hundert, *The Jews in a Polish Private Town: The Case of Opatów in the Eighteenth Century* (Baltimore, 1992); Rosman, *The Lord's Jews*; Moshe Rosman, *Founder of Hasidism: A Quest for the Historical Baʻal Shem Tov* (Berkeley, Calif., 1996); and Shmuel Ettinger, "Hasidism and the *Kahal* in Eastern Europe," in Ada Rapoport-Albert, ed., *Hasidism Reappraised* (London, 1996), 64–75. For a review of the contours of this debate, see Immanuel Etkes, "The Study of Hasidism: Past Trends and New Directions," in Rapoport-Albert, *Hasidism Reappraised*, 447–64.

46. Some proposals to modernize the Polish Jewish community and its autonomy were broached by both Jewish and Polish individuals during the period of the Four-Year Sejm (1788–1792) but came to naught. See Hundert, *Jews in Poland-Lithuania*, 216–31; and Nancy Sinkoff, *Out of the Shtetl: Making Jews Modern in the Polish Borderlands* (Providence, R.I., 2004), 98–105. For an overview of the attitudes of the Prussian, Austrian, and Russian rulers toward Jewish autonomy at the time of partition, see John Doyle Klier, *Russia Gathers Her Jews: The Origins of the "Jewish Question" in Russia, 1772–1825* (DeKalb, Ill., 1986), 38–52.

47. For two excellent overviews, see Israel Bartal, "Autonomie, autonomisme, diasporisme," in Élie Barnavi and Saul Friedländer, eds., *Les juifs et le XXe siècle: dictionnaire critique* (Paris, 2000), 36–46; and Israel Bartal, "Responses to Modernity: Haskalah, Orthodoxy, and Nationalism in Eastern Europe," in Shmuel Almog, Jehuda Reinharz, and Anita Shapira, eds., *Zionism and Religion* (Hanover, N.H., 1998), 13–24.

48. Interestingly, in his famous 1781 call for Jewish emancipation, *Über die bürgerliche Verbesserung der Juden* (On the Civil Betterment of the Jews), Christian Wilhelm Dohm argued for the continued autonomy of the Jewish communities in Prussia—which prompted a dissenting response from Moses Mendelssohn—illustrating an important difference in French and German attitudes. Moses Mendels-

sohn, "On the Curtailment of Jewish Juridical Autonomy," in Paul Mendes-Flohr and Jehuda Reinharz, eds., *The Jew in the Modern World: A Documentary History*, 2nd ed. (New York, 1995), 87–90.

49. Sophia Kemlein, "The Jewish Community in the Grand Duchy of Poznań Under Prussian Rule, 1815–1848," *Polin* 14 (2001): 66.

50. François Guesnet, "*Khevres* and *Akhdes*: The Change in Jewish Self-Organization in the Kingdom of Poland Before 1900 and the Bund," in Jack Jacobs, ed., *Jewish Politics in Eastern Europe: The Bund at 100* (New York, 2001), 5.

51. See Polonsky, *Jews in Poland and Russia*, 1: 273–321; and Theodore R. Weeks, *From Assimilation to Antisemitism: The "Jewish Question" in Poland, 1850–1914* (DeKalb, Ill., 2006).

52. See the classic essay by Salo Baron, "Ghetto and Emancipation," *Menorah Journal* 14 (1928): 515–26.

53. See Simon Dubnov, *History of the Jews*, vol. 3, *From Cromwell's Commonwealth to the Napoleonic Era*, Moshe Spiegel, trans. (South Brunswick, N.J., 1973), 496–501. In a current work in progress, François Guesnet argues that the process of "de-corporating the Jews" in exchange for civil equality began in eighteenth-century France, and its antecedents go further back, to when corporatist traditions in general came under attack by French mercantilists. Guesnet also points out that most French Jews—not least the Ashkenazic community of Alsace, but to a certain extent the Sephardic communities of southern France as well—resisted their decorporation. Eighteenth-century Austria and Prussia, in contrast, favored what Guesnet terms "partial and conservative de-corporation." François Guesnet, "De-Corporating the Jews of Europe," paper presented at the conference "Jewish Politics in Eastern Europe: From *Shtadlanut* to Mass Parties," at the Center for Studies of the History and Culture of East European Jews (Vilnius, 2007).

54. "The Emancipation of the Jews of France (September 28, 1791)," in Mendes-Flohr and Reinharz, *The Jew in the Modern World*, 118.

55. David E. Fishman, *Russia's First Modern Jews: The Jews of Shklov* (New York, 1995), 9–11.

56. Benjamin Nathans, *Beyond the Pale: The Jewish Encounter with Late Imperial Russia* (Berkeley, Calif., 2002), 26. Richard Pipes argues that Catherine and her Senate intended "estate equality" (i.e., equality within the estates) between Jews and Christians. Pipes places the blame for the failure to implement the merging of Jews into the Christian urban and merchant estates on such factors as the appointment of P. G. Passek as governor general of Belorussia in 1782, resistance from the financially hard-pressed merchant and artisan classes, and second thoughts by Catherine and others following the French Revolution. See Richard Pipes, "Catherine II and the Jews: The Origins of the Pale of Settlement," *Soviet Jewish Affairs* 5.2 (1975): 10–17.

57. Heinz-Dietrich Löwe, "Poles, Jews, and Tatars: Religion, Ethnicity, and Social Structure in Tsarist Nationality Policies," *Jewish Social Studies* 6.3 (2000):

59. Löwe makes the convincing argument that Russian imperial policies regarding Jewish integration and autonomy from the late eighteenth to the mid-nineteenth century most closely resemble how the government approached the Tatars (52–96).

58. Klier, *Russia Gathers Her Jews*, 136–37.

59. Gregory Freeze, "The *Soslovie* (Estate) Paradigm and Russian Social History," *American Historical Review* 91.1 (1986): 18–26.

60. Michael Stanislawski, "Russian Jewry, the Russian State, and the Dynamics of Jewish Emancipation," in Birnbaum and Katznelson, *Paths of Emancipation*, 266.

61. For a short history of the "Terms of Integration," see Nathans, *Beyond the Pale*, 72–79.

62. Stanislawski, "Russian Jewry," 271–72.

63. See Nathans, *Beyond the Pale*, 31–38.

64. Klier, "The *Kahal* in the Russian Empire," 39–40; Klier, *Russia Gathers Her Jews*, 116–43. On autonomy and the responsibilities of the *kahal* in imperial Russia, see Isaac Levitats, *The Jewish Community in Russia, 1772–1844* (New York, 1943).

65. Eugene M. Avrutin, *Jews and the Imperial State: Identification Politics in Tsarist Russia* (Ithaca, N.Y., 2010), 32–50. For a comparison of Jews and Muslims in the Russian Empire, see Robert Crews, *For Prophet and Tsar: Islam and Empire in Russia and Central Asia* (Cambridge, Mass., 2006).

66. Klier, *Russia Gathers Her Jews*, 65. The extent to which the Russian imperial government preserved Jewish autonomy in the Russian state both before and after the abolition of the *kahal* system is a matter of some debate, and the different positions are helpfully explained in Klier, "The *Kahal* in the Russian Empire." Klier argues that although Russian officials held a negative view of the *kahal* and its successor institutions, economic considerations trumped all others. In general, the Russian state weakened the corporate rights of the Jews just as it did those of other groups absorbed into the state through territorial expansion.

67. Michael Stanislawski, *Tsar Nicholas I and the Jews: The Transformation of Jewish Society in Russia, 1825–1855* (Philadelphia, 1983), 125.

68. Israel Bartal, *The Jews of Eastern Europe, 1772–1881*, Chaya Naor, trans. (Philadelphia, 2005), 66.

69. Avrutin, *Jews and the Imperial State*, 27.

70. See Stanislawski, *Tsar Nicholas I and the Jews*.

71. Olga Litvak, *Conscription and the Search for Modern Russian Jewry* (Bloomington, Ind., 2006), 35.

72. Litvak, *Conscription*, 35.

73. Litvak, *Conscription*, 38.

74. In theory, Jewish communal responsibilities were assumed by the municipalities. Nonetheless, local government officials frequently complained that the Jews ignored the law abolishing the *kahal* by maintaining a raft of separate communal institutions. See Levitats, *Jewish Community in Russia*, 7–16. Levitats in-

cludes summaries of the significant amendments made to the law abolishing the *kahal* and the regulations for Jewish participation in municipal government.

75. Mordechai Zalkin, "Vilnius," in *YIVO Encyclopedia of Jews in Eastern Europe* (New Haven, Conn., 2008), 2: 1970–77.

76. Antony Polonsky, *The Jews in Poland and Russia*, vol. 2, *1881–1914* (Oxford, U.K., 2010), 192.

77. Levitats, *Jewish Community in Russia*, 62.

78. Levitats, *Jewish Community in Russia*, 62.

79. Because these individuals did not control the *kehila*, they went around it by telling the authorities that the petition represented the will of the *obshchestvo*, which at that point still simply meant community. Steven Zipperstein, *The Jews of Odessa: A Cultural History, 1794–1881* (Stanford, Calif., 1986), 45–46, 56–64.

80. Alexis Hofmeister, *Selbstorganisation und Bürgerlichkeit: Jüdisches Vereinswesen in Odessa um 1900* (Göttingen, 2007), 71–174. Hofmeister's study suggests that the city's extensive Jewish "self-organization" and growing tensions with other nationalities naturally led to Odessa becoming an important center of Jewish nationalism and Russian Zionism (175–225). See also Steven Zipperstein, "Odessa," in *YIVO Encyclopedia of Jews in Eastern Europe* (New Haven, Conn., 2008), 2: 1277–82.

81. Eliyahu Stern, *The Genius: Elijah of Vilna and the Making of Modern Judaism* (New Haven, Conn., 2013), 139–40.

82. Israel Bartal, "From Corporation to Nation: Jewish Autonomy in Eastern Europe, 1772–1881," *Simon Dubnow Institute Yearbook* 5 (2006): 25–26. According to Bartal, Dubnov's secularism prevented him from seeing the role that religious organizations played in preserving Jewish autonomy in Austrian Galicia and throughout the Russian Empire (27–28).

83. Bartal, "From Corporation to Nation," 24–25.

84. According to Lederhendler, "The diffusion of communal responsibility spawned new leadership groups; challenges to the existing communal institutions stimulated the search for new forms of activity; and the loss of the state as a guarantor of the community's structural integrity facilitated the discovery of the 'people's will' as the foundation for a new type of political community" (*Road to Modern Jewish Politics*, 155).

85. See John Klier, *Imperial Russia's Jewish Question, 1855–1881* (Cambridge, U.K., 1995), 263–83.

86. Klier, *Imperial Russia's Jewish Question*, 263–83.

87. Brafman's recommendations were taken up and elaborated on by the governor general of Vilna, Count E. T. Baranov. Remarkably for the time, in 1868 Baranov's successor, A. L. Potapov, allowed the Jews (through official delegates) to compose an official Jewish response to Baranov's so-called Vilna Commission. See Klier, *Imperial Russia's Jewish Question*, 173–81; Lederhendler, *Road to Modern Jewish Politics*, 142–45; and Nathans, *Beyond the Pale*, 174–80. On Brafman's legislative influence, see Levitats, *Jewish Community in Russia*, 10.

88. Simon Dubnov, *History of the Jews*, vol. 5, *From the Congress of Vienna to the Emergence of Hitler*, Moshe Spiegel, trans. (South Brunswick, N.J., 1973), 333–34.

89. Quoted in Eugene Avrutin, "Racial Categories and the Politics of (Jewish) Difference in Late Imperial Russia," *Kritika* 8.1 (2007): 22.

90. Jacob Katz, *A State Within a State: The History of an Anti-Semitic Slogan* (Jerusalem, 1969), 5–6.

91. As Katz argues, such arguments became prevalent precisely when Jewish autonomy was eroding under state power (*State Within a State*, 29–30).

92. See Hilbrenner, "Simon Dubnov's Master Narrative," 159–61.

93. Hilbrenner suggests that Dubnov's position on the *kahal* was a reaction to antisemitic accusations and that he actually appropriated and reinterpreted these arguments (*Diaspora-Natsionalismus*, 184).

94. To Smolenskin, the *kahal* represented the control of the many by the few, which to him was everything that was wrong with Jewish communal life. Instead, Smolenskin looked to the Alliance Israélite Universelle (before the 1880s) to play the role of Jewish national organization ("Am olam," 38–48).

95. Dubnov, "Pis'mo chetvertoe," 79.

96. Dubnov, "Pis'mo chetvertoe," 84–85.

97. Dubnov, "Pis'mo chetvertoe," 178–79, 182.

98. See Weeks, *Nation and State*, 17.

99. Eli Lederhendler suggests that the most notable effect of the abolition of the Council of Four Lands was to deprive the *kahal* system of a means of collective Jewish representation, both in late prepartition Poland and imperial Russia ("Decline of the Polish-Lithuanian *Kahal*," 150–62). See also Lederhendler, *Road to Modern Jewish Politics*.

100. Yokhanan Petrovskii-Shtern, *Evrei v russkoi armii: 1827–1914* (Moscow, 2003), 93–105.

101. David Saunders, *Russia in the Age of Reaction and Reform, 1801–1881* (London, 1992), 239–77. See also Daniel Brower, *The Russian City Between Tradition and Modernity, 1850–1900* (Berkeley, Calif., 1990).

102. There is little evidence to support the widespread idea that factory owners preferred non-Jewish workers to avoid closing on Saturdays as well as Sundays. A steady supply of Jews willing to violate the Sabbath for decent work existed; in places with concentrated Jewish populations, Jewish factory owners could easily employ only Jews and close only on Saturdays, and there were examples of alternative arrangements being made. The best explanation for why Jewish factory owners preferred non-Jewish workers still remains the lower wages they initially had to pay, followed by pressure from non-Jewish workers to maintain their positions afterward. As Eli Lederhendler points out, Jewish factory owners in the United States came to prefer Jewish workers for precisely the same reason, because they were unskilled laborers who would work for lower wages (*Jewish Immigrants and American Capitalism, 1880–1920: From Caste to Class* [Cambridge, U.K., 2009]).

103. Yoav Peled and Gershon Shafir, "From Caste to Exclusion: The Dynamics of Modernization in the Russian Pale of Settlement," in Ezra Mendelsohn, ed., *Studies in Contemporary Jewry*, vol. 3, *Jews and Other Ethnic Groups in a Multi-Ethnic World* (New York, 1987), 100. Peled and Shafir, Lederhendler, Mendelsohn, and Kahan all use the same sources, primarily the studies conducted by the economist Boris Brutskus under the auspices of the Jewish Colonization Society and those on the conditions of Jewish workers by Jacob Lestschinsky. See Jewish Colonization Association, *Recueil de matériaux sur la situation économique des Israélites de Russie* (Paris, 1906); Jewish Colonization Association, *Sbornik materialov ob ekonomicheskom polozhenii Evreev v Rossii* (St. Petersburg, 1904); and Jacob Lestschinsky, *Der yidisher arbayter (in Rusland)* (Vilna, 1906).

104. Lederhendler, *Jewish Immigrants*, 13, 37.

105. Nathans, *Beyond the Pale*, 215.

106. Lederhendler, *Jewish Immigrants*, 218.

107. On Jewish membership in upper-status groups and the size of the Jewish bourgeoisie in 1897, see Arcadius Kahan, "The Impact of Industrialization in Tsarist Russia on the Socioeconomic Conditions of the Jewish Population," in Roger Weiss, ed., *Essays in Social and Economic History*, (Chicago, 1986), 18–19; on the number of Jews educated in Russian institutions, see Nathans, *Beyond the Pale*, 218, 229, 270–71.

108. Nathans, *Beyond the Pale*, 234.

109. Martin Malia, "What Is the Intelligentsia?" *Daedalus* 89.3 (1960): 443.

110. Malia, "What Is the Intelligentsia?" 454–55. Malia suggests that at any given time in the 1870s, the Russian Empire had about 5,000 students in its universities, out of a population of approximately 60 million.

111. A dearth of jobs for the number of educated Poles resulted in a particularly large, frustrated Polish *intelligentsia*, with certain similarities to the Jewish case. See Jerzy Jedlicki, *A Suburb of Europe: Nineteenth-Century Polish Approaches to Western Civilization* (Budapest, 1999), 173–202.

112. See Deborah Hope Yalen, "Red *Kasrilevke*: Ethnographies of Economic Transformation in the Soviet Shtetl, 1917–1939" (PhD diss., University of California, Berkeley, 2007), esp. ch. 1.

113. This process is perfectly illustrated using the available statistics in Kahan, "Impact of Industrialization," 27–31.

114. Shaul Stampfer, "Patterns of Internal Jewish Migration in the Russian Empire," in Yaacov Ro'i, ed., *Jews and Jewish Life in Russia and the Soviet Union* (Ilford, U.K., 1995), 28–47.

115. All figures taken from *Evreiskoe naselenie Rossii po dannym perepisi 1897 g. i po noveishim istochnikam* (Petrograd, 1917).

116. Jane Burbank, "Thinking Like an Empire: Estate, Law, and Rights in the Early Twentieth Century," in Jane Burbank, Mark von Hagen, and Anatolyi Remnev, eds., *Russian Empire: Space, People, Power, 1700–1930* (Bloomington, Ind., 2007), 198.

117. Avrutin, *Jews and the Imperial State*, 10.

118. On this shift, see Lederhendler, *Road to Modern Jewish Politics*; and Brian Horowitz, *Jewish Philanthropy and Enlightenment in Late-Tsarist Russia* (Seattle, 2009).

119. Shaul Stampfer, *Families, Rabbis, and Education: Traditional Jewish Society in Nineteenth-Century Eastern Europe* (Oxford, U.K., 2010), 90–95.

120. Stampfer, *Families*, 285–87.

121. Tamar Kaplan Appel, "Crown Rabbi," in *YIVO Encyclopedia of Jews in Eastern Europe* (New Haven, Conn., 2008), 1: 368–69.

122. Stampfer, *Families*, 292–93.

123. Horowitz, *Jewish Philanthropy*, 17–28.

124. Yvonne Kleinmann, *Neue Orte—neue Menschen: Jüdische Lebensformen in St. Petersburg und Moskau im 19. Jahrhundert* (Göttingen, 2006), 176.

125. See Jonathan Frankel, *Prophecy and Politics: Socialism, Nationalism, and the Russian Jews, 1862–1917* (Cambridge, U.K., 1981); Nathans, *Beyond the Pale*, 7–10; John D. Klier, "The Myth of Zion Among East European Jewry," in Geoffrey Hosking and George Schöpflin, eds., *Myths and Nationhood* (New York, 1997), 170–81; John D. Klier and Shlomo Lambroza, eds., *Pogroms: Anti-Jewish Violence in Modern Russian History* (Cambridge, U.K., 1992); and John D. Klier, *Russians, Jews, and the Pogroms of 1881–1882* (Cambridge, U.K., 2011).

126. Frankel, *Prophecy and Politics*; Israel Bartal, "Lilienblum, Moshe Leib," in *YIVO Encyclopedia of Jews in Eastern Europe* (New Haven, Conn., 2008), 1: 1039–42; and for a short selection of Lilienblum's political writing in English translation, see Arthur Hertzberg, ed., *The Zionist Idea: A Historical Analysis and Reader* (Philadelphia, 1997), 168–77.

127. Benjamin Nathans, "A 'Hebrew Drama': Lilienblum, Dubnow, and the Idea of 'Crisis' in East European Jewish History," *Simon Dubnow Institute Yearbook* 5 (2006): 212.

128. Frankel, *Prophecy and Politics*; Steven Zipperstein, "Representations of Leadership (and Failure) in Russian Zionism: Picturing Leon Pinsker," in Jehuda Reinharz and Anita Shapira, eds., *Essential Papers on Zionism* (New York, 1996), 191–209; David Vital, *The Origins of Zionism* (Oxford, U.K., 1975).

129. Notably, Pinsker wrote this treatise in German rather than Russian, Hebrew, or Yiddish. Both *Autoemanzipation* (in the original German) and D. S. Blondheim's 1906 English translation, *Auto-Emancipation*, are available in full text at books.google.com.

130. Dubnov, "Pis'mo chetvertoe," 76.

131. For example, Nordau stated: "In the ghetto, the Jew had his own world; it was his sure refuge and it provided the spiritual and moral equivalent of a motherland" ("Speech to the First Zionist Congress [1897]," in Hertzberg, *Zionist Idea*, 237).

132. Dubnov, "Pis'mo chetvertoe," 109–10.

133. Shimon Dubnov, "Sod ha-kiyum ve-hok ha-kiyum shel am Yisrael," in *He-'Atid* (Berlin, 1912; reprinted 1922–23), 4: 112–17.

134. Dubnov, "Sod ha-kiyum." In Dubnov's thinking, the Diaspora paradoxically exists as both curse and blessing. As Renée Poznanski suggests, Dubnov's historiography casts the Jews' bloody moments in the Diaspora as the historical engine that drove their emigration and the shifting of hegemonic centers ("Dubnov and the Diaspora," in Kristi Groberg and Avraham Greenbaum, eds., *A Missionary for History: Essays in Honor of Simon Dubnov* [Minneapolis, 1998], 8–9).

135. Pierre Birnbaum and Ira Katznelson, "Emancipation and the Liberal Offer," in their *Paths of Emancipation*, 16.

136. Bartal, "From Corporation to Nation," 30.

137. See Nathans, *Beyond the Pale*, 53.

Chapter 2

1. Derek J. Penslar, *Shylock's Children: Economics and Jewish Identity in Modern Europe* (Berkeley, Calif., 2001), 4. See also David Sorkin, *The Transformation of German Jewry, 1780–1840* (Oxford, U.K., 1987).

2. Eli Lederhendler, "Modernity Without Emancipation or Assimilation? The Case of Russian Jewry," in Jonathan Frankel and Steven J. Zipperstein, eds., *Assimilation and Community: The Jews in Nineteenth-Century Europe* (Cambridge, U.K., 1992), 328.

3. Although many sources say Zhitlowsky was born in 1865, his personal papers indicate that the correct year is 1861. See the archival guide/finding aid to Zhitlowsky's archive located at the YIVO Institute in New York. YIVO, RG 208.

4. For a beautiful telling of An-sky and Zhitlowsky's lifelong friendship as well as a colorful depiction of the entire Russian Jewish revolutionary milieu in exile, see Gabriella Safran, *Wandering Soul: The Dybbuk's Creator, S. An-sky* (Cambridge, Mass., 2010). The best summary of Zhitlowsky's personality and political ideology is still Jonathan Frankel, *Prophecy and Politics: Socialism, Nationalism, and the Russian Jews, 1862–1917* (Cambridge, U.K., 1981), 258–87. Of Zhitlowsky and An-sky's transitions to radicalism, Frankel states: "The biographies of Chaim Zhitlovsky and Shloyme Zanvl Rappoport (An-sky) demonstrate how, even after the pogroms of 1882 and by a paradoxical logic, a commitment to the tenets of Russian revolutionary populism could lead to a simultaneous involvement in Jewish life and politics. Both of these men had arrived by 1905–6 at a similar position, members of the SR [Socialist Revolutionary] party and spokesmen for the revolutionary Left in the Jewish world. But they had followed very different paths in reaching that point" (*Prophecy and Politics*, 260).

5. Frankel, *Prophecy and Politics*, 264. Dubnov skewered *Thoughts on the Historical Fate of Jewry* in a review in *Voskhod*. See Kritikus [Dubnov], "Literaturnaia letopis: ostatki literaturnoi zhatvy 1887 goda," *Voskhod* (December 1887): 6–13.

6. First, in 1885, the group was called Teshuat Israel, and it unsuccessfully sought to create a Jewish wing of Narodnaia Volia. In 1888 the group was recreated as the Society for the Promotion of Life and Learning of the Jewish People (Oscar Janowsky, *The Jews and Minority Rights (1898–1919)* [New York, 1966 (1933)], 53).

7. Zhitlowsky published this long essay in Russian in London. The first three (of five) chapters of "A Jew to Jews" and Zhitlowsky's essay "Why Only Yiddish?" appear in Simon Rabinovitch, ed., *Jews and Diaspora Nationalism: Writings on Jewish Peoplehood in Europe and the United States* (Waltham, Mass., 2012), 83–104.

8. Zhitlowsky, "A Jew to Jews," 86.

9. Zhitlowsky also attended the First Zionist Congress in Basel in 1897, despite being a fierce opponent of political Zionism. On the early Socialist Revolutionary movement, see Manfred Hildermeier, *The Russian Socialist Revolutionary Party Before the First World War* (New York, 2000); and Michael Melancon, "The Socialist Revolutionaries from 1902 to 1907: Peasant and Workers' Party," *Russian History* 1 (spring 1985): 2–47.

10. Janowsky, *Jews and Minority Rights*, 53. For his book *The Jews and Minority Rights*, which was originally published in 1933, Oscar Janowsky interviewed Zhitlowsky in New York and corresponded with Dubnov, who was then living in Berlin. According to Janowsky, "Zhitlowsky believes that the tract *A Jew to Jews* presented the first proposal for Jewish national rights. Dubnow, however, cannot discover in the pamphlet any definite traces of the 'modern concept "autonomism"'" (54). Janowsky wrote *The Jews and Minority Rights* with an agenda to promote and legitimate claims to Jewish national rights and autonomy in Eastern Europe. See James Loeffler, "Between Zionism and Liberalism: Oscar Janowsky and Diaspora Nationalism in America," *AJS Review* 34.2 (2010): 289–308. For a summary of Zhitlowsky's ideological evolution and some comparison to that of Dubnov's, see David Weinberg, *Between Tradition and Modernity: Haim Zhitlowski, Simon Dubnow, Ahad Ha-Am, and the Shaping of Modern Jewish Identity* (New York, 1996), 83–144.

11. Tony Michels, *A Fire in Their Hearts: Yiddish Socialists in New York* (Cambridge, Mass., 2005), 128. Michels nicely summarizes Zhitlowsky's "Progressive Jewish Nationalism" (128–36).

12. Zhitlowsky published the influential essay "Tsionismus oder sotsializmus?" in *Der yidisher arbeyter* in 1898. It appeared later as "Tsionizm oder sotsiyolizm?" in his *Gezamlte shriften* (New York, 1917), 4: 47–76. David E. Fishman suggests that Zhitlowsky may have been the first to use the term *yidishe kultur* ("The Politics of Yiddish in Tsarist Russia," in Jacob Neusner, Ernest Freichs, and Nahum M. Sarna, eds., *From Ancient Israel to Modern Judaism: Essays in Honor of Marvin Fox* [Atlanta, 1989], 4: 156).

13. See Jack Jacobs, *On Socialists and "the Jewish Question" After Marx* (New York, 1992), 36–37.

14. The federally reorganized party, with a common program and All-Austrian

Social Democratic Party congress and executive, was established in 1897. See Arthur A. Kogan, "The Social Democrats and the Conflict of Nationalities in the Habsburg Monarchy," *Journal of Modern History* 21.3 (1949): 206.

15. Ephraim Nimni, "Introduction: The National Cultural Autonomy Model Revisited," in Ephraim Nimni, ed., *National Cultural Autonomy and Its Contemporary Critics* (London, 2005), 5.

16. Kogan, "Social Democrats," 206.

17. Kogan, "Social Democrats," 208. Kogan argues that the Brünn Resolution reflects the continuity of Austrian federalist thought reaching back to the revolution of 1848 (212).

18. Quoted in Kogan, "Social Democrats," 209. For the original, see *Protokoll über die Verhandlungen des Gesamstparteitages der sozialdemokratischen Arbeiterpartei in Österreich* (Vienna, 1899), 85.

19. Kogan, "Social Democrats," 210–15.

20. Ben Ehud [Chaim Zhitlowsky], "Natsional'nyi vopros i sotsializm," *Vozrozhdenie* 3–4 (November 1904): 47. The article originally appeared as "Der Socialismus und die Nationalitätenfrage" in the Viennese journal *Deutsche Worte* 8–9 (1899): 305–43. In the introduction he wrote for the Russian version in *Vozrozhdenie*, Zhitlowsky noted that regarding the question of territory, "which the author dismisses in the first point, he has radically altered his original opinion" (41). An extended version of this essay was published in book form by the Jewish Socialist Labor Party (SERP) as *Sotsializm i natsional'nyi vopros* (Kiev and St. Petersburg, 1906). For Zhitlowsky's notes and outline of this essay, see YIVO, RG 208, f. 1908.

21. Renner also referred to personal autonomy as the "personality principle," to differentiate between his idea and the "territorial principle" on which modern nation-states were based. Renner was influenced by the German historian Friedrich Meinecke (1862–1954), who argued in his most famous work, *Weltbürgertum und Nationalstaat* (Cosmopolitanism and the National State), that personality is the highest form of autonomy. See Ephraim Nimni, "Introduction," in Otto Bauer, *The Question of Nationalities and Social Democracy*, Joseph O'Donnell, trans. (Minneapolis, 2000), xxv–xxvii. A complete English translation of "Staat und Nation" has been published as Karl Renner, "State and Nation," in Nimni, *National Cultural Autonomy*, 15–47. For the original, see Synopticus [Karl Renner], *Staat und Nation: Zur österreichisten Nationalitätenfrage—Staatsrechtliche Untersuchung über die möglichen Principien einer Lösung und die juristischen Voraussetzungen eines Nationalitätengestzes* [State and Nation: On the Austrian Nationalities Question—An Investigation in Constitutional Law of Possible Legal Principles for a Solution and Conditions of a Nationality Law] (Vienna, 1899).

22. Renner, "State and Nation," 22–23.

23. Renner, "State and Nation," 24.

24. Otto Bauer, *Die Nationalitätenfrage und die Sozialdemokratie*, recently translated by Joseph O'Donnell as *The Question of Nationalities and Social Democracy*

(Minneapolis, 2000). See also Enzo Traverso, *The Marxists and the Jewish Question: The History of a Debate, 1843–1943*, Bernard Gibbons, trans. (Atlantic Highlands, N.J., 1990), 76–82.

25. See the section "National Autonomy for the Jews?" in Bauer, *Question of Nationalities*, 291–308. Bauer's adamant opposition to Jewish inclusion in the formula of national rights can be traced to his Jewish origins, much as Adler's Jewish past affected his own views. For more on the question of Austrian socialists and Jewish identity, see Robert Wistrich, *Socialism and the Jews: The Dilemmas of Assimilation in Germany and Austria-Hungary* (Rutherford, N.J., 1982).

26. See Jacobs, *On Socialists*, 86–104. Jacobs observes: "Kautsky realized that the workers of oppressed nations would not wholeheartedly work for the socialist cause unless and until the socialist movement acknowledged and worked against national oppression" (40).

27. Karl Kautsky, *Are the Jews a Race?* (London, 1926), 244.

28. Frankel, *Prophecy and Politics*, 282.

29. See Ben-Adir [Avrom Rozin], "Nash natsional'nyi ideal i nashe natsional'noe dvizhenie," *Vozrozhdenie* 3–4 (November 1904): 39. The idea of a new movement was first broached at a conference of socialist Zionist students in Rovno in the spring of 1903, which led to Vozrozhdenie's foundational conference the following fall. On the origins, conferences, and publications of Vozrozhdenie, see M. Zilberfarb, "Di grupe 'vozrozhdenie,'" *Royter pinkes* 1 (1921): 113–30 (for this reference I am indebted to David Fishman, *The Rise of Modern Yiddish Culture* [Pittsburgh, 2005], 166).

30. The journal was subtitled *Organ evreiskoi revolutsionnoi mysli* (Organ of Jewish Revolutionary Ideas). Frankel says that the conference was divided on various points, but the group that organized the conference also controlled the journal. The members of this faction considered themselves revolutionary socialists and nationalists, favored emigration and territorial concentration, and advocated the use of terrorism (*Prophecy and Politics*, 279).

31. "Nashi zadachi," *Vozrozhdenie* 1–2 (January–February 1904): 1–9. "Nashi zadachi" was written in the form of a manifesto, and although the authors had not officially formed a party, they referred to themselves in the article as the "party of national renaissance of the Jewish people" (6).

32. "Nashi zadachi," 2, 7.

33. "Nashi zadachi," 5–6.

34. See, for example, "O evreiskom voprose na stranitsakh sotsialisticheskoi pechati: Kriticheskie zametki" (On the Jewish Question in the Pages of the Socialist Press: Critical Notes), *Vozrozhdenie* 1–2 (January–February 1904): 12–19; and "Smelost' slova i trusost' mysli (Po povodu "natsionalizma" Bunda)" (Courageous Words and Cowardly Ideas [Regarding the Bund's "Nationalism"]), *Vozrozhdenie* 1–2 (January–February 1904): 19–24.

35. Ben-Adir, "Nash natsional'nyi ideal," 38–42.

36. Many of these ideas are addressed in the collection of essays published under the title *Vozrozhdenie (Evreiskii proletariat i natsional'naia problema): Sbornik Statei* (London, 1905). The book was written by Moyshe Zilberfarb, Avrom Rozin, and Vladimir Fabrikant, with the chapters unsigned (Zilberfarb, "Di grupe 'vozro-zhdenie,'" 127). See especially the chapters (by Zilberfarb) "Printsip natsional'no-politicheskoi avtonomii," 47–59, and "Natsional'naia i territorial'naia avtonomii i interesy evreiskago proletariat," 59–77. This publication actually had greater lon-gevity than one might expect. A letter dated February 20, 1918, from the central bureau of the All-Russian Union of Middle-School Students to the Central Com-mittee of the OESRP (S.S. and E.S.) requested 2,000 copies of "Vozrozhdenie 1905," if they could be spared (presumably referring to the book of collected es-says). In 1918 socialist Zionists obviously still considered the publication to be use-ful for teaching the basics of Jewish autonomism to schoolchildren. TsGAOO/ TsDAHO, f. 41 (Jewish nationalist parties and organizations), op. 1, d. 91.

37. [Zilberfarb], "Printsip natsional'no-politicheskoi avtonomii," 52.

38. "Nashi zadachi," 3–4.

39. SERP applied for organizational unity with the Socialist Revolutionary Party, but by 1907, when the two organizations did officially create an alliance, the relationship was based more on the personal friendship of the two parties' leaders than the generally Marxist inclinations of the broader SERP membership.

40. On SERP's 1906 platform, see *Programmy politicheskikh partii Rossii: Konets XIX–nachalo XX vv* (Moscow, 1995), 194–207. Kalmanovich became an impor-tant Yiddishist and was responsible for translating Dubnov's historical works from Russian into Yiddish.

41. Although Bundists ascribed to themselves a considerable role in the cre-ation of modern Yiddish culture, David Fishman challenges the group's self-pro-claimed founder status in two articles: "The Politics of Yiddish in Tsarist Russia," in Neusner et al., *From Ancient Israel to Modern Judaism*, 155–71; and "The Bund and Modern Yiddish Culture," in Zvi Gitelman, ed., *The Emergence of Modern Jew-ish Politics: Bundism and Zionism in Eastern Europe* (Pittsburgh, 2003), 107–19. In the second article, he states: "Until 1905, the Bund's connection to the language was utilitarian, and not a matter of ideology or principle. Indeed, the top echelon of the Bund's leadership consisted of Russified Jewish intelligentsia, most of whom knew Yiddish quite poorly" (110). The Bund and the language question are dis-cussed further in Chapter 4.

42. Zvi Y. Gitelman, *Jewish Nationality and Soviet Politics: The Jewish Sections of the CPSU, 1917–1930* (Princeton, N.J., 1972), 31.

43. Henry J. Tobias, "The Bund and Lenin Until 1903," *Russian Review* 20.4 (1961): 345.

44. Quoted in Jacob S. Hertz, "The Bund's Nationality Program and Its Crit-ics in the Russian, Polish, and Austrian Socialist Movements," *YIVO Annual* 14 (1969): 57. In some rare instances the development of Jewish nationalism seemed

logical to non-Jewish political theorists because it followed the same laws that applied to other nationalities. For instance, Kazimierz Kelles-Krauz (1872–1905), a sociologist and theorist of the Polish Socialist Party, viewed Zionism and the development of Jewish nationalism positively because it marked a move among Jewish intellectuals to use national culture to reach the masses in the same manner that intellectuals of other nationalities used. See Timothy Snyder, "Kazimierz Kelles-Krauz, 1872–1905: A Polish Socialist for Jewish Nationality," *Polin* 12 (1999): 263.

45. On Mill's use of Kautsky's theories, see Joshua D. Zimmerman, *Poles, Jews, and the Politics of Nationality: The Bund and the Polish Socialist Party in Late Tsarist Russia, 1892–1914* (Madison, Wisc., 2004), 109–15.

46. Jacobs, *On Socialists*, 124–25.

47. Jacobs, *On Socialists*, 126.

48. For a summary of Medem's neutralism, see Yoav Peled, "The Concept of National Cultural Autonomy: The First One Hundred Years," in Jack Jacobs, ed., *Jewish Politics in Eastern Europe: The Bund at 100* (New York, 2001), 256–57.

49. [Zilberfarb], "Printsip natsional'no-politicheskoi avtonomii," 52.

50. [Zilberfarb], "Natsional'naia i territorial'naia avtonomii."

51. Specifically, "the recognition of a nationality as a juridical person is a legal prerequisite for the existence of any and all national rights, which will remain empty noise in the absence of a legal entity to guarantee the inviolability of these rights" ([Zilberfarb], "Printsip natsional'no-politicheskoi avtonomii," 54).

52. Quoted in [Zilberfarb], "Printsip natsional'no-politicheskoi avtonomii," 54.

53. See Jacobs, *On Socialists*, 134–35. As Jacobs points out, however, SERP's leaders' sympathy toward Russian Socialist Revolutionary ideology already put them at odds with Kautsky's orthodox Marxism (138).

54. Thus, also in 1906, Mark Ratner published introductory essays to a Russian translation of the debates on the national question at the Brünn conference and to a Russian translation of Karl Renner's book *Government and National Autonomy in Austria*. M. B. Ratner, "O natsional'noi i territorial'noi avtonomii: vmesto predisloviia k russkomu izdaniiu Sinoptikusa," an essay written "instead of a preface" to Sinoptikus (R. Springer), *Gosudarstvo i natsiia: k natsional'nomu voprosu v Avstrii* (Kiev, 1906); M. B. Ratner "Evoliutsiia sotsialisticheskoi mysli v natsional'nom voprose (vmesto predisloviia)," also written "instead of a preface" to *Debaty po natsional'nomu voprosu na Briunnskom parteitage* (s.l., 1906). Both Springer and Sinoptikus are pseudonyms of Karl Renner.

55. Otto Bauer, *Natsional'nyi vopros i sotsialdemokratiia*, M. S. Panina, trans. (St. Petersburg, 1909).

56. Chaim Zhitlovsky, "O knige Otto Bauera," introduction to Bauer, *Natsional'nyi vopros i sotsialdemokratiia*, ix.

57. Jeffrey Veidlinger states that Dubnov's autonomist doctrine "borrowed primarily from the Austrian Marxists" ("Simon Dubnov Recontextualized: The

Sociological Conception of Jewish History and the Russian Intellectual Legacy," *Simon Dubnow Institute Yearbook* 3 [2004]: 425), and David Fishman explicitly links Dubnov's theory to the ideas of the Austrian socialist Karl Renner. Renner argued that Austria-Hungary should devolve powers over education and cultural matters to the empire's various national groups. According to Fishman, "Renner's theory led Dubnov to conceive of the modern *kehile* as a public and compulsory institution. The scheme of Jewish communal autonomy that he published in December 1905, in the midst of the political euphoria over the revolution, represented a translation of Renner's ideas into Jewish historical terms" (*Rise of Modern Yiddish Culture*, 67). One of Dubnov's biographers, Koppel S. Pinson, believed that in his distinction between state and nationality, Dubnov "follows in the footsteps of the progressive nationalist theories of the late 19th century, especially those of the Austro-Marxist school" ("The National Theories of Simon Dubnow," in Koppel S. Pinson, ed., *Nationalism and History: Essays on Old and New Judaism* [New York, 1970], 340).

58. Tony Michels reaches a more nuanced conclusion: "No doubt Zhitlovsky read Renner and Bauer (who, likewise, probably read Zhitlovsky), but Zhitlovsky had been working up his ideas independently since the late 1880s" (*Fire in Their Hearts*, 290n13).

59. Jacobs, *On Socialists*, 125–27.

60. Zhitlowsky wrote a critical review of Dubnov's *Pis'ma o starom i novom evreistve* in SERP's short-lived journal of political commentary. See Chaim Zhitlowsky, "Dukhovnyi natsionalizm g-na Dubnova," *Serp* 2 (1908): 292–310. Dubnov initially ignored Zhitlowsky's critique, but he eventually responded in his assessment of Zhitlowsky's autonomism, which appeared in a volume in honor of Zhitlowsky's sixtieth birthday. Dubnov credited Zhitlowsky with synthesizing Jewish nationalism and socialism but claimed that when Jewish political movements developed in Russia, autonomism was not yet fully developed in Zhitlowsky's ideology. See Sh. Dubnov, "Zhitlovskis avtonomizm," in *Zshitlovski-zamlbukh: gevidmet Dr. Hayim Zshitlovski zu zayn zekhtsiktsn geburstog* (Warsaw, 1929), 191.

61. Simon Dubnov, "Pis'mo chetvertoe: Avtonomizm, kak osnova natsionalnoi programmy," in S. M. Dubnov, *Pis'ma o starom i novom evreistve (1897–1907)* (St. Petersburg, 1907), 86–87n2.

62. Moira Donald, *Marxism and Revolution: Karl Kautsky and the Russian Marxists, 1900–1924* (New Haven, Conn., 1993), 4. Donald argues that, among other reasons, *Die Neue Zeit*'s preoccupation with theoretical questions (as opposed to local issues) and format (a weekly as opposed to a daily) made the publication both attractive and available to a Russian audience, leading to its becoming the most popular journal among Russian Marxists. On the translation of Kautsky's work into Russian, see pages 5–8 in Donald's book.

63. John Stuart Mill, *Considerations on Representative Government* (repr. New York, 1958), 229.

64. Mill looked to the Constitution of the United States as the inspiration for his formula. See Mill, *Considerations*, 237–49.

65. Renner, "State and Nation," 24.

66. Simon Dubnov, "Pis'mo tret'e: Etika natsionalizma," in Dubnov, *Pis'ma*, 60.

67. The latter part of Renner's "State and Nation" is devoted specifically to creating a legal model that differentiates between different types of sovereignty. See Renner, "State and Nation," 37–40.

68. The idea of using secular culture—folklore, literature, history, and music—was not unique to the autonomists, and is rooted in the thought of the German Romantics' predecessors, such as Johann Gottfried von Herder (1744–1803). In Eastern Europe, Polish Romantics and Russian Slavophiles had long borrowed from their German counterparts in using or creating culture intended to form the basis of national identification.

69. See Simon Dubnov, "Jews as a Spiritual (Cultural-Historical) Nation Among Political Nations," in Rabinovitch, *Jews and Diaspora Nationalism*, 23–44.

70. A. Perel'man, "Avtonomizm," in *Evreiskaia entsiklopediia* (St. Petersburg, 1908), 1: 359. Perel'man was a follower of Dubnov. However, the socialist Mark Ratner, in his history of autonomism in Jewish political parties, also considered Dubnov to have been principally responsible for introducing the idea to a Jewish audience and formulating other early ideas that formed a foundation for the implementation of Jewish autonomism ("Avtonomizm v programmakh evreiskikh politicheskikh partii," *Evreiskii mir* [September 1909]: 58–59).

71. See Simon Dubnov, "Pis'mo piatoe: O natsional'nom vospitanii," in Dubnov, *Pis'ma*, 113–51. This letter includes a detailed plan for educational reform and an appendix of discussions from the so-called Odessa *Kulturkampf* of 1902, when Dubnov and other intellectuals attempted to "nationalize" the educational activities of the Society for the Spread of Enlightenment Among the Jews of Russia. On this issue, see Brian Horowitz, *Jewish Philanthropy and Enlightenment in Late-Tsarist Russia* (Seattle, 2009).

72. Ilya V. Gerasimov, *Modernism and Public Reform in Late Imperial Russia* (Houndmills, U.K., 2009), 23–24.

73. Abbot Gleason, "The Terms of Russian Social History," in Samuel D. Kassow, James L. West, and Edith W. Clowes, eds., *Between Tsar and People: Educated Society and the Quest for Public Identity in Late Imperial Russia* (Princeton, N.J., 1991), 18.

74. Samuel D. Kassow, James L. West, and Edith W. Cloves, "Introduction: The Problem of the Middle in Late Imperial Russian Society," in Kassow et al., *Between Tsar and People*, 19. See also Gregory Freeze, "The *Soslovie* (Estate) Paradigm and Russian Social History," *American Historical Review* 91.1 (1986): 11–36.

75. Gleason, "Terms of Russian Social History," 22. The term *third element* has also been used to describe the rural intelligentsia.

76. David Wartenweiler, *Civil Society and Academic Debate in Russia, 1905–1914* (Oxford, U.K., 1999), 114. The most succinct definition of the word's dual meaning comes from Catriona Kelly and Vadim Volkov: *"obshchestvennost'* meant both the qualities of social engagement, and the sector of society most likely to manifest such qualities, the radical intelligentsia" (*"Obshchestvennost', Sobornost'*: Collective Identities," in Catriona Kelly and David Sheppard, eds., *Constructing Russian Culture in the Age of Revolution: 1881–1940* [Oxford, U.K., 1998], 27).

77. Kassow et al., "Introduction," 3. See also Manfred Hagen, "'Obshchestvennost'": Formative Changes in Russian Society Before 1917," *Sbornik: Papers of the Study Group on the Russian Revolution* 10 (1984): 23–36; and Laura Engelstein, *Slavophile Empire: Imperial Russia's Illiberal Path* (Ithaca, N.Y., 2009), 81–82.

78. Wartenweiler, *Civil Society*, 83–95. *Grazhdanskoe obshchestvo* also referred to the civilian as opposed to the military branch of state service, and it was later used to denote estates. Benjamin Nathans, *Beyond the Pale: The Jewish Encounter with Late Imperial Russia* (Berkeley, Calif., 2002), 74.

79. In Russian, this theory was called *obshchestvennaia teoriia samoupravleniia*. Wartenweiler, *Civil Society*, 88.

80. Joseph Bradley, "Voluntary Associations, Civic Culture, and *Obshchestvennost'* in Moscow," in Kassow et al., *Between Tsar and People*, 139.

81. See Terrence Emmons and Wayne S. Vucinich, eds., *The Zemstvo in Russia: An Experiment in Local Self-Government* (Cambridge, U.K., 1982); Charles E. Timberlake, "The Zemstvo and the Development of a Russian Middle Class," in Kassow et al., *Between Tsar and People*, 164–79; and Gregory L. Freeze, "A National Liberation Movement and the Shift in Russian Liberalism, 1901–1903," *Slavic Review* 28.1 (1969): 81–91.

82. Leopold H. Haimson, "The Problem of Social Identities in Early Twentieth Century Russia," *Slavic Review* 47.1 (1988): 2.

83. Theodore R. Weeks, *Nation and State in Late Imperial Russia: Nationalism and Russification on the Western Frontier, 1863–1914* (DeKalb, Ill., 1996), 133.

84. These provinces included Chernigov, Ekaterinoslav, Kharkov, Kherson, and Poltava.

85. The Jewish example confirms Haimson's argument that not only were class identities in late imperial Russia fluid but also categories and terminology in use could actually shape behavior. In one example, Haimson points to Jewish pharmacists' assistants in Moscow who formed a union in 1905; in order to decide whether they would participate in the social democratic or liberal movement, they first had to decide whether they were "workers" or members of the "intelligentsia" ("Problem of Social Identities," 5–6).

86. Kassow et al., "Introduction," 9.

87. See Samuel D. Kassow, *Students, Professors, and the State in Tsarist Russia* (Berkeley, Calif., 1989).

88. Nathans, *Beyond the Pale*, 74.

89. See P. N. Zyrianov, "Obshchina," in *Obshchestvennaia mysl' Rossii XVIII–nachala XX veka: Entsiklopediia* (Moscow, 2005), 357–61.

90. On Russian populist terminology, see Richard Pipes, "Narodnichestvo: A Semantic Inquiry," *Slavic Review* 23.3 (1964): 441–58.

91. On the application of the terms *natsiia, natsional'nost'*, and *narodnost'* to the Jews in the nineteenth century, see John D. Klier, "The Russian Jewish Intelligentsia and National Identity," in John Morison, ed., *Ethnic and National Issues in Russian and East European History* (New York, 2000), 131–45.

92. Joseph Bradley argues that without voluntary associations in Russia there would have been no *obshchestvennost'* ("Voluntary Associations," 131).

93. Natan Meir, "Jews, Ukrainians, and Russians in Kiev: Intergroup Relations in Late Imperial Associational Life," *Slavic Review* 65.3 (2006): 476, 486.

94. Meir, "Jews, Ukrainians, and Russians," 499.

95. Mark von Hagen commented in 1995: "Today the confederational ideas of Drahomanov are either ignored, rejected as collaborationist, or Drahomanov, in violation of his own written legacy, is transformed into a Ukrainian separatist. Federalist, regionalist and autonomist political thought in general is likely to be one of the casualties of an overly nationalist rewriting of the past that posits a sovereign, national state as the teleological outcome of history" ("Does Ukraine Have a History?" *Slavic Review* 54.3 [1995]: 666). Von Hagen's words proved prescient.

96. See the useful collection of writings about and by Drahomanov in the special issue edited by Ivan L. Rudnytsky, "Mykhaylo Drahomanov: A Symposium and Selected Writings," *Annals of the Ukrainian Academy of Arts and Sciences in the U.S.* 2 (1952).

97. See M. P. Drahomanov, "Free Union: Draft of a Ukrainian Political and Social Program," *Annals of the Ukrainian Academy of Arts and Sciences in the U.S.* 2 (1952): 193–205 (originally published in Geneva in 1884).

98. M. P. Drahomanov to Xavier Ricardi, July 29, 1878, reprinted in *Annals of the Ukrainian Academy of Arts and Sciences in the U.S.* 2 (1952): 176.

99. The similarities between Dubnov and Drahomanov's political philosophies are evident in Ivan L. Rudnytsky, "Drahomanov as Political Theorist," *Annals of the Ukrainian Academy of Arts and Sciences in the U.S.* 2 (1952): 70–130.

100. M. P. Dragomanov [Drahomanov], "Avtobiografiia," *Byloe* 6 (1906), 189–90.

101. George Liber, "Ukrainian Nationalism and the 1918 Law on National-Personal Autonomy," *Nationalities Papers* 15.1 (1987): 29. Liber points out that despite the similarity between Renner's and Bauer's programs and the 1918 Ukrainian law on national-personal autonomy, "the moral and political antecedents of the Ukrainian law remained in the nineteenth century" (29–32).

102. Mark von Hagen, "Federalisms and Pan-Movements: Re-Imagining Empire," in Jane Burbank, Mark von Hagen, and Anatolyi Remnev, eds., *Russian Empire: Space, People, Power, 1700–1930* (Bloomington, Ind., 2007), 494–510.

103. On the ideological diversity of the Russian middle class and its implications in reforming Russian law, see William G. Wagner, "Ideology, Identity, and the Emergence of a Middle Class," in Kassow et al., *Between Tsar and People*, 149–63.

104. The association between modernity and the West is problematic in a Russian context. See Gerasimov, *Modernism*, 18–20.

105. [Zilberfarb], "Printsip natsional'no-politicheskoi avtonomii," 55.

106. [Zilberfarb], "Printsip natsional'no-politicheskoi avtonomii," 59.

Chapter 3

1. On Dubnov's Odessa years (1890–1903), see S. M. Dubnov, *Kniga zhizni: Vospominaniia i razmyshleniia, materialy dlia istorii moego vremeni* (St. Petersburg, 1998), 153–245; and Sofie Dubnov-Erlich, *The Life and Work of S. M. Dubnov: Diaspora Nationalism and Jewish History*, Judith Vowles, trans., and Jeffrey Shandler, ed. (Bloomington, Ind., 1991), 90–119. See also Anke Hilbrenner, "Nationalization in Odessa: Simon Dubnow and the Society for the Dissemination of Enlightenment Among the Jews in Russia," *Simon Dubnow Institute Yearbook* 2 (2003): 223–39; and Alexander Orbach, "Jewish Intellectuals in Odessa in the Late 19th Century: The Nationalist Theories of Ahad Ha'am and Simon Dubnov," *Nationalities Papers* 6.2 (1978): 109–23.

2. Dubnov and the lawyer Grigorii Ia. Krasnii-Admoni (1881–1970) published a collection of documents on the wave of anti-Jewish violence: *Materialy dlia istorii antievreiskikh pogromov v Rossii*, 2 vols. (Petrograd, 1919–23). For a detailed account of the events of Kishinev and the pogroms that followed in Gomel, see Shlomo Lambroza, "The Pogroms of 1903–1906," in John Klier and Shlomo Lambroza, eds., *Pogroms: Anti-Jewish Violence in Modern Russian History* (Cambridge, U.K., 1992), 195–247; and Edward H. Judge, *Easter in Kishinev: Anatomy of a Pogrom* (New York, 1992).

3. See Robert Seltzer, "Simon Dubnow: A Critical Biography of His Early Years" (PhD diss., Columbia University, 1970), 182–84.

4. Vladimir Ze'ev Zhabotinskii [Jabotinsky], *O zheleznoi stene: rechi, stat'i, vospominaniia* (Minsk, 2004), 32.

5. Alice Stone Nakhimovsky, *Russian-Jewish Literature and Identity: Jabotinsky, Babel, Grossman, Galich, Roziner, Markish* (Baltimore, 1992), 48; Michael Stanislawski, *Zionism and the Fin de Siècle: Cosmopolitanism and Nationalism from Nordau to Jabotinsky* (Berkeley, Calif., 2001), 159–60. Stanislawsky suggests that Jabotinsky resisted ascribing significance to Kishinev in his own path to Zionism, when in fact the event led him to the Sixth Zionist Congress in Basel, and then Rome, from whence he returned a committed Zionist. According to Stanislawsky, Jabotinsky left for Basel at a period in his life when he felt frustrated as a literary figure, and when he returned from Rome, he turned his attention to Zionism (160–77).

6. Quoted in Monty Noam Penkower, "The Kishinev Pogrom of 1903: A Turning Point in Jewish History," *Modern Judaism* 24.3 (2004): 194.

7. Jabotinsky translated Bialik's poem into Russian and, according to Michael Stanislawski, was largely responsible for its popularization (Stanislawski, *Zionism*, 183–202).

8. M. A. Krol', *Stranitsy moei zhizni: Tom pervyi* (New York, 1944), 302–3.

9. Before the Kishinev pogroms of 1903, as Renée Poznanski points out, Dubnov referred to the Diaspora by the Russian term *rasseianie* (dispersion) and used the Hebrew term *galut* (exile) only to describe the Zionists' attitude toward the Diaspora ("Dubnov and the Diaspora," in Kristi Groberg and Avraham Greenbaum, eds., *A Missionary for History: Essays in Honor of Simon Dubnov* [Minneapolis, 1998], 7).

10. Shmuel Galai, "The Jewish Question as a Russian Problem: The Debates in the First State Duma," *Revolutionary Russia* 17.1 (2004): 35; and Shmuel Galai, *The Liberation Movement in Russia, 1900–1905* (Cambridge, U.K., 1973), 168–69.

11. On the general Russian case and the western provinces in the period leading up to the 1905 revolution, see Klaus Fröhlich, *The Emergence of Russian Constitutionalism, 1900–1904: The Relationship Between Social Mobilization and Political Group Formation in Pre-Revolutionary Russia* (The Hague, 1981).

12. Samuel Kassow, *Students, Professors, and the State in Tsarist Russia* (Berkeley, Calif., 1989), 271.

13. Gregory L. Freeze, "A National Liberation Movement and the Shift in Russian Liberalism, 1901–1903," *Slavic Review* 28.1 (1969): 90.

14. The Jewish Historical-Ethnographic Society, established in St. Petersburg in 1908, collected documents concerning the revolutionary events of 1905 that related to Jewish and non-Jewish political parties, including various resolutions of Jewish students and Russian lawyers, joint statements by prominent Russians and Jews, and letters from the revolutionary leader, Father Gapon. TsGIA SPb, f. 2129, op. 3, d. 36 and 37.

15. See Sergei Podbolotov, "'. . . And the Entire Mass of People Leapt Up': The Attitude of Nicholas II Towards the Pogroms," *Cahiers du monde russe* 45.1–2 (2004): 197.

16. See Gilbert S. Doctorow, "The Government Program of 17 October 1905," *Russian Review* 34.2 (1975): 125–33. A detailed analysis of the revolutionary process that led to the creation of the Duma, including Jewish participation in this process, is too large a subject for the confines of this chapter. See Abraham Ascher's two volumes, *The Revolution of 1905: Russia in Disarray* (Stanford, Calif., 1988) and *The Revolution of 1905: Authority Restored* (Stanford, Calif., 1992); Dmitrii Borisovich Pavlov, ed., *Liberal'noe dvizhenie v Rossii, 1902–1905gg.* (Moscow, 2001); Gerald Dennis Surh, *1905 in St. Petersburg: Labor, Society, and Revolution* (Stanford, Calif., 1989); and Laura Engelstein, *Moscow 1905: Working-Class Organization and Political Conflict* (Stanford, Calif., 1982).

17. Lambroza, "Pogroms of 1903–1906," 228, 242. For an analysis of one of the worst outbreaks of violence, see Robert Weinberg, "The Pogrom of 1905 in Odessa:

A Case Study," in Klier and Lambroza, *Pogroms*, 248–89. For an account of the relationship between the autocracy and right-wing political movements, see Hans Rogger, *Jewish Policies and Right-Wing Politics in Imperial Russia* (Berkeley, Calif., 1986). Rogger argues that far from encouraging anti-Jewish violence, the authorities feared that if "pogroms and pogrom agitation were to serve anti-revolutionary ends, this weapon, it was quickly realized, could also be turned against its inventors" (28).

18. Quoted in Lambroza, "Pogroms of 1903–1906," 234.

19. See Yitzhak Maor, *Ha-tenu'a ha-Tsiyonit be-Rusya: me-reshita ve-'ad yamenu*, 2nd rev. ed. (Jerusalem, 1986); Stanislawski, *Zionism*; and Jonathan Frankel, *Prophecy and Politics: Socialism, Nationalism, and the Russian Jews, 1862–1917* (Cambridge, U.K., 1981).

20. See Andreas Kappeler, *The Russian Empire: A Multiethnic History*, Alfred Clayton, trans. (Harlow, U.K., 2001), 328–41.

21. Kappeler, *Russian Empire*, 329–34; Ascher, *Revolution of 1905: Russia in Disarray*, 152–74. Kappeler and Ascher describe the same events; however, Kappeler stresses their roots in national discontent, whereas Ascher gives considerably more credence to their social and economic genesis.

22. Cited in Rimantas Miknys, "Vilnius and the Problem of Modern Lithuanian Statehood in the Early Twentieth Century," *Lithuanian Historical Studies* 2 (1997): 111. On the Lithuanian national movement and the 1905 revolution, see Egidijus Motieka, "The Great Assembly of Vilnius, 1905," *Lithuanian Historical Studies* 1 (1996): 84–96.

23. During negotiations for a joint resolution on Lithuanian autonomy, other Polish, Belorussian, and Jewish representatives refused to endorse the concept of "ethnic" as opposed to "historic" Lithuania (Miknys, "Vilnius," 113).

24. Miknys, "Vilnius," 110.

25. Motieka, "Great Assembly of Vilnius," 84, 90. By 1909 the LSDP's "minimum program" called for "a democratic Lithuanian republic with a sejm in Vilna, joining on its own invitation with other countries in a federal union" (*Programmy politicheskikh partii i organizatsii Rossii kontsa XIX–XX veka* [Rostov-on-Don, 1992], 21). The Ukrainian Revolutionary Party demanded the implementation of Ukrainian autonomy through *sejm*s in its 1903 program, as did the Ukrainian Social Democratic Workers' Party and the Ukrainian-Democratic Radical Party, both in 1905 (*Programmy politicheskikh partii*, 55, 76, 168–69).

26. Šarūnas Liekis, *A State Within a State? Jewish Autonomy in Lithuania, 1918–1925* (Vilnius, 2003), 37. See also *Programmy politicheskikh partii*, 324.

27. Toivo U. Raun, "The Nationalities Question in the Baltic Provinces, 1905–17," in John Morison, ed., *Ethnic and National Issues in Russian and East European History* (New York, 2000), 125–26.

28. On Dmowski and the Polish National Democrats before the war, see Antony Polonsky, *Politics in Independent Poland, 1921–1930: The Crisis of Constitutional Government* (Oxford, U.K., 1972), 54–56.

29. Quoted in *Programmy politicheskikh partii*, 15–16.

30. Paul Robert Magocsi, *A History of Ukraine* (Toronto, 1996), 380–81. The Prosvita Society in the Russian Empire was based on the one founded by Ukrainians in Austrian Galicia in 1868, which developed a vast program for educational and economic development. In 1906 the Prosvita Society had 10,000 members in Galicia, with 39 affiliates or branches and 1,700 reading rooms (442).

31. Robert D. Crews, *For Prophet and Tsar: Islam and Empire in Russia and Central Asia* (Cambridge, Mass., 2006), 343–46; Adeeb Khalid, *The Politics of Muslim Cultural Reform: Jadidism in Central Asia* (Berkeley, Calif., 1998), 231; Kappeler, *Russian Empire*, 337–38; Vladimir Levin, "Common Problems, Different Solutions: Jewish and Muslim Politics in Late Imperial Russia," paper presented at the conference "Jews and Muslims in the Russian Empire and the Soviet Union" (Munich, 2013).

32. Polish autonomy was to be accompanied by guaranteed rights for its minorities (*Programmy politicheskikh partii*, 330–31).

33. See G. Anoprieva and N. Erofeev, "Partiia sotsialistov-revoliutsionerov," in *Politicheskie partii Rossii: Konets XIX–pervaia tret' XX veka—Entsiklopediia* (Moscow, 1996), 433–52; and *Programmy politicheskikh partii*, 58–66.

34. Simon Dubnov, "Uroki strashnyhk dnei," *Voskhod* (1 December 1905): 6.

35. An incomplete version ("fragments") of this text is included in S. M. Dubnov, *Pis'ma o starom i novom evreistve (1897–1907)* (St. Petersburg, 1907), 294–320.

36. Kappeler, *Russian Empire*, 335.

37. Terence Emmons, *The Formation of Political Parties and the First National Elections in Russia* (Cambridge, Mass., 1983), 357. On Koło, see Zygmunt Łukawski, *Koło Polskie w rosyskiej Dumie Państwowej w latach 1906–1909* (Wrocław, 1967); and Mirsoław Wierzhowski, *Sprawy Polski w III i IV Dumie Państwowej* (Warsaw, 1966).

38. Galai, "Jewish Question," 38–39.

39. Sidney S. Harcave, "The Jewish Question in the First Russian Duma," *Jewish Social Studies* 6.2 (1944): 168. See also M. M. Vinaver, *Konflikty v pervoi Dume* (St. Petersburg, 1907), 147–83.

40. *Kotimaa* (20 December 1906); *Helsingin Sanomat* (12 December 1906); *Wiipuri* (13 December 1906); *Hufvudstadsbladet* (8 December 1906).

41. Quoted in Freeze, "National Liberation Movement," 84.

42. The long name of the union led to its members being called attainers. On the significance of the organization's name, see Vladimir Levin, "Politics at the Crossroads: Jewish Parties and the Second Duma Elections, 1907," *Leipziger Beiträge zur jüdischen Geschichte und Kultur* 2 (2004): 130.

43. The election laws of August 6 and December 11, 1905, provided for broad but not universal suffrage. Besides setting property or professional qualifications, the laws denied the vote to women, men under the age of 25, soldiers and policemen, students in secondary school or university, propertyless workers in facto-

ries with fewer than fifty employees, and members of certain other categories. See Vladimir Levin, "Russian Jewry and the Duma Elections, 1906–1907," *Jews and Slavs* 7 (2000): 234–35.

44. "Delo ob organizatsii i rabote 1-go s"ezda evreiskikh deiatelei v g. Vil'no i uchrezhdenii 'Soiuza dlia Dostizheniia Polnopraviia Evreiskogo Naroda v Rossii,'" RGIA, f. 1565, op. 1, d. 54.

45. Vinaver, Sliozberg, the lawyer Mikhail Kulisher, and the other organizers wrote directly to Dubnov to request his participation in Vilna. The meeting was to be held in Vilna because the organizers could not receive permission to hold it in St. Petersburg. Letter, February 16, 1905, CAHJP, P1/3.

46. Quoted in A. Perel'man, "Avtonomizm," in *Evreiskaia entsiklopediia* (St. Petersburg, 1908), 1: 362.

47. On this controversy, see Oscar Janowsky, *The Jews and Minority Rights (1898–1919)* (New York, 1966 [1933]), 92.

48. "Rezoliutsii S"ezda evreiskikh obshchestvennykh deiatelei, sostoiavshogosia v g. Vil'ne 25–27 Marta 1905 g.," CAHJP, P1/3.

49. Simon Dubnow, "Pis'mo tretie: Etika natsionalizma," in Dubnov, *Pis'ma*, 61. The influence of Vladimir Solov'ev is evident here. See Jeffrey Veidlinger, "Simon Dubnov Recontextualized: The Sociological Conception of Jewish History and the Russian Intellectual Legacy," *Simon Dubnow Institute Yearbook* 3 (2004): 425.

50. Dubnov, "Pis'mo tretie," 61.

51. The similarity is evident in any comparison between Dubnov's "Pis'mo chetvertoe: Avtonomizm, kak osnova natsional'noi programmy" (in Dubnov, *Pis'ma*, 74–112) and the Vilna platform of the Union for Full Rights, published in *Voskhod* (6 April 1905): 17.

52. See Christoph Gassenschmidt, *Jewish Liberal Politics in Tsarist Russia: The Modernization of Russian Jewry* (New York, 1995), 21–22.

53. See the letters from Iulii Gessen to Dubnov from May 4, June 23, and June 30, 1905, CAHJP, P1/3.

54. Janowsky, *Jews and Minority Rights*, 93. Whereas Janowsky argues that the creation of the Union for Full Rights was intended to legitimize the already de facto role of a group of Jewish elites as official spokesmen for the Jews of Russia, Christoph Gassenschmidt argues that the low membership fee and open membership policies suggest the Union's desire to "mobilize and politicize the masses" (*Jewish Liberal Politics*, 91).

55. The Bund, Poalei Zion, and SERP, all of which boycotted the elections to the First Duma, had candidates in the elections to the Second Duma but failed to win any seats. See Levin, "Politics at the Crossroads," 140–45.

56. The rules establishing franchise resulted in disappointment that the Jews would not be likely to have a large number of representatives in the Duma, although in certain cities, such as Minsk, Gomel, and Vilna, Jews were dispropor-

tionately overrepresented among those eligible to vote because of the electoral system. See Sidney S. Harcave, "Jewish Political Parties and Groups and the Russian State Dumas from 1905–1907" (PhD diss., University of Chicago, 1943), 58. See also Harcave, "Jewish Question," 155–76; and Sidney S. Harcave, "The Jews and the First Russian National Election," *American and Slavic East European Review* 9.1 (1950): 33–41.

57. Jabotinsky discusses the idea of a national assembly, or *sejm*, in "Bund i natsional'noe sobranie," *Khronika evreiskoi zhizni* 2 (17 January 1906): 7–9. *Khronika everiskoi zhizni* was succeeded briefly by *Evreiskii narod* in 1906 and then by the better known Russian-language Zionist journal *Rassvet*, which was published from 1907 to 1919.

58. "Ukazy ob uchrezhdenii Gos. Dumy, polozhenie o vyborakh; tsirkuliary i instruktsii TsK Obshchestva polnopraviia . . . 1905–1907 gg.," RGIA, f. 1565, op. 1, d. 11.

59. *Protokoly tret'ego delegatskogo s"ezda Soiuza dostizheniia* (St. Petersburg, 1906). The Union accepted the resolution's proposal that Jewish deputies in the national faction be allowed to remain in their general parties but not to join other national factions; however, it declined to institute the "national parliamentary group." See the adopted resolutions of February 13, 1906, and the Dubnov-Goldberg-Brutskus unaccepted resolution ("Tekst nepriniatoi rezoliutsii"), CAHJP, P1/3.

60. "Postanovlenie tret'iago delegatskogo s"ezda Soiuza dlia dostizheniia polnopraviia evreiskogo naroda v Rossii, 10–13 Fevralia 1906 goda," CAHJP, P1/3.

61. Most of the Jewish deputies were members of the Kadet Party before the election; some joined the Kadets in the Duma after the elections; and one, Moisei Ostrogorskii, technically never joined any faction but voted with the Kadets. The three others joined the Trudovik faction once in the Duma. See Levin, "Russian Jewry," 237–38.

62. "Rezoliutsiia, priniataia v vecherniem zasedanii S"ezda 12 Fevralia," CAHJP, P1/3.

63. Dubnov to Ahad Ha'am, March 30, 1905, Ahad Ha'am Archives, JNUL, Jerusalem. Dubnov begged Ahad Ha'am in numerous letters to take part in the Union's activities to help bolster the autonomists and swing the intellectual balance against the "assimilators." See letters of March 20, 1905, and January 31, 1906, Ahad Ha'am Archives, JNUL, Jerusalem.

64. Although this was the last "congress," the Union for Full Rights held a "conference" in March 1907 to debate whether or not it should continue to exist, and if so, in what form. A letter from the Central Committee, St. Petersburg, dated January 28, 1906 (CAHJP, P1/3), includes the seven points on the agenda for the congress to be held in St. Petersburg on February 10–12, 1906. The program for the fourth congress included a more modest number of issues for discussion, but at the top of the agenda were the tasks of the Jewish deputies to the Duma and

a discussion of the question of a national group in the Duma. Letter from Central Committee, St. Petersburg, April 11, 1906, CAHJP, P1/3.

65. Janowsky, *Jews and Minority Rights*, 97; and Harcave, "Jewish Political Parties," 103–5.

66. "K evreiskomu obshchestvu (Ot Tsentral'nogo biuro Soiuza dlia dostizheniia polnopraviia evreiskogo naroda v Rossii)," CAHJP, P1/3.

67. Genrikh [Henryk] Borisovich Sliozberg, *Dela minuvshikh dnei: zapiski russkogo evreia* (Paris, 1934), 3: 171.

68. Sliozberg, *Dela minuvshikh dnei*, 3: 171.

69. See Gassenschmidt, *Jewish Liberal Politics*, 21–22.

70. "Obshchee sobranie chlenov Tsentral'noe Komiteta 30 Sentiabria 1906 g.," TsGIA SPb, f. 2049, op. 1, d. 43. The series of resolutions essentially demanded that the Central Committee resolve its differences and agree on a platform.

71. Dubnov, *Kniga zhizni*, 284.

72. Announcement relating to the "question of the organizational form of the Union for Full Rights," TsGIA SPb, f. 2049, op. 1, d. 49.

73. Letter from the Central Committee dated April 19, 1907, CAHJP, P1/3. It is worth noting that any belief that the Union for Full Rights could ever reach a compromise was mocked in the Yiddish press, which seemed to prefer that the parties recognize the inevitability of factionalism rather than make the futile attempts at compromise given so much attention in the Russian-language Jewish press. See Sarah Abrevaya Stein, "Faces of Protest: Yiddish Cartoons of the 1905 Revolution," *Slavic Review* 61.4 (2002): 753–56.

74. Dubnov, *Kniga zhizni*, 287. On the dissolution of the Union for Full Rights and the resulting new parties, see Vladimir Levin, "Ha-politika ha-Yehudit ba-Imperya ha-Rusit be-idan ha-re'aktsiya 1907–1914" (PhD diss., Hebrew University of Jerusalem, 2007), 128–73.

75. Just when the Union for Full Rights began to disintegrate, a twice-weekly newspaper appeared in St. Petersburg that was devoted solely to covering the Union's affairs. *Evreiskii izbiratel'* chronicled the Union's collapse as its factions, which were then forming into parties and groups, published their appeals to voters in the journal. See, for example, *Evreiskii izbiratel'* (5 December 1906).

76. "Proekt programmy evreiskogo natsion. (narod.) Soiuza," CAHJP, P1/3.

77. Ironically, Vinaver did not need the assistance of the Union for Full Rights to win election to the Duma. As Vladimir Levin points out, Vinaver was elected in St. Petersburg, where the Jewish population was not significant enough to influence the results ("Russian Jewry," 237).

78. See Simon Dubnov, "Pis'mo deviatoe: Razdroblennaia i ob"edinennaia natsional'naia partiia," in Dubnov, *Pis'ma*, 227–44.

79. Dubnov, *Kniga zhizni*, 284. The Folkspartey published its complete platform as the pamphlet "Volkspartei: 'Evreiskaia Narodnaia Partiia'" (St. Petersburg, 1907). In Russian party publications the name of the party was often written

in Latin letters as "Volkspartei" (the transliteration of the Yiddish name), along with the full Russian name. A version of the party's platform with Dubnov's letter of introduction was initially published in January 1907 in Russian in *Rassvet* and in Yiddish in *Der fraynd*, but I have used here their complete official platform published privately shortly after. The introduction to the platform was published as "O zadachakh 'Volkspartei' (Evreiskai Narodnaia Partiia)," in Dubnov, *Pis'ma*, 337–50. Before officially consecrating itself as a party, the Folkspartey published a short program in *Evreiskii narod* titled "Programma Evreiskoi Natsional'noi Gruppy (Folkspartei)," *Evreiskii narod* (8 December 1906): 11–13.

80. Meir Kreinin, "Zikhronot," JNUL, MF 40 1416, p. 46. After leaving Russia for Berlin in 1921 and then moving to Paris in 1927, Kreinin settled in Jerusalem in 1934, where he died five years later. At the time of his death, he was in the process of composing his memoirs (*zikhronot*). The mix of handwritten and incomplete typescripts is now in the archive and manuscript section of the Jewish National and University Library.

81. "Ot organizatsionnogo komiteta 'Volkspartei' ('Evreiskoi narodnoi partii')," *Evreiskii izbiratel'* (16 January 1907): 31.

82. Dubnov, *Kniga zhizni*, 284.

83. Simon Dubnov, "K sporu o tipe evreiskoi obshchiny," *Evreiskii mir* (28 January 1910).

84. David Fishman argues that the debate over how to define Jewish nationality and membership in the Jewish community that arose within the Folkspartey and in the general Jewish political sphere as a result of Dubnov's call for the reinstitution of the *kehila* revolved primarily around "the status of Jewish converts to Christianity, many of whom had embraced Christianity to advance their education and careers but still identified with Jewry" (*The Rise of Modern Yiddish Culture* [Pittsburgh, 2005], 69; see also 62–79). According to the Folkspartey's original platform, "Every Jew that did not declare otherwise shall be considered a member of the community" ("Volkspartei," 27 [special directive 5]). Although the Russian Zionists felt similarly, this one small line in the party platform represented the most significant difference between Dubnov's vision and the vision of other liberal groups who took up autonomism. See Kurt Stillschweig, "Nationalism and Autonomy Among East European Jewry," *Historia Judaica* 6 (1944): 34. It is in fact a principle that Dubnov had articulated in his first letter, where he stated: "As long as he does not advocate national assimilation, lack of faith does not tear the Jew away from his people; but the fact of officially converting to another belief denotes *in fact*, in the conditions of the Diaspora, leaving the Jewish nation, if not for the renegade himself, than for his progeny, who have no choice but to merge their nationality with the surrounding non-Jewish population" ("Pis'mo pervoe: Teoriia evreiskago natsionalizma," in Dubnov, *Pis'ma*, 19).

85. "Volkspartei," 27–28 (special directives 9 and 10). My emphasis.

86. "Volkspartei," 4.

87. "Volkspartei," 27–28 (special directive 9).

88. Dubnov described Kreinin as "a straightforward man with a clear and practical intellect" (*Kniga zhizni*, 284). Zalkind apparently had been a member of a revolutionary party and was forced by the Black Hundreds to seek the relative safety of St. Petersburg. Dubnov mentions only in passing the other founders of the party, the two lawyers (Mandel' became president of the Society for Jewish Folk Music in 1914). The party's paid announcements in *Der fraynd* directed all correspondence to Kreinin. These announcements began with the February 5, 1907, issue of *Der fraynd* and appeared periodically through March 1907. See also Meir Kreinin, "Neobkhodimoe raz"iasnenie: voprosy dnia" (A Necessary Explanation: Questions of the Day), *Khronika evreiskoi zhizni* (21 February 1906).

89. Kreinin, "Zikhronot."

90. See Brian Horowitz, "The Society for the Promotion of Enlightenment Among the Jews of Russia and the Evolution of the St. Petersburg Russian Jewish Intelligentsia, 1893–1905," *Studies in Contemporary Jewry* 19 (2003): 195–213.

91. Brian Horowitz, "Victory from Defeat: 1905 and the Society for the Promotion of Enlightenment Among the Jews of Russia," in Stefani Hoffman and Ezra Mendelsohn, eds., *The Revolution of 1905 and Russia's Jews* (Philadelphia, 2008), 79–95. See also Frankel, *Prophecy and Politics*, 160; and I. M. Cherikover [Tcherikower], *Istoriia Obshchestva dlia rasprostraneniia prosveshcheniia mezhdu evriami v Rossii, 1863–1913* (St. Petersburg, 1913). Kreinin was an early and devoted proponent of a Jewish national school. He wrote a five-part article for *Voskhod* over the course of 1901 titled "O s"ezde po narodnomu obrazovaniiu" (About a Congress for National Education) (*Voskhod* [1901], nos. 57, 62, 64, 73, 78). See also Meir Kreinin, "Soiuz evreiskikh uchitelei i deiatelei po narodnomu obrazovaniiu" (Union of Jewish Teachers and Their Work for National Education), *Khronika evreiskoi zhizni* (24 January 1906). Others who later joined the Folkspartey, such as Leontii Bramson and the historian Yisroel Tsinberg, were also among those attempting to democratize the OPE.

92. I have not described this conflict in detail here because it has been analyzed at length in Fishman, *Rise of Modern Yiddish Culture*, 33–47.

93. "Ot organizatsionnogo komiteta 'Volkspartei,'" 30.

94. On the membership and leadership of these groups, see "Evreiskaia demokraticheskaia gruppa," "Evreiskaia narodnaia gruppa," and "Evreiskaia narodnaia partiia," in *Evreiskaia entsiklopediia* (St. Petersburg, 1908), 7: 437–40.

95. Vladimir Zhabotinskii [Jabotinsky], "K voprosu o nashei politicheskoi platforme," *Evreiskaia zhizn'* (November 1905): 43.

96. Zhabotinskii, "K voprosu o nashei politicheskoi platforme," 43.

97. M. Shvartsman, "Natsional'noe samoupravlenie," *Evreiskaia mysl'* 6 (9 November 1906): 1.

98. Shmarya Levin, *The Arena*, Maurice Samuel, trans. (New York, 1932), 270. Levin also describes Dubnov as the liaison between the nationalist and nonnationalist factions in the Union for Full Rights (280).

99. S. M. Dubnov, "Osnovnyia nachala evreiskogo natsionalizma," *Evreskaia zhizn'* (August–September 1906): 23–51.

100. See Joseph Goldstein, "Jabotinsky and Jewish Autonomy in the Diaspora," *Studies in Zionism* 7.2 (1986): 224–32. According to Goldstein, Jabotinsky's conception of *samoupravlenie*, in which Jewish autonomist institutions would act as intermediaries between Russian Jewry and the government, was "moderate" compared with the "extremist" autonomism of Abraham Idelson, the editor of *Khronika evreiskoi zhizni*, and Yitshak Grinbaum, the editor of the Polish-language journal *Glos zydowski*, which advocated full national self-government (231).

101. *Evreiskaia mysl'*, based in Odessa, was a forum for many of Russia's most prominent Zionist ideologues. It balanced demands for a national program in Russia (a Jewish national assembly, *obshchina* [communal governing body], and rights to self-government and self-determination) with considerable discussion of emigration.

102. On *Dos yudishe folk*, the Helsingfors Program, and Zionism and national rights in Russia between 1905 and 1907, see Janowsky, *Jews and Minority Rights*, 98–113. David Vital argues that the new national agenda of the Russian Zionists was established primarily through closed meetings run by Jabotinsky, Idelson, and Grinbaum (*Zionism: The Formative Years* [Oxford, U.K., 1982], 466–67).

103. Asher D. Biemann, "Aesthetic Education in Martin Buber: Jewish Renaissance and the Artist," in Michael Zank, ed., *New Perspectives on Martin Buber* (Tübingen, 2006), 87–95; Jeffrey Veidlinger, *Jewish Public Culture in the Late Russian Empire* (Bloomington, Ind., 2009), 13–14. Buber's essay "Gegenwartsarbeit" was originally published in *Die Welt* 5.6 (8 February 1901): 4–5.

104. The entire December 2, 1906, issue of *Evreiskii narod* was devoted to reporting the resolutions and activities of the seven days of the Helsinki conference (held November 21–27, 1906). A number of articles in *Evreiskii narod* before the conference indicated that national rights would be one of its major topics. Most important among these articles was Abraham Idelson's "Svoboda lichnosti i natsional'noe samoupravlenie," *Evreiskii narod* 3 (3 November 1906): 7–11.

105. *Helsingin Sanomat* (12 December 1906).

106. Alexander Goldstein, "Programmnye voprosy vserossiiskogo s"ezda," *Evreiskii narod* 4 (10 November 1906): 9.

107. M. Shvartsman, "Pod kakim flagom?" *Evreiskaia mysl'* 2 (12 October 1906): 8–9. Shvartsman pointed to Austria, where a Jewish People's Party had been formed that united nationalists while also having the goal of building up Palestine (9).

108. Moisei Galinskii, "K voprosu o nashei taktike: Tol'ko pod svoim flagom," *Evreiskaia mysl'* 5 (2 November 1906): 6.

109. During debates over the issue, "Volkspartei" (written in Latin letters) was used to denote Dubnov's party and "Folkspartei" (also written in Latin letters, but in quotation marks) denoted the possible combined party.

110. Galinskii, "K voprosu o nashei taktike," 7.

111. Galinskii, "K voprosu o nashei taktike," 8.

112. A. M. Borukhov, "Ne vo flage delo," *Evreiskaia mysl'* 5 (2 November 1906): 9.

113. Borukhov, "Ne vo flage delo," 9.

114. See David Rechter, "A Nationalism of Small Things: Jewish Autonomy in Late Habsburg Austria," *Leo Baeck Institute Yearbook* 52 (2007): 87–109; and Joshua Shanes, *Diaspora Nationalism and Jewish Identity in Habsburg Galicia* (New York, 2012), 197–277.

115. Leila P. Everett, "The Rise of Jewish National Politics in Galicia, 1905–1907," in Andrei S. Markovits and Frank E. Sysyn, eds., *Nationbuilding and the Politics of Nationalism: Essays on Austrian Galicia* (Cambridge, Mass., 1982), 158.

116. For Birnbaum's essays "The Jewish Renaissance Movement" and "Jewish Autonomy" (and my introduction to them), see Simon Rabinovitch, ed., *Jews and Diaspora Nationalism: Writings on Jewish Peoplehood in Europe and the United States* (Waltham, Mass., 2012), 45–55. For a helpful explanation of the context for these two essays, see Jess Olson, *Nathan Birnbaum and Jewish Modernity: Architect of Zionism, Yiddishism, and Orthodoxy* (Stanford, Calif., 2013), 123–38 and 158–76.

117. Birnbaum, "Jewish Autonomy," 55.

118. Maor, *Ha-tenu'a ha-Tsiyonit be-Rusya*, 303–20. Maor devotes remarkably little attention to the Helsinki conference and the Helsingfors Program.

119. Following the Kishinev pogrom in 1903, Dubnov devoted a letter to the question of emigration. In it he affirmed the central importance of the emigration movement and called for organizational help in facilitating Jewish emigration. Consistent with his earlier and later positions, however, Dubnov argued that because most of Russian and East European Jewry would remain in those regions, efforts should be concentrated on bettering the situation for the Jews there. See S. M. Dubnov, "Istoricheskii moment (Emigratsionnyi vopros)," in Dubnov, *Pis'ma*, 281–93.

120. An open letter in *Der fraynd* challenged Dubnov about the contradictions in his and the Folkspartey's platform on the issue of emigration. See Dr. Ch. D. Hurwitz [Horovits], *Der fraynd* (21–22 February 1907). For Dubnov's response, see Simon Dubnow [Dubnov], "The Emancipation Movement and the Emigration Movement (A Reply to Dr. Ch. D. Hurwitz)," in Koppel S. Pinson, ed., *Nationalism and History: Essays on Old and New Judaism* (New York, 1970), 235. This article was Dubnov's first to appear in Yiddish, and he later translated it into Russian himself in order to publish it with his letters.

121. The influence of Ahad Ha'am on Dubnov is obvious here.

122. Dubnow, "Emancipation Movement," 235.

123. "Evreiskaia narodnaia partiia," *Evreiskaia mysl'* 12 (21 December 1906): 1–3; Shvartsman, "Natsional'noe samoupravlenie," 3.

124. "Evreiskaia narodnaia partiia" (in *Evreiskaia mysl'*), 1–3; Shvartsman, "Natsional'noe samoupravlenie," 3.

125. Benjamin Nathans, "Integration and Modernity in Fin de Siècle Russia," in Zvi Gitelman, ed., *The Emergence of Modern Jewish Politics: Bundism and Zionism in Eastern Europe* (Pittsburgh, 2003), 29.

126. The decision by the Russian Zionists to leave the organizational framework of the Jewish liberal political struggle met with some opposition (e.g., from Leo Motzkin and Shmarya Levin) and was later openly regretted by some supporters (such as Daniel Pasmanik, Iulii Brutskus, and Boris Goldberg). See Levin, "Politics at the Crossroads," 139–40.

127. On Bramson's Trudovik activities and the protocols of the Trudovik Party in the Duma, see TsGIA Ukraine, f. 992, op. 1, d. 17; and L. M. Bramson, *K istorii Trudovoi Partii: Trudovaia gruppa pervoi gosudarstvennoi Dumy*, 2nd ed. (Petrograd, 1917).

128. "Vozzvanie Evreiskoi demokraticheskoi gruppy: Fevral' 1905 g. Peterburg," YIVO, RG 87 (Simon Dubnov Archive), f. 985.

129. Bramson's papers at TsGIA Ukraine are a record of the breadth of his communal activism, with materials from his work in nearly every Jewish communal society, cultural organization, and political endeavor of the late imperial period, in addition to speeches and other evidence of his role in the Trudovik Party.

130. Quoted in Brian Horowitz, *Jewish Philanthropy and Enlightenment in Late-Tsarist Russia* (Seattle, 2009), 91.

131. Horowitz, *Jewish Philanthropy*, 110–11.

132. Members of the Central Committee of the Union for Full Rights first met to discuss the formation of a national group on November 24, 1906. This initial national group, however, was intended as a nationalist faction within the Union. See letter from Maksim Vinaver to Mikhail Sheftel', November 23, 1906, TsGIA SPb, f. 2049, op. 1, d. 44. Sheftel''s personal archive is located at TsGIA SPb and contains a number of items related to the Union for Full Rights, including his notes for a speech he gave to the Central Committee outlining the program of the Evreiskaia Narodnaia Gruppa ("Konspekt rechi Sheftel'ia [na zasedaniia Tsentral'nogo Komiteta soiuza polnopraviia evreiskogo naroda v Rossii] s izlozheniem programmy 'Evreiskoi Narodnoi Gruppy,'" TsGIA SPb, f. 2049, op. 1, d. 57). Perhaps the best summary of Shternberg's political views during this period is his "Natsional'nyia techeniia v russkom evreistve," *Svoboda i ravenstvo* 2 (14 January 1907): 6–9, and 5 (25 January 1907): 2–6. See also Sergei Kan, *Lev Shternberg: Anthropologist, Russian Socialist, Jewish Activist* (Lincoln, Neb., 2009).

133. "Vozzvanie Evreiskoi Narodnoi Gruppy: K grazhdanam evreiam," *Evreiskii izbiratel'* 8–9 (4 January 1907): 25–28; *Svoboda i ravenstvo* 1 (9 January 1907): 13–15. See also "Vozzvanie Evreiskoi Narodnoi Gruppy. No. 3. S kem vstupat' v izbiratel'nia soglasheniia?" *Svoboda i ravenstvo* 2 (14 January 1907): 15–16.

134. "Vozzvanie Evreiskoi Narodnoi Gruppy" (4 January 1907), 26.

135. The Folksgruppe was, at the time, also committed to maintaining the Union for Full Rights. See "Vozzvanie Evreiskoi Narodnoi Gruppy" (4 January

1907), 26. See also M. L. Trivus (Shmi), "Evreiskaia Narodnaia Gruppa," *Svoboda i ravenstvo* (14 January 1906): 5–6.

136. See Dubnov and Kreinin's letters in *Evreiskii golos* (16 February 1907): 6, and (23 February 1907): 7; *Der fraynd* 120 (28 December 1906); and *Evreiskii izbiratel'*, which published simultaneously the announcement "Vozzvanie evreiskoi narodnoi gruppy" (Appeal of the Jewish People's Group), 8–9 (January 1907): 25–28. See also Dubnov, *Kniga zhizni*, 285–86. *Svoboda i ravenstvo* devoted extensive space to critiquing the Folkspartey and Dubnov specifically. See, for example, "Sekuliarizatsiia natsional'nosti," *Svoboda i ravenstvo* 7 (1 February 1907): 1–3; [Trivus-]Shmi, "Volkspartei," *Svoboda i ravenstvo* 9 (8 February 1907): 4–6; "Iz zhizni Evreiskoi Narodnoi Gruppy," *Svoboda i ravenstvo* 8 (4 February 1907): 13; and Trivus, "Evreiskaia Narodnaia Gruppa," 5–6.

137. See *Dos yudishe folk* (24 May 1906): 19–22. For a more critical assessment of Koło from a Zionist perspective, see "Pol'skoe Kolo," *Khronika evreiskoi zhizni* 28 (20 July 1906): 4–7.

138. "Proekt avtonomii Pol'shi," *Svoboda i ravenstvo* 23 (19 April 1907): 1–5. Although Polish liberals were not as openly hostile toward Jews as the National Democrats, relations between Polish liberals and Jews were complicated by the rise of Jewish nationalism. As Maciej Janowski points out, for liberals and nationalists equally, national consciousness was exclusivist; one could only be either a Pole or a Jew (*Polish Liberal Thought Before 1918*, Danuta Przekop, trans. [Budapest, 2004], 232).

139. David Vital points out that with 12 deputies out of 486 in the First Duma, Jews were underrepresented compared to their proportion of the empire's population, and the lack of success in the Kingdom of Poland contributed to that disparity (*A People Apart: A Political History of the Jews in Europe, 1789–1939* [Oxford, U.K., 1999], 593).

140. Jacob G. Frumkin, "Pages from the History of Russian Jewry (Recollections and Documentary Material)," in Jacob Frumkin, Gregor Aronson, and Alexis Goldenweiser, eds., *Russian Jewry (1860–1917)*, Mirra Ginsburg, trans. (New York, 1966), 38.

141. See Scott Ury's insightful chapter on the elections to the First and Second Duma in Warsaw in his *Barricades and Banners: The Revolution of 1905 and Warsaw Jewry* (Stanford, Calif., 2012), 172–213. Ury explains the difficulty Jewish leaders and the press in Warsaw had in explaining the electoral process to a confused Jewish public. In Warsaw the Zionists were unsure whether or not to embrace *Gegenwartsarbeit*, the elite were "handcuffed by Polish sensibilities," and the revolutionary parties boycotted (like everywhere else), leaving Jews without clear leadership (182).

142. See *Evreiskii izbiratel'* 3 (12 December 1906): 6; 6 (22 December 1906): 15–16; 7 (29 December 1906): 11–14; 15 (1 February 1907): 17–19; and 13–14 (23 January 1907): 21.

143. "Proekt avtonomii Pol'shi," 5.

144. Maksim Vinaver, "Evreiskii vopros v pervoi Gosudarstvennoi Dume," *Svoboda i ravenstvo* 2 (14 January 1907): 1–5; 3 (18 January 1907): 2–6; and 9 (8 February 1907): 1–4.

145. See Leonard Schapiro, "The Role of the Jews in the Russian Revolutionary Movement," *Slavic and East European Review* 40 (1961): 148–67.

146. See Harcave, "Jewish Political Parties," 80.

147. Harcave, "Jewish Political Parties," 80.

148. Frankel, *Prophecy and Politics*, 167.

149. See Henry J. Tobias, "The Bund and Lenin Until 1903," *Russian Review* 20.4 (October 1961): 344–57; Frankel, *Prophecy and Politics*, 227–46; Mordechai Altshuler, "The Attitude of the Communist Party of Russia to Jewish National Survival, 1918–1930," *YIVO Annual of Jewish Social Science* 14 (1969): 68–86; and Zvi Y. Gitelman, *Jewish Nationality and Soviet Politics: The Jewish Sections of the CPSU, 1917–1930* (Princeton, N.J., 1972), 39–46, and, on internal disagreements within the Bund over national-cultural autonomy, 53–66.

150. Jacob S. Hertz, "The Bund's Nationality Program and Its Critics in the Russian, Polish, and Austrian Socialist Movements," *YIVO Annual* 14 (1969): 57.

151. Quoted in Gitelman, *Jewish Nationality*, 46.

152. Levin, "Russian Jewry," 244.

153. Frankel, *Prophecy and Politics*, 283.

154. Khaim Zhitlovskii [Chaim Zhitlowsky], "'Dukhovnyi' natsionalizm g-na Dubnova," *Serp* 2 (1908): 292–310.

155. Zhitlovskii, "'Dukhovnyi' natsionalizm," 302.

156. "Nashi zadachi," *Vozrozhdenie* 1–2 (January–February 1904): 3.

157. "K evreiskomu obshchestvu (Ot Tsentral'nogo biuro Soiuza dlia dostizheniia polnopraviia evreiskogo naroda v Rossii)," CAHJP, P1/3. A Yiddish version of this circular was published as "Tsu der Yidisher Gezelshaft." Dubnov had been drafted to the commission to write the circular, intended as an appeal for a unified organization for the elections to the Duma, along with Genrikh Sliozberg, Maksim Vinaver, Mark Ratner, and Leontii Bramson. See letter from Iulii Gessen to Dubnov, St. Petersburg, August 29, 1905, CAHJP, P1/3.

158. Simon Dubnov, "Predislovie," in Dubnov, *Pis'ma*, iv; emphasis in original.

159. Vinaver was disqualified from running because he was a signatory to the Vyborg Appeal. All the Jewish deputies to the First Duma signed this call for passive resistance to the government through avoidance of taxation and military conscription. All were then disqualified from running for the Second Duma, and a number of them, including Vinaver and Sheftel', spent three months in prison. See M. M. Vinaver, *Istoriia Vyborgskogo vozzvaniia* (Petrograd, 1917).

160. Dubnov, *Kniga zhizni*, 285–86.

161. "Volkspartei," 17; emphasis in original.

162. Dubnov, *Kniga zhizni*, 288–89.

163. See Robert Weinberg, "The Russian Right Responds: Visual Depictions of Jews in Postrevolutionary Russia," in Hoffman and Mendelsohn, *Revolution of 1905*, 55–69.

Chapter 4

1. Alfred Levin, *The Third Duma: Election and Profile* (Hamden, Conn., 1973), 3–6.

2. Geoffrey A. Hosking, *The Russian Constitutional Experiment: Government and Duma, 1907–1914* (Cambridge, U.K., 1973), 48–49.

3. Quoted in Abraham Ascher, *P. A. Stolypin: The Search for Stability in Late Imperial Russia* (Stanford, Calif., 2001), 166.

4. Ascher, *Stolypin*, 168.

5. Stolypin personally opposed such measures and fought to have the quotas raised. He also rejected barring Jews from the armed forces and prevented the enforcement of banishment for Jewish merchants in Russia. See Hans Rogger, *Jewish Policies and Right-Wing Politics in Imperial Russia* (Berkeley, Calif., 1986), 96.

6. Samuel D. Kassow, *Students, Professors, and the State in Tsarist Russia* (Berkeley, Calif., 1989), 298–99.

7. Simon Dubnov, *History of the Jews*, vol. 5, *From the Congress of Vienna*, Moshe Spiegel, trans. (South Brunswick, N.J., 1973), 769.

8. See Ascher, *Stolypin*; Mary Schaeffer Conroy, *Peter Arkad'evich Stolypin: Practical Politics in Late Tsarist Russia* (Boulder, Colo., 1976); and Hosking, *Russian Constitutional Experiment*. Ascher describes Stolypin's tactics after 1909 as attempts to "please the right without offending the center" (*Stolypin*, 293). He also argues that Stolypin's "nationalist initiatives," such as curtailing Finnish autonomy and incorporating the Kholm into the Russian Empire, should not be considered "a cynical ploy to curry favor with the rightists" (320).

9. See Peter Waldron, *Between Two Revolutions: Stolypin and the Politics of Renewal in Russia* (London, 1998), 165–75. For example, Stolypin allowed one of his most important and trusted advisers to use a pseudonym to publish polemics that accused the Kadets and Trudoviks of being dominated by the supposedly Russia-hating Jewish intelligentsia (Ascher, *Stolypin*, 124–25).

10. Jeffrey Veidlinger, *Jewish Public Culture in the Late Russian Empire* (Bloomington, Ind., 2009), 118.

11. Those who in their speeches negated the connection between politics and the Jewish national question would only be called in as witnesses. GARF, f. 102, op. 7 d-vo, 1910 g., d. 218, l. 3–9.

12. Francis William Wcislo, *Reforming Rural Russia: State, Local Society, and National Politics, 1855–1914* (Princeton, N.J., 1990), 208.

13. Wcislo, *Reforming Rural Russia*, 277–79.

14. Mary Schaeffer Conroy, "Stolypin's Attitude Toward Local Self-Government," *Slavonic and East European Review* 46.107 (1968): 451–52.

15. Wcislo, *Reforming Rural Russia*, 148. Stolypin's alienation of the Octobrists (when he courted more extreme nationalist elements) combined with his heavy-handed methods in pushing through the Western Zemstvo Bill (which angered conservative elements in the State Council), at a time when Nicholas II seems to have lost faith in his prime minister, effectively spelled the end of Stolypin's career, even before his assassination in September 1911. See Waldron, *Between Two Revolutions*, 173–75. See also Ben-Cion Pinchuk, *The Octobrists in the Third Duma, 1907–1912* (Seattle, 1974), especially 137–58.

16. Hosking, *Russian Constitutional Experiment*, 106.

17. Hans Rogger, *Russia in the Age of Modernisation and Revolution, 1881–1917* (London, 1983), 233.

18. See Yanni Kotsonis, "'Face-to-Face': The State, the Individual, and the Citizen in Russian Taxation, 1863–1917," *Slavic Review* 63.2 (2004): 221–46.

19. Kotsonis, "Face-to-Face," 229.

20. Kotsonis, "Face-to-Face," 226–27. Taxation, particularly the poll tax, was for much of Russian history the most significant indicator of legal status. See Gregory Freeze, "The *Soslovie* (Estate) Paradigm," *American Historical Review* 91.1 (1986): 21–22.

21. Alexander Vucinich, "The State and the Local Community," in Cyril Black, ed., *The Transformation of Russian Society: Aspects of Social Change Since 1861* (Cambridge, Mass., 1960), 196.

22. See Isaac Levitats, *The Jewish Community in Russia, 1772–1844* (New York, 1943), 38–45.

23. See Chapter 1.

24. A report on the conference, including transcripts of speeches, was published as "Otchet o soveshchanii evreiskikh obshchestvennykh deiatelei, proiskhodivshem v Kovne 19–22-go noiabria 1909 g.," *Evreiskii mir* (November–December 1909): pt. 2, 32–61. A stenographic report was also prepared and is available in the YIVO library. This report was published as *Soveshchanie evreiskikh obshchestvennykh deiatelei v g. Kovne 19–22 Noiabria 1909 g.: Stenograficheskii otchet* (St. Petersburg, 1910), 7–10.

25. Christoph Gassenschmidt, *Jewish Liberal Politics in Tsarist Russia: The Modernization of Russian Jewry* (New York, 1995), 86.

26. See the list of delegates in *Soveshchanie*, 7–10.

27. "Otchet," 32. A slight discrepancy exists between the transcript published in St. Petersburg, accounting for 120 representatives from 46 locales, and the account published in *Evreiskii mir*, which claimed that the conference was attended by 115 representatives from 51 locales.

28. "Otchet," 32; *Soveshchanie*, 10.

29. See A. Perel'man, "Kovenskii S"ezd," *Evreiskii mir* (November–December 1909): pt. 2, 1–9.

30. Perel'man, "Kovenskii S"ezd," 4. My emphasis.

31. *Soveshchanie*, 17–18.

32. "Otchet," 35–36; *Soveshchanie*, 19–33.

33. "Otchet," 45.

34. Interestingly, Sliozberg favored compulsory membership in the community, whereas Bramson favored voluntary membership.

35. *Soveshchanie*, 104.

36. *Soveshchanie*, 178.

37. *Soveshchanie*, 124.

38. Gassenschmidt, *Jewish Liberal Politics*, 89.

39. Eli Lederhendler considers the calling of conferences and constituency organizations into being by Jewish political leaders a radically democratic departure from previous methods. For example, referring to Herzl and the Zionist Congress, Lederhendler states: "No traditional shtadlan ever sought a popular mandate by convening a congress, putting before it a program for its endorsement, and establishing the machinery, in full public view, for the mobilization of a mass membership" (*The Road to Modern Jewish Politics: Political Tradition and Political Reconstruction in the Jewish Community of Tsarist Russia* [New York, 1989], 157).

40. "Otchet," 36.

41. G. B. Sliozberg, *Dela minuvshikh dnei* (Paris, 1934), 3: 263. In his memoirs Sliozberg depicts the Kovno conference as an extension of the Union for Full Rights work.

42. See Sliozberg's fifteen points on the reorganization of the *obshchiny* in *Soveshchanie*, 42–44.

43. *Soveshchanie*, 33.

44. *Soveshchanie*, 48.

45. The resolutions are in *Soveshchanie*, 215–19. They are printed in English in Levitats, *Jewish Community in Russia*, 20–21.

46. This was more than a hypothetical question as conversion reached a growing number of families among the Jewish intelligentsia in late imperial Russia, including Dubnov's. On Dubnov's reaction to his daughter Olga's intermarriage and conversion to Russian Orthodoxy, see Joseph Goldstein, "Fathers and Daughters: Dubnov and Ahad Ha-am," in Avraham Greenbaum, ed., *A Missionary for History: Essays in Honor of Simon Dubnow* (Minneapolis, 1998), 35–40.

47. *Soveshchanie*, 215.

48. Sliozberg, *Dela minuvshikh dnei*, 3: 263.

49. ChaeRan Y. Freeze, *Jewish Marriage and Divorce in Imperial Russia* (Hanover, N.H., 2002), 245.

50. Freeze, *Jewish Marriage*, 245. See N. Pereferkovich, *Religioznye voprosy u sovremennykh evreev v Rossii: Razbor "zakliuchenii" Osobago S"eszda pri Ravvinskoi Kommissii 1910 g.* (St. Petersburg, 1911). For a brief summary of the Rabbinic Commission's proceedings, see "Ravvinskaia kommissia," *Evreiskaia nedelia* 1–2 (16

April 1910): 33–37. The Rabbinic Commission of 1910 is also discussed in Gassenschmidt, *Jewish Liberal Politics*, 93–97.

51. At a conference convened in St. Petersburg in March 1910, in which the Rabbinic Commission and communal leaders participated, Sliozberg, the conference secretary, managed to gain the acceptance of most of the statements passed at the Kovno conference, despite opposition from Hasidic and mitnagdic conservatives.

52. "Otchet," 61.

53. "Otchet," 61.

54. They were also upset that the Folksgruppe members held a majority in the resulting Kovno committee. See S. M. Dubnov, *Kniga zhizni: Vospominaniia i razmyshleniia, materialy dlia istorii moego vremeni* (St. Petersburg, 1998), 307.

55. "Nashi zadachi," *Evreiskaia nedelia* 1–2 (16 April 1910): 1. *Evreiskaia nedelia* was a continuation of *Novy voskhod*, which was founded in January 1910 but was suspended for several months by the authorities.

56. M. G. Morgulis, "Organizatsiia evreiskoi obshchiny," *Evreiskaia nedelia* 10 (17 June 1910): 4.

57. Two works by Vladimir Levin address the changing approach to the Jewish community and bourgeois Jewish politics on the part of the Jewish socialist parties: "The Jewish Socialist Parties in Russia in the Period of Reaction," in Stefani Hoffman and Ezra Mendelsohn, eds., *The Revolution of 1905 and Russia's Jews* (Philadelphia, 2008), 111–27; and "Ha-politika ha-Yehudit ba-Imperya ha-Rusit be-idan ha-re'aktsiya 1907–1914" (PhD diss., Hebrew University of Jerusalem, 2007).

58. M. Zilberfarb, "Neotlozhnyia zadachi evreiskoi obshchiny," *Evreiskii mir* (July 1909): pt. 2, 4–6.

59. Zilberfarb, "Neotlozhnyia zadachi evreiskoi obshchiny," 11. Zilberfarb still had biting words for the Union for Full Rights that he and the other *vozrozhdentsy* had boycotted, referring to "the distinctive logic of Jewish life found in the Jewish activists who formed the Union for Full Rights in the manner of a union of different professions, as if the Jewish nation constitutes a shop organization" (2).

60. Zilberfarb, "Neotlozhnyia zadachi evreiskoi obshchiny," 10.

61. David E. Fishman, *The Rise of Modern Yiddish Culture* (Pittsburgh, 2005), 74.

62. Vladimir Medem, "Di yidishe kehile," *Tsayt-fragen* 2 (March 1910): 24–37; A. Litvak, "Fragn fun der idisher kehile," *Tsayt-fragen* 3–4 (August 1910): 47–59.

63. Vladimir Medem, *The Life and Soul of a Legendary Jewish Socialist*, Samuel A. Portnoy, trans. (New York, 1979), 466.

64. Medem, *Life and Soul*, 471. Vladimir Levin considers the elections to the Second Duma the most important factor leading to the crisis of confidence among Jewish socialists: "During the elections, the leaders of the Jewish socialist parties suddenly discovered that socialist ideas, which enjoyed success among working-class youth and the young intelligentsia, did not influence the broader masses of Jews outside these two narrow strata of society. This dealt a hard blow to the

perception that the 'proletariat' was the leading force of the revolution and that the 'petit bourgeois' Jewish masses were subject to its leadership and influence" ("Politics at the Crossroads: Jewish Parties and the Second Duma Elections, 1907," *Leipzige Beiträge zur jüdischen Geschichte und Kultur* 2 [2004]: 143).

65. Joshua D. Zimmerman, *Poles, Jews, and the Politics of Nationality* (Madison, Wisc., 2004), 227. See also Levin, "Jewish Socialist Parties."

66. Quoted in Zimmerman, *Poles, Jews*, 233.

67. Zimmerman, *Poles, Jews*, 236.

68. Levin, "Jewish Socialist Parties."

69. V. Medem, "Natsionalizm oder 'neytralizm,'" *Tsayt-fragen* 3–4 (August 1910): 15–25. Litvak attended the Kovno conference and reported on it in *Tsayt-fragen* 1 (November 1909): 1–14.

70. V. Medem, "Vsemirnaia evreiskaia natsiia," in *Teoreticheskie i prakticheskie voprosy evreiskoi zhizni* (St. Petersburg, 1911), 104. See this essay, translated as "The Worldwide Jewish Nation," and my introduction in Simon Rabinovitch, ed., *Jews and Diaspora Nationalism: Writings on Jewish Peoplehood in Europe and the United States* (Waltham, Mass., 2012), 105–24.

71. "Nashi zadachi," *Vestnik evreiskoi obshchiny* 1 (August 1913): 3.

72. "Nashi zadachi" (1913), 3.

73. "Nashi zadachi" (1913), 4; emphasis in original.

74. S. Dubnov, "Problema obshchiny v noveishei istorii evreistva," *Vestnik evreiskoi obshchiny* 1 (August 1913): 10; emphasis in original.

75. Dubnov, "Problema obshchiny," 10.

76. Dubnov, "Problema obshchiny," 10.

77. Dubnov, "Problema obshchiny," 12.

78. See the regular columns in *Vestnik* by Zilberfarb ("Ocherki obshchinoi politiki"), Efroikin (under the name Efren, "Ocherki mestechkovoi-obshchinoi zhizni"), and Aizenberg ("Iz praktiki obshchinnogo prava").

79. See *Soveshchanie*, 146–47.

80. Fishman, *Rise of Modern Yiddish Culture*, 68. Fishman states of Dubnov's 1905 plan: "On the one hand, it proposed that the Jewish National Assembly consist of three hundred delegates, each representing a district of ten thousand adult Jews. On the other hand, it skirted over fundamental questions of constituency, authority, and operation" (68). While true in terms of Dubnov's theoretical writings, many of these issues were clarified in the Folkspartey's 1906 platform.

81. "Zadachi momenta," *Novyi voskhod* 1 (6 January 1910): 1.

82. A. Perel'man, "*Evreiskii mir* (Glava iz vospominanii)," *Vestnik Evreiskogo Universiteta v Moskve* 18.2 (1998): 228–33. See also Aron Perel'man, *Vospominaniia* (St. Petersburg, 2009).

83. Dubnov, *Kniga zhizni*, 296. On An-sky's contribution to *Evreiskii mir*, see Gabriella Safran, *Wandering Soul: The Dybbuk's Creator, S. An-sky* (Cambridge, Mass., 2010), 154–83.

84. Perel'man, "*Evreiskii mir* (Glava iz vospominanii)," 231. Idelson attacked the editors of *Evreiskii mir* for what he considered their false nonpartisanship and anti-Zionism. See *Rassvet* (8 March 1909).

85. Ben-Adir [Avrom Rozin], "Bor'ba natsional'noi i assimiliatsionnoi ideologii," *Evreiskii mir* 3 (March 1909): 21.

86. See Dubnov, *Kniga zhizni*, 300–301. See also Trivus-Shmi, "Evreiskaia Narodnaia Gruppa," *Svoboda i ravenstvo* 2 (14 January 1907): 5–6.

87. Pasmanik was a proponent of *Gegenwartsarbeit* (until 1908) and was on the editorial boards of *Evreiskaia zhizn'* and *Rassvet*. He was also a contributor to *Evreiskii mir*.

88. "Ot redaktsii," in *Teoreticheskie i prakticheskie voprosy evreiskoi zhizni* (St. Petersburg, 1911), 4.

89. See Joshua A. Fishman, "Attracting a Following to High-Culture Functions for a Language of Everyday Life: The Role of the Tshernovits Language Conference in the 'Rise of Yiddish,'" in Joshua A. Fishman, ed., *Never Say Die! A Thousand Years of Yiddish in Jewish Life* (The Hague, 1981), 369–94.

90. Quoted in Fishman, "Attracting a Following," 374.

91. The conference's prospective agenda appears in translation in Emanuel S. Goldsmith, *Architects of Yiddishism at the Beginning of the Twentieth Century: A Study in Jewish Cultural History* (Rutherford, N.J., 1976), 184.

92. Birnbaum, whose mother tongue was German, had not yet mastered oral Yiddish at the time of the conference. For an intellectual biography of Birnbaum, see Jess Olson, *Nathan Birnbaum and Jewish Modernity: Architect of Zionism, Yiddishism, and Orthodoxy* (Stanford, Calif., 2013).

93. See Rabinovitch, *Jews and Diaspora Nationalism*, 45–55. "Proekty evreiskoi natsional'noi avtonomii," *Evresikii mir* (1909).

94. Olson, *Nathan Birnbaum and Jewish Modernity*, 174–76.

95. Quoted in Goldsmith, *Architects*, 184.

96. Goldsmith, *Architects*, 184.

97. Despite being one of the initiators, Pinski also did not attend.

98. Goldsmith, *Architects*, 193.

99. Quoted in Dovid Katz, *Words on Fire: The Unfinished Story of Yiddish* (New York, 2004), 268–69. My emphasis.

100. Katz, *Words on Fire*, 268–69.

101. See Zhitlowsky's essay "Why Only Yiddish?" in Rabinovitch, *Jews and Diaspora Nationalism*, 96–104.

102. Quoted in Tony Michels, *A Fire in Their Hearts: Yiddish Socialists in New York* (Cambridge, Mass., 2005), 138.

103. Michels, *Fire in Their Hearts*, 139.

104. N. Shtif, "Oytobiografye," *YIVO bleter* 5.3–5 (1933): 206. For selections published in English, see Nokhum Shtif, "How I Became a Yiddish Linguist," in Lucy S. Dawidowicz, ed., *The Golden Tradition: Jewish Life and Thought in Eastern*

Europe (Syracuse, N.Y., 1996), 257–63. For an intellectual biography of Shtif and an assessment of his role in the development of Yiddish, see Barry Trachtenberg, *The Revolutionary Roots of Modern Yiddish, 1903–1917* (Syracuse, N.Y., 2008), 135–57.

105. A. Perel'man, "K voprosu o iazyke," *Evreiskii mir* 1 (January 1909): pt. 2, 89.

106. A. Perel'man, "Evreiskii iazik v diaspore," *Evreiskii mir* 1 (8 January 1910): 8.

107. On Mieses, see Katz, *Words on Fire*, 272–74; and Goldsmith, *Architects*, 139–58, 200–208.

108. Perel'man, "Evreiskii iazik v diaspore," 9.

109. Perel'man, "Evreiskii iazik v diaspore," 9.

110. Dubnov, *Kniga zhizni*, 297.

111. Dubnov, *Kniga zhizni*, 316–17. The literary critic Samuel (Shmuel) Niger-Charney attributed Dubnov's dislike for Peretz to his Litvak (Lithuanian Jewish) temperament. Peretz's Polish neo-Hasidism in his literature, according to Niger-Charney, was too romantic for Dubnov's rational outlook. Samuel Niger-Charney, "Simon Dubnow as a Literary Critic," *YIVO Annual* 1 (1946): 316–17.

112. On Engel (known as the father of Jewish music), the Jewish Folk Music Society, the creation of "Jewish music," and the relationship between music and Jewish national self-consciousness in late imperial Russia, see James Loeffler, *The Most Musical Nation: Jews and Culture in the Late Russian Empire* (New Haven, Conn., 2010).

113. From the typescript of a lecture delivered on November 8, 1915, at a Moscow concert organized by the Jewish Folk Music Society. See Iuly (Yoel) Engel, "Jewish Folksongs: The Ethnographic Expedition," in *The Upward Flight: The Musical World of S. An-sky*, addendum to Gabriella Safran and Steven J. Zipperstein, eds., *The Worlds of S. An-sky: A Russian Jewish Intellectual at the Turn of the Century* (Stanford, Calif., 2006).

114. Dubnov, *Kniga zhizni*, 297. Peretz made the identical distinction at the Czernowitz conference.

115. S. M. Dubnov, "Utverzhdenie golusa," *Evreiskii mir* 5 (May 1909): 58.

116. Niger-Charney, "Simon Dubnow as a Literary Critic," 311–12. Dubnov later published a number of his essays on Yiddish literature and literary figures in *Fun "zhargon" tsu Yidish un andere artiklen: literarish zikhroynes* (Vilna, 1929).

117. Dubnov, *Kniga zhizni*, 313–14.

118. See Zimmerman, *Poles, Jews*, 248–51.

119. "Decisions on the Nationality Question (1899, 1901, 1905, 1910)," in Paul Mendes-Flohr and Jehuda Reinharz, eds., *The Jew in the Modern World: A Documentary History*, 3rd ed. (New York, 2011), 401.

120. Medem, "Vsemirnaia evreiskaia natsiia," 103; Medem, "Worldwide Jewish Nation," 121.

121. Benjamin Harshav, *Language in Time of Revolution* (Stanford, Calif., 1993), 25.

122. Harshav, *Language*, 26.

123. TsGIA SPb, f. 2049, op. 1, d. 33.

124. At this time Dubnov for the most part withdrew from editing and organizing the publication.

125. See Solomon Volkov, *St. Petersburg: A Cultural History*, Antoninia W. Bouis, trans. (New York, 1995), 153.

126. The issue of *Di yidishe velt*'s party affiliation is not entirely clear. According to Dubnov, the publication was founded as a party organ (*Kniga zhizni*, 322). Barry Trachtenberg suggests, however, that *Di yidishe velt* was programmatic in its support for Yiddish, Jewish communalism, and folklore but was not partisan, especially under the editorship of Shmuel Niger ("From *Zhargon* to *Visnshaft*: The Generation of 1905 and the Transformation of Yiddish" [PhD diss., University of California, Los Angeles, 2004], 177; *Revolutionary Roots*, 70–75). With *Di yidishe velt*'s move to Vilna in 1913 and the ascension of Niger as editor, the original political purpose of the journal may have receded into the background (or simply became irrelevant), but the content of the publication remained consistent with its original mission of diaspora nationalism, cultural revival, and reaching out to the folk.

127. "Unzer veg," *Di yidishe velt* 1 (1912): 1–6.

128. "Unzer veg," 2.

129. Fishman, *Rise of Modern Yiddish Culture*, 14; Kenneth Moss, "Jewish Culture Between Renaissance and Decadence: *Di Literarishe Monatsshriften* and Its Critical Reception," *Jewish Social Studies* 8.1 (2001): 161, 163. See also Trachtenberg, *Revolutionary Roots*, 82–107.

130. Eli Lederhendler, *Jewish Responses to Modernity: New Voices in America and Eastern Europe* (New York, 1994), 14; emphasis in original.

131. Y. Efren [Efroikin], "*Kehile*, folk un inteligentsie," *Di yidishe velt* 2 (April 1912): 49–50.

132. Efren, "*Kehile*, folk un inteligentsie," 51.

133. Efren, "*Kehile*, folk un inteligentsie," 52.

134. Gerhard Brunn, Miroslav Hroch, and Andreas Kappeler, "Introduction," in Andreas Kappeler, ed., *The Formation of National Elites* (New York, 1992), 4. See also Miroslav Hroch, *Social Preconditions of National Revival in Europe: A Comparative Analysis of the Social Composition of Patriotic Groups Among the Smaller European Nations*, Ben Fowkes, trans. (Cambridge, U.K., 1985).

135. Viktoriia [Victoria] Khiterer, *Dokumenty sobrannye Evreiskoi istoriko-arkheograficheskoi kommissiei Vseukrainskoi akademii nauk* (Kiev, 1999), 294.

136. See David Wartenweiler, *Civil Society and Academic Debate in Russia, 1905–1914* (Oxford, U.K., 1999), 114.

137. "Evreiskoe literaturnoe obshchestvo," in *Evreiskaia entsiklopediia* (St. Petersburg, 1908–13), 7: 450.

138. Loeffler, *Most Musical Nation*, 122–33. See also James Loeffler, "Society for Jewish Folk Music," in *The YIVO Encyclopedia of Jews in Eastern Europe* (New Haven, Conn., 2008), 2: 1770–71.

139. These early members included Kreinin, Bramson, Vinaver, Sheftel', and the banker Mark Varshavskii (Loeffler, *Most Musical Nation*, 123).

140. Jeffrey Veidlinger, "'Emancipation: See Anti-Semitism': The *Evreiskaia entsiklopediia* and Jewish Public Culture," *Simon Dubnow Institute Yearbook* 9 (2010): 404–26.

141. "Ot izdatelei," in *Evreiskaia entsiklopediia*, 1: iii. For more on the debates on organizing the encyclopedia (from Dubnov's rather frustrated perspective), see Dubnov, *Kniga zhizni*, 287–88, 295.

142. S. M. Dubnow [Dubnov], *Jewish History: An Essay in the Philosophy of History* (Philadelphia, 1903), 29. This essay, intended as an introduction to an abridged Russian edition of Graetz's *History of the Jews*, was originally published as "Chto takoe evreiskaia istoriia? Opyt filosofskoi kharakteristiki," *Voskhod* 10/11 (October 1893).

143. The 1888 tract was published in book form as S. M. Dubnov, *Ob izuchenii istorii russkikh evreev i ob uchrezhdenii russko-evreiskogo istoricheskogo obshchestva* (St. Petersburg, 1891).

144. Brian Horowitz, "The Society for the Promotion of Enlightenment Among the Jews of Russia and the Evolution of the St. Petersburg Russian Jewish Intelligentsia, 1893–1905," *Studies in Contemporary Jewry* 19 (2003): 202.

145. On the founding of the Jewish Historical-Ethnographic Society, see Simon Rabinovitch, "Positivism, Populism, and Politics: The Intellectual Foundations of Jewish Ethnography in Late Imperial Russia," *Ab Imperio* 3 (2005): 245–46.

146. TsGIA SPb, f. 2129, op. 1, d. 54. Syrkin and Sev had graduated from law school but did not work as lawyers. See Levin, "Ha-politika ha-Yehudit," 136.

147. Benjamin Nathans, *Beyond the Pale: The Jewish Encounter with Late Imperial Russia* (Berkeley, Calif., 2002), 311–20; Benjamin Nathans, "On Russian-Jewish Historiography," in Thomas Sanders, ed., *Historiography of Imperial Russia: The Profession of Writing History in a Multinational State* (Armonk, N.Y., 1999), 404.

148. Louis Greenberg, *The Jews in Russia* (New Haven, Conn., 1953), 2: 117. The documents in *Regesty i nadpisi* were collected by Vinaver, Sev, A. G. Gornfel'd, and M. G. Syrkin. According to Dubnov, *Regesty i nadpisi* resulted from an inquiry by Vinaver about how he might help in achieving the goals outlined in Dubnov's 1891 essay. See *Regesty i nadpisi: svod materialov dlia istorii v Rossii (80 g.–1800 g.)*, 3 vols. (St. Petersburg, 1899–1913).

149. See M. Vinaver, "Kak my zanimalis' istoriei," *Evreiskaia starina* 1 (1909): 41–54.

150. Minutes of the meeting of November 23, 1908, TsGIA SPb, f. 2129, op. 1, d. 54.

151. Minutes of the meeting of November 23, 1908, TsGIA SPb, f. 2129, op. 1, d. 54. The connectivity of Jewish cultural projects is demonstrated by the fact that this speech was reproduced in the inaugural issue of *Evreiskii mir*.

152. S. Dubnov, "Protsessy gumanizatsii i natsionalizatsii v noveishei istorii evreev," *Evreiskii mir* 1 (January 1909): 48.

153. S. Dubnov, "Uchreditel'noe sobranie i publichnyia zasedaniia Evreiskogo Istoriko-Ethnograficheskogo Obshchestva," *Evreiskaia starina* 1.1 (1909): 157.

154. Jeffrey Veidlinger discusses the significance of the Jewish Historical-Ethnographic Society in three works: "The Historical and Ethnographic Construction of Russian Jewry," *Ab Imperio* 4 (2003): 165–84; "Popular History and Populist History: Simon Dubnov and the Jewish Historical Ethnographic Society," in Avraham Greenbaum, Yisrael Bartal, and Dan Haruv, eds., *Safra ve-saifa: Shimon Dubnov, historyon ve-ish tsibur* (Jerusalem, 2010), 71–86 (English side); and *Jewish Public Culture in the Late Russian Empire* (Bloomington, Ind., 2009). See also Benjamin Nathans, "Russian-Jewish Historiography," 411–19.

155. Gessen, although not a lawyer, participated in the Union for Full Rights as a prominent liberal. Like Dubnov, he was at the time attempting to write a synthetic history of Russian Jewry. Gessen initially joined the Folksgruppe but became disillusioned and left it in 1907. Braudo was a librarian, journalist, and communal activist.

156. Dubnov seems to have been in complete control of the society's publications and their finances. TsGIA SPb, f. 2129, op. 1, d. 54.

157. Dubnov, *Kniga zhizni*, 310.

158. Veidlinger, "Historical and Ethnographic Construction," 167.

159. The minutes of a meeting of the Jewish Historical-Ethnographic Society's Publications Committee held on January 30, 1911, report that Vinaver and Dubnov had set aside their earlier disagreement on the kinds of materials suitable for *Evreiskaia starina* and that they would work out their differences of opinion at meetings of the Editorial Committee in order to gradually establish the journal's character. TsGIA SPb, f. 2129, op. 1 d. 54.

160. TsGIA SPb, f. 2134 (Evreiskaia starina), op. 1, d. 1.

161. TsGIA SPb, f. 2134, op. 1, d. 2.

162. See Rabinovitch, "Positivism," 247. For a number of essays touching on An-sky's ethnographic efforts, see Safran and Zipperstein, *Worlds of S. An-sky. Perezhitoe* was edited by S. M. Ginzburg and Yisroel (Sergei) Tsinberg and, although unlike *Evreiskaia starina* it was not an official journal of the Jewish Historical-Ethnographic Society, it had many of the same participants.

163. TsGIA SPb, f. 2129, op. 1, d. 54.

164. Letter from Semyon An-sky to Shmuel Niger, St. Petersburg, March 1, 1913, YIVO, RG 360, f. 57. See also Eleanor Mlotek, comp., *S. Ansky (Shloyme-Zanvl Rappoport), 1863–1920, His Life and Works: Catalogue of an Exhibition* (New York, 1980). An-sky solicited help from wealthy Moscow Jews and, through Zhitlowsky, American Jews as well. See Benjamin Lukin, "'An Academy Where Folklore Will Be Studied': An-sky and the Jewish Museum," in Safran and Zipperstein, *Worlds of S. An-sky*, 287.

165. Lukin, "Academy," 284.

166. Vladimir Gintsburg took an active role in planning the expedition. See the correspondence of An-sky and Gintsburg in "Perepiska: Barona Gintsburga i S. An-Skogo po povodu etnographicheskikh ekspeditsii v cherte evreiskoi osedlosti," *Ab Imperio* 4 (2003): 429–72. The Gintsburgs had previously attempted to use ethnography for the purpose of improving the Jews' situation in Russia when, in 1884, Naftali Horace Gintsburg hired the Russian writer Nikolai Leskov to publish a series of articles about Judaism and Jewish rituals in order to convince the Russian public that Jews posed no threat to Christians. An-sky called Gintsburg's commissioning of Leskov a form of Jewish ethnography in "self-defense" (S. Anskii [An-sky], "Evreiskoe narodnoe tvorchestvo," *Perezhitoe* 1 [1908]: 277). See also Gabriella Safran, "Ethnography, Judaism, and the Art of Nikolai Leskov," *Russian Review* 59.2 (2000): 235–51.

167. Benyamin Lukin, "An-ski Ethnographic Expedition and Museum," in *YIVO Encyclopedia of Jews in Eastern Europe* (New Haven, Conn., 2008), 1: 48–51.

168. Several thoughtful interpretations of An-sky's ethnographic work—its context and meaning to An-sky—have been published in recent years. See Eugene M. Avrutin and Harriet Murav, "Introduction," in Eugene M. Avrutin, Valerii Dymshits, Alexander Ivanov, Alexander Lvov, Harriet Murav, and Alla Sokolova, eds., *Photographing the Jewish Nation: Pictures from S. An-sky's Ethnographic Expeditions* (Waltham, Mass., 2009), 3–25; Nathaniel Deutsch, *The Jewish Dark Continent: Life and Death in the Russian Pale of Settlement* (Cambridge, Mass., 2011), 6–71; and Safran, *Wandering Soul*, 186–224.

169. In addition to An-sky, the committee consisted of M. I. Kulisher, Lev Shternberg, and M. G. Syrkin. They were aided by S. M. Ginzburg, M. M. Margolin, and Yisroel (Sergei) Tsinberg. Protocols of the meeting held November 21, 1915, TsGIA SPb, f. 2129, op. 1, d. 60.

170. A small exhibit of material objects collected on the first two expeditions opened for a few months in the spring of 1914. See Valerii Dymshits, "The First Jewish Museum," and photographs of the exhibit, in Avrutin et al., *Photographing the Jewish Nation*, 191–97, 202–3. An-sky's collection of material objects on his expedition led him to see the educational and national value of Jewish museums. See Lukin's articles in Safran and Zipperstein, *Worlds of S. An-sky*; and in the *YIVO Encyclopedia*.

171. According to the minutes of a planning session, "S. A. Rapoport [An-sky] counts on managing the museum until the end of his life, if one doesn't mind this position" (TsGIA SPb, f. 2129, op. 1, d. 60).

172. Frug and Dubnov were close friends. For Dubnov's memories of Frug, see S. Dubnov, "Vospominaniia o S. G. Fruge," *Evreiskaia starina* 8.4 (1916): 441–59.

173. Brian Horowitz argues that as a poet, Frug appealed to a wide range of people because his poems reflected a number of the day's political currents and readers tended to project their own views on his poetry. See Brian Horowitz,

"Poet and Nation: Fame and Amnesia in Shimon Frug's Literary Reputation," in Brian Horowitz, *Empire Jews: Jewish Nationalism and Acculturation in 19th- and 20th-Century Russia* (Bloomington, Ind., 2009), 51–64. Frug also wrote the poem "Shtey oyf," which, according to Yohanan Petrovsky-Shtern, might have become a Jewish national anthem had it been written in Hebrew instead of Yiddish. Yohanan Petrovsky-Shtern, *The Anti-Imperial Choice: The Making of the Ukrainian Jew* (New Haven, Conn., 2009), 49.

174. S. Frug, "Molodniak," *Evreiskii mir* 1 (January 1909): 13.

175. S. Dubnov, "Kakaia samoemantsipatsiia nuzhna evreiam?" *Voskhod* (May–June 1883): 219–46, and (July–August 1883): 1–30.

176. Dubnov, "Kakaia samoemantsipatsiia nuzhna evreiam?" (May–June 1883): 246, 238; (July–August 1883): 15.

177. See Dubnov's preface to his memoirs, *Kniga zhizni*, 17–18.

178. An early Hebrew work by Sholem Yankev Abramovich (Mendele Moykher-Sforim), titled *The Fathers and the Sons: A Love Story*, related a different story but a similar message. See Olga Litvak, *Conscription and the Search for Modern Russian Jewry* (Bloomington, Ind., 2006), 111.

179. "Otchet," 43; *Soveshchanie*, 81.

180. "Ot redaktsii," *Vestnik obshchestva rasprostraneniia prosveshcheniia mezhdu evreiami v Rossii* 1 (November 1910): i.

181. "Ot redaktsii" (1910), i.

182. As Nathaniel Deutsch observes, "The category of culture became the conceptual glue that bound otherwise disparate elements within Russian Jewish society together and helped enable protean figures like Simon Dubnow and S. An-sky to move between spheres that might otherwise have remained separate" ("When Culture Became the New Torah: Late Imperial Russia and the Discovery of Jewish Culture," *Jewish Quarterly Review* 102.3 [summer 2012]: 461).

Chapter 5

1. Shimon Dubnov, "Sod ha-kiyum ve-khok ha-kiyum shel am Yisrael," *He-'Atid* 4 (1912):114–15.

2. Regarding Jewish responses to the war in Germany, see Amos Elon, *The Pity of It All: A Portrait of the German-Jewish Epoch, 1743–1933* (New York, 2002), 297–354; and for an overview among all belligerents, see the recent book by Derek Penslar, *Jews and the Military: A History* (Princeton, N.J., 2013), 145–57.

3. See Steven J. Zipperstein, "The Politics of Relief: The Transformation of Russian Jewish Communal Life During the First World War," *Studies in Contemporary Jewry* 4 (1988): 22–40.

4. See Eric Lohr, *Nationalizing the Russian Empire: The Campaign Against Enemy Aliens During World War I* (Cambridge, Mass., 2003); Peter Gatrell, *A Whole Empire Walking: Refugees in Russia During World War I* (Bloomington, Ind.,

1999); and Peter Holquist, *Making War, Forging Revolution: Russia's Continuum of Crisis, 1914–1921* (Cambridge, Mass., 2002).

5. Arguably, this "continuum of crisis" began even earlier, with the lead-up to the 1905 revolution.

6. Holquist, *Making War*, 4.

7. A riveting and thoughtful account of anti-Jewish violence during the war, and the attending politics, can be found in Gabriella Safran, *Wandering Soul:* The Dybbuk's *Creator, S. An-sky* (Cambridge, Mass., 2010), 225–57. The most detailed assessments to date can be found in two recent dissertations: Semion Gol'din, "Russkoe evreistvo pod kontrolem tsarskikh voennykh vlastei v gody Pervoi mirovoi voiny" (PhD diss., Hebrew University of Jerusalem, 2005); and Polly M. Zavadivker, "Blood and Ink: Russian and Soviet Jewish Chroniclers of Catastrophe from World War I to World War II" (PhD diss., University of California, Santa Cruz, 2013). See also Eric Lohr, "1915 and the War Pogrom Paradigm in the Russian Empire," in Jonathan Dekel-Chen, David Gaunt, Natan M. Meir, and Israel Bartal, eds., *Anti-Jewish Violence: Rethinking the Pogrom in East European History* (Bloomington, Ind., 2011), 41–51; Peter Holquist, "The Role of Personality in the First (1914–1915) Russian Occupation of Galicia and Bukovina," in Dekel-Chen et al., *Anti-Jewish Violence*, 52–73; John Klier, "Kazaki i pogrom: Chem otlichalis' 'voennyi' pogromy?" in O. V. Budnitskii, O. V. Belova, V. E. Kel'ner, and V. V. Mochalova, eds., *Mirovoi krizis 1914–1920 godov i sud'ba vostochnoevropeiskogo evreistva* (Moscow, 2005), 47–70; and Konrad Zieliński, "The Shtetl in Poland, 1914–1918," in Steven T. Katz, ed., *The Shtetl: New Evaluations* (New York, 2007), 102–20.

8. Lohr, *Nationalizing the Russian Empire*, 18–21.

9. Semion Goldin, "Deportation of Jews by the Russian Military Command, 1914–1915," *Jews in Eastern Europe* 41.1 (2000): 42.

10. Eric Lohr, "The Russian Army and the Jews: Mass Deportation, Hostages, and Violence During World War I," *Russian Review* 60.3 (2001): 406.

11. Semion Gol'din, "Russkoe komandovanie i evrei vo vremiia Pervoi mirovoi voiny: prichiny formirovaniia negativnogo stereoptipa," in Budnitskii et al., *Mirovoi krizis*, 29–46. In 1912 the Ministry of War surveyed Russia's commanders on whether the Jews should serve in the military and received many emphatically negative responses from the army's top officers (30).

12. S. Ansky, *The Enemy at His Pleasure: A Journey Through the Jewish Pale of Settlement During World War I*, Joachim Neugroschel, ed. and trans. (New York, 2002), 5, see also 16–17.

13. An-sky also dismissed the possibility that many Jews, though not responsible for spying, did in fact place their sympathies with the Germans. Safran, *Wandering Soul*, 229–35.

14. Goldin, "Deportation of Jews," 70.

15. Goldin, "Deportation of Jews," 40–73.

16. Russian anti-Jewish violence and the war's depravations are covered extensively in An-sky's account of his time as a representative first of the Union of Zemstvos in Poland and then of the Red Cross in the war zone, especially Galicia. In English, see Ansky, *Enemy at His Pleasure*. In the original Yiddish, see S. An-sky, "Der yudisher hurbn fun Poylen Galitsye un Bukovina fun tog bukh 674–677, 1914–1917," in *Gezamelte shriften*, vols. 4–6 (Warsaw, 1925). An important collection of materials relating to Russian Jews in the first half of the war is "Iz 'chernoi knigi' rossiiskogo evreistva: Materialy dlia istorii voiny 1914–1915 g.," *Evreiskaia starina* 10 (1918): 195–296. See in particular a description of the practice of taking Jewish hostages in the section "Zalozhniki: russkie evrei," 254–64.

17. See Holquist, "Role of Personality"; and Klier, "Kazaki i pogrom."

18. Alexander Prusin, *Nationalizing a Borderland: War, Ethnicity, and Anti-Jewish Violence in East Galicia, 1914–1920* (Tuscaloosa, Ala., 2005), 24–27.

19. Quoted in Mordechai Altshuler, "Russia and Her Jews: The Impact of the 1914 War," *Weiner Library Bulletin* 27 (1973–74): 12.

20. *Rapport sur la Question Juive: Présenté par M. Vinaver Ancien Député à la Douma au nom du Comité Central du Parti Constitutional-Démocrate a la conference des délégués du parti et de son groupe parliamentaire tenue à Moscou les 19 et 21 Juin 1915* (Paris, n.d.), 6. Vinaver's speech to the Kadet Party Central Committee and the conference's resolutions are also reproduced in "Iz 'chernoi knigi' rossiiskogo evreistva," 197–227.

21. For a good example, see Sergei Kan, *Lev Shternberg: Anthropologist, Russian Socialist, Jewish Activist* (Lincoln, Neb., 2009), 224–25.

22. Simon Dubnov, *Kniga zhizni: Vospominaniia i razmyshleniia, materiali dlia istorii moego vremeni* (St. Petersburg, 1998), 334–37.

23. *Rapport sur la Question Juive*, 43–44; "Iz 'chernoi knigi' rossiiskogo evreistva," 219.

24. This speech appeared in full in *Rech'* on August 3, 1915, and, remarkably, in the *New York Times* on September 23, 1915. It was reprinted in the report by the American Jewish Committee titled *The Jews in the Eastern War Zone* (New York, 1916), 111–17.

25. *Jews in the Eastern War Zone*, 111–17.

26. YIVO, Lucien Wolf and David Mowshowitch Papers, RG 348, f. 111b.

27. See Yohanan Petrovsky-Shtern, *Jews in the Russian Army, 1827–1917: Drafted into Modernity* (Cambridge, U.K., 2009), 252–57.

28. Quoted in *Jews in the Eastern War Zone*, 22. The quote is from the minutes of an August 4, 1915, meeting of the Council of Ministers.

29. The nearly complete minutes of the meetings of the Council of Ministers, along with the notes on other secret meetings, were translated (from I. V. Gessen, ed., *Arkhiv Russkoi Revolutsii*, vol. 17 [Berlin, 1926]) and reproduced in Michael Cherniavsky, *Prologue to Revolution: Notes of A. N. Iakhontov on the Secret Meetings of the Council of Ministers, 1915* (Englewood Cliffs, N.J., 1967). Iakhontov's notes

in the original Russian were also published as *Sovet Ministrov Rossiskoi imperii v gody Pervoi mirovoi voiny: Bumagi A. N. Iakhontova—zapisi perepiska* (St. Petersburg, 1999).

30. Cherniavsky, *Prologue to Revolution*, 57–63, 72. Counterintuitively, some ministers also believed that the interior of the empire would benefit from an influx of economic competition (66).

31. Cherniavsky, *Prologue to Revolution*, 86.

32. Sam Johnson, "Breaking or Making the Silence? British Jews and East European Jewish Relief, 1914–1917," *Modern Judaism* 30.1 (2010): 106–7.

33. Alexander Orbach, "The Jewish People's Group and Jewish Politics, 1906–1914," *Modern Judaism* 10.1 (February 1990): 8. Despite the limited franchise, there were two Jewish deputies in the Third Duma: Naftali Fridman and Lazar Nisselovich (1856–1914). For a firsthand account of their efforts, see the pamphlet by L. N. Nisselowitsch [Nisselovich], *Die Judenfrage in Russland* (Berlin, 1909), especially 41–45.

34. See *Politicheskie partii Rossii (pervaia chetvert' XX v.): Spravochnik* (Briansk, Russia, 1993), 73. The Progressive Bloc was made up of six Duma caucuses. The Kadets, Progressists, and Left Octobrists were on most issues considered the Bloc's "liberal" wing, whereas the Centrists, Zemstvo Octobrists, and Progressive Nationalists constituted the Bloc's conservatives. For a description of the caucuses that composed the Progressive Bloc, see Michael F. Hamm, "Liberal Politics in Wartime Russia: An Analysis of the Progressive Bloc," *Slavic Review* 33.3 (1974): 453–68. For new research on Kadet and Octobrist policies (in general, not regarding the Jews) on the eve of the war, see Leopold H. Haimson, "'The Problem of Political and Social Stability in Urban Russia on the Eve of War and Revolution' Revisited," *Slavic Review* 59.4 (2000): 860–63. For new research on the Progressive Bloc, see Haimson, "Political and Social Stability," 866–73. As Haimson observes, during the war the Bloc was reluctant to oppose the tsar in a meaningful way for fear of impeding the war effort.

35. See "Progressivnyi blok i evreiskii vopros," *Evreiskaia nedelia* 15 (30 August 1915): 1–3. There was also considerable dissatisfaction with the Kadets' participation in the Progressive Bloc on the part of party members who believed that the Kadets were sacrificing their liberal principles and agenda and becoming indistinguishable from the Octobrists. See Melissa Kirschke Stockdale, *Paul Miliukov and the Quest for a Liberal Russia, 1880–1918* (Ithaca, N.Y., 1997), 229. See also Raymond Pearson, "Miliukov and the Sixth Kadet Congress," *Slavonic and East European Review* 52 (April 1975): 210–29.

36. Resolution of the Central Committee of the Constitutional-Democratic Party, from the conference of June 6–8, 1915; *Rapport sur la Question Juive*, 54–57; "Iz 'chernoi knigi' rossiiskogo evreistva," 225–27.

37. The circulars affair is described in detail in Michael F. Hamm, "Liberalism and the Jewish Question: The Progressive Bloc," *Russian Review* 31.2 (1972): 163–

72; R. Ganelin, "Gosudarstvennaia duma i antisemitskie tsirkuliary 1915–1916 go-dov," *Vestnik Evreiskogo Universiteta v Moskve* 10.3 (1995): 4–37; and Jacob G. Frum-kin, "Pages from the History of Russian Jewry (Recollections and Documentary Material)," in Jacob Frumkin, Gregor Aronson, and Alexis Goldenweiser, eds., *Russian Jewry (1860–1917)*, Mirra Ginsburg, trans. (New York, 1966), 76–78. The circulars affair and the actions of the Jewish Duma members and the Kadet Party were covered in depth during the winter and spring of 1916 in *Evreiskaia zhizn'* and *Evreiskaia nedelia*. See also L. M. Bramson, "Primenenie na praktike Shcherbato-vskogo tsirkuliara o rashirenii 'cherty,'" *Novyi put'* 1 (21 January 1916): 4–9.

38. Transcript of an Executive Committee plenum held on March 17, 1916, Ts-GIA SPb, f. 2049, op. 1, d. 192.

39. Letter from Reuben Blank to Mr. [Claude] Montefiore and Mr. [David] Alexander, June 23, 1916, YIVO, RG 348, f. 24. On Miliukov during the circulars affair, see Gol'din, "Russkoe evreistvo," 371–74.

40. Frumkin, "Pages," 80.

41. Frumkin, "Pages," 69.

42. Hamm, "Liberalism and the Jewish Question," 165. On the weakness of Russian liberalism's appeal to Jews, see Robert Seltzer, "Jewish Liberalism in Late Tzarist Russia," *Contemporary Jewry* 9.1 (1987–88): 51. See also Charles E. Timber-lake, ed., *Essays on Russian Liberalism* (Columbia, Mo., 1972); and Michael Kar-povich, "Two Kinds of Russian Liberalism: Malakov and Miliukov," in Ernest J. Simmons, ed., *Continuity and Change in Russian and Soviet Thought* (Cambridge, Mass., 1955), 129–43.

43. Quoted in Oleg Budnitskii, "Russian Liberalism in War and Revolution," *Kritika* 5.1 (2004): 153. In this review of the wealth of recently published Kadet Party archival records, Budnitskii suggests that as the Kadets began to lose control and become disillusioned, they also increasingly looked to a military dictatorship as a solution. According to Budnitskii, these documents suggest that the differ-ence between the right and the Kadets completely disappeared during the civil war (154).

44. "Konferentsiia fraktsii narodnoi svobody," *Evreiskaia nedelia* 5 (21 June 1915): 3.

45. Safran, *Wandering Soul*, 236–38.

46. A number of writers, artists, and political figures—from neo-Orthodox Christian philosophers to Maxim Gorky—came together to publish a volume of essays against antisemitism called *The Shield* (*Shchit: Literaturnyi sbornik*). Accord-ing to Laura Engelstein, "*Shchit* was conceived as an expression of moral and civic consciousness on the part of the non-Jewish intelligentsia, not merely for the ben-efit of the Jews, but on behalf of the Russian cultural nation" (*Slavophile Empire: Imperial Russia's Illiberal Path* [Ithaca, N.Y., 2009], 221).

47. Laura Engelstein, "Against the Grain: Russian Intellectuals in Defense of the Jews," paper presented at the AAASS Annual Conference (Boston, 2009). En-

gelstein is currently working on a project that intends to revise our understanding of Russian liberal intellectuals during the revolutionary years from 1905 to 1925 and in particular emphasizes their moral resistance to antisemitism, including during the war years.

48. Even after the tsar's abdication, the Kadets preferred to blame the Bolsheviks or imaginary German agents for anti-Jewish violence rather than the people carrying out the attacks. During the civil war, when the Whites were responsible for far more pogroms than the Bolsheviks, the Kadets took to blaming the Jews themselves, internalizing popular antisemitism. At their conference in Kharkov in November 1919, the Kadets openly blamed widespread anti-Jewish violence on Jewish support for the Bolsheviks. See William G. Rosenberg, *Liberals in the Russian Revolution: The Constitutional Democratic Party, 1917–1921* (Princeton, N.J., 1974), 426; and O. V. Budnitskii, *Rossiiskie evrei mezhdu krasnymi i belymi (1917–1920)* (Moscow, 2006), 344–67.

49. The Political Bureau was originally founded during the 1905 revolution.

50. "Executive Committee," TsGIA SPb, f. 2049, o. 1, d. 192.

51. "Executive Committee," TsGIA SPb, f. 2049, o. 1, d. 192. In these minutes Dubnov stated: "Before us are two tasks: historical and political. If in one meeting it was possible to settle both questions, I would have been very pleased, but as we can have no success with this, I suggest we engage these questions, like how to react to the incident, and not in so doing to run ragged its value."

52. *Reports Received by the Joint Distribution Committee of Funds for Jewish War Sufferers* (New York, 1916), 11. Most of the information in this publication comes from a transcript of the Obshchiia Svedeniia EKOPO for February 1916 and from a translation of this document titled "Jewish Committee for the Relief to Victims of War: Special Conference for the Organization of War Refugees," JDC NY, collection 1914–1918, f. 143-1. For a general description of EKOPO's activities, see Ilya Trotzky, "Jewish Institutions of Welfare, Education, and Mutual Assistance," in Frumkin et al., *Russian Jewry*, 432.

53. *Otchet Tsentral'nago Evreiskago Komiteta pomoshchi zhertvam voiny s nachala deiatel'nosti (Avgust 1914 goda po 30-e Iunia 1917 goda* (Petrograd, 1918), 12–14, 93–94. EKOPO's report of its wartime activities, issued after the war, details both the plight of refugees in wartime and the scope of the organization's activities.

54. *Otchet Tsentral'nago Evreiskago Komiteta,* 7.

55. Sliozberg claimed in his memoirs that he was EKOPO's originator and that he founded the organization for the purpose of aiding Jewish soldiers and their families (*Dela minuvshikh dnei* [Paris, 1934], 3: 326–28).

56. Zipperstein, "Politics of Relief," 25. Zipperstein's essay is still the most thorough and significant account of EKOPO's activities and significance during the war. See also Mikhail Beizer, *Evrei Leningrada, 1917–1939: Natsional'naia zhizn i sovetizatsiia* (Moscow, 1999), 236–44; Yevgeniya Pevzner, "Jewish Committee for the Relief of War Victims (1914–1921)," *Pinkas* 1 (2006): 114–42; and Anasta-

siia Sergeevna Tumanova, "Evreiskie obshchestvennye organizatsii v gody pervoi mirovoi voiny (na primere Tambovskoi gubernii)," in Budnitskii et al., *Mirovoi krizis*, 124–41.

57. Thomas Fallows, "Politics and the War Effort in Russia: The Union of Zemstvos and the Organization of the Food Supply, 1914–1916," *Slavic Review* 37.1 (1978): 72–73.

58. Fallows, "Politics," 82. For a detailed description of the issue (albeit lacking analysis of Russia's food supply problems), see P. B. Struve, ed., *Food Supply in Russia During the World War* (New Haven, Conn., 1930).

59. See "Pomoshch' zhertvam voiny," *Evreiskaia nedelia* 6 (28 June 1915): 23–27.

60. A complete list is included in *Reports Received by the Joint Distribution Committee*, 28–37.

61. *Reports Received by the Joint Distribution Committee*, 46.

62. *Reports Received by the Joint Distribution Committee*, 19.

63. "Ot redaktsii," *Pomoshch* 1 (24 December 1915): 2; emphasis in original.

64. "Ot redaktsii," 2–3; emphasis in original.

65. See, in particular, the editorials in *Delo pomoshchi* during the summer and fall of 1916.

66. *Otchet Tsentral'nago Evreiskago Komiteta*, 37–48.

67. *Otchet Tsentral'nago Evreiskago Komiteta*, 43. See also Pevzner, "Jewish Committee," 125–26.

68. *Otchet Tsentral'nago Evreiskago Komiteta*, 43–44.

69. *Otchet Tsentral'nago Evreiskago Komiteta*, 44.

70. *Otchet Tsentral'nago Evreiskago Komiteta*, 45.

71. *Otchet Tsentral'nago Evreiskago* Komiteta, 45; emphasis in original.

72. On the Information Bureau, see Zavadivker, "Blood and Ink," 142–47.

73. "Instruktsii 'obsledovateliam,'" TsGIA Ukraine, Fridman Papers, f. 1010, op. 1, d. 135, l. 1–9. (I am indebted to Semion Gol'din for this material.)

74. "Instruktsii 'obsledovateliam.'"

75. Zavadivker, "Blood and Ink," 88–157. Chapters 2 and 3 are respectively on An-sky and Dubnov during World War I.

76. As Gabriella Safran suggests, An-sky was the perfect person to collect information from the front on behalf of EKOPO: He had already undertaken ethnographic expeditions in Volynia and Podolia, which were on the border with Austria-Hungary; he had good local Jewish contacts and relationships with liberal and non-Jewish relief organizations; and he was unmarried and childless (and was going to head into the war zone regardless) (*Wandering Soul*, 228).

77. S. An-sky, I. L. Peretz, and Yankev Dinezon, "Appeal to Collect Materials About the World War," in David Roskies, ed., *The Literature of Destruction: Jewish Responses to Catastrophe* (Philadelphia, 1988), 209–10 (originally published in *Haynt*, 1 January 1915). In this appeal the three authors directly connected managing the Jewish historical record to the postwar settlement: Without evidence of

how their blood was shed, Jews would be unable to defend themselves against slander and "neither people nor history will owe us anything."

78. Zavadivker, "Blood and Ink," 80–83 and *passim*.

79. *Otchet Tsentral'nago Evreiskago Komiteta*, 13.

80. JDC NY, Collection 1914–1918, f. 143-1. U.S. Jews had previously proved willing to exert pressure on their government to defend Russian Jews. For example, when Russia refused to offer Jewish and non-Jewish Americans equal access to Russian visas and protection, the American Jewish Committee successfully forced Congress to revoke the existing treaty governing Russo-American commercial ties. See J. Bruce Nichols, *The Uneasy Alliance: Religion, Refugee Work, and U.S. Foreign Policy* (New York, 1988), 33.

81. See "A New Ambassador and the Duma," *New York Times* (24 February 1916): 12; and "Francis Seeks New Treaty with Russia," *New York Times* (18 April 1916): 3.

82. Arthur A. Goren, *New York Jews and the Quest for Community: The Kehillah Experiment, 1908–1922* (New York, 1970), 215–17.

83. Arthur A. Goren, *The Politics and Public Culture of American Jews* (Bloomington, Ind., 1999), 25.

84. Goren, *Politics*, 25.

85. Oscar Janowsky, *The Jews and Minority Rights (1898–1919)* (New York, 1966), 172. For detailed assessments of the American Jewish Congress movement, see Janowsky, *Jews and Minority Rights*, 161–90; and Jonathan Frankel, *Prophecy and Politics: Socialism, Nationalism, and the Russian Jews, 1862–1917* (Cambridge, U.K., 1981), 509–51.

86. Janowsky, *Jews and Minority Rights*, 176.

87. Frankel, *Prophecy and Politics*, 509–10.

88. Frankel, *Prophecy and Politics*, 548–49.

89. "Financial Report from July 1916," EKOPO Central Committee, JDC NY, Collection 1914–1918, f. 143-1.

90. Polly Zavadivker points out that because Mowshowitch had close ties to the Political Committee in Petrograd and was an able translator, much of the materials that he collected were in fact translations of documents collected and archived by the Political Bureau ("Blood and Ink," 141).

91. YIVO, RG 348, f. 57.

92. In Lucien Wolf's opinion, "The belligerent communities risk being held responsible for all that is done by the neutral communities, and this is calculated sometimes to estrange from them the sympathies of their respective governments." Lucien Wolf to Reuben Blank, July 20, 1916, YIVO, RG 348, f. 24.

93. YIVO, RG 348, f. 57. The Alliance Israélite Universelle, headed by Jacques Bigart, was even less receptive to Tchlenov and Sokolov when they visited Paris in February 1915. Bigart sought to coordinate his rebuff with that of Lucien Wolf. See Eugene C. Black, *The Social Politics of Anglo-Jewry, 1880–1920* (Oxford, U.K., 1988), 338.

94. Sir George Buchanan to Sir Edward Grey, March 10, 1915, cited in Carole Fink, *Defending the Rights of Others: The Great Powers, the Jews, and International Minority Protection, 1878–1938* (New York, 2004), 72n29.

95. Maurice de Bunsen to Lucien Wolf, March 3, 1916, YIVO, RG 348, f. 54j.

96. See Mark Levene, *War, Jews, and the New Europe: The Diplomacy of Lucien Wolf* (Oxford, U.K., 1992), 128–59.

97. *Jewish Chronicle* (27 October 1916).

98. Lucien Wolf to Zalman Dywien, January 11, 1916, YIVO, RG 348, f. 27e.

99. Levene, *War*, 168.

100. See YIVO, RG 348, f. 57.

101. Like Wolf, Adler would also eventually attend the Paris Peace Conference in 1919.

102. Cyrus Adler to Lucien Wolf, July 30, 1915, and Wolf to Adler, September 15, 1915, YIVO, RG 348, f. 2.

103. "Jewish Committee for the Relief to Victims of the War: Special Conference for the Organization of War Refugees," JDC NY, Collection 1914–1918, f. 143-1.

104. *Reports Received by the Joint Distribution Committee*, 9, 14. In the thirteen months between December 23, 1914, and February 9, 1915, the Petrograd Committee received $1,085,000 from the Joint. The Joint paid the ICA office in Petrograd directly, which then turned all its funds over to EKOPO—an amount totaling $1.8 million between January 1915 and August 1916.

105. *Reports Received by the Joint Distribution Committee*, 11–12, 42.

106. *Reports Received by the Joint Distribution Committee*, 24. Between August 1914 and July 1917, OZE opened 90 clinics, 19 hospitals, 19 feeding stations, 9 children's soup kitchens, 125 kindergartens, and 10 "Drop of Milk" children centers (Beizer, *Evrei Leningrada*, 239).

107. "Jewish Committee for the Relief to Victims of the War: Special Conference for the Organization of War Refugees," JDC NY, Collection 1914–1918, f. 143-1; *Reports Received by the Joint Distribution Committee*, 39. The Committee of the District of Moscow also raised some funds for redistribution, but it eventually spent them all and had to ask for assistance from the Petrograd Committee (*Reports Received by the Joint Distribution Committee*, 42, 45).

108. *Otchet Tsentral'nago Evreiskago Komiteta*, 7.

109. *Otchet Tsentral'nago Evreiskago Komiteta*, 10.

110. *Reports Received by the Joint Distribution Committee*, 42.

111. "Financial Report from July 1916," EKOPO Central Committee, JDC NY, Collection 1914–1918, f. 143-1.

112. The Petrograd Committee officially controlled EKOPO as of the first conference on communal affairs held in Vilna on January 6–8, 1915, and further centralized EKOPO activities at the following conference in Petrograd on May 14–16, 1915. See *Otchet Tsentral'nago Evreiskago Komiteta*, 9, 37–38.

113. A. Ginzburg [Gintsburg] to American Jewish Relief Committee, February 12–25, 1916, JDC NY, Collection 1914–1918, f. 143-1.

114. Lohr, *Nationalizing the Russian Empire*, 419.

115. See the mission statement in *Vestnik trudovoi pomoshchi sredi evreev* 1 (December 1915): 1.

116. Zipperstein, "Politics of Relief," 33.

117. Zipperstein, "Politics of Relief," 32.

118. Beizer, *Evrei Leningrada*, 237.

119. Gatrell, *Whole Empire Walking*, 148–49.

120. *Reports Received by the Joint Distribution Committee*, 11.

121. Brian Horowitz, "The Society for the Promotion of Enlightenment Among the Jews of Russia and the Evolution of the St. Petersburg Russian Jewish Intelligentsia, 1893–1905," *Studies in Contemporary Jewry* 19 (2003): 196.

122. Horowitz, "Society for the Promotion of Enlightenment," 196–97.

123. Horowitz, "Society for the Promotion of Enlightenment," 206. See also Horowitz's history of the OPE: *Jewish Philanthropy and Enlightenment in Late-Tsarist Russia* (Seattle, 2009). On attempts to democratize the OPE and Jewish welfare institutions in Kiev, see Natan M. Meir, *Kiev, Jewish Metropolis: A History, 1859–1914* (Bloomington, Ind., 2010), 284–309.

124. Leon Shapiro, *The History of ORT: A Jewish Movement for Social Change* (New York, 1980), 54.

125. "A Report on the Expediency of Subsidizing the Activity of the Provisional Committee for the Establishment of a Society for the Promotion of Handicrafts and Industrial and Agricultural Work Among Jews in Russia," in ORT Union, *80 Years of ORT: Historical Materials, Documents and Reports* (Geneva, 1960), 86; Shapiro, *History of ORT*, 68.

126. Shapiro, *History of ORT*, 60–67.

127. Gennady Estraikh, "A Quest for Integration: Nikolai Bakst and 'His' ORT, 1880–1904," and "Building a Jewish Economy: The Last Decade of the Russian Empire," in Rachel Bracha, Adi Drori-Avraham, and Geoffrey Yantian, eds., *Educating for Life: New Chapters in the History of ORT* (London, 2010), 36–37 and 52–53.

128. Estraikh, "Building a Jewish Economy," 55.

129. *Reports Received by the Joint Distribution Committee*, 23, 43–44, 59.

130. Jewish Colonization Association, *Séances du Conseil d'administration: proces-verbaux*, vol. 6 (10 January 1914). I refer here to the complete administrative minutes located at Tel Aviv University, Sourasky Library.

131. For example, in 1904 the ICA voted to grant Baron Gintsburg 316,000 rubles for the OPE to open forty new primary schools and forty new adult schools and to organize other courses and libraries. The ICA funded thirteen girls' vocational schools in the Russian empire between 1910 and 1916. The ICA also frequently gave grants to cooperative loan funds in dozens of cities in the Russian Empire (thirty-four in 1914 alone). The ICA channeled its funds to the Varshavskii

Banking House, which then distributed the money to the cooperative loan funds. Jewish Colonization Association, *Séances du Conseil d'administration: proces-verbaux*, vol. 3 (1 May 1904).

132. The request was granted on the conditions that no new payments would be made without receipts and reports and that new spending required approval from the Paris board. See Jewish Colonization Association, *Séances du Conseil d'administration: proces-verbaux*, vol. 7 (December 23, 1917).

133. On the OPE's creation of schools for refugees during the war and the attending political controversies over the language of instruction, the mixing of sexes, and so on, see Horowitz, *Jewish Philanthropy*, 211–16.

134. Zipperstein, "Politics of Relief," 35–36.

135. Zipperstein, "Politics of Relief," 35–36.

136. Sacha [Baron Aleksandr Gintsburg] to Felix Warburg, May 20, 1916, JDC NY, Collection 1914–1918, f. 143-1.

137. Baron Gunzburg [Gintsburg], "Letter on Jewish Affairs in Russia," and David Mowshowitch, "Some Remarks on Baron Gunzburg's Letter on the Jewish Affairs in Russia," YIVO, RG 348, f. 115.

138. Gunzburg, "Letter on Jewish Affairs in Russia"; Mowshowitch, "Some Remarks."

139. *Reports Received by the Joint Distribution Committee*, 51–58. To be exact, EKOPO and OZE employed thirty physicians, forty assistant surgeons, two sanitation officers, and eight dietitians. In addition, forty-seven kindergarten teachers and forty-four kindergarten assistants were responsible for establishing and maintaining children's "homes" (56).

140. See an overview in *Otchet Tsentral'nago Evreiskago Komiteta*, 15–36.

141. These statistics are from tables that appear, in order, in *Pomoshch* 1 (25 December 1915): 9; *Delo pomoshchi* 1–2 (20 January 1917): 11–14; and *Delo pomoshchi* 12 (20 November 1916): 49–54.

142. See tables in *Vestnik trudovoi pomoshchi sredi evreev* 1 (December 1915): 7, and 3–4 (February–March 1916): 12–17. We also can see in these tables and many others that appear in this publication that men were employed in only somewhat higher proportion than women (54 percent versus 43.4 percent, respectively, overall) and that the most commonly held trades were in the clothing and leather industry (30–35 percent depending on place).

143. See the tables in *Pomoshch* 1 (25 December 1915): 9, and 4 (15 February 1916): 4; and in *Delo pomoshchi* 1 (1 June 1916): 3–5, and 1–2 (20 January 1917): 11–14.

144. In one sample of more than 30,000 people looking for work, less than one-fourth of people in office and commercial work, liberal professions, and trade found new employment compared to more than 60 percent for all other categories. Thus, even though the office, trade, and professional workers made up nearly one-third of everyone looking for work, they made up less than 15 percent of the total people who had found work. *Vestnik trudovoi pomoshchi sredi evreev* 3–4 (February–March 1916): 14.

145. "Samopomoshchi i samodeiatel'nosti," emphasis in original; *Otchet Tsentral'nago Evreiskago Komiteta*, 37.

146. "Iz itogov minuvshago soveshchaniia," *Vestnik trudovoi pomoshchi sredi evreev* 3–4 (February–March 1916): 2.

147. See David Rechter, *The Jews of Vienna and the First World War* (Oxford, U.K., 2001).

148. See Antony Polonsky, *The Jews in Poland and Russia*, vol. 3, *1914–2008* (London, 2012); Ezra Mendelsohn, *Zionism in Poland: The Formative Years, 1915–1926* (New Haven, Conn., 1982); Marsha Rozenblit, *Reconstructing a National Identity: The Jews of Habsburg Austria During World War I* (Oxford, U.K., 2001); and Carole Fink, *Defending the Rights of Others*.

149. See Gatrell, *Whole Empire Walking*, 141–70.

150. "V 'Evreiskom Istoriko-Etnograficheskom O-ve,'" *Novyi voskhod* 8 (27 February 1915): 33. Vinaver was paraphrased by the author of this article.

151. "V 'Evreiskom Istoriko-Etnograficheskom O-ve,'" 33–34.

Chapter 6

1. Rex A. Wade, *The Russian Revolution, 1917* (Cambridge, U.K., 2000), 42–43. There is an enormous literature in English detailing the revolutionary events of 1917. Together, Wade's *Russian Revolution* and his edited anthology, *Revolutionary Russia: New Approaches* (New York, 2004), represent a synthesis of some of the most important recent scholarship on the revolution.

2. See Tsuyoshi Hasegawa, *The February Revolution: Petrograd, 1917* (Seattle, 1981), 520. Geoffrey Hosking describes the division between the two revolutionary authorities as one between *obshchestvennost'* (the Provisional Government and its supporters among the educated professionals) and the *narod* (the Soviets and their supporters among the workers, peasants, and soldiers). See Geoffrey Hosking, *Russia: People and Empire, 1552–1917* (London, 1997), 481.

3. S. Ansky, *The Enemy at His Pleasure: A Journey Through the Jewish Pale of Settlement During World War I*, Joachim Neugroschel, ed. and trans. (New York, 2002), 288–89.

4. Most Poles and Finns at this point would accept nothing less than complete independence, a result guaranteed by Russian military performance during the war. The Lithuanians, Latvians, Estonians, and Ukrainians, whose fate was still quite undecided, were working for territorial autonomy within a Russian federation by unilaterally establishing proto-parliaments. I focus on European Russia here, but movements for territorial autonomy were also developing in Transcaucasia and Central Asia.

5. Ronald G. Suny, "Nationality Policies," in Edward Acton, Vladimir Cherniaev, and William G. Rosenberg, eds., *Critical Companion to the Russian Revolution, 1914–1921* (Bloomington, Ind., 1997), 659–66. See also Oliver Radkey, *The Agrar-*

ian Foes of Bolshevism: Promise and Default of the Russian Socialist Revolutionaries, February–October 1917 (New York, 1958); and Manfred Hildermeier, *The Russian Socialist Revolutionary Party Before the First World War* (New York, 2000).

6. Richard Pipes, *The Formation of the Soviet Union*, rev. ed. (Cambridge, Mass., 1997), 31.

7. During the second coalition of the Provisional Government, the Socialist Revolutionaries trimmed their earlier promises of Ukrainian autonomy and opposed Finnish independence. Oliver Radkey is particularly unforgiving in his assessment of the Great Russian nationalism that crept into the Socialist Revolutionary Party (*Agrarian Foes*, 352–55). The Socialist Revolutionaries became the champions of nationalities once again only after the Bolshevik Revolution. See Oliver Radkey, *The Sickle Under the Hammer: The Russian Socialist Revolutionaries in the Early Months of Soviet Rule* (New York, 1963), 309–10.

8. The Kadets softened their opposition to decentralization while remaining adamantly committed to maintaining Russian territorial integrity. Pavel Miliukov reported to the Eighth Party Congress that "the Party of People's Freedom [Kadets] will endeavor to find a solution that, while giving an opportunity to the various regions of Russia to create their local autonomy on the principle of local legislation, will not at the same time destroy the unity of the Russian State" (Robert Paul Browder and Alexander F. Kerensky, eds., *The Russian Provisional Government 1917: Documents* [Stanford, Calif., 1961], 1: 317). Miliukov's speech originally appeared in *Rech'* 108 (10 May 1917): 3.

9. See Henry J. Tobias, "The Bund and Lenin Until 1903," *Russian Review* 20.4 (October 1961): 345; and Mordechai Altshuler, "The Attitude of the Communist Party of Russia to Jewish National Survival, 1918–1930," *YIVO Annual of Jewish Social Science* 14 (1969): 68–86.

10. S. M. Dubnov, *Kniga zhizni: Vospominaniia i razmyshleniia, materialy dlia istorii moego vremeni* (St. Petersburg, 1998), 411.

11. Vinaver observed that An-sky never felt any antagonism between his Russian and Jewish activities and that he saw Russian, Hebrew, and Yiddish as playing different roles in Jewish life (*Nedavnee [Vospominaniia i kharakteristiki]* [Paris, 1926], 290–91). This view is not entirely supported by An-sky's own words (see David Roskies, "S. Ansky and the Paradigm of Return," in Jack Wertheimer, ed., *The Uses of Tradition* [New York, 1992], 243–60), but there is no doubt that An-sky continued to see himself as a *narodnik* even after his turn to Jewish affairs.

12. Dubnov, *Kniga zhizni*, 412.

13. Letters from Yudel Mark to Dubnov dated August 24, 15 (no month, but most likely August), and no date, CAHJP, P1/4. Letter from Pinhas Dubinskii to Dubnov, Petrograd, June 12 [1917], CAHJP, P1/4.

14. Letter from Pinhas Dubinskii to Dubnov, Petrograd, June 12 [1917], CAHJP, P1/4.

15. "Der seder ha-yom fun der konferents fun der 'Idisher Demokratisher Fareynigung'" (n.d.), CAHJP, P1/4.

16. Dubnov, *Kniga zhizni*, 381.

17. At that meeting it was decided that Pinhas Dubinskii would run as a candidate for the new autonomous Ukrainian parliaments, the Maly Rada and the Central Rada (*Evreiskaia nedelia* 36–37 [September 12, 1917]: 26). *Evreiskaia nedelia*, a Moscow-based weekly (and a reincarnation of the second *Novy voskhod* and separate from the earlier St. Petersburg–based *Evreiskaia nedelia*), was liberal in its orientation but unaffiliated with any party. It covered Zionist and folkist affairs quite thoroughly, and in 1917–18 it covered the new Jewish communal politics more extensively than any other Jewish paper.

18. Dubnov, *Kniga zhizni*, 387.

19. S. M. Dubnov, *Chego khotiat evrei* (Petrograd, 1917), 17–18.

20. Laserson wrote extensively on legal theory and minority rights.

21. *Proekt platformy Evreiskogo Demokraticheskogo Ob"edineniia* (Petrograd, 1917), 5. In addition to the platform of the Jewish Democratic Union, this publication also includes a number of speeches from the party's organizational congress, although unfortunately these speeches are not attributed to specific individuals.

22. *Proekt platformy Evreiskogo Demokraticheskogo Ob"edineniia*, 5.

23. Dubnov, *Chego khotiat evrei*, 18.

24. "Idishe Folkspartei (Evreiskoe Demokraticheskoe Ob"edinenie)" (flier), YIVO, RG 30 (Revolutionary Russia and USSR), f. 221–23 (Folkspartey folders).

25. "Folkspartey. Iden!" (flier), YIVO, RG 30, f. 221–23.

26. "Di Idishe Folkspartey (Demokratishe Fareynigung): Evreiskaia demokraticheskaia narodnicheskaia partiia" (flier), YIVO, RG 1400, MG-9/MG-10, f. 293.

27. *Dos folk* 2 (December 1917): 4. *Dos folk* was established in December 1917 by the Folkspartey. Although it was presented as a newsletter about the Jewish Congress, it actually was an organ of the Folkspartey, attacking the religious party, the Zionists, and the socialists.

28. "'Idishe Folkspartei': K evreiskoi intelligentsii" (flier), YIVO, RG 30, f. 221–23.

29. "'Idishe Folkspartei': K evreiskoi intelligentsii," YIVO, RG 30, f. 221–23.

30. Flier from Galiupol titled "S evreiskogo grazhdane-evrei!" YIVO, RG 30, f. 221–23; emphasis in original.

31. Poltava region commission for elections to the Ukrainian Constituent Assembly, TsGAVO/TsDAVO, f. 3261, op. 1, d. 73.

32. Poltava region commission for elections to the Ukrainian Constituent Assembly, TsGAVO/TsDAVO, f. 3261, op. 1, d. 73.

33. YIVO, RG 30, f. 221–23.

34. "Idishe Folkspartey: Petrogradskii Komitet" (dated October 26, 1917) (flier), YIVO, RG 30, f. 221–23. In August 1917, Samuel O. Gruzenberg initiated a "Free Jewish Theater" (V. Lebedeva-Kaplan, "Evrei Petrograda v 1917 g.," *Vestnik*

Evreiskogo Universiteta v Moskve 2 [1993]: 14). Samuel Gruzenberg was Oskar Gruzenberg's brother and the editor of *Bunduchnost'*. On the idea of a Jewish people's
theater, see A. Berkhifand, "Evreiskii Narodnyi teatr," *Novyi put'* 3 (5 February
1916): 30–31.

35. Y. Efroikin, "Rech' predstavitsia 'Evreiskoi Narodnicheskoi Partii' I. R.
Efroikina na Demokraticheskom Soveschanii," *Evreiskaia nedelia* 38–39 (29 September 1917): 5–6.

36. For an overview of Efroikin's involvement in *Dos yidishe folksblat* and his
intellectual response to the 1917 revolutions, see Joshua Karlip, "The Center That
Could Not Hold: *Afn Sheydveg* and the Crisis of Diaspora Nationalism" (PhD
diss., Jewish Theological Seminary, 2006), 184–204.

37. Dubnov's detachment from *Dos yidishe folksblat* further indicates his limited
involvement in the Folkspartey in 1917. Dubnov occasionally contributed to *Dos
yidishe folksblat*, as he did to *Di yidishe velt*, but the party organ was not under his
direct editorship nor did it particularly interest him (he mentions it only once in
his memoirs), most likely because the paper was in Yiddish instead of Russian.
Dubnov's first contribution to *Dos yidishe folksblat* did not come until the eighth
issue, when he started his series "Der nayer mabul" (The New Deluge) (*Dos yidishe
folksblat* 8 [December 1917]: 5–8).

38. N. Shtif, "A veltlikher un a religiozer yidishe kehile," *Dos yidishe folksblat* 1 (3
October 1917): 7.

39. Efroikin, "Rech' predstavitsia," 5–6.

40. "'Idishe Folkspartei': K evreiskoi intelligentsii," YIVO, RG 30, f. 221–23.

41. "'Idishe Folkspartei': K evreiskoi intelligentsii," YIVO, RG 30, f. 221–23.

42. Mikhail Beizer, "The Petrograd Jewish Obshchina (Kehilla) in 1917," *Jews
and Jewish Topics in the Soviet Union and Eastern Europe* 10 (1989): 7.

43. TsGIA SPb, f. 2130 (Petrograd Jewish community assembly, 1916–1918), op.
1, d. 1.

44. TsGIA SPb, f. 2130, op. 1, d. 2–6.

45. Beizer, "Petrograd Jewish Obshchina," 8–10.

46. "Tezisy k dokladu M. N. Kreinina po finansogo-organizatsionnomu voprosu. 7/xii 1916 g.," TsGIA SPb, f. 2049, o. 1, d. 107.

47. "Obshchee sobranie petrogradskoi obshchiny," *Evreiskaia nedelia* 2 (1917):
26–27.

48. "Idishe Folkspartey: Petrogradskii Komitet," YIVO, RG 30, f. 222. This
flier is stamped 26 October 1917—coincidentally, the day after the Bolshevik seizure of power. After the *obshchina*'s democratization, support of Jewish cultural
endeavors did, as the Folkspartey had urged, become a major component of its responsibilities. As one example, the Petrograd *obshchina* granted Dubnov a stipend
of 10,000 rubles to reestablish *Evreiskaia starina* (apparently he also counted on a
stipend of similar size from the Moscow *obshchina*) (Protocols of the meeting of
July 28, 1918, TsGIA SPb, f. 2129, op. 1, d. 60).

49. "Idishe Folkspartey: Petrogradskii Komitet," YIVO, RG 30, f. 222.

50. In his assessment of the battles fought over the Petrograd *obshchina*'s democratization in 1917, Mikhail Beizer presents this transformation as a dual and overlapping struggle between secular and Orthodox Jews and, in parallel, between the prerevolutionary Jewish leadership and the radical democratizers and autonomists ("Petrograd Jewish Obshchina," 5–29 *passim*; and Mikhail Beizer, *Evrei Leningrada, 1917–1939: Natsional'naia zhizn i sovetizatsiia* [Moscow, 1999], 172–91). Yitshak Grinbaum described a similar struggle in the Warsaw community beginning in 1899 in "Borby za vlast' v varshavskoi evreiskoi obshchine," *Vestnik evreiskoi obshchiny* 4 (November 1913): 3–12, and 5 (December 1913): 10–26.

51. The Petrograd *obshchina*'s communal council was involved in planning the All-Russian Jewish Congress from the beginning and was sent drafts outlining the goals of the preliminary conference (Statute of June 19, 1917, TsGIA SPb, f. 2132, op. 1, d. 1).

52. The secretary of the Odessa party then wrote Dubnov and Kreinin, asking them to pressure Gruzenberg to accept the proposition. See letter from Shapiro to Dubnov (undated but likely September 1917), CAHJP, P1/9. The folkists' desire to bring Gruzenberg onto the Folkspartey list reflects their understanding of the importance of prominent names in order to win Jewish votes.

53. In return, Gruzenberg enlisted those he defended, as well as others, such as Lev Tolstoy and Vladimir Solov'ev, to attack the government's anti-Jewish policies. See Benjamin Nathans, *Beyond the Pale: The Jewish Encounter with Late Imperial Russia* (Berkeley, Calif., 2002), 329.

54. Gruzenberg also worked extensively with Vinaver and Sliozberg on legal affairs. Gruzenberg's memoirs, written in exile in France, focus on his upbringing, university experiences, and most of all his legal career. In these memoirs he does not mention his political activities of 1917 or the fact that he was elected to the All-Russian Constituent Assembly. See O. O. Gruzenberg, *Vchera: Vospominaniia* (Paris, 1938). The complete English translation (minus a few biographical sketches) was published as O. O. Gruzenberg, *Yesterday: Memoirs of a Russian-Jewish Lawyer*, Don C. Rawson and Tatiana Tipton, trans. (Berkeley, Calif., 1981). A volume that includes a selection of Gruzenberg's speeches, essays, and correspondence was published after his death by a group of his colleagues as O. O. Gruzenberg, *Ocherki i rechi* (New York, 1944). See also M. Dazerson, "Dukhovnii oblik O. O. Gruzenberga (1866–1941)," in *Evreiskii Mir: Sbornik 1944 goda* (New York, 1944; repr. Jerusalem, 2001), 409–14.

55. I. A. Naidich, "O. O. Gruzenberg i Russkoe evreistvo," in Gruzenberg, *Ocherki i rechi*, 37.

56. Kerenskii's Provisional Government attempted to appoint both Gruzenberg and Bramson senators, but only Gruzenberg accepted the offer.

57. A collection of Lozinskii's papers from 1912–39 are located in the Manuscript Division of the State Museum of the History of Religion in St. Petersburg (for-

merly the St. Petersburg State Museum of the History of Religion and Atheism), where Lozinzkii worked for many years during the Soviet period. These papers include a one-page biography describing Lozinskii's expulsion from the university in Kiev for revolutionary activities and his work for the publisher Brokhaus-Efron between 1908 and 1918 and for *Evreiskaia starina* after 1914. Lozinskii also contributed an analysis of the Austrian parliamentary elections of 1907 to the short-lived publication *Serp* ("K parlamentskim vyboram v Avstrii," *Serp* 2 [1908]: 167–78).

58. The party's Central Committee included Jacob Latskii-Bertoldi, Aron Perel'man, Yisroel Efroikin, Nokhem Shtif, Kh. G. Korobkov, P. M. Klinchin, and M. I. Ginzburg. See "'Idishe Folkspartei': K Vserossiiskomu Evreiskomu S"ezdu," YIVO, RG 30, f. 221–23.

59. Boris Ivanovich Kolonitskii, "'Democracy' in the Political Consciousness of the February Revolution," *Slavic Review* 57.1 (1998): 95–96.

60. "'Idishe Folkspartei': K evreiskoi intelligentsii," YIVO, RG 30, f. 221–23.

61. "Izvlechenie iz protokolov Petrogradskogo soveschaniia po podgotovke Vserossiiskogo Evreiskogo S"ezda" and the minutes of meetings from March 30 and April 14, 1917, GARF, f. 9528, op. 1, d. 2.

62. "Izvlechenie iz protokolov Petrogradskogo soveschaniia" and minutes of meetings, GARF, f. 9528, op. 1, d. 2.

63. See the closing statute of the Seventh Russian Zionist Conference, in "The Russian Zionist Conference," *Zionist Review* 1.2 (June 1917): 50.

64. See Yitzhak Maor, *Ha-Tenu'a ha-Tsiyonit be-Rusya: me-reshita ve-'ad yamenu*, 2nd ed. (Jerusalem, 1986), 460–65.

65. See Maor, *Ha-Tenu'a ha-Tsiyonit be-Rusya*; and Yitshak Grinbaum, *Ha-Tenu'a ha-Tsiyonit be-hitpatkhuta* (Jerusalem, 1954), 4: 98–108. The Seventh Congress of Russian Zionists was also covered extensively in *Evreiskaia zhizn'* and *Evreiskaia nedelia* in May and June 1917. For the conference program, see *Evreiskaia zhizn'* 19 (14 May 1917): 5.

66. Lebedeva-Kaplan, "Evrei Petrograda," 7.

67. See "K Vserossiiskomu evreiskomu s"ezdu," *Evreiskaia nedelia* 22 (4 June 1917): 18–20. Kreinin describes his role in organizing the new Folkspartey and the Congress in Meir Kreinin, "Zikhronot," JNUL, MF 40 1416 (section 4 of part 2).

68. S. Dubnov, "Chto meshaet sozyvu evreiskogo s"ezda?" *Evreiskaia nedelia* 19–20 (21 May 1917): 7–8.

69. "Vserossiiskaia evreiskaia konferentsiia: Otkrytie," *Evreiskaia nedelia* 29 (23 July 1917): 15–17.

70. "Statute of 19 June, 1917" of the Petrograd Organizing Committee for elections to the All-Russian Jewish Congress, TsGIA SPb, f. 2132, op. 1, d. 1.

71. *Evreiskaia nedelia* 29 (23 July 1917): 15.

72. *Evreiskaia nedelia* 29 (23 July 1917): 15.

73. *Evreiskaia nedelia* 29 (23 July 1917): 17. See also "The Russian Jewish Congress," *Zionist Review* 1.7 (November 1917): 119.

74. "Vozvanie komiteta po organizatsii vserossiiskogo evreiskogo s"ezda: Ko vsem evreiam v Rossii," *Evreiskaia nedelia* 35 (3 September 1917): 11–13.

75. "Vozvanie komiteta po organizatsii vserossiiskogo evreiskogo s"ezda," 11–13.

77. For the parallel debate over the American Jewish Congress, see Jonathan Frankel, *Prophecy and Politics: Socialism, Nationalism, and the Russian Jews, 1862–1917* (Cambridge, U.K., 1981), 548–49; and on the Austrian Jewish Congress, see David Rechter, *The Jews of Vienna and the First World War* (Oxford, U.K., 2001), 137–60.

78. GARF, f. 9528, which is devoted to the All-Russian Jewish Congress, lacks the rather important component of complete election results but does include some interesting, if random, materials relating to the campaign. GARF, f. 9528 op. 1, d. 3, includes party posters, lists of candidates, and electoral materials from a number of districts, including Moscow, Petrograd, and Kharkov. GARF, f. 9528, op. 1, d. 4, includes lists of candidates (though the inventory calls them delegates) for election to the Congress in Gomel, Simferopol, Odessa, Voronezh, Iaroslav, Irkutsk, Penza, Ekaterinburg, and a few other locales. The elections were designed based on the All-Russian Constituent Assembly elections, as a combination of proportional representation and representation by district. Candidates were able to run in multiple districts, and parties could order their lists as they pleased from district to district (which usually resulted in a mix of national and local figures). Once elected, a candidate could represent only one district, which meant that if he or she was elected in more than one place, additional seats would fall to the next person on the list of the candidate's party. See "Polozhenie o vyborakh na Vserossiiskii Evreiskii S"ezd" (Petrograd, 1917), TsGIA SPb, f. 2132, op. 1, d. 1. This set of rules to the Congress elections also includes a list of electoral districts.

79. See Oleg Budnitskii, *Rossiiskie evrei mezhdu krasnymi i belymi (1917–1920)* (Moscow, 2005), 72–73.

80. Gershon C. Bacon, *The Politics of Tradition: Agudat Yisrael in Poland, 1916–1939* (Jerusalem, 1996), 30–31.

81. Vladimir Levin argues that in adopting demands for equality and economic betterment, Knesset Yisrael was a fundamentally liberal political organization. See Vladimir Levin, "Ha-Politika ha-Yehudit ba-Imperya ha-Rusit be-idan ha-re'aktsiya 1907–1914" (PhD diss., Hebrew University of Jerusalem, 2007), 209–22. On the brief life and death of Knesset Yisrael, see Vladimir Levin, "'Knesset Yisrael': ha-miflaga ha-politit ha-ortodoksit ha-rishona ba-Imperya ha-Rusit," *Tsiyon* 74.1 (2010): 29–62.

82. Quoted in Levin, "Knesset Yisrael," 48. See also David Vital, *A People Apart: A Political History of the Jews in Europe, 1789–1939* (Oxford, U.K., 1999), 637.

83. I rely here on the figures in Zvi Y. Gitelman, *Jewish Nationality and Soviet Politics: The Jewish Sections of the CPSU, 1917–1930* (Princeton, N.J., 1972), 79 (based on M. Zipin, "Der idisher kongress in rusland," *Di tsukunft* 27.1 [January 1919]). There seems to have been little information about the results available

at the time, as I have been unable to independently verify them through other sources.

84. Beizer, *Evrei Leningrada*, 60.

85. *Jewish Chronicle* (22 March 1918): 10.

86. This process is described in great detail in Gitelman, *Jewish Nationality*, 105–48.

87. *Jewish Chronicle* (12 April 1918): 8. The Bolsheviks took similar measures against the Electoral Committee of the All-Russian Constituent Assembly.

88. Mordechai Altshuler, "Ha-Nisayon le-argen kinus kelal-Yehudi be-Rusya ahar ha-Mahpekha," *He-'Avar* 12 (May 1969): 85. Altshuler's calculations of voter participation are somewhat lower than what appeared in the Jewish press at the time because his estimates of Jewish populations are higher. For example, *Evreiskaia nedelia* (1–2 [January 18, 1918]: 20) reported that 44 percent of eligible voters took part in Odessa.

89. Dubnov, "Chto meshaet sozyvu evreiskogo s"ezda," 8.

90. Evidently this union was never established. See "Zadachi; 'Evr. Narodn. Soiuza' 1917g.," IVRAN SPb, Tsinberg Archive, f. 86, op. 3, d. 98.

91. GARF, f. 9528, op. 1, d. 2, contains materials on the role of the Petrograd central committees of the various Jewish organizations in the proposed All-Russian Jewish Congress.

92. The significant exception appears to be in Odessa, where the Jewish National Democratic Party (which became the Odessa Folkspartey) was second (with 7,568 votes) only to the Zionists (with 12,068 votes) and received 24 percent of the votes cast. See *Evreiskaia nedelia* 1–2 (18 January 1918): 20.

93. Jonathan Frankel, "The Paradoxical Politics of Marginality: Thoughts on the Jewish Situation During the Years 1914–1921," *Studies in Contemporary Jewry* 4 (1988): 16.

94. Lev Grigor'evich Protasov, "The All-Russian Constituent Assembly and the Democratic Alternative: Two Views of the Problem," in Wade, *Revolutionary Russia*, 248.

95. On the origins of the idea of an all-Russian constituent assembly, see L. G. Protasov, *Vserossiiskoe uchreditel'noe sobranie: istoriia roszhdeniia i gibeli* (Moscow, 1997), 11–32.

96. In Oliver Radkey's assessment, by insisting on the deferment of all matters to the future Constituent Assembly, the Socialist Revolutionaries shared no small portion of the blame for the assembly's failure (*Sickle Under the Hammer*, 280).

97. Voting in most districts occurred as scheduled on November 12–14, 1917, but it had to be postponed for up to three months in some areas and completely failed to take place in others. A number of factors, both logistical and political, make a complete picture of the results impossible, and so the results should be approached with caution. Disruptions in the telegraph system created communication problems between central electoral commissions and local district commis-

sions, and the new Bolshevik regime made no effort to cooperate with these commissions, whose members had been appointed by the Provisional Government. At the height of the campaign, the Council of People's Commissars even liquidated the All-Russian Electoral Commission, destroying not just the electoral machinery but also much of the historical record. Accepting the possible problems, because the vast majority of Russia's Jews lived in the western provinces, where voting was relatively complete, what exists of the voting results of Jewish voters should be treated seriously. See Oliver H. Radkey, *Russia Goes to the Polls: The Election Results to the All-Russian Constituent Assembly, 1917* (Ithaca, N.Y., 1990), 3–5; and Protasov, "All-Russian Constituent Assembly," 257.

98. By far the most complete tabulation of election results is produced in L. M. Spirin, *Rossiia 1917 god: Iz istorii bor'by politicheskikh partii* (Moscow, 1987), 273–328. Other sources that include statistics and analysis of election results are Radkey, *Russia Goes to the Polls*; L. M. Spirin, *Krushenie pomeshchich'ikh i burzhuaznykh partii v Rossii (nachalo XX v.–1920 g.)* (Moscow, 1977); and N. V. Sviatitskii, "Itogi vyborov vo Vserossiiskoe Uchreditel'noe Sobranie (predislovie)," in *God Russkoi Revoliutsii (1917–1918 gg): Sbornik Statei* (Moscow, 1918), 104–19. Many of the later studies build on the original computations of Sviatitskii, who was a Socialist Revolutionary deputy. Spirin uses local newspapers as well archival holdings in Russia, Ukraine, and Belarus to supplement Sviatitskii's calculations, whereas Radkey primarily uses only local newspapers.

99. For further analysis and comparative tables, see Simon Rabinovitch, "Russian Jewry Goes to the Polls: An Analysis of Jewish Voting in the All-Russian Constituent Assembly Elections of 1917," *East European Jewish Affairs* 39.2 (2009): 205–25.

100. It is impossible to know the number of eligible Jewish voters living in Russian territory in November–December 1917, but the population was considerably diminished by the loss of the Baltic region and Poland, which were at the time controlled by Germany. Using a median from the 1897 and 1926 censuses, Altshuler estimates that, in 1918, 400,000 Jews lived in Belorussia, constituting 10 percent of the population, and that 1.5 million Jews lived in Ukraine, constituting 7 percent of the population. See Altshuler, "Attitude of the Communist Party," 75. The Jewish Statistical Society estimates that 3,387,000 Jews lived in European Russia in 1917, a figure that is almost certainly too high. See S. Ettinger, "The Jews in Russia at the Outbreak of the Revolution," in Lionel Kochan, ed., *The Jews in Soviet Russia Since 1917*, 3rd ed. (Oxford, U.K., 1978), 15.

101. Ezra Mendelsohn, *The Jews of East Central Europe Between the World Wars* (Bloomington, Ind., 1983), 51.

102. Mendelsohn, *Jews of East Central Europe*, 51.

103. "Vegen 'natsionalen blok' tsu der grindungs-farzamlung," *Dos yidishe folksblat* 1 (3 October 1917): 12.

104. Russian accounts, beginning with that of Sviatitskii, referred to these co-

alitions as Jewish nationalist parties and the vote for nonsocialist Jewish parties generally as "nationalist." I refer to these coalitions as Jewish "national" coalitions and parties, both because their composition was not entirely nationalist and because "national" is the term that they consistently incorporated into their names.

105. A list of the names of every representative elected to the Constituent Assembly, with their parties and districts, is included in M. N. Pokrovskii and Ia. A. Iakovlev, eds., *1917 g. v dokumentakh i materialakh (Arkhiv oktiabrskoi revoliutsii): Vserossiiskoi uchreditel'noe sobranie* (Moscow, 1930), 116–38.

106. Vladimir Levin, "Russian Jewry and the Duma Elections, 1906–1907," *Jews and Slavs* 7 (2000): 240, 250.

107. Vladimir Levin, "Politics at the Crossroads: Jewish Parties and the Second Duma Elections 1907," *Leipziger Beiträge zur jüdischen Geschichte und Kultur* 2 (2004): 144. Furthermore, according to Levin, the huge number of nonpartisan electors demonstrates the extent to which, despite politicization, "the majority of the Jewish population continued to consider Jewry a unified entity and adhered to the traditional and deeply-rooted idea of the solidarity of Jews in the face of Gentiles" ("Russian Jewry," 247).

108. The elections to the Polish Sejm in 1919 also seem generally to support this pattern. Because the Folkspartey and non-Zionist Orthodox League ran separately in the elections to the Polish Sejm and because the national coalition was more clearly Zionist (though it was for Jewish national autonomy in Poland and included some prominent independents), it is also somewhat easier to gauge Zionist support. The Temporary Jewish National Council won a plurality of the votes for Jewish parties, but it did not win a majority. The Folkspartey won approximately one-third the number of votes as the Temporary Jewish National Council but had a plurality of votes in Warsaw. The Orthodox League won just over half the number of votes as the Temporary Jewish National Council. Furthermore, Zionist support was much stronger in the previously Austrian western part of Galicia than in the previously Russian Polish provinces. See Ezra Mendelsohn, *Zionism in Poland: The Formative Years, 1915–1926* (New Haven, Conn., 1981), 107–8.

109. Some have interpreted the Zionist strength in the various elections in Russia as directly stemming from the timing of the Balfour Declaration. See Gitelman, *Jewish Nationality*, 75. The *Jewish Chronicle* stated of the Petrograd communal elections: "The great Zionist success was undoubtedly a result of the effect which the British Declaration regarding Palestine has made on the public" ([1 February 1918]: 8).

110. See Protasov, "All-Russian Constituent Assembly," 259–61. As William Dando suggests, the Kadets may have fared poorly in terms of popular support, but the fact that their 2 million votes were heavily concentrated in the urban areas of western Russia, the same areas where the Bolsheviks had the most support, contributed to their underrepresentation in the apportionment of seats in the Constituent Assembly. See William A. Dando, "A Map of the Election to the Russian Constituent Assembly of 1917," *Slavic Review* 25.2 (1966): 316.

111. The one partial exception was Petrograd, where Jewish nationalists chose to support the Kadet Party instead of run against it.

112. See Levin, "Russian Jewry," 246.

113. The complete electoral rules were published by the Provisional Government's Constituent Assembly Commission as "Polozhenie o vyborakh v Uchreditel'noe Sobranie: S Nakaza, raspisaniia chisla chlenov Uchreditel'nogo Sobraniia i postanovlenii Vremennogo Pravitel'stva" (Petrograd, 1917).

114. "Gorodskie vybory v Minske," *Evreiskaia nedelia* 34 (27 August 1917): 21. The strength of the Jewish nonsocialists in Minsk is particularly telling, given that Minsk was in the heart of the region where Jewish workers first established militant trade unions known as *kases*, which acted as the pioneers of the Jewish labor movement. See Ezra Mendelsohn, "The Russian Jewish Labor Movement and Others," *YIVO Annual of Jewish Social Science* 14 (1969): 88; and Ezra Mendelsohn, *Class Struggle in the Pale* (Cambridge, U.K., 1970), x–xi, 16, 64. The voting statistics for Minsk may reflect the impact of the emigration movement as the vast majority of those Jews who left Russia in the early twentieth century were the very same artisan workers who had planted the seeds of the Russian Jewish labor movement.

115. Leopold H. Haimson, "The Problem of Social Identities in Early Twentieth Century Russia," *Slavic Review* 47.1 (1988): 9.

116. "Deklaratziia Moskovskoi Sionistskoi Organizatii (k vyboram v Moskovskuiu Obshchinu)," YIVO, RG 30, f. 80.

117. S. Gepshtein, "Organizatsiia obshchiny," *Evreiskaia zhizn'* 19 (14 May 1917): 6.

118. Peter Gatrell, *A Whole Empire Walking: Refugees in Russia During World War I* (Bloomington, Ind., 1999), 17–23, 145–50.

119. For the resolutions and platform of the Ukrainian Socialist Revolutionary Party in 1917, see *Programmnye dokumenty natsional'nykh politicheskikh partii i organizatsii Rossii (konets XIX v.–1917 g.): Sbornik dokumentov* (Moscow, 1996), 138–48.

120. William G. Rosenberg, *Liberals in the Russian Revolution: The Constitutional Democratic Party, 1917–1921* (Princeton, N.J., 1974), 30–31. Timothy Snyder observes: "The Achilles heel of peasant nations, and the weak point of ethnic politics, is the city" (*The Reconstruction of Nations: Poland, Ukraine, Lithuania, Belarus, 1569–1999* [New Haven, Conn., 2003], 134).

121. Salo W. Baron, *The Russian Jew Under Tsar and Soviets*, 2nd ed. (New York, 1976), 87.

122. William G. Rosenberg, "The Russian Municipal Duma Elections of 1917: A Preliminary Computation of Returns," *Soviet Studies* 21.2 (October 1969): 142–43.

123. See Steven L. Guthier, "The Popular Basis of Ukrainian Nationalism in 1917," *Slavic Review* 38.1 (March 1979): 32.

124. Ronald G. Suny, "Nationalism and Class in the Russian Revolution: A Comparative Discussion," in Edith Rogovin Frankel, Jonathan Frankel, and Baruch Knei-Paz, eds., *Revolution in Russia: Reassessments of 1917* (Cambridge, U.K., 1992), 229.

125. Suny, "Nationalism and Class," 229.

126. Yoav Peled, *Class and Ethnicity in the Pale: The Political Economy of Jewish Workers' Nationalism in Late Imperial Russia* (New York, 1989), 28. Peled suggests that in the late nineteenth and early twentieth centuries, Jews and Russians in the cities and towns of the Pale of Settlement were heading down quite different paths of economic development. In essence, Russian workers were employed in large, technologically advanced, and strategically important factories and mines, whereas Jews were almost entirely employed by other Jews in small, unmechanized workshops, where they received considerably lower wages than Russian workers.

127. Voters could choose between a strongly Ukrainian autonomist joint list of Ukrainian and Russian Socialist Revolutionary candidates and a second list of Ukrainian Socialist Revolutionaries (UPSR) and the All-Ukrainian Peasants' Union (Selians'ka Spilka). Approximately 80 percent of the votes were cast for one of these two lists, and of those votes, almost 80 percent were cast for the more nationalist-oriented All-Ukrainian Peasants' Union. See Spirin, *Rossia 1917 god*, 302. The results in Poltova Province are also perhaps the most complete and official record from the elections. Radkey calls them "a rare exception to the rule" (*Russia Goes to the Polls*, 31–32).

128. The voting breakdown for the city itself did not survive, but we know that 28,154 votes were cast in the city, and in all probability a significant percentage of the Jewish national votes (and Kadet votes) in the province as a whole were cast in the city. See Spirin, *Rossia 1917 god*, 302.

129. Levin, "Russian Jewry," 250.

130. Abraham Revutsky, *Wrenching Times in Ukraine: Memoir of a Jewish Minister*, Sam Revusky and Moishe Kantorowitz, trans. (St. John's, Canada, 1998), 10.

131. See Henry Abramson, *A Prayer for the Government: Ukrainians and Jews in Revolutionary Times, 1917–1920* (Cambridge, Mass., 1999), 34–39.

132. The nearly 1,000-member Central Rada created a smaller legislative council known as the Mala (Little) Rada, which in turn created the General Secretariat as its executive cabinet. Jewish socialists were allocated 4 percent of the seats in the Central Rada, and all Jewish parties combined were allocated a full quarter of the seats in the Mala Rada. The Second Universal, issued on July 16, recognized an agreement made between the Ukrainian General Secretariat and the Provisional Government that the organizational framework of an autonomous Ukraine would be established through consultation with and agreement by non-Ukrainian minorities. See George Liber, "Ukrainian Nationalism and the 1918 Law on National-Personal Autonomy," *Nationalities Papers* 15.1 (1987): 26–27. See also Paul Robert Magocsi, *A History of Ukraine* (Toronto, 1996), 471–77; and Orest Subtelny, *Ukraine: A History*, 2nd ed. (Toronto, 1994), 345–53.

133. Poltava Jewish Democratic Union, "Evrei-Izbiratel'" (24 June 1917), YIVO, RG 1400, MG9/MG10, 293.

134. Kenneth B. Moss, "'A Time for Tearing Down and a Time for Building

Up': Recasting Jewish Culture in Eastern Europe, 1917–1921" (PhD diss., Stanford University, 2003), 48.

135. Moss, "Time for Tearing Down," 49. For further elucidation of these ideas, and in particular, Moss's assessment of the revolution's role in transforming Jewish culture, see his book *Jewish Renaissance in the Russian Revolution* (Cambridge, Mass., 2009).

136. *Evreiskaia nedelia* 38–39 (29 September 1917): 5.

137. "Attitude of the Executive Committee of the Petrograd Soviet on the Question of Participation in the Provisional Government," in Martin McCauley, ed., *The Russian Revolution and the Soviet State: Documents* (London, 1975), 18 (this essay was originally published in *Izvestia*, 3 March 1917). This demand was approved by the Executive Committee as an amendment to the first set of recommendations.

138. This statement, it was recorded, met with applause from the center and the right of the chamber (*Uchreditel'noe Sobranie: Stenograficheskii otchet* [Petrograd, 1918], 13).

139. On the session of the Constituent Assembly and its dissolution, see Radkey, *Sickle Under the Hammer*, 386–455.

Chapter 7

1. Letter from Louis Brandeis to Lucien Wolf, May 16, 1916, YIVO, RG 348, f. 63, l. 5319. Brandeis would be confirmed as an associate justice on the U.S. Supreme Court less than three weeks later, on June 5, 1916.

2. See Jonathan Schneer, *The Balfour Declaration: The Origins of the Arab-Israeli Conflict* (New York, 2010).

3. Yuri Slezkine, "The USSR as a Communal Apartment, or How a Socialist State Promoted Ethnic Particularism," *Slavic Review* 53.2 (1994): 427. Slezkine argues that Bolshevik nationalities policies should be understood as earnest rather than pragmatic. This argument has been further developed in recent works, such as Terry Martin, *The Affirmative Action Empire: Nations and Nationalism in the Soviet Union, 1923–1939* (Ithaca, N.Y., 2001). Both Slezkine and Martin have more recently been challenged by Francine Hirsch, *Empire of Nations: Ethnographic Knowledge and the Making of the Soviet Union* (Ithaca, N.Y., 2005). Hirsch argues that Soviet nationalities policy was earnest only in its devotion to Marxist theory. Whatever Bolshevik motivations were with regard to nationalities policies, the Jews remained an exception whose right to self-determination was as limited and pragmatically granted as it was short-lived.

4. On the conflict between the "national" and "economic" principles in organizing the early Soviet Union, see Francine Hirsch, "State and Evolution: Ethnographic Knowledge, Economic Expediency, and the Making of the USSR, 1917–1924," in Jane Burbank, Mark Von Hagen, and Anatolyi Remnev, eds., *Russian Empire: Space, People, Power, 1700–1930* (Bloomington, Ind., 2007), 139–65.

5. Slezkine, "USSR as a Communal Apartment," 419–20.

6. Slezkine, "USSR as a Communal Apartment," 425.

7. Quoted in Yohanan Petrovsky-Shtern, *Lenin's Jewish Question* (New Haven, Conn., 2010), 79. V. I. Lenin, *Polnoe sobranie sochinenii* (Moscow, 1966–1970), 24: 394.

8. J. Stalin, "Marxism and the National Question," Marxists Internet Archive, http://marxists.org/reference/archive/stalin/works/1913/03.htm.

9. V. I. Lenin, *On National Liberation and Social Emancipation* (Moscow, 1986), 93; emphasis in original. For a cursory look at Bolshevik and Soviet approaches to Jewish national autonomy, see Benjamin Pinkus, "The Development of Jewish National Autonomy and Its Application in the Soviet Union from Lenin to Gorbachev," *Shvut*, n.s., 1–2 (1995): 80–123.

10. Quoted in Pinkus, "Development of Jewish National Autonomy," 104; emphasis in original.

11. Mordechai Altshuler, "The Attitude of the Communist Party of Russia to Jewish National Survival, 1918–1930," *YIVO Annual of Jewish Social Science* 14 (1969): 75.

12. Altshuler, "Attitude of the Communist Party," 76.

13. TsGIA SPb, f. 2130, op. 1, d. 11.

14. TsGIA SPb, f. 2130, op. 1, d. 11. Voter participation, however, was relatively low, with only 5,315 votes cast. On the elections, see Mikhail Beizer, *Evrei Leningrada, 1917–1939: Natsional'naia zhizn i sovetizatsiia* (Moscow, 1999), 183–88.

15. Semion Aleksandrovich Charnyi, "Evreiskie religioznyie obshchiny i vlast' v Rossii v period grazhdanskoi voiny (1918–1920)," in O. V. Budnitskii, O. V. Belova, V. E. Kel'ner, and V. V. Mochalova, eds., *Mirovoi krizis 1914–1920 godov i sud'ba vostochnoevropeiskogo evreistva* (Moscow, 2005), 234.

16. TsGA SPb, f. 75, op. 1, d. 100, l. 161; TsGA SPb, f. 75, op. 2, d. 39a. Starving Jewish intellectuals, including the folkists Shmuel Niger and Zelig Kalmanovich, were compelled by necessity to work for Evkom in 1918 and 1919. Kalmanovich even translated *State and Revolution* into Yiddish for the Third Congress of Soviets (although he refused to have his name appear on the title page). As Zvi Gitelman states, "The rations which the Commissariat provided literally saved the lives of some starving intelligentsia. *Paiok* (rations) won out over principle" (*Jewish Nationality and Soviet Politics: The Jewish Sections of the CPSU, 1917–1930* [Princeton, N.J., 1972], 127, see also 135). Niger shared the podium with S. Ia. Rapoport, the commissar for Jewish affairs in Petrograd, during at least one meeting of Der Idisher Arbeiter Club, where Niger lectured on the history of Jewish literature (TsGA SPb, f. 75, o. 1, d. 100, l. 6).

17. David Shneer, *Yiddish and the Creation of Soviet Jewish Culture: 1918–1930* (Cambridge, U.K., 2004), 28–29. Shneer suggests that the writers who Dimanshtein gathered became the new *shtadlonim*, cultural and political intermediaries between the Jews and the new powers that be. The problem with this metaphor,

however, as Shneer accedes, is that "these new intercessors *were* the state when it came to articulating a vision of Soviet Jewish culture" (15–16).

18. Beizer, *Evrei Leningrada*, 55–66; David Vital, *A People Apart: A Political History of the Jews in Europe, 1789–1939* (Oxford, U.K., 1991), 708–10.

19. Letter dated December 12, 1918, TsGA, f. 75, op. 1, d. 100, l. 75.

20. TsGA SPb, f. 75, o. 1, d. 100, l. 74.

21. Second letter dated December 12, 1918, TsGA, f. 75, op. 1, d. 100, l. 76.

22. By January 1919 the nationalities commissariats received instructions to fight the counterrevolutionaries in their sections, especially the "national bourgeois governments" (TsGA Spb, f. 75, o. 1, d. 29, l. 154).

23. On the politics of Jewish autonomy in independent Ukraine, see Henry Abramson, *A Prayer for the Government: Ukrainians and Jews in Revolutionary Times* (Cambridge, Mass., 1999); Henry Abramson, "Jewish Representation in the Independent Ukrainian Governments of 1917–1920," *Slavic Review* 50.3 (1991): 542–50; Arie Zaidman, "Ha-otonomya ha-le'umit ha-Yehudit be-Ukraina ha-'atsma'it ba-shanim 1917–1919" (PhD diss., Tel Aviv University, 1980); and Jonathan Frankel, "The Dilemmas of Jewish National Autonomism: The Case of Ukraine 1917–1920," in Howard Aster and Peter J. Potichnyj, eds., *Ukrainian-Jewish Relations in Historical Perspective*, 2nd ed. (Edmonton, Canada, 1990), 263–79.

24. Moses Silberfarb [Moyshe Zilberfarb], *The Jewish Ministry and Jewish National Autonomy in Ukraine*, David H. Lincoln, trans. (New York, 1993), 81–82.

25. On the Kultur-Lige, see Simon Rabinovitch, ed., *Jews and Diaspora Nationalism: Writings on Jewish Peoplehood in Europe and the United States* (Waltham, Mass., 2012), 140–51; and Kenneth Moss, *Jewish Renaissance in the Russian Revolution* (Cambridge, Mass., 2009).

26. See the helpful documentary collection edited by L. B. Miliakova, *Kniga pogromov: Pogromy na Ukraine, v Belorussii i evropeiskoi chasti Rossii v period Grazhdanskoi voiny 1918–1922 gg. Sbornik dokumentov* (Moscow, 2007). See also the documents, published in Yiddish and Russian in Berlin between 1923 and 1932 and compiled by Elias Tcherikower (Elye Tsherikover, 1881–1943) and others, at the Ostjüdsches Historisches Archiv. For a list of volumes and one view of the later uses of this material, see the "Bibliographic Postscriptum" to Abramson, *Prayer for the Government*. For a general outline of the anti-Jewish violence in Ukraine during the civil war, see O. V. Budnitskii, *Rossiiskie evrei mezhdu krasnymi i belymi (1917–1920)* (Moscow, 2006), 344–67; and Abramson, *Prayer for the Government*, 109–140. For the broader context, see Piotr Wróbel, "The *Kaddish* Years: Anti-Jewish Violence in East Central Europe, 1918–1921," *Simon Dubnow Institute Yearbook* 4 (2005): 211–36.

27. Frankel, "Dilemmas of Jewish National Autonomism," 268.

28. See the firsthand accounts by the Jewish participants in the various Ukrainian national governments, in particular Zilberfarb's (Silberfarb, *Jewish Ministry*) and the accounts by Solomon Goldeman (*Jewish National Autonomy in Ukraine*

1917–1920, Michael Luchkovich, trans. [Chicago, 1968]) and Abraham Revutsky (*Wrenching Times in Ukraine: Memoirs of a Minister for Jewish Affairs*, Sam Revusky and Moishe Kantorwitz, trans. [St. John's, Canada, 1998]).

29. Carole Fink, *Defending the Rights of Others: The Great Powers, the Jews, and International Minority Protection, 1878–1938* (New York, 2004), 28–38.

30. All the following works offer detailed accounts of the conflicts between the Jewish delegations in Paris and the creation of the Minorities Treaties: Jacob Robinson, Oscar Karbach, Max M. Laserson, Nehemiah Robinson, and Mark Vichniak, *Were the Minorities Treaties a Failure?* (New York, 1943); Nathan Feinberg, *La question des minorities a la conférence de la paix de 1919–1920 et l'action Juive en faveur de la protection international des minorities* (Paris, 1929); Oscar Janowsky, *The Jews and Minority Rights (1898–1919)* (New York, 1933); Mark Levene, *War, Jews, and the New Europe: The Diplomacy of Lucien Wolf* (Oxford, U.K., 1992); Fink, *Defending the Rights of Others*; Vital, *A People Apart*; and Eugene C. Black, "Lucien Wolf and the Making of Poland: Paris, 1919," *Polin* 2 (1987): 5–36. The notes and bibliographies of these works attest to the considerable documentary record available. For a long time Janowsky's account was the standard treatment, but the ideological aspect of his division of the players at Versailles into bad assimilationists and good nationalists is brought to light in two works: James Loeffler, "Between Zionism and Liberalism: Oscar Janowsky and Diaspora Nationalism in America," *AJS Review* 34.2 (2010): 289–308; and Mark Levene, "Resurrecting Poland: The Fulcrum of International Politics, 1917–1919," *Simon Dubnow Institute Yearbook* (2002): 29–40.

31. See David Engel, "Minorities Treaties," in *The YIVO Encyclopedia of Jews in Eastern Europe* (New Haven, Conn., 2008), 2: 1176–77.

32. And aided, perhaps, by the vacuum left by the absence of politically well-connected members of the German and Russian Jewish elite. See Levene, "Resurrecting Poland," 37.

33. "Die Forerungen des jüdischen Volkes," CZA, Z3/101-2T.

34. Janowsky, *Jews and Minority Rights*, 264–68.

35. YIVO, RG 348, f. 81.

36. YIVO, RG 348, f. 81.

37. On the Jewish delegations at Versailles, see Robinson et al., *Were the Minorities Treaties a Failure*; Feinberg, *La question des minorities*; Janowsky, *Jews and Minority Rights*; Levene, *War, Jews, and the New Europe*; Fink, *Defending the Rights of Others*; Vital, *A People Apart*; and Black, "Lucien Wolf."

38. Black, "Lucien Wolf," *passim*; Levene, *War, Jews, and the New Europe*, 186–226.

39. Levene, "Resurrecting Poland," 34–35.

40. See the appendix "Woodrow Wilson's Fourteen Points" in Margaret MacMillan, *Paris 1919: Six Months That Changed the World* (New York, 2002), 495–96.

41. Fink, *Defending the Rights of Others*, 74–82.

42. Joanna Beata Michlic, *Poland's Threatening Other: The Image of the Jews from 1880 to the Present* (Lincoln, Neb., 2006), 72.

43. Jewish political life in interwar Poland has been the subject of a large number of studies. See, for example, Kalman Weiser, *Jewish People, Yiddish Nation: Noah Prylucki and the Folkists in Poland* (Toronto, 2011); David Fishman, *The Rise of Modern Yiddish Culture* (Pittsburgh, 2005); Jack Jacobs, *Bundist Counterculture in Interwar Poland* (Syracuse, N.Y., 2009); Gershon Bacon, *The Politics of Tradition: Agudat Yisrael in Poland, 1916–1939* (Jerusalem, 1996); Antony Polonsky, *The Jews in Poland and Russia*, vol. 3, *1914–2008* (Oxford, U.K., 2012); *Polin* 8 (2004), focusing on "The Jews in Independent Poland, 1918–1939"; and three books by Ezra Mendelsohn: *The Jews of East Central Europe Between the World Wars* (Bloomington, Ind., 1983); *Zionism in Poland: The Formative Years, 1915–1926* (New Haven, Conn., 1982); and *On Modern Jewish Politics* (New York, 1993).

44. Antony Polonsky, "The New Jewish Politics and Its Discontents," in Zvi Gitelman, ed., *The Emergence of Modern Jewish Politics: Bundism and Zionism in Eastern Europe* (Pittsburgh, 2003), 48; Simon Rabinovitch, "The Dawn of a New Diaspora: Simon Dubnov's Autonomism, from St. Petersburg to Berlin," *Leo Baeck Institute Yearbook* 50 (2005): 273–74. For a detailed assessment of Jewish autonomy in interwar Lithuania, see Šarūnas Liekis, *A State Within a State? Jewish Autonomy in Lithuania, 1918–1925* (Vilnius, 2003), 37.

45. For a discussion of Dubnov's relationship with Jewish political figures in the Lithuanian Republic, see Verena Dohrn, "State and Minorities: The First Lithuanian Republic and S. M. Dubnov's Concept of Cultural Autonomy," in Alvydas Nikžentaitis, Stefan Schreiner, and Darius Staliūnas, eds., *The Vanished World of Lithuanian Jews* (Amsterdam, 2004), 155–73.

46. S. M. Dubnov, *Kniga zhizni: Vospominaniia i razmyshleniia, materialy dlia istorii moego vremeni* (St. Petersburg, 1998), 485–86. On Dubnov's Berlin years, see Rabinovitch, "Dawn of a New Diaspora." On the other folkists and diaspora nationalists who settled in Berlin and their efforts to found what became the YIVO Institute for Jewish Research, see Cecile Esther Kuznitz, *YIVO and the Making of Modern Jewish Culture: Scholarship for the Yiddish Nation* (New York, 2014).

47. On anti-Jewish violence in Ukraine, see Miliakova, *Kniga pogromov*; documents compiled by Elias Tcherikower and others at the Ostjüdsches Historisches Archiv; Budnitskii, *Rossiiskie evrei mezhdu krasnymi i belymi*, 344–67; Abramson, *Prayer for the Government*, 109–140; and Wróbel, "*Kaddish* Years."

48. See Michael R. Marrus, *The Unwanted: European Refugees in the Twentieth Century* (New York, 1985), 61–68.

49. For a published account by the Comité of how the information became known, see the preface to Comité des délégations juives, *The Pogroms in the Ukraine Under the Ukrainian Governments (1917–1920): Historical Survey with Documents and Photographs* (London, 1927), vi–viii.

50. Comité des délégations juives, *Pogroms in the Ukraine*, xi–xii.

51. Quoted in Weiser, *Jewish People*, 178.

52. For the full text of the treaty, see the appendix to Levene, *War, Jews, and the New Europe*, 312–15.

53. Gershon Bacon, "Polish Jews and the Minorities Treaties Obligations: The View from Geneva (Documents from the League of Nations Archives)," *Gal-Ed* 17 (2002): 145–76. Bacon suggests that the League's bureaucrats in its Minorities Section had, in any event, a limited view of the Section's mandate and were more sympathetic to Polish than Jewish concerns. See also Robinson et al., *Were the Minorities Treaties a Failure?*

54. YIVO, RG 87, f. 1007.

55. The significant exception to the rule here is the Bund, which supported Jewish national-cultural autonomy and opposed Zionism.

56. YIVO, RG 87, f. 1007. Dubnov made this statement to the Jewish Telegraph Agency (JTA) in Berlin on July 6, 1927. The JTA translated the statement into German (presumably from Russian), and thus the translation here is from the German.

57. In using the term *Kaddish*, Dubnov refers here to the prayer for mourners. S. M. Dubnow, "The New Jewish Diplomacy," *The American Hebrew* (5 October 1929): 9.

58. Robinson et al., *Were the Minorities Treaties a Failure*, 248.

59. For examples, see the essays in Rabinovitch, *Jews and Diaspora Nationalism*, by Horace Kallen ("Democracy Versus the Melting Pot: A Study of American Nationality," 155–68), Mordecai Kaplan ("The Future of Judaism," 169–81), and Simon Rawidowicz ("Jerusalem and Babylon," 217–32). See also Simon Rabinovitch, "Diaspora, Nation, and Messiah: An Introductory Essay," in Rabinovitch, *Jews and Diaspora Nationalism*, xv–xli; Loeffler, "Between Zionism and Liberalism"; and Noam Pianko, *Zionism and the Roads Not Taken* (Bloomington, Ind., 2010).

60. Polonsky, *Jews in Poland and Russia*, 3: 259–62.

61. See Zvi Gitelman, *A Century of Ambivalence: The Jews of Russia and the Soviet Union, 1881 to the Present*, 2nd ed. (Bloomington, Ind., 2001), 74–114; Benjamin Pinkus, *The Jews of the Soviet Union: The History of a National Minority* (Cambridge, U.K., 1988); and Shneer, *Yiddish and the Creation of Soviet Jewish Culture*, 1–59.

62. David Shneer, "Birobidzhan," in *The YIVO Encyclopedia of Jews in Eastern Europe* (New Haven, Conn., 2008), 1: 187–89. The creation of Birobidzhan was established following significant Jewish agricultural colonization that occurred first in the Crimea. See Jonathan Dekel-Chen, *Farming the Red Land: Jewish Agricultural Colonization and Local Soviet Power, 1924–1941* (New Haven, Conn., 2005).

63. See Stuart Finkel, *On the Ideological Front: The Russian Intelligentsia and the Making of the Public Sphere* (New Haven, Conn., 2007).

64. Oscar Janowsky obtained this story through an interview with Ussishkin but points out that it does not appear in the minutes of the meeting (Janowsky, *Jews and Minority Rights*, 301).

65. The Paris Sanhedrin, "Doctrinal Decisions (April 1807)," in Paul Mendes-Flohr and Jehuda Reinharz, eds., *The Jew in the Modern World: A Documentary History*, 3rd ed. (New York, 2011), 158.

Conclusion

1. S. M. Dubnov, *Kniga zhizni: Vospominaniia i razmyshleniia, materialy dlia istorii moego vremeni* (St. Petersburg, 1998), 199.

2. Several scholars have examined the applicability of the Dubnovian model to Jewish scholarship today, Jewish nationalism today, and even minority rights writ large in the post-Soviet Commonwealth of Independent States. See, respectively, Eli Lederhendler, *Jewish Responses to Modernity: New Voices in America and Eastern Europe* (New York, 1994), 189–97; Allan Arkush, "From Diaspora Nationalism to Radical Diasporism," *Modern Judaism* 29.3 (2009): 326–50; and Michael Beizer, "Simon Dubnov's Theory of Autonomism and Its Practicability in the CIS," in Avraham Greenbaum, Yisrael Bartal, and Dan Haruv, eds., *Safra ve-saifa: Shimon Dubnov, historyon ve-ish tsibur* (Jerusalem, 2010), 87–102 (English side).

3. "Evreiskaia narodnaia partiia," *Evreiskaia mysl'* 12 (21 December 1906): 3.

4. YIVO, RG 87, f. 1024.

5. My thanks to David Myers for focusing my mind on the question of autonomism's viability when he was chair of a recent roundtable on diaspora nationalism at the 2012 Association for Jewish Studies conference. My thanks also to the other panelists—Joshua Karlip, James Loeffler, Joshua Shanes, and Kalman Weiser—whose thoughts on these questions undoubtedly have made their way into this conclusion.

6. Arieh Saposnik, *Becoming Hebrew: The Creation of a Jewish National Culture in Ottoman Palestine* (New York, 2008).

7. See Assaf Likhovski, *Law and Identity in Mandate Palestine* (Chapel Hill, N.C., 2006); and Yosef Gorni, *From Binational Society to Jewish State: Federal Concepts in Zionist Political Thought, 1920–1990, and the Jewish People* (Leiden, 2006).

8. See Simon Rabinovitch, "Diaspora, Nation, and Messiah: An Introductory Essay," in Simon Rabinovitch, ed., *Jews and Diaspora Nationalism: Writings on Jewish Peoplehood in Europe and the United States* (Waltham, Mass., 2012), xv–xli; and Yisrael Bartal, *Kozak ve-Bedvi: "Am" ve-"erets" ba-le'umiyut ha-Yehudit* (Tel Aviv, 2007).

Index